Death Rituals and Life in the Societies of the Kula Ring

DEATH RITUALS
and
LIFE
in the
SOCIETIES
of the
KULA RING

Edited by
Frederick H. Damon and
Roy Wagner

Northern Illinois University Press
DeKalb   1989

© 1989 by Northern Illinois University Press
Published by the Northern Illinois University Press, DeKalb, Illinois 60115
Manufactured in the United States of America using acid-free paper
Design by Julia Fauci

Library of Congress Cataloging-in-Publication Data

Death rituals and life in the societies of the kula ring / edited by
    Frederick H. Damon and Roy Wagner.
        p. cm.
        Bibliography: p.
        ISBN 0-87580-151-X
        ISBN 0-87580-546-9 (pbk)
        1. Massim (Melanesian people)—Funeral customs and rites. 2. Kula exchange. 3. Funeral rites and
    ceremonies—Papua New Guinea—Milne Bay. 4. Milne Bay (Papua New Guinea)—Social life and
    customs.
    I. Damon, Frederick H. II. Wagner, Roy.
    DU740.42.D43 1989
    393'.0899950541—dc20   89-8611
                            CIP

Contents

Contents

vi

Acknowledgments

♦ The papers presented here were initially prepared for the Internal Exchange session of the Second International Conference on the Kula: History and Internal Exchange, held at the University of Virginia in 1981. Papers presented in the History session appear in the *Journal of Pacific History* 18, nos. 1–2 (1983). All papers in this volume were revised for publication, some substantially rewritten in 1988.

For financial assistance we thank the Esperanza Trust Fund for Anthropological Research, the National Science Foundation, the Wenner-Gren Foundation for Anthropological Research, and the provost and dean of the Graduate School of Arts and Sciences at the University of Virginia.

We also thank Mr. Scott Parker for help in preparing the maps and diagrams, and Dr. Mary Lincoln of Northern Illinois University Press for her encouragement and help with this project.

In addition to this volume's contributors, attending the conference were Mr. Donald Affleck; Dr. Christopher Gregory; Mr. Wari Iamo; Drs. Geoffrey Irwin, Janet Landa, Nancy Munn, Annette Weiner, and John Waiko; and Mr. John Woichom. Professor William Davenport served as an outside critic and discussant throughout the conference. His contribution was greatly appreciated. At the conference's concluding session he correctly asked us to synthesize our complex material. Aware of their shortfalls, the editors have initiated such an endeavor in their respective Introduction and Conclusion.

F. H. D.
R. W.

Death Rituals and Life in the Societies of the Kula Ring

Frederick H. Damon

Introduction

• This volume describes mortuary practices in nine locations
of Milne Bay Province, Papua New Guinea, an area known as the *Massim*,
the region of the Kula Ring. The volume is one of a number of steps designed to achieve an understanding of the area as a complex regional system.
It provides detailed accounts of mortuary rituals because Massim societies
hold these activities to be unique, most representative of their distinctive-
ness. These are rites that motivate and organize many other aspects of social
life, political, economic, moral, etc. Perhaps two exceptions aside, mortuary
rituals are the "total social facts" of the individual Kula Ring and greater
Kula Ring societies.

Although Malinowski's *Argonauts of the Western Pacific* (1922) may
have had a greater influence on the development of social anthropology than
any other single monograph (Leach 1983:1), and the Kula may be the best
known primitive exchange system in the anthropological world (Persson
1983:32), for the Kula's direct and indirect participants mortuary rituals
are of significance equal to or greater than that of the Kula for the organization and perpetuation of daily life. No description of any single Massim society, and no understanding of the region as a whole, can approach com-
pleteness until these rituals are understood. The earliest ethnographic
descriptions noted them (Seligman 1910), but Malinowski's Trobriand ethnography gave little indication of their scale and import. For him they were

3

"perhaps the most difficult and bewildering aspect of Trobriand culture for the investigating sociologist" (Malinowski 1929:148). It was not until Weiner published *Women of Value, Men of Renown* (1976) that we received any idea of what Malinowski found so bewildering and, consequently, had a new image of Trobriand society that made previous interpretations obsolete. All future work in the area will have to come to terms with the material presented in these essays.

This volume is this group's third joint publication.[1] In this Introduction I relate it to its predecessors, place the individual contributions, and discuss some ethnographic and theoretical issues relating to our focus, the significance of mortuary phenomena in the Massim.

INTERNAL EXCHANGE

The Massim is a complex regional system, or, perhaps, a complex of regional systems. By focusing on what we call *internal exchange*, these essays highlight one feature of the region and raise the question of how different groups relate to the larger whole.

Internal exchange is opposed to *external exchange,* the main focus of our first joint publication, *The Kula: New Perspectives on Massim Exchange* (Leach and Leach 1983). *The Kula* presents data on parts of the Kula Ring not described by the original ethnographers (Armstrong 1928; Fortune 1932; Malinowski 1922; Seligman 1910), assesses some changes in the area since the time of the earlier reports, and interprets both the old and the new data given recent changes in anthropological theory. All ethnographic papers in the volume[2] are firmly located in the realities of the writers' research locales. But the book does not deal systematically with the major differences between one area and another. Hence we created a distinction between external and internal exchange to try to capture these societies' different if complementary foci.

The external/internal exchange opposition that defines the relationship between our first and this third publication is not to be taken too rigidly. For some groups directly engaged in Kula exchange it corresponds to indigenous usages. Some of these people, for example, believe the Kula operates, or should operate, the same way everywhere. But they know that mortuary practices change significantly from one island or part of an island to another. In other groups, for example Vanatinai (Sudest Island), external exchange, now at least, seems negligible. What there is of it is motivated largely by the mortuary system, the dynamics we label internal. In Goodenough, Bwaidoka, external exchange is underplayed, but it bears formal resemblance to the Kula. The practice goes by a term, *niune,* that is probably cognate to *kula* (*kun* or *kune* in many eastern and southern Kula

societies [Macintyre and Young 1982; Young 1983a]). Even for the societies in which the distinction affords the greatest utility, those directly involved in the Kula, Vakuta, Muyuw, Tubetube, and Lobada in this volume,
the distinction does not so much refer to the spatial parameters of exchange
as it connotes culturally inscribed motivations and forms. As is evident from
Campbell's paper, Kula valuables enter Vakutan mortuary exchanges, but
their purposes are somewhat different from normal Kula and her informants indicate that they have to circumvent if not disrupt their Kula for
this use of external items in internal exchange processes. Although internal
exchange processes are motivated by local value systems, in some groups,
Muyuw and Tubetube for example, they nevertheless draw on resources
from far beyond the confines of the local setting. Pigs consumed in mortuary
rituals of both Muyuw and Tubetube may be provided to one by the other
or by a more distant group.

Our distinction between external and internal exchange is a simple heuristic with lesser or greater relevance to each particular society. It will be
evident, however, that in those societies where the distinction is the most
finely drawn the relationship between the two modes seems also to be the
most complementary.

THE PRESENT VOLUME

The map included here locates the groups described in this volume. Three
papers about the Northern Massim come first,[3] four for the south second.
Chowning's paper on the Molima mediates the northern and southern sets.
The southern set begins in its center, Tubetube, and heads west toward
Goodenough on the one hand and then east toward Rossel Island (Yela) on
the other. This arrangement takes the reader from what might be more familiar to what is less, and it maximizes ethnographic and theoretical questions the Massim region poses.

The collection begins with two selections from the Trobriand Islands.
Both Montague's paper about Kaduwaga village on Kaileuna Island, and
Campbell's on Vakuta, far western and southern Trobriands, respectively,
build on the new Trobriand ethnography Weiner's publications defined.
Weiner's work was located in the north central Trobriands. Leach wrote
(1957:120) that Malinowski's signal contribution to social anthropology
was to teach us that ethnographic description had to make internal sense.
One of Weiner's contributions is to demonstrate that Malinowski's description did not fulfill its avowed promise. Weiner has told us what was so "bewildering" about Trobriand mortuary practices; Montague and Campbell
help make those complex activities considerably less bewildering. This is not
to suggest that everywhere Trobriand mortuary practices are identical; they

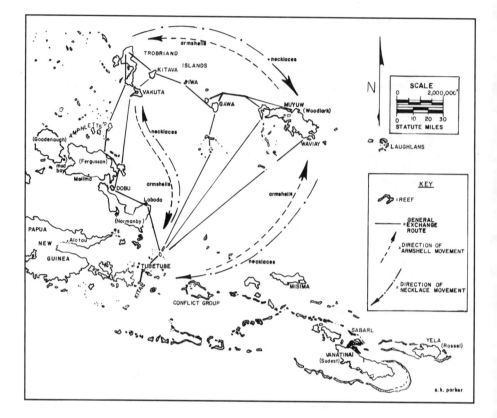

are not. But the three areas for which we now have good data mutually inform one another.

Montague's paper describes the ethics of eating and the symbolism of food as both relate to the forms in which and through which Kaduwagans are born and die. But her brilliant and suggestive paper goes beyond a presentation of Trobriand mortuary performances. She describes the Trobriand understanding of "mind" and "intentionality" so that the reader begins to learn not just what is happening, but why it is happening: why the actors are doing what they are doing. Campbell's paper has a different sense. Her description of Vakuta's mortuary rites provides the most complete and detailed account yet available for any Massim society. My paper concludes the set dealing with the northern Massim. Although I provide an overview of the whole Muyuw mortuary system, I explain how one particular ritual functions. Muyuw people say this ritual, the *lo'un*, ends the marriage between a deceased's parents; I try to show how it accomplishes this task.

To effect a transition between the northern and southern Massim I next place Chowning's paper on the Molima, a group well out of the main Kula flow on the southern side of Fergusson Island. The Molima exhibit typical Massim mortuary patterns, but their descent regime is unusual. According to Chowning they have a cognatic rather than a unilineal descent system. Chowning explores these similarities and differences through an examination of linguistic parallels between the Molima and other nearby southern peoples. This endeavor is very useful for thinking about the adequacy of anthropological categories that become especially problematic in a volume of this kind. For all Massim societies the production of children is a principal activity, and the establishment of conditions to reproduce them is an important outcome of mortuary rites. Everywhere a marriage's matrilateral and patrilateral sides participate in these processes. Variations in descent ideology should be viewed in light of variations in these structures.

After Chowning's paper is Macintyre's on Tubetube, the center of the southeastern corner of the main Kula circuit. Both her paper and Thune's on Normanby, which follows, provide us with the first developed pictures of the kinds of patterns Fortune described for Dobu ([1932] 1962). Both papers show the *susu* (matrilineal clan) as coming to the fore through each group's cycle of mortuary practices. The quotes Macintyre provides from her informant Panetan make it seem as if only now, in the face of massive change, do the "boundaries" of the *susu* so clearly emerge. But there is reason to believe that long ago Tubetube mortuary practices distilled one domain out of the confluence of several others.

Macintyre describes the actualities of Tubetube mortuary rituals as they reflect the sociogeography of Tubetube society. Although in principle similar descriptions could be made of all these societies, Thune's paper suggests that geographic ideas may be the major means for representing social relationships in much of the southern Massim. Thune interprets Lobadan, northeast Normanby, mortuary rituals as progressively transforming the antisocial experience of history onto an ideal static landscape with the *susu*, represented by stones and bones, squarely in the center of the hamlet. This extraordinary paper thus provides some of the social and symbolic sense that would appear to lie behind the concentric village structures Fortune described for Dobu.

Young's discussion of Bwaidoka, on Goodenough Island, is next. Among Massim societies Goodenough is unique in that it alone has a patrilineal ideology for its descent form. This fact and others illustrate profound discontinuities between Goodenough and the rest of the region, but there are equally significant continuities. Similar to the Lobada people Thune described (and several other southern Massim societies [Seligman 1910:463–65]), "permanent lithic symbols" (Young 1971:22), are employed to represent descent group unity. However, Normanby and Dobu mortuary practices tend to work to deny intergenerational relationships, whereas

7

these seem to be quite important in Goodenough culture. I refer here to Goodenough culture's classification of uterine generations into the consecutive categories *tubuya, dala, weyo, bu'u,* and *sese* (Young *infra.* 1971:36–40). Among other things these categories distinguish between impossible (*tubuya, dala,* and *weyo*) and possible (*bu'u* and *sese*) marriages as understood in generational terms. The way marriage relates to these categories suggests affinities with intergenerational relationships found in the northern Massim. Recall the ideal FZD marriage of the Trobriands and the ritual, *lo'un,* I focus upon in my Muyuw paper. Muyuw's ritual has alternate descending generations ending the marriages of an alternate ascending generation. It thereby sets up conditions for new marriages. Yet whatever affinities one finds between this and that Goodenough custom and other Massim practices, the total Goodenough configuration is radically different than elsewhere. Consequently, Young's paper illustrates in the extreme the ways in which these cultures may vary.

The variation found west from Tubetube toward Goodenough is paralleled by that which runs from Tubetube east to Vanatinai, Sabarl (not discussed separately in this work), and Rossel Island. Lepowsky's paper on Vanatinai returns us to more familiar Massim mortuary patterns, but structures she describes differ significantly from Tubetube's. The categories of persons giving and receiving in Tubetube are brother/sister pairs. In Vanatinai, and Sabarl, they are cross-cousins reclassified into symbolic father/child relationships. Pigs, which are the most important medium of exchange in Muyuw and Tubetube, are replaced by large stone axes in Vanatinai.[4]

Moving east from Tubetube produces a shift in both the exchange relationships in mortuary systems and the things exchanged in them. This pattern reaches its extreme with our last ethnographic contribution, Liep's discussion of Rossel Island, Yela culture. Yela people are the farthest southeast of all of the Massim cultures, they have their own exceedingly complex exchange system, and they speak a non-Austronesian language. Their production of *bagi,* one of the two principal Kula valuables, makes them indispensable to the Kula system. Yet virtually every other aspect of their ethnography isolates them from the region. Liep's important thesis is that the relative absence of Yela mortuary activity derives from the island's attempt to deny the hierarchy that lurks around every other Massim society. It is likely that the disjunctions and conjunctions Yela has with the larger area are as much a product of the total Massim regional system as they are of Yela's unknown history. It may be then that Liep's thesis is just to the point of Yela's place in the larger system: Yela culture attempts, perhaps, to deny a hierarchy that encompasses it.

Roy Wagner concludes the volume by forging a synthesis among discussions in all the papers. He finds an opposition between the northwest and southeast societies. Affinities between Muyuw and Tubetube, northern and southern representatives of the Kula circuit, mediate this opposition. Significantly, the noted affinity between these two groups concerns how *kitoum* (personally owned Kula valuables) enter each group's mortuary system. The volume thus concludes by returning to the system of external exchange, the Kula, by means of processes internal to these cultures.

INTERPRETING MASSIM MORTUARY RITUAL

Our volume's purpose is to describe the activities Massim societies hold to be the most important. But a collection such as this presents a number of general ethnographic and analytical problems that have consequences beyond its particular area. I raise questions for further consideration here under the subheadings History, Language, and Comparison.

History

The archaeology of this area is in its infancy so little can be stated about Massim prehistory other than that for a long time these islands have been connected by long-distance trade. The cultures our papers describe are not and never were social isolates.

Aspects of colonial history are better known and have a major bearing on the societies and institutions we experienced. My historical account begins by drawing liberally from J. W. Leach's overview in our first publication (Leach 1983:12–16).

The Spanish may have entered this part of the Pacific in the early seventeenth century. But more sustained European contact began with English and French exploration during the latter part of the eighteenth century. Whalers probably frequented the Massim from the first part of the nineteenth century; Woodlark Island and the Marshall Bennetts (Gaw, Kweywata, Iw) are named for whalers that visited there in the early 1830s. Unsuccessful missions started on several islands during the midcentury (Affleck 1983:57–72; 132–33). However, the region is only brought into the orbit of the modern world system during the major expansion of world trade with the last quarter of the nineteenth century. The Massim's contribution to this worldwide activity came from the export of raw materials such as copra and luxury products such as pearls, and gold after 1890. Massim material culture that began to appear in European museums about this time, and shortly thereafter ethnographic reports, should also be classified as luxury products given their uses in the dominating European cultures.

From about 1890 to 1914 the region was one of the centers of European activity in what is now Papua New Guinea. By 1918 or so it was becoming one of the backwaters. Although many indigenous peoples began their own copra production in the 1920s, subsequently this work has been fitful at best. Little gold was found in the region after about 1940. And only with the dramatic rise in the price of gold during the 1970s did intensive exploration and some mining begin again. Gold exploration in the early 1980s was predicated on gold's being priced at or above U.S.$500 per ounce.

After 1920 the Australian colonial administration had a continuing presence in many areas and, along with missions, began to insinuate its morals into the local cultures, in many cases nominally for hygienic reasons. World War II brought a new set of Australian administrators and thousands of American troops to some islands; airstrips on Goodenough, the Trobriands, and Muyuw date from that war. Government activities; mission schools, many of which were later taken over by the government; and some European commerce intensified after 1950, and more dramatically in the 1960s and 1970s. In the early colonial years only Goodenough and Rossel islands produced much labor for the European economy (Young 1983b; Liep 1983). Their contribution might be related to their marginal location in the region as a whole. Nevertheless, after 1960 other areas entered this phase of incorporation, church and government schools funneling youths out of their elders' system into the European one.

By 1980 another significant shift in the area's relationship to the European world economy may have come about. Before then Australian-based companies such as Burns Philps and Steamships had interisland trawlers that periodically deposited European imports in mostly European-run tradestores as they picked up copra from small-scale indigenous producers and, as it appears now, often underfinanced Europeans. The region was also dotted with European-owned mills producing lumber for the local area. Since 1980 Burns Philps and Steamships have largely, but not completely, withdrawn; many of the local lumber mills have closed; and on Muyuw and near Alotau, the provincial capital, highly financed lumber concerns have begun exporting uncut logs to mostly Asian markets.

The last one hundred years vitally affected all of these societies. With regard to mortuary practices several changes may be noted. Secondary internment was widely practiced throughout the region. It no longer is and many of us learned little about it. Forms of commodity production underlie or participate in most societies' ceremonies. Australian white flour and rice are often added to or replace some ritual exchange items. In Vakuta cloth dresses complement traditionally produced coconut or banana leaf skirts. Pigs, which play a major or minor role in every group's practices, are sometimes just bought with money rather than exchanged in a like-for-like manner. This does not necessarily affect the way the pigs are handled within the confines of the rituals, but it denotes a transformation in the networks that facilitate them. These rituals are not about the production of commodities, but now commodity production is used in their meaning and functioning.

There are other, perhaps more subtle, changes. Particular locales are gradually becoming defined more by their largely opaque relations to distant European metropoles than their transparent relationships to each other.[5] The importance of this switch may be illustrated with one dramatic ethnographic problem. The major exchange items in the southeastern corner of the region, represented in this volume by Lepowsky's paper on Vanatinai, are large ceremonial stone axes. Most of these stone products came from the Sulog quarries and production sites on Muyuw, Woodlark Island. But because of a demographic collapse and the increasing availability of iron Muyuw stopped producing these materials about 1870. Now, however, Vanatinai and other people believe that their stone axes come out of the water, that they are not products of human agents. Is this belief a product of relations created or recreated by colonial circumstances? Or is it a feature of the "traditional" organization of regional production and reproduction? It should be noted that in virtually every other locale the producer of an exchange item and the craftsmanship with which the item is produced are significant aspects of mortuary ritual exchange dynamics. Such considerations seem to be disappearing.

Another set of facts ties together questions of historical change and a regional perspective. Goodenough and Rossel cultures are similar in that in neither do mortuary rites constitute the crystallizing events that such rituals do elsewhere. Goodenough culture speaks an Austronesian language but its descent system is atypically patrilineal. Rossel has a normal Massim matrilineal regime but its language is non-Austronesian. But both cultures play inversely paradoxical roles in the larger system. In the past enormous pig tusks were an additional and important exchange article in the Kula circuit. Now they have virtually fallen out of the system, kept only by the occasional elder to show youths about past times. The origins of these items and the exact way they were employed are both poorly understood. Equally poorly understood is the bizarre fact that as they left the Kula circulation thousands of them were deposited on Goodenough. What is, or was, the structure of the whole region such that by historical change one important item drained into an island that for some time has hardly participated in the interisland exchange system at all? Rossel Island does not participate in the Kula either. Yet it produces one of the main Kula valuables, *bagi*, what Malinowski called *soulava* (necklaces). For all of this century *bagi* production has been mediated if not encouraged by Europeans. The exact significance of this for the Kula, in Malinowski's time and our own, is not known. But old "Kula valuables" went into Goodenough; new ones come from Rossel. Why?

How the region's history is being incorporated into the views people have of their societies also deserves consideration. Especially on the southern side of the Massim one often finds statements to the effect that in the past people were cannibals, but now pigs, important mortuary exchange items, replace humans. A variant of this expression concludes Young's paper on Bwaidoka (Goodenough): Bwaidokans "believe that before Europeans came, and indeed before pigs were in general use, mother's brothers used to kill, cook, and eat their sister's firstborn child as brideprice" (p. 198). From such statements one needs to ask whether colonial relations have generated fundamental changes in the structure and content of these societies. Or, do such expressions reflect structural principles connected with the interrelationships between persons and things that absorb, so to speak, the content of the last one hundred years for their symbolic expression? A historical perspective seems necessary for an interpretation of the meanings of many of these cultures' beliefs.

Language

As the history of this region introduces many problems for its comparative understanding, so does its linguistic makeup. As in much of Papua New Guinea, Massim linguistic diversity is legendary. According to Lithgow (1976), Milne Bay Province has as many as forty different Austronesian languages divisible into some twelve families and eight non-Austronesian groups. The linguistic diversity in the region covered in these essays is somewhat less, yet it is substantial. Indigenous people relatively easily negotiate their east-to-west language differences, but north-to-south differences require study before they transcend them. Capell (1969) distinguishes the northern and southern Massim languages as two types (object-dominated and event-dominated, respectively). Further linguistic research will refine our understanding of the area, but it will not change the problem language presents social anthropology.

Social anthropology demands that the anthropologist learn the language of the culture he or she investigates. A residue of this practice is one language, one culture. In wide-ranging comparative work this circumstance is not a problem because linguistic complexities must be ignored for comparison to proceed. However, in a place like the Massim where the cultures are both contiguous to one another and interconnected by numerous exchanges the relationship between language and institutions demands investigation. Frequently two or more cultures share the same word form, which has slightly different meanings; in other cases different words have identical meanings and functions. Investigation is needed to determine whether these similarities and differences evoke some larger configuration, a random or unknowable history, or peculiarities resulting from a particular area's naming practices. I discuss two of many cases where these questions seem particularly pertinent.

In most if not all of these societies the word for breast and often breast milk is *susu* or some close variant. In the Trobriands, for example, it is *nunu*. In Massim cultures the production of the person is richly elaborated sociologically and symbolically. It is not surprising then that the *susu* term takes on significant sociological content. But it varies tremendously. In many southern societies (for instance, Tubetube, Lobada, and Dobu), it refers to the most important aspect of matrilineal descent ideology: hence "clan" or "lineage" is an initial translation of *susu*. In Goodenough the analogous descent notion is *unuma*, and this may be cognate to *susu*. However, Goodenough descent ideology is patrilineal rather than matrilineal. Nevertheless the exact linguistic cognate of *susu* occurs. It refers to one's mother's descent line (Young 1971:38). A Goodenough person calls his mother's descent group (*unuma*) by the same term *susu* by which people to the east call their own. Is there a logical pattern inherent in this difference that defines other aspects of Goodenough's relationships to these societies?

In northern Kiriwina Weiner (1976:92) writes that the Trobriand *nunu* can be used in place of the more common *dala; dala* is translated "subclan" in the Malinowskian tradition. However, in Vakuta, the southern Trobriands, *nunusi* merely refers to people of the same mother. It does not imply the more inclusive *dala* (Campbell personal communication). Although these Trobriand usages bear family resemblances to the southern *susu*, the descent category in the Trobriands partakes of a significantly different system than the southern one. As the Tubetube and Lobada data in this volume indicate, the *susu* notion strains toward achieving a kind of ultimate, if primarily ideological, autonomy. In the Trobriands (and east to Muyuw), on the contrary, descent groups are represented as part of a totality, whether this totality is defined by a consciously hierarchical system or by the inclusion of *dala* in a larger and more embracing clan (*kumila* or *kum*) system, or both systems. Nevertheless a form of this near pan-Massim term turns up in another context, in northern Kiriwina at least. In the form of *nununiga* it refers to the banana leaf bundles that are the most important medium of exchange in northern Kiriwina mortuary ceremonies. If Weiner's attempt to define *nununiga* by its constituent parts ("breast" and "share" [1976:92]) is correct, then the term connotes relating units. This is contrary to the southern usage, which tends toward exclusiveness. The meaning of *nununiga* merges with that in Muyuw, although there the cognate refers neither to descent units nor to any exchange medium such as the Trobriand banana leaf bundles. In Muyuw the word just means "breast" or "breast milk," and, as in the Trobriands, in its verbalized form, *-sus*, "to suck." However, Muyuw understand breast milk as transformed male labor, the fish and garden food a man has produced and given to his wife that she then transforms and passes on to their children. So although it has neither the sociological referent of the south nor the symbolic use of the Trobriand

nununiga, the Muyuw term is embedded in productive processes that constitute the essence of the production of children. Such notions are at the heart
of the Muyuw mortuary system.

A second linguistic example contrasts the use of an apparent cognate in
Tubetube, and straight north of Tubetube, Muyuw culture. The Tubetube
word is *lowalowa*, the Muyuw *lawalov*. In both cultures the term refers to
the exchange of *kitoum* (or *kitomwa*) following a death. In brief, *kitoum*
are personally owned Kula valuables crucial to the operation of the Kula.
From Macintyre's discussion it appears that the Tubetube *lowalowa* always
goes between intermarried clans. This is frequently but not necessarily true
in Muyuw. In both Tubetube and Muyuw the *kitoum* must be returned to
the original giver although restitution may take several years. Thus the
word, the occasion for its usage, and the content of the exchange are all
virtually identical. However, the Tubetube practice takes far greater significance than the Muyuw one. In Tubetube clan resources are tied to the return
of the *kitoum*; if it is not returned, things such as clan land must be given
in its place. This does not occur with respect to the Muyuw *lawalov*. However, in Muyuw the giving and receiving of pigs in the mortuary system create debts that are tied to clan resources in the same way that they are tied
to *kitoum* in the Tubetube *lowalowa*.

In her contribution to this volume Chowning traces linguistic and cultural cognates for several of the southern societies. She thus initiates an important level of inquiry that requires the skills of both linguists and social
anthropologists. This endeavor will alter our understanding of the relationships between these societies and, just as importantly, alter the use of some
traditional anthropological categories.

Comparison

Comparison in anthropology now refers to at least two different procedures. The oldest form of comparative analysis follows from the creation
of ideal types and their use in ferreting out unsuspected relations or processes in the specified data or in trying to determine what kinds of external
relationships realize the particular form. Eggan's "controlled comparison"
called for these long ago (1954). And of course van Wooden [1935] 1968)
sketched one for eastern Indonesia even earlier. There are others (Fox 1980;
Maybury-Lewis 1979). For the papers collected here the most important
work follows from Hertz's famous essay on death (1960). I shall relate this
collection's papers to Hertz's work through a brief discussion of two recent
volumes that extend and redefine Hertz: Huntington and Metcalf's *Celebrations of Death* (1979) and Bloch and Parry's *Death and the Regeneration
of Life* (1982).

Huntington and Metcalf's *Celebrations* attempts to readjust the "grammar" of mortuary rites Hertz originally outlined. As did Hertz, they view death and its attendant rituals as transitions variously affecting the deceased's corpse, its soul, and the mourners who must take up life again. They, especially Metcalf (chap. 3, fig. 2), suggest that the sequence of rites and beliefs associated with the corpse, its soul, and the mourners will be homologous to one another. Since none of the papers in this volume specifically addresses this model, and since secondary internment practices have been eradicated in fact and in many peoples' memory, not all of the details of the form are witnessed in the Massim societies. However, readers will be able to identify the likelihood of its former existence in the papers by Montague, Damon, Macintyre, Thune, and Lepowsky. Although he does not engage the Hertz paradigm, Thune constructs his paper on the principle that mortuary rites are rites of transition. In the beginning of the Lobadan— and other areas' practices too—ritual sequence the deceased is dressed up to express the essence of life. Mourners, or some of them, appear dead. By the end of the ritual pattern this inversion is inverted. The mourners are brought back to life and the deceased is reduced to a pile of bones. One might note that it is precisely as a pile of bones that the Lobadan descent category, *susu*, achieves its ultimate and perhaps only realization of autonomy.

A difficulty in applying the grammar of mortuary rites put forth by *Celebrations* is that it supplies no ready way for moving from the particular forms of one place to those of another. Showing that there are concordances among beliefs about the soul, manipulations of the corpse, and transformations among the living in each of these societies would be a valuable exercise. However, how does such a plan deal with differences between them? For example, many of the central exchanges in the Trobriands are between women allied by marriage, whereas in Muyuw they are between male affines; in Tubetube and Lobada (and Dobu), they are between pairs of brother/sister units; in Vanatinai (and Sabarl), they are between cross-cousins reclassified into symbolic father/child relations.

Huntington's discussion of the Bara, a society in Madagascar (1979: chap. 4), poses the question of transition and death in a way that may help focus upon Massim variability. In departing from the Hertzian model Huntington asks why Bara mortuary rites are accompanied by such a profuse demonstration of sexuality and sexual symbolism. His answer is that many Bara values turn on an opposition between "order" and "vitality." Order is variously represented by "male," "bone," "sterility," "tomb," and the like; vitality is incarnated by "female," "flesh," and "womb." Bara existence must combine these contrasting elements, but death effectively promotes too much "order." Hence mortuary rituals attempt to restore balance by giving society too much vitality, female sexuality. This summary of a provocative and subtle description is sufficient to suggest a line of inquiry into both Trobriand and Muyuw death practices.

What is so striking about Trobriand mortuary practices, from Weiner's initial presentation (1976) to those Montague and Campbell provide in this volume, is the place women hold in the rituals and the profusion of female products, skirts, and banana leaf bundles, that women produce for and manipulate in them. Montague adds an important fact about Trobriand death notions. According to her, Trobriand people (those in Kaileuna at least) believe that it is men who kill, who bring death into the world. One might suggest then that Trobriand rituals attempt to reorder a world too dominated by male capacities by temporarily dominating it with female capacities.

The exact opposite could be said of Muyuw. In its first and third mortuary rituals vegetable food and pig are assembled on a grand scale. These products are conceived to be male-produced, just the opposite of Trobriand female wealth. Also just the opposite of the Trobriands is the Muyuw belief that virtually all death results from female witchcraft. In Muyuw mortuary rituals women maintain very subservient roles, especially during the main distributions, when they go to the periphery while men make all of the decisions as to who gets what and why at the event's center. In this culture these rituals provide the only context in which male and female persons and attributes are not explicitly intertwined. So since death is usually conceived as a consequence of having too much feminine activity the rituals might be interpreted as supplying a countervailing male dominance.

To be fully convincing this interpretation would have to integrate more details than I have presented, and, more important, it would be necessary to show how it could be transported to the cultural configurations in the southern Massim. But the effort may be worthwhile.

Space considerations prevent me from commenting on anything more than the long introduction (pp. 1–44) to Bloch and Parry's *Death and the Regeneration of Life* (1982). The editors' point of departure is, to some extent, Huntington's discussion of the Bara. Like Huntington they ask why beliefs and symbols of fertility are so commonly found in mortuary rites. However, Bloch and Parry are more concerned with how mortuary rituals legitimize the social order than with the rituals' form or grammar. And they think Hertz was more concerned with the sociology of emotion, with how the biological individual is kept in society, than with the structuralist reading that Huntington and Metcalf provide. Bloch and Parry deal with what gives rise to complex mortuary rites, not with the actual rites themselves. This shift in emphasis is useful for this volume, especially because they employ two Massim societies, Dobu (pp. 27–32) and the Trobriands of Malinowski (pp. 8, 29), to illustrate aspects of their thesis.

16

Bloch and Parry's main thesis is that mortuary rites serve to mediate the contradictory relationship between the biological individual, a product and victim of largely contingent events, and a hierarchical and static social order. In those societies where there is no or little hierarchy, and in those societies where the social order itself is conceived to be a product of a contingent history, one would not expect to find elaborate mortuary rites. But in other societies mortuary rites mediate the individual/society, event/form contradiction by placing in the hands of the authorities a symbolic system that attempts to say that they, the authorities, are responsible for the reproduction of life. Mortuary rites frequently exhibit sexual themes precisely because they devalue individuals' productive capacities while appropriating them for larger, or higher, systems of control.

This is an engaging and fruitful point of view for Massim studies. One set of facts, more discussed during our conference than described in our papers, immediately suggests its relevance. For many Massim peoples the first reaction to elders' deaths is the assertion of their uniqueness and irreplacability: "nobody will be able to do what that person did." But, as the rituals begin, people become swept up in details, and as the rites mount in material and social complexity people replace the memories of the deceased's creativity by their own. Massim mortuary practices rid the living of the active memory of the dead.

However, to become applicable to the Massim area, the Bloch and Parry perspective needs serious criticism. The version of society they present seems a very fragile one, as if any fact running counter to a particular design for living is likely to topple that form of domination. Such a point of view hardly describes the Massim, where a significant number of people in any one area know that on the next island things are done much differently. Massim political authority is not dependent upon knowing only one way to construct images for peoples' lives.

But what is really at issue here is the artificialist view of culture that pervades their introduction. For Bloch and Parry what is real is the "biological" person and hierarchy. Culture, in this instance mortuary rites, merely makes real people consent to the hierarchy. The place of the individual, of biology, in their essay needs critical discussion. Significantly they draw on Leach's initiation of the Trobriand Virgin Birth controversy (Leach 1966). But Leach's attempt to focus on the varying ways cultures construct reality is converted by them into showing how cultures lie about reality. Although it is true that many Massim societies ignore or underplay the way a child is conceived, they pay great attention to the way men and women combine their labors to produce children both in and ex utero. Sexual symbolism plays important roles in Massim mortuary ceremonies not because people are devaluing sexuality, but because the dependencies created by the production of children are being paid back at death, and

17

the conditions for the reproduction of children in the future are being established.

• The kind of comparative analyses just reviewed will remain useful for further probing the complexities of Massim mortuary rites and beliefs. But to them must be added the most recent comparative perspective, that associated with Lévi-Strauss. This practice traces transformations between collectivities differentiated in space or time, or both. Recent work by Rosman and Rubel (1978) for New Guinea and Kuper (1982) for southern Africa provides examples worthy of consideration for the Massim. Formal models play their roles here. However, the method analyzes variability not to demonstrate causation but to define societal objects and limits. The ease with which some Massim people can specify their differences yet also establish identities with one another is one kind of social fact that lends credibility to this kind of approach. Complex regional systems like the Massim's are legion throughout Melanesia and other places, so the method needs more attention. For the Massim, Wagner's Conclusion to the present volume should be taken as a point of departure for this analytical mode. The volume as a whole will afford, we hope, other students the opportunity to pursue different avenues for the understanding of one of anthropology's classic areas.

NOTES

1. Published independently but simultaneously with the Leach and Leach volume is Macintyre's *The Kula: A Bibliography* (1983), an invaluable source on a hundred years of writing about the Massim. The annotated bibliography is complete to about 1978. For critical comments on previous versions of this Introduction I thank John Liep, Martha Macintyre, Susan Montague, Nancy Munn, Roy Wager, Michael Young, and several anonymous reviewers. Nevertheless, I am alone responsible for the views expressed here. This publication is a joint effort. However, my Introduction and Wagner's Conclusion were conceived and produced after the 1981 Kula Conference and should be understood as our individual syntheses.

2. The 1983 volume contains comparative essays by several anthropologists with library research on the Massim: R. Firth, C. Gregory, A. Strathern, and S. Tambiah. G. Irwin (1983), the lone archaeologist in the group, makes an important contribution to Massim studies that social anthropologists should not overlook. The regional systems perspective of the present Introduction owes much to Irwin's paper and his participation in the 1981 conference.

3. Although she attended the 1981 conference, Nancy Munn did not submit a paper for publication. Chapters 7 and 8 of her book (Munn 1986) present material similar to that of this volume. Gawa is located between the Trobriands and Muyuw, and its mortuary rites (chapter 7) and community entertainments (chapter 8), respectively, resemble the mortuary activities of these two areas.

4. Lepowsky's rich paper describes the social relationships manifested in her area's mortuary rites. Although Vanatinai and Sabarl cultures are not identical, readers might wish to read Battaglia's discussion of the symbolism of stone axes on Sabarl along with Lepowsky's contribution here (Battaglia 1983).

5. Such categories as "economics," "religion," and "politics" are not informative when discussing traditional systems, but they are when discussing colonial relations. Colonial agents use these terms. It may be argued that political and religious domination is not opaque since Massim people understand who dominate them if not the sense of their dominators' messages. But some Massim people, astute strategists concerning their own productive forms, find the imposed Western economic system baffling.

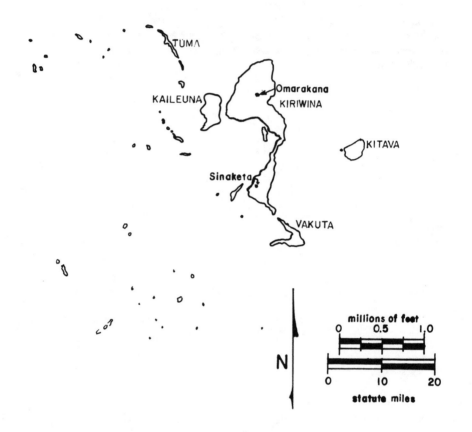

PART ONE

The Northern Massim

KWAIAWATA

GAWA

MUYUW

n a y e m

wamwan

muyuw

YANABA

YEGUMA.

NASIKWABU

s. k. parker

Susan P. Montague

To Eat for the Dead

Kaduwagan Mortuary Events

We eat for the living, and we eat for the dead, whereas you just
bury your dead and eat for yourselves alone.

   ◆   When I took up residence in 1971 in Kaduwaga village,
Kaileuna Island, the Trobriand Islands, I was soon struck by the lavish feasting that followed upon the death of any villager.

I naively assumed that it would be easy to ascertain why Kaduwagans
(and other Trobriand Islanders) think it appropriate to cope with death by
staging an elaborate cycle of feasting and gift giving. So I asked about this.
But I got no answer beyond statements such as "It is our custom" and "We
wonder why you foreigners do not have these customs." It was not until
I returned to Kaduwaga in 1980 that a friend, pushed to the edge of emotional endurance by the death of a close relative, erupted into anger and
said the words I have quoted. As he tried to make amends for his rude out-
burst, he said that he did not mean to indict me personally for gross selfish-
ness. It is only that he cannot understand how our mortuary customs work,
given that they seem so thoroughly grounded in failure to perceive or act
upon proper human considerations. As I pursued his remarks with other
villagers, I discovered that they too shared his perceptions about the inade-
quacy of our mortuary practices. To Kaduwagans we appear to be people
who selfishly eat for ourselves rather than for others and who carry this
wrong-minded behavior to the extreme of failing even to eat for our recently
deceased consociates.

This paper describes the mortuary observances at Kaduwaga village. It begins with a discussion of why Kaduwagans think that people should eat for others, living and dead, an idea that follows from their view of cosmic process, some of which I explain in that discussion. I then present my data on the mortuary observances themselves and, as I do that, explore three other issues, also generated from the Kaduwagan view of cosmic process, that also enter into these observances.

Trobriand funerals are immensely elaborate by Western standards, and many kinds of considerations enter into them. Some already have been analyzed in the ethnographic literature. I have chosen not to reanalyze those here because of spatial limitations. Interested readers should look at Malinowski's (1929) comments on the ways in which mourning practices are designed to forestall sorcery accusations and Weiner's (1976) comments on how mortuary observances are structured so as to maintain matrilineages, as well as her comments on how they are used to reconstruct exchange networks rent apart by death.

To assist my readers, I append a list of the main Kaduwagan mortuary events. It can also be used to compare Kaduwagan funerals with those found at Vakuta. (See the essay by Campbell in this volume.) A description of the first two sections of the Kwaibwaga village funeral observances from northern Kiriwina Island is available in Weiner (1976).

EATING FOR OTHERS IN THE
TROBRIAND ISLANDS

Malinowski (1929:170–72) indicated that Trobriand Islanders know each person to be a *baloma* (spirit), inhabiting a *wowo* (body). I will hence forth substitute *mind* for Malinowski's *spirit* since Kaduwagans do not draw any spirit/mind distinction, and I prefer to reserve the term *spirit* for some aspect of an animate being that exists apart from its mind. The Trobriand mind originates in the nonsubstantial world of the dead, inside the earth. It is sent out to the substantial world of the living, on the earth's surface, by another mind residing in the world of the dead. The mind that is sent out is a *waiwaia* (infant mind). In order to become a new living person, the *waiwaia* must obtain an encapsulating body. In order to do that it must enter into a woman's womb. There, with proper application of *kanua* (human body building food), which consists of yams and taro, the woman's menstrual blood (itself a digestive product of *kanua*) is augmented and grows into a new infant body.

The infant is born as the food dependent of two people, a man and a woman. The man provides the requisite *kanua* to build the new infant body. The woman processes that food into the new infant body, first by cooking it and second by eating and digesting it.

The infant remains a food dependent, usually of the same man and woman, throughout its childhood and adolescence. When it reaches adulthood, its dependency status changes, but not because it becomes self-sufficient in terms of food provisioning. It changes as, continuing its food-related dependency on others, the adult begins also to produce food and give it to others. In short, adulthood is marked by the acquisition of one's own food dependents.

The adult combination of simultaneously being a food dependent and having food dependents is a crucial derivative of Trobriand ideas about cosmic process. Life is a game set up by minds that naturally inhabit the world of the dead. These minds, which include yours and mine, are all-seeing, all-knowing, and all-powerful. It is as if the Mind of God did not exist in a vacuum, but in a milieu where there were many minds like His. These minds find their natural state boring. When you are all-seeing, all-knowing, and all-powerful, you do not have much to think about. So these minds got together and invented a game with which to amuse themselves, the game of life.

The game of life is simple in its conceptual basics, though not at all simple in its play. The idea is to see how much control you can exercise over other minds in a context wherein all of the minds that are playing have temporarily restricted their vision, knowledge, and prowess.

The restrictions are produced in two ways. First, each *waiwaia* (infant mind) is an adult mind that has temporarily done away with all of its conscious knowledge. This is why infants are born knowing nothing. Second, each mind that enters into life surrounds itself with a physical shell, a body. The body provides a perceptual barrier to the mind's intake of information, limiting vision and, thereby, knowledge. It also limits the contained mind's effective ability to use its innate powers to do virtually anything it wants.

To make the game of life more problematical, the minds that set it up agreed upon several other conventions. They agreed to make the field of play sufficiently small that only a few of the many minds wanting to play can play at any given point in time. They agreed that each player must exit from play when the bodily shell encapsulating his mind dies. And they agreed that no player will either manufacture or sustain his own bodily shell. The last point is the one that mandates the continuation of each player's being dependent on others for food throughout his lifetime.

To help gain an initial sense of what all this looks like on the ground, let us consider an event that occurred at Kaduwaga when I was there in 1981. I and my host family were sitting in our house after dinner when some visitors from Kaibola Village (on northern Kiriwina Island) dropped in to chat. The conversation focused on the peculiar doings of a Frenchman who recently had built himself a house in the bush near the beach owned by Kaibola Village. He was living alone and had indicated to the villagers that he did not desire social interaction with anyone. He told them to leave him alone. He also told them that he currently possessed enough food to get by until his first garden was grown, and that he intended to live out the rest of his life all by himself in his bush house.

The recounting of this story caused a lot of excited chatter, most of which I could not follow. After a bit, someone turned to me and said, "Susan, you too are a foreigner. What do you make of this man?" Since I was not sure what all the chatter was about I returned the question, asking one of the Kaibola women, "What do *you* make of him?" She said, "We're scared! We think he must be a murderer!" Since Kaduwagans often indicate that deaths are caused by sorcerers, I said, "You mean that he sorcerized someone and they died?" She said, "No! I mean that he hit someone and killed them. You know, the English word, *murderer*! Why else would he live alone and not grow food for anyone but himself? He must have murdered one of his fellow villagers, and they drove him out of their village. Now he has come here, and maybe he will murder one of us!"

This man was death walking. No Kaduwagan who wants to live would possibly consider voluntarily doing as he had done. Even if he could physically survive very long all on his own, something that is doubtful, there is no point to doing that. Physical isolation only produces mental isolation, which in turn produces a high state of boredom. If a mind wants to be bored, it has no reason to attempt to remain in the world of the living. Since it has no reason to do that, his mind cannot have voluntarily made the choice to reside in isolation. So it must have been forced into that position. The sole reason why other minds would force it into that position is that he manually killed someone outside the field of battle and the consociate minds in the village wherein he was playing banished him from their presence for doing that. That is the sole form of killing that will result in someone's being banished from a village because it is the sole form of killing that happens too fast for the victim to have had a reasonable chance of self-defense. The banishment is not in aid of the victim, but of the remaining consociates who do not themselves want to fall victim to this type of killing, just as the Kaibolans, now that the banishee had come to reside near them, also did not want to fall victim to it. Not surprisingly it did not take long for them to persuade the local branch of the national government to deport the Frenchman.

When Kaduwagans say that *buena* (organized) people eat for others, they are saying that people who correctly perceive how it is that life processes work eat in ways that consistently honor and flatter the people who provide them with *kanua* (human body building food). To do otherwise is virtually to ask to die, because an unappreciated food provider will quickly turn away and supply the food instead to someone else, someone who will *be* appreciative.

Eating for others involves several sorts of approaches to *kanua*. *Kanua*

26

is never to be tossed on the ground. It is never to be thrown away, unless it is rotten. A person who is carrying *kanua* must never be physically attacked, nor must anyone who is eating it. As a person consumes *kanua*, she or he should chew with the mouth open. One woman commented, "The person who chews with a shut mouth is a selfish, stingy person." Finally, *kanua* crops are all dedicated to the recently dead. As I toured Kaduwaga's gardens at harvest time in 1981, man after man showed me his plot, saying, "All that you see here is for mortuary distribution!" That is not literally true, but sentiment is what counts.

Trobriand Islanders do not literally give all their *kanua* away in the sense that they do not alienate all of it from their own household consumption (although they do alienate most of it). Nonetheless, they are careful never to eat their own *kanua* even when eating that small portion that is retained for their own household consumption. In 1980 my hostess, Itagoma, said, "I am glad that on this visit you are living in our house rather than in your own as you were on your first visit. Then you ate your own food. Now you eat food that I give you." I pointed out that I was still mostly eating my own (store-bought) food. She said, "No. Now all of the food you eat is cooked on my hearth, and any food cooked on my hearth has been given to me. So now you are eating food that I have given (back) to you." Another woman pointed out to me that some of the food in her husband's garden plot had been grown by their son for his parents. Since the son in question was only three years old, I said, "How can that be?" She said, "Oh, I and his father helped him with the actual labor. Isn't it nice to have a son who works to build your body as you work to build his!" The toddler was present as she said this and beamed at her praise of him.

Despite the fact that Kaduwagans always do eat for others as they want others to continue to maintain their bodies so that they can go on actively playing life, death is a necessity given the nature of the game. What death ultimately boils down to is food deprivation, the cessation of provisioning the body so that it can continue to live. However, this point is obscured to most novice Western outsiders looking in at the game because Trobriand Islanders do not kill people by overtly refusing to give them food. They do it by adulterating the food they do give in ways that are invisible to the recipient and that destroy the food's utility for building and sustaining the recipient's body. This practice of covert refusal to give food is what is generally referred to in the anthropological literature on the Trobriands as sorcery.

To understand why Trobriand Islanders kill mostly through covert food deprivations it is necessary to realize that death does not only enter the game as the way to cycle minds out of life so that other minds can cycle into it. Death plays an additional role because the problematics of the game are enhanced by making it the case that each player can play only so long as he can manage at least to convince some other mind(s) to provide him with the food necessary to sustain his body. If, at any point in the period of time allotted to a player in any given round of play, he cannot do that, he is knocked out of the game.

The most that any player can hope for is to stay in the game for fifty to sixty years. That is the amount of time provided for any one mind to participate in any one round of play before it must give up playing so that another mind can take its place. But most players do not stay in the game that long. Most are knocked out in a shorter period as other players find it strategic to remove them in order to advance their (the other players') immediate position.

I want to stress that the rules of the game *do not* preclude the removal of other players to enhance one's own immediate position in the game. They only make it risky. But then risk is central to problematics, and problematics are what the game is all about. However, as they *do* make it risky, they also set up a situation wherein it is very unwise to present one's self as overtly attempting to kill the body of another player. The player who can see you coming will, at least, take steps to deflect your attack, or, at most, try to kill your body so that you are no longer in the game to mount an attack against his.

To close this section, it is necessary to add one point about death. Whether a player survives the amount of time allotted to a single round of play of the game of life or not, his or her body is always killed by another living mind. The rules of the game preclude dead minds from killing bodies because dead minds have a conflict-of-interest insofar as they are eager to cycle into life.

With this background on Trobriand construals of eating, life, and death, let us turn to a consideration of two specific issues to be kept in mind as I present my mortuary data and of a third that I will actively explore in that presentation.

THREE ISSUES FOR CONSIDERATION IN THE PRESENTATION OF THE MORTUARY DATA

The first issue is the departure of the mind of the deceased person out of the world of the living. Malinowski (1929) indicated that Trobriand funerals seemed overly elaborate in that the mind of the deceased person is thought to have departed this world rapidly after death and thereby not to be present to witness the lengthy proceedings. However, he was mistaken in his apparent assumption that minds that are off in the world of the dead cannot thereby witness proceedings in the world of the living. But the more important point is that part of the reason why Trobriand funerals are so lengthy is that, as Weiner (1976) indicates, they cover what is thought to be the amount of time required for the living to rearrange their lives in order to compensate for the void caused by the death. This amount of time is thought to be about a year and a half. This also is the amount of time the body requires to decay into a mere assemblage of bones. This coincidence is not fortuitous. Minds organize bodily decay, just as they organize everything else, and have chosen to time it that way.

I divide my mortuary data into three sections because most of the events I describe occur at one of three points along the continuum of bodily decay. The first events take place shortly after the person has died. They center upon the burial of the corpse. The second section takes place three to four months later, at the time when the corpse's flesh has sufficiently decayed so that the body is visually unrecognizable as that of the person who died. These events center on the cessation of mourning for the deceased. The last events take place a year or so after that, at the time when the corpse has decayed into an assemblage of bones. They center on the cessation of having to rearrange one's life to fill the void caused by the death.

    • The second issue is that of the mechanics of holding a Kaduwagan funeral. Like most Western funerals they are catered events that involve hiring people and paying them to perform death-related labor. Under normal circumstances the person who holds the funeral is the deceased's strongest male matrilineal consociate. It is he who determines how elaborate the funeral will be, a function of how much labor he is willing and able to hire, and he who pays for it. He is called *tolikariga* (the source of the death man). This is for two reasons. One is that the death is only as socially significant as he says it is, as he decides to hold a larger or smaller funeral. The other is that he is the most likely person actually to have caused the death. Let us look at why this is.

Only men kill in the Trobriand world. Only men possess bodies that are sufficiently *kasai* (hard or solid) to have any chance of fending off serious attempts at vengeance. This is not to say that no Trobriand woman ever actually kills someone. Instead, it is to say that no Trobriand woman kills someone without herself being under the protection of some man or men. For that protection to exist, some man or men have to sanction the death, and, thereby, some man or men ultimately cause it.

Second, men who venture to cause deaths are likely to be stronger than most of their male consociates. If they are not that, their risk of dying from vengeance is too high. They always do run this risk, but the stronger they are, the harder it is for other men to kill them.

Third, the likelihood is greatest that any given death will be caused by a matrilineal consociate. The man who kills out of the cosmic need for death to occur is very wise to confine his action to his matrilineal consociates because each matrilineage construes itself as a unique pool of people who handle ultimate cosmic cycling as a closed subunit of the larger cycling system. If he extends his efforts outward and kills someone from another matrilineage, he risks much more danger from attempted vengeance than he does if he confines those efforts to his own matrilineal consociates.

The man who kills to enhance his own immediate life position also tends to confine his action to his own matrilineal consociates for another reason. Given how the game of life is structured, most of his leverage over other minds is bound up with his ability to possess *kanua*. Most of the people he wants to remove are those who stand in the way of his maximization of control over that resource. Although not all of the people who stand in his way are his matrilineal consociates, the ones who most *directly* stand in his way usually are. Therefore they are the ones upon whom he tends to focus his attempts at removal.

As the man who holds the funeral is also the single most likely person to have caused the death, he faces a very interesting problematic. While he determines how elaborate the funeral will be, he runs a very high risk of attempted vengeance by his own male matrilineal consociates unless he decides to make it sufficiently elaborate that its cost exceeds his own wealth. But if he decides to make it that elaborate, he must turn first of all to them to help him pay for it. This means that he must turn to those same male matrilineal consociates because, if they will not help him in this respect, no other man will. How he copes with this situation is one of problematics that Kaduwagans find most interesting about their funerals.

The third issue concerns the ways in which mortuary procedures incorporate village level concerns. This is the issue to which I will devote most attention in the actual presentation of my mortuary data. Trobriand villages have not received much analytical attention in the anthropological literature, largely because they have been viewed as mere clumps of contiguous matrilineal hamlets. Although it certainly is true that each Trobriand village contains a number of matrilineages, it also is true that their contiguous aggregation is not what makes them into a *vanu* (village). What makes them into that is a higher level of centralized organization.

The centralized organization turns on the mechanics of land ownership. Malinowski to the contrary, Trobriand garden land is not owned by corporate matrilineages. It is owned by individual men. Additionally, it is owned by very few individual men. This is because Trobriand garden land is organized into a series of *kwabila* (large fields). At Kaduwaga there are only five large fields and four large-field owners (one man owns two of them). Each large field is big enough that a sufficient amount of *kanua* can be grown on it alone to feed the entire village population of three hundred for one year. In any given year, only one *kwabila* is put into production. They are gardened in rotation on a five-year cycle to ensure maximal crop yields.

There are numerous tenancy arrangements among the four large-field owners and the seventy or so landless Kaduwaga men who garden on their land. For instance, in one arrangement the tenant has the right to garden a particular plot in a particular field for the rest of his life. But all of the tenancy arrangements are subject to two conditions. The tenant can only garden on the land in a year when the large-field owner agrees to put the field into production, and the tenant must stop gardening on the land if the large-field owner announces that he is taking the field out of production, as the owner is free to do at any time.

The centralized organizational structure that makes the village a village consists of the agreement of the large-field owners to make their land available on a rotational basis and to make it available to all of the rest of the village's male populance. However the structure is fragile, as any owner(s) can withdraw from this arrangement at any time, even if the withdrawal means the destruction of entire *kanua* crop currently under cultivation. Large-field owners are not fools. They are well aware that they are likely to be killed if they engage in capricious withdrawals of their land from the rest of the village populace. But there is one circumstance wherein they do make those withdrawals. They make them when a villager dies.

The reason they do this is that the death creates the distinct possibility that there is an unidentified killer loose in the village who may attempt to kill them next. They are the most obvious targets for murder because theirs is the second-most desirable position for any man to occupy in life (the most desirable position is that of a "chief," the man among the large-field owners who manages to own the most large fields).

As the large-field owners withdraw their land from access by their tenants, the village comes to a halt. It literally goes out of existence. It only comes back into existence as the funeral holder, leveraged by this ploy, manages to offer them adequate assurance that the man who caused the current death and who, of necessity, still remains unidentified for the time being will not turn and attack them in the period between when the death occurs and when an adequate investigation has been carried out to identify the killer. Once the killer has been identified, they can cope with him themselves.

A DEATH OCCURS: THE FIRST SECTION OF KADUWAGAN MORTUARY OBSERVANCES

Most Kaduwagans die inside a house, surrounded by friends and relatives. After the death, matrilineal consociates bathe the corpse, plug its orifices, dress it, and decorate it. When these acts have been performed, one or two of the consociates loudly begin the wailing characteristic of mourning. As it is heard, the cry is taken up by others. It quickly spreads throughout the village. Now everyone is welcome to come and view the corpse.

After a few hours of viewing, the corpse is wrapped in a fine mat. Then it is held on the outstretched legs of women sitting crosswise from one another in the house where the death occurred. The women are drawn from any clan other than that of the deceased.

Ordinarily the corpse is buried the morning after the death. Burial traditionally was in the center of the village. Missionary objections caused it to be relocated to the strip of bush adjacent to the village. All those who wish may go to the grave. There is a brief (Christian) graveside service, and then the corpse is untied in its wrappings and placed face down in the grave to discourage the mind from attempting to stay with it. The grave is filled in with dirt and topped with coral rocks. Then the people who have attended the burial return to the village.

If the deceased is a married man survived by his wife, she is carried back from the grave to the house of mourning (usually the house wherein the death occurred). This is because, as *nakakau* (widow), she has as her appropriate role *ikarikariga* (to do active death) for the deceased, and no one who is doing active death can walk in the center of the village. No one does active death for either a married woman or an unmarried person of either sex. This is not a matter of differences in social status between a dead married man and other dead people. It is a matter of pragmatics. No man can actively do death for his wife because doing it requires that he not work in the gardens until the second section mortuary events have been held, some three months later. Additionally, the main female mourner for either a married woman or an unmarried person is a matrilineal consociate of that person, not an affine from another matrilineage. As a matrilineal consociate, she needs to be free to move about in the center of the village as she participates in making women's payments for mortuary labor in both the first and the second section events.

After the burial, people once again gather outside the house of mourning. They continue to cry and wail, and, as they do this, they watch the main female mourner perform a dance, called *vesali*. This is a slow hopping dance that she does to display her grief publically. As she does it, she carries some item that belonged to the deceased and cries and wails over it. This lasts for about half an hour. Then she and the other people, male and female alike, who will become secluded mourners go inside a designated house of mourning. The audience members disperse.

On the two nights following the burial people gather at the house of mourning to sing. The women who held the corpse on their legs go inside and sing with the secluded mourners. The others sing outside. The singing lasts all night and is designed both to comfort the mourners and to discourage the newly dead mind from attempting to enter the house to be with its closest loved ones.

On the second or third day following the death the *sagali* (mortuary distributions) begin. All of these events combine two elements: the making of payments for death-related labor and the feasting of all who attend as the payments are made. All are put on by the *tolikariga* (source of the death man), the male matrilineal consociate of the deceased who is holding the funeral.

The first section *sagali* consist of five major events. They are *sekokwau*, *puya*, *sagali kanua*, *sagali veguwa*, and *govana vanu*.

Sekokwau (give-get) is a *sagali* wherein the deceased's female matrilineal consociates give *doba* (fiber skirts) and *nunuga* (fiber bundles) to pay the people who held the corpse, the people who dug the grave, the people who carried the corpse to the grave and buried it, the man who gave the graveside service, and the people who went to the house of mourning to sing at night.

For each payment a *pieta* (round basket) is set on the ground, and the name of the payment is called out along with the name of the recipient. Then skirts and bundles are piled onto the basket, and it is carried away by a female matrilineal consociate of the recipient. It is not customary for actual recipients at this or any other *sagali* to pick up their own payments. To do so might imply greed.

Although the give-get involves an extensive list of payments, it is a rather perfunctory event. One woman I asked about this said, "At give-get we give rubbish skirts and bundles. We haven't had time to make new ones and to gather together good ones. Later, at the skirt trimming ceremony [in the second section], we give out fine skirts and bundles."

When the give-get is finished, the man who is holding the funeral gives out *puya*. *Puya*, which is cooked *kanua* plus areca nut, is given to the women who organized the give-get for their work in holding it. They are the funeral holder's female matrilineal consociates.

After the *puya* has been distributed, the funeral holder performs the *sagali kanua*. He gives raw *kanua* to all of the women who are not his female matrilineal consociates but who also contributed skirts and bundles to help the women who are. These are women who in the past had eaten *kanua* supplied by either the man who is holding the funeral or one of the men assisting him. Finally, the funeral holder distributes more cooked food to feast all the people who have gathered for the combined series of events.

The next *sagali* is *sagali veguwa* (payment of men's valuables). The valuables include shells and shell ornaments, greenstone axe blades, Amphlett clay cooking pots, coconut trees, areca trees, garden land, village house plots, and money. This sagali is "backward" in that the payment of men's valuables is made *to* the funeral holder, not by him. It is made by the deceased's closest male affine, either his father, if he was not married, or his wife's brother, if he was. The most prominent payment in this *sagali* is *kunututu*, also called *ninabuena* (organized mind). This payment is quite large. It generally consists of either the temporary alienation of some land rights or something of equivalent value.

Since the funeral holder is staging the men's valuables payment, just as he is staging all of the other mortuary events, he must pay the man who paid him the valuables for coming to make that payment. He pays in two kinds of *kanua* pudding, *mona uli* (taro pudding) and *mona taitu* (yam pudding). As he does this he combines the food payment with the feasting component of the event. He can do this because *kanua* puddings are more costly to produce than are other forms of cooked *kanua*.

The final *sagali* of the first section is *govana vanu* (to make a cheerful noise in the center of the village). The deceased's major affine organizes a boat load of men to go out fishing. When they return they give their catch to the funeral holder, who distributes it throughout the village households. He then pays them and feasts them with another form of *kanua* pudding, called *loilo*. The fishermen consume the pudding in the center of the village, talking and laughing loudly as they do so.

Apart from having the corpse buried, the funeral holder's main priority in the first section of mortuary events is to work to get the village going again, if only on a temporary basis. What he needs to do is to convince the large-field owners to agree once again to make their land available to their tenants. To do this, he needs to offer them an adequate amount of assurance that the killer will not shortly attempt to kill them. But before he turns his attention to the construction of that assurance, he must work at something else: persuading the village's women to indicate that they are willing at least to consider the possibility of going on living and working in the village if the large-field owners bring the village back into existence. Otherwise, no matter how much assurance he offers them about their own physical safety, they will not bother making their land available to the same combination of tenants who were gardening on it when the death took place. Instead, they will turn their efforts toward the recruitment of a new combination of tenants, with whom the women will live and work, because a village without women is a village on the road to extinction.

The funeral holder would be quite happy if he could get a firm commitment from the village's women to go on in the village if the large-field owners do agree to restore it to existence, but, as both he and all of the other men know, he has no hope of doing that in the first section of mortuary events. Let us look at why.

Remember that I indicated that men are the *kanua* producers. As Malinowski (1929) and Weiner (1976) correctly note, women do work in the *kanua* gardens. But that work does not give them any claim to any portion of the subsequent crop. Their work is construed as *pilasi* (help to the men) and is compensated by an equal amount of help offered by men when they are pregnant and thereby cannot perform the heavier portion of their normal work load.

Remember too that I indicated that the Trobriand adult is someone who is both dependent upon someone else for his or her own food and produces food that he or she, in turn, gives to others, making them dependents. But this situation only really holds for men. Women too do give food to others, but it is not food that they produced. It is food that they got from men. In short, women are dependent upon men both for the food they eat and for the food they give to others.

Trobriand women do not like to be at the total mercy of men as they need food. So they take action to change that aspect of their lives. What they do is to insist that as women's ultimate productive labor, childbearing, is more dangerous than is men's ultimate productive labor, *kanua* growing, and as it is men who kill the bodies that women have produced at great danger to themselves, they will only go on living with the men of their village after a death occurs if the men compensate them by alienating a considerable amount of *kanua* to them, enough *kanua* that they do not have to ask some man for *kanua* every time that they need to give some away.

The reason why the funeral holder has no chance of inducing the village's women actually to commit themselves to going on living and working with the village's men in the first section of mortuary observances is that, at the moment, he does not possess anything near the amount of *kanua* that they are going to insist on receiving in return for their continued cooperation. It will take him most of the next three months, the interval between the first and second section events, to gather together that much *kanua*.

When the funeral holder begins his payments by having women pay the death/burial workers in skirts and bundles, he is showing the large-field owners that he has succeeded in persuading the women to consider the possibility of going on with the village's men. Now he is free to turn his attention to the task of offering them sufficient assurance that they will be physically safe if the village comes back into existence that they will once again make their land available to their former tenants.

Since most deaths are caused by a male matrilineal consociate of the victim, the first thing he must do is assure the large-field owners that none of the current victim's male matrilineal consociates is going to attack them. This is a bit tricky, given that he is the one among those consociates who is most likely to have caused the death. He plays on two factors: One is the idea that, as he is willing to expend a great amount of his own wealth, time, and labor to hold a lavish funeral for the victim, it is highly unlikely that he killed that person, unless he did so out of cosmic necessity. If he had killed that person because of a concern for advancing his own immediate life interests, he would not value that person's life enough to take on the immense amount of cost that is involved in holding a lavish funeral.

Given that he has no reason to kill any of the large-field owners out of cosmic necessity, and given that he did not kill this victim, the large-field owners have nothing to fear from him.

The other idea he plays on is that, since he can only hold a lavish funeral with the cooperation of his fellow male matrilineal consociates, the fact that he *is* holding this lavish funeral means that he can exercise a very great degree of influence over those men, enough to prevent any of them from attempting to kill the large-field owners, even if one of them did cause the death, for whatever reason, of the current victim.

The large-field owners may greet these ideas with jaundiced eyes, considering the source. But they are willing to concede that the man who presents them probably is not going to attack them, at least not in the immediate future, and that he is not going to allow any other of his male matrilineal consociates to attack them in the immediate future.

But the funeral holder's job of reassuring the large-field owners is still not yet done. Although most deaths are caused by male matrilineal consociates, "most" means about 60 to 70 percent; 30 to 40 percent are still outstanding.

Fortunately for the funeral holder almost all of the remaining deaths are caused by an affine. This is fortunate in that it reduces the pool of potential killers to manageable size for him. What he now needs to do is to indicate to the large-field owners that he has sufficient influence over the victim's affines to prevent any of them from attacking those owners.

He does this by turning on the deceased's closest male affine, the father, if the deceased is unmarried; the husband (of a woman) or wife's brother (of a man) if the deceased is married. He accuses the deceased's closest male affine of having caused the death and indicates that his anger over the death is sufficiently great that he will wreak vengeance on that person unless he appeases his anger by alienating a considerable amount of wealth to him. The payment of men's valuables to him is the event that proclaims to the large-land owners that he has won this confrontation. That proclamation carries with it the rider that, as he can exact all this wealth from the affine, he can exercise a great deal of influence over that man, just as he can over his own male matrilineal consociates.

The cost to the affine is very high, partly because the amount of the payment is a sign of just how much influence the funeral holder can exercise over that man. The larger the amount of the payment, the more influence the funeral holder shows himself to be able to exercise, the more likely it is that he can prevent that man from attacking the large-land owners, and the safer they are. Partly, too, it is high because the actual affine in question is only one in a pool of affines, and protection against the entire pool is necessary. This can only be achieved by making the price sufficiently high that the strongest man in that pool, the man who can ride herd on the others, must provide a considerable portion of the payment.

Once the funeral holder has brought off the payment of men's valuables, he can stage *govana vanu* (the event wherein men eat and make cheerful noises in the center of the village). This event announces that the large-field owners have agreed once again to make their land accessible to their former tenants.

"MOURNING CEASES": THE SECOND SECTION OF MORTUARY OBSERVANCES

The second mortuary section is generically referred to as *nisanadabu* (she trims the bottom of her mortuary skirt). The name refers to trimming the lower edge of the skirts that will be placed on the mourners to signal the end of their period of mourning. Trimming the lower edge of a skirt is the finishing touch, equivalent to hemming a skirt in the Western world. Like the first mortuary section, the second is made up of a series of feasts centered around payments to the hired mortuary laborers. Weiner (1976) describes these in detail, so I will only mention the high points.

The second mortuary section focuses on the return of hired mourners to normal life, which also is to full village life. This is not to say that most of the mourners have spent the last three to four months wholly outside normal life. They started out that way, but gradually the funeral holder has paid them off for engaging in various of the more severe mourning restrictions. He has done so for two pragmatic considerations. One is that he would be hard-pressed to find people to hire for most of the mourning roles if those roles did involve their not being able to resume certain life functions well before three months had gone by. The other is that he would have to pay them a truly exorbitant amount if they did agree to observe all of the initial restrictions for three months. The Trobriand labor market is not one wherein even the wealthiest and most influential man can afford to hire ten or eleven people on a full-time basis for three months.

Two public events have led up to the skirt trimming ceremony: *vatu sepwana* (sewing a *sepwana* skirt) and *nitutula sepwana* (thinning a *sepwana* skirt). A *sepwana* skirt is a distinctive mortuary skirt made of a fiber called *sepwana*. It is long, untrimmed, and conical in shape. It is worn by one of the deceased's female matrilineal consociates. As she dons it she pledges to attempt to organize the women's end of the skirt trimming ceremony. The woman who dons the *sepwana* is one of the funeral holder's matrilineal consociates.

The *sepwana* is sewn by women who are clan consociates of the male mourner(s). There may be more than one of them, and therefore more than one *sepwana*. The funeral holder pays the women who sew the *sepwana* in raw *kanua* and then feasts all the women who attend the event in cooked *kanua*.

The *sepwana* are sewn on one day and thinned on another day, about a week later. In the interim they are held by the wife of the man who is holding the funeral.

More women participate in the skirt thinning than in the skirt sewing. Their appearance at the skirt trimming indicates to the *sepwana* wearers that there is a reasonable likelihood that they will cooperate with the skirt trimming ceremony.

Again, the funeral holder pays all of the women who attend the skirt trimming in *kanua* and feasts them.

Now we are ready for the big day, the day upon which the skirt trimming ceremony is held. By ten o'clock in the morning the center of the village is filled with women, most of them sitting on the ground and chatting cheerfully with one another. Virtually all of the village's women are there, as well as at least an equal number who have come from neighboring villages. As they sit and chat, they chew betel and smoke. They laugh and joke a lot. As Weiner (1976) indicates, this, above all, is their day, and well they know it. As each woman is accompanied by a large load of fiber skirts and fiber bundles, the center of the village is distinctly crowded.

As the women sit, a number of men are building wooden racks around the periphery of their gathering. As each rack is completed, it is loaded with raw *kanua* and betel. The women sit for at least a couple of hours, casually watching the evergrowing display of food as they seem generally to ignore it. Only as it becomes sufficiently large to please them does the eldest of the *sepwana* wearers stand up and say, "*Bogwa desi*" ("Enough"). Then the women's casual chatter dies down as they turn their attention to the first order of business.

Their first act is to trim the skirts that will be placed on the mourners, bringing a halt to their mourning. This takes a while as the skirts must be selected from the total number of skirts and as each must be admired while being modeled by the person who temporarily dons it so that it can be properly trimmed.

Their second act is to distribute skirts and bundles to each of the mourners to pay them for their work. As in the give-get, a round basket is placed on the ground for each payment, the name of the recipient is called, and the basket is removed by a friend or relative of that person. The skirts that are given out are not like the *sepwana*; they are generally red with a ruff at the top.

Their third act is to join men who are carrying men's valuables and walk over to the two houses wherein the most significant male and the most significant female mourner are respectively sitting. These two people have both already been paid in baskets of skirts, but they receive more. The man is given the male valuables, and the woman is given more, very fine skirts. The valuables are put on the man, signifying that his period of mourning has fully ended, and the finest of the skirts is put on the woman, signifying the same thing.

The women return to the center of the village and proceed to put skirts on all the other mourners. They do not literally put skirts on the other male mourners; they use female stand-ins instead. This act signifies that mourning is ended for all of these other people.

Now the funeral holder gives out raw *kanua* and areca nut to each woman who has contributed skirts to the skirt trimming ceremony. Then he gives out cooked *kanua* to everyone who has attended the event.

As Weiner (1976) notes, the sheer amounts of skirts, bundles, and raw *kanua* presented on the occasion of the skirt trimming ceremony are awesome. We easily can see why that is so with regard to the *kanua*: Women are using this occasion largely to gain enough *kanua* for themselves so that they do not have to keep turning to this or that man to beg it from him every time they want some to give away to others. That requires a lot of food. But why so many skirts and bundles?

The skirts are the currency of pregnancy. The women are insisting that men alienate *kanua* to them as compensation for the risks that they have run by engaging in the task of childbearing. Some women have run more risks than others because they have put themselves at risk more times than have others. They thus deserve more compensation than do others.

As a woman's pregnancy advances, she becomes progressively less able to take on the more physically laborious tasks in her daily routine, such as walking out to the gardens and carrying home food and firewood. Her male partner takes over these tasks in return for the help she has provided him in his *kanua* garden at times when she was not pregnant. This frees some of her time, and she uses that time to engage in the sedentary activity of creating skirts and bundles. The more times that she engages in a pregnancy that advances to the point of freeing her from some of her daily work tasks, the more skirts and bundles she can manufacture: thus the more skirts and bundles she has to present at the skirt trimming ceremony and the more raw *kanua* she can receive for them.

Weiner (1976) correctly notes that all women work at skirt and bundle manufacture in their free time, whether they are pregnant or not. They do this because it is the total of each woman's skirt and bundle holding that determines how much *kanua* she receives. For a woman to fail to manufacture skirts and bundles in her nonpregnant free time is to allow some other woman to surpass her and claim a larger portion of the available *kanua* than she can claim.

Skirts and bundles "work" as the currency of pregnancy only because

39

each manufacturer ultimately receives as many skirts and bundles as she gives away, so that the sum of her manufacture is available to her each time she "exchanges" it for food. No man who is paid for labor in skirts and bundles ever actually receives them. They are taken by one of his female matrilineal consociates and redistributed among the givers in proportion to the number of skirts and bundles each gave. A woman who is paid for labor in skirts and bundles *does* receive, and keep, them. But the resource imbalance this produces is only temporary, as women cycle themselves through the performance of that labor in an equalized manner.

I mentioned that at least an equal number of women appear for the skirt trimming ceremony from other villages as the number who participate from the village in which it is being held. The number of men from other villages who attend is also equal to the number of men from that village. That arrangement ensures that the village's women can safely leave the village if they decide that they do not want to go on living and working with the village's men. It is not so much a matter of concern over actually removing them if they do make that choice as it is of ensuring that their decision to stay is a matter of free choice rather than physical coercion.

VENGEANCE OR NO? THE THIRD SECTION OF MORTUARY OBSERVANCES

Once the skirt trimming ceremony is over, the deceased is no longer publically mourned. But that does not mean that there is no continuing public recognition accorded to that person. There is, in the form of continued relic wearing and grave tending, as now begins the period when people are expected to begin personally to cope with the void in their lives caused by the removal of the deceased from the world of the living. This period lasts for somewhat more than a year, the time necessary for the corpse to disintegrate into an assemblage of bones. At its end, the funeral holder puts on a final series of feasts/payments, the third section events.

The major third section events consist of *kailagina, lagila, katupwakau laka,* and *dani. Kailagina* leads off.

The word *kailagina* means "hearth." In this event the funeral holder pays the wives of the men who have assisted him in putting on the funeral because these women have cooked all the food that has been served as he has repeatedly feasted people. The payment consists of raw *kanua.*

Kailagina is followed by *lagila* (pouring). The name comes from the fact that areca nut is "poured" onto the ground for each grave tender. The symbolic message is that the village is an especially fine one, one well worth reconstructing, since it produces a great deal of wealth above what is actually needed for the physical survival of its citizens. Note the contrast between the handling of the areca nut and that of *kanua*: survival wealth can never be "poured" on the ground. That can only be done with wealth exceeding that needed for survival.

Although the event takes its name from the pouring of areca nut, its more important component in terms of the actual value of the commodities paid out is the payment of raw *kanua* to the relic wearer. This, the final payment to that woman for her labor, consists of a literal tower of raw *kanua*.

The next event is *katupwakau laka* (grave cleaning). It is the final payment to the grave tenders for keeping the grave clean and decorated with flowers. They are given a large amount of the most expensive form of *kanua* pudding. The pudding consists of *kanua* dumplings that are bathed in coconut oil. This is the most expensive form of *kanua* pudding because a great many coconuts are needed to yield the requisite amount of oil to provide the sauce.

The final event is *dani* (squeezing). The name alludes to the fact that the relic wearer has been wearing fingernails that were squeezed off the corpse. It consists of skirts, which are not paid to her because of the labor she has performed by wearing the relic, but are paid to get her to relinquish possession of that relic. A day or so after *dani*, another woman who is a female matrilineal consociate of the dead person goes to her and takes the relic from her. That woman then secretly buries the relic somewhere. The funeral is over.

The third section events differ from those of the first and second sections in that they are "group" events rather than "individual" events. Each is held simultaneously for all the dead people from a given clan since that same event was last held for the dead people of that clan. The internal structure is still the same as in the first and second section events. The funeral holder for each dead person puts on the portion of the larger event that is dedicated to that person.

These are "group" events as a result of their position in the progressive reestablishment of the village. The men have agreed to go on, the women have agreed to go on, but as yet there has been no formal investigation to determine the identity of the killer. This investigation is held by a series of people called *kayao*. The *kayao* have been preselected by the victim from among his or her clan consociates. They work anonymously, and the "group" aspect of these events helps to preserve their anonymity, since many more clan consociates simultaneously appear on the scene as each event is held for several dead people at once than would if each were held for one dead person at a time.

Each Trobriand adult wants to avoid dying at the hands of someone who kills in order to advance his own immediate position in life. The fundamental precaution that each can take against this occurrence is to hire someone to investigate his or her death. The investigator(s) is charged with determining the identity of the killer, determining the killer's motivation in causing the death, and punishing the killer if the motivation was enhancement of his own immediate position in life.

The investigator(s) is called *kayao*. Investigators are almost always selected from those of the hirer's clan consociates who are not thereby also his or her matrilineal consociates. There are four classes of people on the Trobriand landscape from whom he or she can choose: matrilineal consociates, affines, clan consociates who are not matrilineal consociates, and nonrelatives. Matrilineal consociates and affines are ruled out as the killer is one of them. Nonrelatives are ruled out as too distant to be willing to accept the employment, which involves considerable personal danger to whoever does accept it. Clan consociates who are not matrilineal consociates remain the only alternative.

It may seem a little strange to Westerners that the official investigation into the death is conducted anonymously, but that cannot be avoided given the way that the Trobriand game of life is structured. Remember that killing to enhance one's own immediate life position is not wrong under its rules. It is risky, but then the game is about problematics and problematics involve risk. The major risk that someone who kills to advance his own immediate life position engages is due to his victim's *kayao* since their mandate is that of avenging the death if the death was motivated by the killer's seeking his own immediate gain. The others, like the large-land owners, who have good reason to fear that they may be next on his list of potential victims, have not accepted that mandate and will not exercise it. They want to know who he is, but only so that they can take suitable precautions to deflect any attack that he may mount against them.

The result is that the *kayao* are in a very dangerous position as they work to exercise their mandate. If *their* identity becomes known to the killer he will do one of two things. If it becomes known to him before they have identified him, he will kill them to prevent the identification. If it becomes known to him after they have identified him, he will take suitable precautions to deflect their attacks on him.

Even though the *kayao* remain anonymous, they are perceived as generally doing their job. The information they collect from the other villagers during the third section mortuary events is the information upon which they act. If everyone is quite sure that a certain man caused the death and did it out of self-advancing motivation, that man soon falls ill or dies as they attack him.

Or maybe he does not. But if not, he must be a very strong man indeed, as the game once again turns in on its grounding in problematics and couches the problematic of keeping one's self in the field of play as the greatest problematic of all.

CONCLUSIONS

To eat for others, whether living or dead, is a central part of the Trobriand game of life. The game, set up by bored minds to amuse themselves, is highly problematic. One of the ways in which it is problematic is that it always fundamentally turns on each player's ability to maintain himself in the field of play by exercising enough influence over the minds of the other players that they will keep him there. Another of the ways in which it is problematic is that, as each player's goal is to increase the amount of influence he has over the minds of the other players, each positive step he makes in this direction also gives the players against whom he makes it additional reasons to try to remove him from the field of play.

Trobriand funerals appear to novice Western onlookers to be both rather mysterious and overly elaborate events. That is because those same onlookers do not understand the Trobriand game of life, the game through which the funerals are generated. This essay constitutes a step toward the attainment of that understanding.

APPENDIX: MORTUARY EVENTS

Unless otherwise noted, all the payments are made by the man who is holding the funeral.

FIRST SECTION

Sekokwau	Skirts given to people who have various sorts of mortuary labor
Puya	Cooked *kanua* given to the women who give out the skirts
Sagali kanua	Raw *kanua* given to the women who *vakabiyamina* at the *sekokwau*
Sagali veguwa	Male valuables given to the funeral holder by the deceased's affines
Govana vanu	Fish given to the funeral holder, who distributes them throughout the village; *kanua* pudding given to the fishermen, who eat the fish in the center of the village while making celebratory noises

INTERIM EVENTS	Various payments to create the semirelease of secluded mourners
Vatu sepwana	*Sepwana* skirt sewn for each of the men who were secluded mourners
Nitutula sepwana	Thinning of each *sepwana* skirt

SECOND SECTION

Nisanadabu	Skirt trimming ceremony
Sagali	Skirts and bundles paid to secluded mourners, relic wearers, and grave tenders
Sagali buwa	Areca nuts given to the grave tenders
Sagali kanua	Raw *kanua* given to all the women participants in the skirt and bundle distributions

Sagal mona	*Kanua* pudding given to the women who organized the skirt trimming ceremony and skirt and bundle distributions
INTERIM EVENTS	Various small payments to grave tenders and relic wearers

THIRD SECTION

Kailagina	Raw *kanua* given to the women who cooked the food served at the previous events
Lagila	Areca nut given to the grave tenders, a tower of raw *kanua* given to each relic wearer
Katupwakau laka	*Kanua* pudding given to the grave tenders
Dani	Skirts given to the relic wearers

ACKNOWLEDGMENTS

My Trobriand Island fieldwork was made possible by grants from the National Institute of Mental Health, the Dean's Fund at Northern Illinois University, and the National Endowment for the Humanities. I wish to thank them all. In addition I want to thank Katubai, Itagoma, Boyomu, and Nakovivi, as well as the many other Trobriand Islanders who worked so hard to educate me about mortuary observations and other aspects of Trobriand life. Finally, I wish to thank Edwin and Donna Hutchins for allowing me access to their dictionary of Kilivilan, the Trobriand language, and for devoting time to assisting me to decode the meaning of various of the names of mortuary events, and Drs. Debora Battaglia, Fred Damon, Carol Goldin, and John Kirkpatrick for reading and commenting on earlier drafts of this essay.

Shirley Campbell

A Vakutan
Mortuary Cycle

INTRODUCTION

♦ Northern Kiriwina, in the Trobriand Islands, has recently come under closer scrutiny since the work of Annette Weiner in her analysis of Kiriwinan mortuary practices (1976). Until the publication of her book, mortuary observances in the Trobriand Islands went almost entirely unnoticed. Although Malinowski published a considerable number of monographs and essays dealing with various aspects of Trobriand language, culture, and society, mortuary practices received very little attention. Indeed, the most notable descriptions of the events surrounding a death are to be found in only thirteen pages (1929:31–32, 128–139). When Weiner's book was published and the detailed description of elaborate mortuary observances together with extensive distributions was available for the first time, interest in Trobriand ethnography was rekindled.

It is not that we now have a detailed description and analysis of a northern Massim mortuary sequence, comparable to that of the Soi of the southern Massim, first described by Seligman in 1910 and later mentioned by Roheim (1937), that is of prime significance. Weiner's analysis demonstrates that the role of women in these affairs particularly, and in social life generally, is far more integral to the maintenance of the life cycle as it is perceived by northern Kiriwinans than was previously thought. In essence, Weiner argues that women are the prime caretakers of *dala* (subclan) identity, property, and regeneration, and that it is in the elaborate mortuary displays, exchanges, and associated activities that the position of women in these matters is asserted.

Mortuary observances in other parts of the Trobriand Islands also place emphasis on the role of women and their significance to the regeneration of *dala*. Montague (this volume) reports similar mortuary sequences from Kaileuna Island while also noting significant shifts in the focus of certain ceremonies. While I was on a brief visit to Kitava Island in 1977 for the purpose of Kula, a death occasioned the initial stages of mortuary observances enabling me to question people about the overall sequence of events that play out obligations of the living to the deceased. The sequence was generally comparable to that described by Weiner for northern Kiriwina, again, however, with some differences. While resident on Vakuta Island from October 1976 to January 1978 I was present at the time of the deaths of four village members. I also witnessed mortuary events concerned with deaths that had occurred prior to my arrival on the island. Much of what is described by Weiner for the northern Kiriwinan mortuary sequence is similar to that utilized by Vakutans. There are, however, differences that range from technical divergencies and terminological differences to, perhaps more significantly, differences in the focus of specific stages. For example, Weiner discusses the importance of "bundles" of banana leaves in northern Kiriwinan mortuary exchanges. On Vakuta bundles are not used as women's wealth. Rather, women manufacture banana leaf materials for the construction of skirts only. Fully made skirts are women's primary items of exchange on Vakuta.[1] The absence of bundles on Vakuta and the inflationary potential that bundles allow Kiriwinan women illustrate the different scope to which Vakutan mortuary customs operate. Although the population density of northern Kiriwina may demand a wider exchange field in the sheer numbers of relationships it involves, the Vakutan population of some six hundred persons does not require an exchange item that can be numerically increased with relative ease to accommodate wider networks of exchange relations. Vakutan women direct all their energies toward the production of skirts. Another difference in the scope of the obligations toward a deceased member of the society is in the variety of people who mourn a death on Kiriwina as compared to the relatively select group who take on mourning obligations on Vakuta. Many more people shave their heads and wear mourning skirts and/or relics of the deceased in northern Kiriwina than on Vakuta Island. Finally, there is a significant shift of focus from *dala* to clan in the mortuary sequence of Vakuta. In contrast, Weiner stresses the importance of *dala* identity and the corresponding solidarity of the members of the deceased's *dala*.[2] These and other differences will be compared as each stage of the Vakutan mortuary cycle is discussed. The purpose of this essay is to provide comparative data from the Vakutan mortuary cycle. In the following account I will proceed through the sequence of events as they occur, describing each stage in some detail.

THE VAKUTAN MORTUARY CYCLE

The sequence of events following a death is fixed. Particular ceremonies and exchanges must occur before others can happen; thus each stage in the mortuary cycle must occur at the appropriate time. The entire mortuary sequence from beginning to end can be divided into three phases. This tripartite structure is based upon the timing of particular events following a death and the associated motives ascribed to each stage of the sequence. What I have defined as the first phase, or the *yawari* (crying) phase of the mortuary sequence, occurs within the first few days after a death. The principal motive behind each stage within the first phase is for village life to return to normal as soon as possible. At the moment of death all normal activity ceases. With the gradual unfolding of phase one this period of initial restrictive mourning is redressed and all but the principal mourner are released to continue a relatively normal existence. In the next set of ceremonies constituting phase two, or the *vakakaiya* (bathing) phase, the emphasis is on the gradual shedding of restrictions placed upon the principal mourner. The time lapse from the moment of death is approximately one to ten months. Phase three, or the *doba sagali* (skirt distribution) phase, is markedly different from phases one and two. Whereas in the first and second phases all stages are directed toward the relief of mourning caused by one death, in phase three the ceremonies are related to a number of deaths within a particular clan. This phase can occur from one to twenty years after any particular death within the clan. The basic three-phased structure will emerge more clearly as the entire sequence is broken up into individual events and a description of each is given.

Tables 1, 2, and 3 present the entire three-phase sequence of distributions following a death. The temporal relationship between the moment of death and the occurrence of each stage is given together with a brief description. A more detailed account of each stage follows in the text. Let us now focus on the village and the scene at a particularly tragic moment for all concerned.

PHASE I: *YAWARI* (CRYING)

It is a truism that sound, for example, speech, provides a very efficient means of communication. Even the absence of certain sounds can be effective. The sounds that fill a village at particular times during a normal day provide information about the well-being of life in general. The natural sounds of leaves rustling as trees and palms sway under a gentle breeze are almost unnoticed. And the music of the birds as they call to each other or complain about an intrusion is only momentarily acknowledged and only then to confirm normality. The incessant grunting of pigs together with the cackling of domestic chickens provides the background noise to the sounds of humans going about their daily tasks. Imagine this orchestration of sound and hear the laughter of children playing while men and women chatter away, some in animated discourse, others in hushed tones of secrecy. Suddenly a scream intrudes upon life's symphony: the ritualized mourning cry takes up the traditional tempo and announces a death in the village. Normal life stops as everyone is summoned to participate in some way in the mourning of the newly deceased among them.

The sorrowful cry of those close to the dying, following immediately upon the death of the loved one, communicates most effectively to the rest of the village the loss of one of their members. That single, ritualized cry of anguish heralds the onset of yet another cycle of mortuary ceremonies and exchanges to honor the newly deceased. These ceremonies enmesh every individual in the Vakutan community, consisting of four interrelated villages.[3] Individuals from other villages on Kiriwina, Kitava, and Dobu islands who had relationships with the deceased may also become involved. All stop whatever task they are engaged in and embark upon a series of activities that identifies their past relationship with the deceased.

Uterine kin of the deceased's spouse and father become the mourners. They go directly to the house where the corpse lies, enter, and proceed to mourn actively through ritualized crying. Although the cries follow a well established pattern, the real sorrow is no less diminished. Women make up the majority of mourners in the house. Only men who have direct blood ties with the deceased's spouse and father enter and participate in this form of active mourning, which is called *yawari* (crying). Other men remain outside the house, listening in silence to the sorrowful wail emitting from the house (Table 1).

Conspicuously absent from the house in which their dead kin lies among prostrate, wailing figures are the uterine kin of the deceased. All people of the same clan, and particularly of the same *dala*, try to maintain a grieved but controlled manner. They do not enter the house to participate in mourning activity. Some enter occasionally to oversee the proceedings, take refreshment to the mourners, or take note of who is mourning for their dead kin. When I asked why those who to our minds would be most emotionally affected were in fact retaining a degree of decorum, I was told that they cannot afford to express their sadness and mourn their dead: "They feel very sad for the death of their kin, but they have much work to do, they must cook for those who mourn their dead kin, and they must make plans for the mortuary distributions" (Kunabu, Vakuta village; see also

TABLE I

Phase I: *Yawari* 'crying'

Stages in Mortuary Cycle	Period after Death	Item (s) Distributed	Description	Purpose
Yawari	0	Ritual mourning	The physical, ritualized mourning of the deceased by his or her closest affines and any other person who wishes to contribute, other than someone from the deceased's *dala*	To mourn and bury the deceased
Biribusi	0–1 days*	Physical mourning	Spouse or father of deceased moves into *torikariga's* house with helpers; a wall (*ribu*) is built to isolate the principal mourner	To isolate the principal mourner from living society, thus simulating principal mourner's association with deceased who has just been interred
Bigibataula or *Bivivisa*	1–2 days	Uncooked food	The principal mourner's clan gives uncooked food to the *torikariga's* clan	To solicit the *torikariga* to allow the principal mourner to commence eating, drinking, chewing betel nut, and smoking
Mwagula Valu	1–5 days	Fish	All men other than the deceased's clansmen go fishing; fish are brought back to the village and given to *torikariga*, who then distributes this to his clan	To release the village from *borabora*, a restriction on normal village noise, such as laughter, singing, and dancing
Youwisa wa Bagula	1–5 days	Garden labor	Principal mourner's kinsmen spend one day working the gardens of the deceased's kinsmen, after a death	To release everyone in the village from the restriction prohibiting garden work
Kulututu or *Ninaboila*	1–5 days	Men's valuables particularly *Kula* shell valuables	Giving of men's valuables to the *torikariga* and his kinsmen by the principal mourner's kinsmen	To allay sorcery accusations

TABLE I (continued)

Stages in Mortuary Cycle	Period after Death	Item (s) Distri- buted	Description	Purpose
Sakulakola	3–5 days	Fish	The principal mourner's kinsmen go fishing, return- ing with the catch and giv- ing it to the *torikariga*, who distributes the fish among his clan	To allow the principal mourner to resume mini- mal bathing
Katulaguva or *Nagabu*	2, 3, or 4 days	Mature coconuts or un- cooked yams	Deceased's clansmen give mature coconuts (or yams) to all participants in the *yawari*	To reciprocate for mourn- ing activity at the *yawari*
Sikwokwau	2, 3, or 4 days	Skirts	Deceased's clanswomen give skirts to all partici- pants in the *yawari*	To reciprocate for mourn- ing activity at the *yawari*
Kaptunila Papa	4–8 days	Skirts	The *ribu* wall is broken by the deceased's clans- women; skirts are given by the deceased's clanswomen to the principal mourner, who distributes these among his clan	To allow the principal mourner to reemerge into living society
Biulusila Yamala+	2–3 weeks	Garden labor	The principal mourner, helped by his or her clans- men, goes to the gardens of the deceased's clansmen and works them for one day	To reassert the principal mourner's role in the re- sponsibility of nurturing life's sustenance: the yam garden

*The timing of specific activities associated with mourning following a death is dependent upon several factors and can vary widely because of particular circumstances. The timing given here is a general estimate based upon the stages witnessed during fieldwork.

+Although many of these activities are similar to those practiced in northern Kiriwina and the main aim of the entire sequence of events within this stage, which focuses upon the relaxation of broader mourn- ing restrictions, is shared between the two districts, dissimilarity is evident in the terminological details, focus of specific ceremonies, and people involved (cf. Weiner 1976:64–76).

Malinowski 1929:127–29). Although the kin are not allowed to join the ritual mourning of their dead kin, they move with red-rimmed eyes around the outside of the house, carrying out the various chores to be done while the chorus of cries, rising and falling in intensity, issues from the house. The atmosphere is very tense for those outside who are trying to maintain control over any direct display of emotion. While the village is divided between those who go about the business of mourning, and those preparing food for the mourners, a few young men who are not kin to the deceased dig the grave and prepare the coffin. They also remove hair or fingernails from the corpse.[4] These relics are woven into a necklace called *mwagula* and worn by a close affine of the dead person. He or she who puts on the mourning necklace becomes the principal mourner for the deceased. It is because of *mwagula* that the kin of the deceased must perform all the stages in the mortuary cycle, particularly those in the third phase. Until all the remains of their dead kinsman or woman are buried, the deceased's kinsmen are obliged to maintain a demanding exchange relationship with the wearer of the mourning necklace and her or his kin. The exchange is demanding because they must amass great amounts of wealth in the form of yams, coconuts, betel nut, pigs, skirts, and Kula shell valuables.[5] These they must periodically give to the wearer of the mourning necklace and her or his kin in exchange for their mourning activity and for care of the remains of the deceased. The spouse or father (depending upon whether the deceased is married or not) has the right to wear the mourning necklace. If the deceased's spouse or father is too old, the primary mourning responsibilities will be taken on by a close relative of the spouse or father such as a daughter, son, brother, or sister.

When burial is imminent, all the personal belongings of the deceased are put into the coffin with the body. Many of these articles will be removed again before interment (cf. Malinowski 1922:512–13). *Bobwailila* (gifts) are also put into the coffin by friends and affines[6] and removed before burial. These are gifts denoting love and affection for the deceased by people not in a kinship relationship to her or him. The gifts consist of valuables and may include Kula shell valuables. The deceased's kin will remove what they want prior to burial. Careful note is taken of who gave gifts so that those who contribute *bobwailila* are repaid at a later date.

The climax of *yawari* involves the final parting as the corpse is interred. All but the remains that are worn around the neck of the principal mourner are buried. It is at this point that emotions reach a climax. As the pallbearers attempt to lower the corpse into the coffin, and then the coffin into the grave, people violently try to prevent it. The most overtly violent are close kin of the principal mourner. Hands snatch at the corpse as it is lowered into the coffin. Other people must be restrained from jumping into the grave or from preventing the coffin's progress as it is lowered into the grave. The emotion that swells the already heavy atmosphere at the grave site turns into hysteria as villagers catch their last glimpse of the corpse. Resigned sobbing follows as the falling earth resounds loudly, resonating with each heavy thud on the lid of the coffin as it lies in the grave. The *yawari* finishes.

The closest affines move directly from the grave site to the house of the head of the deceased's *dala*.[7] The senior man of the *dala* takes on the responsibility of organizing the sequence of events that make up the mortuary cycle. His responsibilities begin with the burial of his kinsperson and the seclusion (*biribusi*) of the primary mourners in his house. (*Biribusi* is the verb specifying the action of this particular stage in the mortuary cycle. The stem -*ribu*- is also used as a noun referring to the wall behind which the mourners remain). When the mourners, together with the principal mourner, move into the house, a wall is erected to hide them from the public. Here mourning continues. By the separation of the principal mourner from the public domain, the mourner publically announces her or his commitment to mourning the deceased. In the past this commitment involved extreme hardship for the principal mourner, particularly if she was a widow. She would remain enclosed in the *ribu* for ten to twelve months and prohibited from speaking to anyone and from leaving the confines of the *ribu* even to defecate or bathe (cf. Malinowski 1929:134).[8] Today mourners remain in seclusion for a few days only. However several restrictions begin for the mourner in the *ribu*, as her or his seclusion marks the beginning of the restrictive mourning period that is accepted by all the closest affines of the deceased. Although the restrictions placed upon the principal mourner follow social convention (that is, everyone knows what a principal mourner can and cannot do) the fiction is maintained that the mourner embraces restrictive mourning voluntarily. In other words, the mourner presents herself or himself as so afflicted with grief that she or he cannot (or will not) continue with normal everyday living activities such as talking, drinking, smoking, chewing betel nut, eating, and gardening. With each successive stage more and more of these restrictions are shed and the mourner gradually returns to normal village life.

Once the mourner has entered into seclusion, her or his *dala* collect betel nut and uncooked yams. These are taken to the senior member of the deceased's *dala*, or *torikariga* (*tori:* owner, ruler; -*kariga:* death). This gift is called *bigibataula* or *bivivisa*. The senior member of the deceased's *dala* then redistributes this among the *kariga* clan. (I use *kariga*, here to identify the clan to which a death belongs.)[9] The giving of *bigibataula* to the *kariga* clan solicits the latter to allow the mourner to resume eating, drinking, chewing, and smoking. The consumption of principal foodstuffs such as yams, taro, mature sweet bananas, fish, and pig, however, remains prohibited.

Upon death a blanket restriction is placed upon the village prohibiting

loud noise, laughter, song, dance, and so on. In short, there is a general prohibition on the resumption of normal activities. This is in consideration for
the *kariga* clan, who, it is said, are experiencing extreme grief. To release
the entire village from this veil of gloom (called *borabora*) all men other than
the *kariga* clansmen go fishing after the lapse of a dignified number of days
following the death. The number of days between a death and *mwagula
valu*, as this stage is called (similar to *katuyuvisavalu* in northern Kiriwina,
cf. Weiner 1976:77), depends upon many criteria: for example, the age and
social position of the deceased, the timing of death in relation to the garden
cycle, Kula events, or other village activities. The aim of *mwagula valu* is
to release the village from *borabora* restrictions so it can resume normal
daily activities. The entire catch is taken to the *torikariga*, who distributes
it to his clansmen. These latter have prepared cooked food for the fishermen
in anticipation of their return. After this transaction, village life is resumed.
The principal mourner, however, remains bound by mourning restrictions.
These restrictions are discarded one by one as each successive stage of the
cycle unfolds.

In conjunction with *mwagula valu*, the mourner's kinsmen spend a day
working in each garden belonging to the dead person's kinsmen. The purpose of this day of communal labor (*youwisa wa bagula*) by affines of the
deceased is to release everyone in the village from the restriction prohibiting
garden work.

At marriage a spouse publicly takes on the responsibility for and care
of his or her partner. Until marriage, the father is acknowledged to be the
one responsible for the well-being of his children, although they are "other
people's" kin. When a death, particularly that of a child, occurs, the father
feels an acute sense of shame toward his affines. Upon the death of their
partner, husbands and wives also feel shame because it was to them that
their affines gave over the care and responsibility for the well-being of their
kin. Associated with these feelings of shame is a more basic fear that they,
as affines to the deceased, may become prime targets for sorcery accusations by the deceased's kin. It is said to be for these reasons that affines
present valuables to the *torikariga*, who distributes them among his *dala*.
There are two ways in which this can be termed. If a death occurred through
accident or sickness, the exchange would be called *kulututu*. But if the cause
of death was suspected sorcery the valuables would be called *ninaboila*. This
term signifies a shift in the collective attitude by the kin of the deceased toward their affines. Following death by accident or a long illness, the affines
wish to comfort the "minds" of the deceased's kin. By giving *kulututu* valuables the affines are saying they are sorry for their negligence in looking after
the deceased. In giving *ninaboila*, however, the affines communicate to the
deceased's kin their innocence of his or her death. *Ninaboila* communicates,
first, that no one in their group brought about the death of their affine

through sorcery or witchcraft and, second, that they apologize for the death by sorcery or witchcraft should the attack have been a surrogate one made because of jealousy of material possession or status acquired by someone in their own group. In this way the affines of the deceased attempt to ward off any sorcery or witchcraft accusations that may be directed to them. The content of the *ninaboila* and *kulututu* is the same. Kula shell valuables predominate; clay pots, items of clothing and body decoration, together with axes or adzes may also be given. The *ninaboila* and *kulututu* are not returned in kind, but through the various exchanges that follow.[10] This is different from what occurs in northern Kiriwina, where the *wayala kaybila* (roughly equivalent to the Vakutan *kulututu* and *ninaboila*) is a "short-term exchange" in which the valuables are returned to the original givers (cf. Weiner 1976:70).

It is interesting to note that the *ninaboila* and *kulututu* payments consist of men's wealth and not women's wealth and that the focus is upon the death and its cause. This is the only exchange within the mortuary cycle that has such a retrospective focus and that involves only men's wealth. In all the other exchanges the focus is upon the resumption of normal life by the survivors and reconstruction of social relationships dramatically severed by death. These latter exchanges involve primarily, if not exclusively, women's wealth (skirts) and combined *dala* wealth (yams, taro, pigs, and so on). This differing focus highlights an ideological distinction between male and female on Vakuta (Campbell 1984). Whereas women are generally associated with the perpetual regeneration of society in ways that cut across generational boundaries, men are central to the concerns of each generation, manipulating political and economic circumstances for individual gain. (Weiner makes similar associations between the differing, but complementary focuses of the genders [1976]).

Several days following the death come and go. The village has returned to normal life. All but the principal mourner go about their daily activities. The spouse or father of the deceased remains enclosed within the *ribu* in accordance with prescribed mourning restrictions. The principal mourner has begun to smoke, drink, chew betel nut, and eat "rubbish food" but has not been allowed to move from the enclosure. Soon the principal mourner's kinsmen (belonging to the same *dala*) go fishing. At the end of the day they take the catch to the *torikariga*'s house, where the principal mourner has been secluded for several days. This is called *sakulakola* and is intended to permit the principal mourner to resume bathing. The fish is distributed among the deceased's *dala*.

The first major exchange by the *kariga* clan to all mourners takes place several days after the interment of the corpse. Two exchanges are held on the same day, one by the men of the *kariga* clan and the other by the women of the *kariga* clan. The first one to occur, early in the morning, is the carrying of strung coconuts to every individual who took part in the *yawari*. The number of coconuts given depends upon the type of participation.

Main mourners, such as a sister of the deceased's spouse, are given ten to twelve mature coconuts for their contribution to the *yawari*. A mourner who is only related indirectly as an affine is given six to seven mature coconuts because the contribution to a *yawari* is generally less than that of an affine more closely related to the deceased. Someone who helped prepare the body in any way (binding, making the coffin, digging the grave) receives twenty to thirty mature coconuts. The principal mourner receives thirty to forty mature coconuts. The giving of mature coconuts to participants in the *yawari* is called *katulaguva* and is the sole activity of the men in payment to the mourners of their deceased kinsperson. If coconuts are not available, yams are given. This alternative is called *nagabu*. Mature coconuts, however, are the "correct" exchange item for this stage.[11]

Later in the day women of the *kariga* clan gather in front of the *torikariga*'s house bearing skirts. Once all the women have gathered, they begin ritual crying followed by the distribution of the skirts. Like the men's distribution earlier in the day, the women's distribution includes all who participated in the *yawari*. The number and quality of the skirts given to each individual depend upon his or her kind of participation in the *yawari*. This exchange is called *sikwokwau*. It is of interest to note that the term for fingernail—one of the main relics of the deceased to be worn by the mourner—is *sikwekwela*. The *sikwokwau* exchange marks the commencement of yet another mortuary cycle, which is concerned with the return of the relics of the deceased, usually fingernails, to her or his *dala* kin for burial. The majority of skirts go to the wearer of the mourning necklace. Following the distribution of skirts women then distribute uncooked vegetables that have been given to them by their kinsmen. This is payment by the men for the work of their kinswomen and is called *kaimelu*. This "payment" follows every distribution the women make. In these exchanges women are distributing men's wealth given to them to distribute among themselves.[12]

The way is now clear for removal of some of the more restrictive mourning requirements from the principal mourner. The next stage, called *kaptunila papa*, entails the breaking of the *ribu* wall. The principal mourner is ceremonially readmitted to society in that she or he can now move to the verandah as well as about the immediate village. She or he has access to other villagers and vice versa. The principal mourner, however, must stay away from central village areas. Prior to the breaking of the *ribu* wall, ritual crying can be heard from the house. The mourner together with some helpers who have joined him or her for this occasion renew their sorrowful wail. Accompanied by the ritual cry of the mourners, *kariga* clan women bring skirts and place them in the *ribu*. Women of the principal mourner's *dala* remove these and distribute them to their clanswomen. This stage can alternatively be called *risaladabu* by Vakutans.[13]

Once the principal mourner emerges from seclusion the way is open to move gradually into normal village activities such as cooking and gardening. This is done via the successive stages of the cycle. From the moment someone becomes identified as the principal mourner that person takes on a degree of association with the dead. The mourner retains some remnant of the deceased. The principal mourner secludes herself or himself behind a wall (*ribu*) specially erected for the purpose immediately after the burial of the deceased in the grave (*riku*). Normal living activities, such as bathing, defecating in the bush, gardening, and cooking, cease. More significantly, eating, drinking, smoking, and chewing of betel nut are stopped. Like the deceased, the principal mourner, in close association with the dead, ceases to behave in a manner considered essential to the living. This association is greatest and most direct for the first couple of days following the death. As the various mortuary activities are completed, the principal mourner is gradually readmitted to the village of the living. The breaking of the *ribu* wall is the first decisive step in returning the principal mourner to the world of the living. *Biulusila yamala* is one further step in this process: The principal mourner, helped by her or his *dala* members, goes into the gardens of the members of the deceased's *dala* to work each in turn. The mourner is symbolically expressing her or his position with the living by working at life's mainstay, the garden.

PHASE II: *VAKAKAIYA* (BATHING)

The preceding stages occur within a few days following a death. They have as their principal aim the return to normal village life. Throughout this period the principal mourner has maintained close association with the deceased by adopting many deathlike characteristics. It now remains to readmit the principal mourner to society. The next set of mortuary distributions places an emphasis on the gradual shedding of the restrictions on the principal mourner, which symbolize less an association with death than a denial of certain pleasures symbolic of one's sorrow at the loss of a loved one. These restrictions include *kawagala*, a prohibition on eating yams, taro, and ripe bananas; *saigala*, the wearing of dark unattractive clothes, growing a beard, not combing one's hair, together with a general neglect of one's appearance; and finally *vaigula*, a prohibition on remarriage and the pursuit of sexual partners (Table 2).

At some time following a death the principal mourner's clanswomen gather at the house of the principal mourner's *dala* head to make a *saipwala*.[14] A *saipwala* is a special skirt made of undyed banana leaf strands

TABLE 2

Phase II: *Vakakaiya*

Stages in Mortuary Cycle	Period after Death	Item (s) Distributed	Description	Purpose
Saipwala	1–3 months	Special mourning skirt	Making of the *saipwala*, a special skirt, by the principal mourner's clanswomen and the giving of the skirt to the *torikariga*	To solicit the *vakakaiya* ceremony (see entry below)
Biritutulasi Saipwala	Several weeks after receipt of the *saipwala*	Fibers from the *saipwala*	Dismantling of the *saipwala* by the deceased's clanswomen	To obligate the deceased's clanswomen to make skirt to give at the *vakakaiya* (see entry below)
Kawasa	1–2 (or more) months	Taro pudding	Cooking of taro pudding by the principal mourner's clansmen and giving it to the deceased's clan	To solicit the performance of *ulusila wadola* for their clansman or clanswoman who is principal mourner
Mapula Kawasa	3–5 days after *kawasa*	Taro pudding	Cooking of taro pudding by the deceased's clansmen and giving it to the principal mourner's clan	To reciprocate *kawasa*
Ulusila Wadola	2–3 months	Yam pudding	Giving yam pudding to the principal mourner by the deceased's clansmen	To release the principal mourner from restriction on eating yams
Vakakaiya	3–10 months	Skirts	Ritual cleansing of the principal mourner and distribution of skirts by the deceased's clanswomen to the principal mourner and his or her clanswomen	To effect final release of all mourning restrictions a principal mourner has sustained for a particular death; the principal mourner can now remarry

prepared in the same way as the *dubalela* (underskirt) of *debumwoya* skirts. The fibers in the *saipwala*, however, are joined together to make a skirt five or six times longer than a *debumwoya* (normal skirt). This stage is called *saipwala ivatusi* (they bind together the *saipwala*). The purpose is to solicit the *vakakaiya* ceremony. The women are given cooked and uncooked food by their kinsmen to distribute as *kaimelu* (payment) for their work on the *saipwala*.

When completed, the *saipwala* is given to the *torikariga*, who houses it until his clanswomen (women of the same *dala*/clan of the deceased) gather to dismantle it. This is called *biritutulasi saipwala* and occurs several weeks after the *saipwala* has been presented to the *kariga* clan. The skirt is taken apart from the bottom up, until the skirt is a suitable length, with the hemline falling almost to the ground. The woman who receives it is either the principal mourner herself or the sister or daughter of a male principal mourner. The individual bands of the skirt, separated from the main skirt, are distributed among the *kariga* clan women. Those who receive a band must make a skirt to give at the *vakakaiya* ceremony that follows several months later. The women are again given payment in the form of *kaimelu* (cooked and uncooked food) by their clansmen.

Like the clanswomen of the principal mourner, her or his clansmen must also perform certain tasks to solicit ceremonies designed to remove particular restrictions. *Kawasa* is the cooking of *mona* (taro pudding: a special food made of beaten taro and coconut cream) and the giving of this pudding to the *kariga* clan to distribute among themselves. The purpose is to induce the *kariga* clan to perform *ulusila wadola* (discussed later) on the principal mourner.

Some time after the cooking of taro pudding, the *kariga* clansmen repay the principal mourner's clansmen by collectively cooking taro pudding and returning it to them. This is simply called *mapula kawasa*. After these preliminary activities the stage is set for *ulusila wadola* and *vakakaiya*, the lifting of the final restriction on the principal mourner.

The offering of *ulusila wadola*, (yam pudding) to the principal mourner is a symbolic reintroduction of "proper" food to her or his diet. The yam pudding is called *toamata*. It is of interest to compare *toamata* with the noun for corpse, *tomata* (*to-* is the masculine prefix; *-mata* means to go out, to be extinguished as a flame or fire). The pale yellow color of the yam pudding is likened to the pallor of a corpse. It is this pudding that the principal mourner is to eat. (See also the essay by Montague in this volume.) Ideologically the most onerous restriction assumed by the principal mourner is the denial of "good" food such as yams, taro, and ripe bananas. With the performance of *ulusila wadola* this restriction is removed. In eating *toamata*, the principal mourner internalizes her or his close association with the deceased, thus allowing the external being of the principal mourner, which

59

has remained visually associated with the deceased since death, to begin the process of returning to the living.[15] The *kariga* clan head makes the *toamata* and with the help of other kinsmen tries to persuade the mourner to eat it. It is not an easy task to convince the mourner to resume eating yams again, thereby internalizing his grief. One man mourning the loss of his son resisted three attempts by his wife's kinsmen to persuade him to accept the *toamata*. He was still refusing yams when I left the village. If the mourner refuses the *toamata*, it is simply reintroduced at a later date until she or he accepts the spoon of yam pudding and thus sheds another restriction (*kawagala*).

The final ceremony in the second phase of the mortuary cycle is *vakakaiya*, and it corresponds roughly to the final stage in northern Kiriwina called *lisaladabu* (Weiner 1976:62). As in northern Kiriwina the purpose of the *vakakaiya* ceremony is to release the principal mourner and others who have elected to take on the *saigala* restriction from further restrictive mourning. *Saigala* is the deliberate neglect of one's appearance. The *vakakaiya* ceremony is also designed to pay back all those who wore *kuwa* (a thin black band around the upper arm or neck). The principal mourner, however, retains his or her mourning necklace.

The participants, comprising the men and women of the *kariga* clan together with the mourning clan and anyone else who wishes to attend, gather at the house where the principal mourner has resided throughout her or his mourning (usually the *torikariga*'s house). The *kariga* clanswomen bring skirts, and the men bring material, valuables, and money to distribute to the mourning clan. The women commence the proceedings by allocating skirts for distribution to the various mourners who accepted behaviors and work associated with mourning: those who deliberately neglected their appearance, those who adorned themselves with *kuwa*, women who prepared the *saipwala* skirt, and the principal mourner who wears the *mwagula*. The men busy themselves with the distribution of their valuables to *saigala* wearers. While this is going on outside the *torikariga*'s house, the principal mourner remains inside, helped by other mourners of her or his *dala* and clan. They commence the ritual cry, reminding everyone of the loss of a relative and friend. It is the job of the deceased's clanswomen to end the "crying" and recurring mourning of the deceased by bathing the principal mourner and dressing her or him in clothes symbolizing the new status of the mourner. Once the skirts are satisfactorily distributed by *kariga* women outside the house they enter the house to join the principal mourner. With them they take a prepared mixture of scraped coconut and scented herbs. This they rub onto the skins of the principal mourner and her or his helpers. In this way they are ritually "bathed" and the external signs of mourning removed. *Kuwa* are cut off and new skirts given to the principal mourner. If the latter is a woman a new, bright-red skirt is put on and cut short: the attire of a sexually available female. If the mourner is a man, a new cloth is tied around his loins by *kariga dala* men, and he is given a razor with which to shave his beard. Symbolically, the mourners are cleansed of their closeness to death. They are entreated to rejoin the society of the living and to prepare themselves for the reemergence of their sexuality. This ends the actual *vakakaiya*. Everyone gathers outside the house to partake of the cooked food prepared by the wives of the *kariga dala*/clan men. Uncooked vegetables are distributed to the *kariga dala*/clan women by their kinsmen in payment for their work in preparing the skirts and doing the work of the preceding mortuary ceremonies.

The completion of the *vakakaiya* ceremony marks a structural break in the mortuary cycle as a whole; all mortuary ceremonies that have been concerned with an individual's death are now finished. Village life for everyone returns to normal and the two individuals for whom all the preceding ceremonies have been conducted are freed of most of their responsibilities to each other; one may rest in peace, temporarily separated from living society, while the other rejoins it. The two are freed, however, only from the central stage of village life. They must reemerge together at a later date when the *mwagula* (mourning necklace), which still binds them together, is laid to rest at the grave site.

PHASE III: *DOBA SAGALI*
(SKIRT DISTRIBUTION)

It is because of the mourning necklace into which some remnant (be it fingernails, hair, or teeth) of the deceased is woven that the third phase must take place. As long as the mourning necklace remains above ground and in the hands of the affines of the deceased, the deceased's *dala* is obligated to carry out one more phase of the mortuary cycle. Whereas the first two phases of the cycle are associated with an individual's death, phase three is related to a number of deaths that have accumulated to a *dala* and clan. It is phase three that offers the most significant divergencies from mortuary observances in northern Kiriwina. The only tradition shared between Vakuta and northern Kiriwina at this stage of the mortuary cycle is the long-term privately maintained economic tie between close kin of the deceased and close affines who wear the mourning necklaces of the dead. Whereas the major public ceremonies to a mortuary cycle in northern Kiriwina end with the women's distribution of their wealth in *lisaladabu* (Weiner 1976:91–120), its equivalent on Vakuta, the *vakakaiya*, only finishes the major ceremonies related to a single death. There remains a final sequence of mortuary ceremonies that have as their objective the massive payment of women's wealth and men's wealth in large public distributions to all of a clan's affines who wear the relics of its deceased around their necks.

Whereas the focus of the mortuary sequence prior to the *vakakaiya* ceremony (*lisaladabu* in northern Kiriwina) is upon one death and affines related to the deceased, phase three on Vakuta is concerned with an entire clan's obligations to their deceased's affines who retain the relics.

With the accumulation of deaths in the passing of ten or more years a clan will decide it is time to finalize all mortuary commitments that have accumulated. This means they must finally pay those who possess the mourning necklaces of the dead. In northern Kiriwina this is done more or less privately by the deceased's *dala* and the individuals who look after the relics (Weiner 1976:84); Vakutans accomplish this by two elaborate distributions of wealth that involve the entire population. The final payment to the affines by the clan who is to sponsor the last mortuary rites can take several years (Table 3).

The men of a clan agree to begin the final phase of the mortuary cycle by declaring the coming year *kaiyasa* (a competitive yam harvest). The sponsoring clan not only tries to grow as many yams as it can, but also entreats everyone else to do the same. Every household on the island (including Giribwa villagers) prepares and nurtures its yam gardens with extra zeal, for there is now acute competition among them to harvest as many yams as possible. The sponsoring clan is responsible for periodically refueling this zest throughout the year by holding communal eating ceremonies. After the harvest, the sponsoring clan receives most of the yams through various categories of exchanges. These yams are next redistributed to those affines who retain the mourning necklaces of their dead kin. The wearers of the mourning necklaces then redistribute the yams among those who have in some way helped them since the commencement of mourning. Although most of the harvested yams in the *kaiyasa* year go to the clan who is sponsoring the competitive yam harvest, thereby enabling them to pay the *mwagula* wearers of the sponsoring clan's dead kin, these yams are finally recycled back to the rest of the village. One could simplify this by saying B gives yams to A in yam harvest exchanges so that A can give them back to B in mortuary exchanges (see fig. 1 for diagram). The payment of yams to those who wear mourning necklaces at the *kaiyasa* yam festival is said to be men's *sagali* (distribution). The clansmen are giving their wealth (pigs and yams) to the wearers of their dead kin's relics. Women's *sagali* has yet to follow.

The initiative to begin the final phase in a *dala*/clan's mortuary cycle generally comes from the senior man of a *dala* that has an accumulation of dead kin whose relics remain with affines. This senior man becomes the chief organizer and sponsor for the entire clan's final mortuary phase. No one man, however, can bring the skirt exchange to a climax without the help of his clansmen and women. Fellow clansmen are solicited and agreement is accomplished before the process of finalizing the clan's communal mortuary ceremonies is set into motion.

TABLE 3
Phase III: *Doba sagali*

Stages in Mortuary Cycle	Period after Death	Item (s) Distributed	Description	Purpose
Kaiyasa	1–10 (or more) years	Uncooked yams, cooked foods, and male valuables	A competitive yam harvest and festival in which the deceased's clansmen receive yams to distribute among their deceased's principal mourners	To repay the principal mourners of a clan's dead kin with male wealth and to finalize the exchange relationship between a clan's deceased and their spouses (or fathers)
Katumova Urikudu	1–10 (or more) years	Cooked food	Deceased's clansmen prepare and distribute cooked food to all women of the village(s)	To obligate all women who receive food to work hard on the production and accumulation of skirts
Dobobu	1–10 (or more) years		Deceased's clanswomen gather to cut the hemlines of the new *debumwoya* skirts	To preview the new prestigious skirts that will be distributed at the *doba sagali*; the few women who can make *debumwoya* receive acclaim
Luvaosa	1–10 (or more) years		Deceased's clanswomen gather to display their skirts in a competitive manner	To determine who of the deceased's clanswomen maintains most social relationships, allowing her to accumulate most prestigious skirts
Doba Sagali	1–10 (or more) years	Skirts	The final skirt distribution by the deceased's clanswomen to the former's affines in payment for their mourning activities; after the skirt distribution the clansmen distribute cooked and uncooked food to the women participants	To pay back the principal mourners of a clan's dead kin with female wealth and to finalize the exchange relationship between a clan's deceased and their spouses (or father)

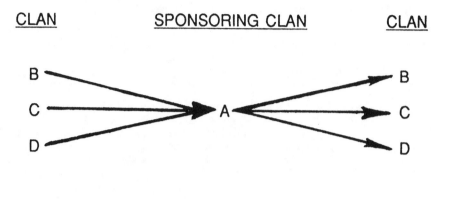

CLAN   SPONSORING CLAN   CLAN

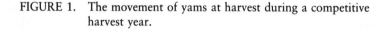

gives yams at   gives yams as
harvest for *kaiyasa*   mortuary payments

FIGURE 1.   The movement of yams at harvest during a competitive harvest year.

To begin the chain of events that will end in the women's skirt exchange, the clansmen organize a communal feeding of all the women of the island's four villages. *Katumova urikudu*, as this communal feeding is called, is meant to obligate all women, especially the clanswomen of the sponsoring clan, to acquire or make as many skirts as possible for the big skirt distribution. *Katumova urikudu* literally means the preparation of the string that binds the skirt strands into the skirt band. The string that binds the coconut or banana leaf strands into the skirt band is twisted from fiber taken from the *iem* (the aerial root of the pandanus tree). *Katumova urikudu*, the binding of many disparate strands into one skirt band, symbolically binds women to each of their respective clans so they will cooperate as one. Communal eating also symbolizes unity of a corporate group. There are four groups gathered, each affiliated to one of the four clans and each separated from the other three. It is significant that *iem* not only refers to the pandanus tree (itself redolent of femininity because it provides numerous materials for skirt production) and to the twisted string used to bind the fibers into the skirt but it is also used metaphorically to refer to women.

The communal eating of food prepared by the wives of *kariga* clansmen heralds the onset of the women's final mortuary ceremony in which hundreds of skirts are distributed to those who wear the remains of their dead kin. Many months will lapse, however, between the *katumova urikudu* and the final skirt distribution. Before the final payment can be accomplished, skirts must be accumulated, and the obvious way for a woman to acquire them is to make them herself.

It is not as simple as this, however. The vast social network that Vakutans are continually at pains to maintain must be attended to in the final mortuary ceremony as well as in the associated activities leading up to it. If women were simply to make their own skirts for the distribution, the opportunity for binding others to them through exchange obligations would be lost. Women of the sponsoring clan share the greatest burden. Not only do they make skirts for themselves but they also prepare the materials for making skirts so that they can give these to other women to make. This is called *vawawa* and the women who make up the skirts are given *vakapula* (cooked food, betel nut, and tobacco) for their work.[16] *Vawawa* should not be confused with *valova* exchanges in northern Kiriwina (Weiner 1976:78–80). Whereas *valova* involves the "exchange of objects for bundles" (ibid:78), and the objects' being "sold" in an immediate transaction for equivalent payment in bundles, *vawawa* is not an exchange of objects nor is its payment immediate or equivalent. Indeed, *vawawa* is not a transaction. The deceaseds' clanswomen gather the necessary materials for skirt construction and give these to women of their husbands' clans: sisters, mothers, and/or sisters' daughters. It is significant that these women belong to the same group as those affines who retain the mourning necklaces and for whom the sequence of ceremonies in phase three are performed. By receiving *vawawa* materials, however, these women are also drawn into the preparation of skirts for the final mortuary distribution, thus aiding the sponsoring clanswomen. During their labor the women who have received *vawawa* materials are given *vakapula*. The final payment for their labor comes after the skirt distribution when their brother, sons, mothers' brothers, and so on (husbands of the *vawawa* givers and therefore affines to the deceased's clan) cook a special taro or yam pudding and give this to female relatives who supported their wives in the accumulation of skirts for the *doba sagali*. The more valuable the skirt, the greater the *vakapula* during construction and final payment. Skirts are classified into a hierarchy of value according to certain criteria. More specifically, there is a basic division between *sainuya* (coconut leaf skirts) and *debumwoya* (banana leaf skirts). The *debumwoya* are more highly valued than the *sainuya*. *Debumwoya* fall into named types, each exhibiting specific design features. These types are further classified hierarchically. Not every woman can make the *debumwoya*. Only a few have received the magic (*sopi*) that enables them to make the more highly valued skirts. Hence, this is a source of prestige and small economic gain for those acknowledged as masters of *debumwoya* skirt creativity.

It is the aim of the sponsoring clanswomen to collect as many skirts as possible.[17] They are the leading actors in the final attempt to lay their dead to rest. Extra clanswomen become involved (as they are obliged to by *katumova urikudu*) by making skirts to give as *dodiga bwala* (a general exchange term which involves the giving of some item required for a distribution to an affine). In this case, a woman makes a skirt and gives it to a sponsoring woman through the latter's husband or father. In other words, a woman will give her brother's wife or daughter skirts to contribute to the final distribution. She is later paid back in the form of *kaimelu* (consisting of a particularly favorite cooked food, yams, pigs, betel nut, or valuables) by the man through whom they are linked. In one way or another, all the women of Vakuta are involved in making skirts for the final skirt distribution following *katumova urikudu*.

When preparations have been made, the skirts all finished and collected by the sponsoring clanswomen, and when the sponsoring clansmen have accumulated enough yams, bananas, sugarcane, betel nut, and tobacco, and fattened pigs, the *doba sagali* (skirt distribution) is imminent.

There are three stages of the skirt distribution: *dobobu, luvaosa,* and the *doba sagali* itself. The staging of these activities generally corresponds to the time when there are many yams in the village immediately after the yam harvest in September.

The *dobobu* is a comparatively minor activity preceding the skirt distribution. It occurs a couple of days before the final ceremony and involves cutting the lengths of the *debumwoya* skirts that have been newly made for distribution. The sponsoring clanswomen come together with all the *debumwoya* they have made themselves, received as *vawawa*, or obtained through *dodiga bwala*. Together with these women are the *debumwoya* makers, who usually cut the skirts. Other women gather to watch the proceedings and get a preview of the new *debumwoya* about to be circulated in the village. The *debumwoya* makers receive acclaim for their efforts at this showing. All women present at the *dobobu* are fed taro pudding made by the sponsoring clansmen.

Luvaosa is a competitive display of each women's collection of skirts. In this, every woman competes against her own clanswomen. Sister against sister, mother against daughter compete in a bid for public acclaim as the woman who can mobilize the greatest number of social obligations by amassing skirts. The amount of skirts a single woman displays not only shows her own industriousness but also reflects her own social position and that of her husband (or father, should she be unmarried). It demonstrates their combined wealth in being able to mobilize a wide social network. This intraclan competition was also noted by Weiner in the *lisaladabu* distribution and given much consideration (1976:103–20).

On a specified day, the sponsoring clanswomen bring their skirts in special containers called *bubuwaga* (*waga* means boat) made and decorated by their husbands. The more finely decorated stand off the ground on legs. They have branches from the upper four corners that are decorated with strips of material, colored leaves, flowers, colored paper, tobacco, betel nut, and so forth. Once everyone has arrived with her skirts the display begins with a crowd of female watchers nearby and male onlookers in the far distance. Each woman pulls a skirt from her *bubuwaga* and puts it on the ground in front of her, declaring aloud whether she made it or acquired it through some other means (principally through *vawawa* or *dodiga bwala*). She shouts out the name of the person, indicating the relationship. When the last woman has shown her skirts, all women sit down to cooked food prepared by the wives of the sponsoring clansmen. In *luvaosa* there is competition between the sponsoring clanswomen. Although the woman who "wins" is not treated differently nor publicly congratulated, everyone is fully aware of who she is. The criteria by which the competition is individually judged rest upon the number of skirts amassed, the proportion of *debumwoya* to *sainuya*, and the number of cloth skirts and dresses also acquired. Whereas these women were bound together in *katumova urikudu*, they demonstrate in *luvaosa* their individual identity, separated from clan or dala identity, and their place in society as individuals. In *luvaosa* the sponsoring clanswomen are in competition with each other to display their social importance symbolically through skirts. Two to three days later they work as a unified group to distribute the accumulated skirts principally to those people who have looked after the relics of their dead brothers, sisters, uncles, children, and mothers.

The *doba sagali* is the final public ceremony in the mortuary cycle on Vakuta. The purpose of this ceremonial distribution is for the women of the sponsoring clan to pay off the *mwagula* wearers. The men complete their obligations in the *kaiyasa* yam harvest, so it remains to the women to do the final honors by distributing women's wealth, the symbols of femininity and the ultimate standard for Vakutan matrilineal values.

In the same manner as the men's yam distribution, the women of the sponsoring clan hold a meeting one night prior to the skirt distribution so as to determine who is wearing the mourning necklace of their dead kin. They must also establish who will "hold" each of the wearers of the mourning necklaces; that is, one woman will contribute the majority of skirts to a particular *mwagula* wearer. This is generally determined by the woman's closeness to the deceased. For example, a woman "holds" her father, who wears the *mwagula* of her mother or sister (if the latter were married, the deceased's husband would be more likely to possess his wife's *mwagula*). In this way the distribution is organized, with the result that each *mwagula* wearer is guaranteed an equitable number of skirts, and all the women distributing know exactly how many skirts they can give to each wearer of the mourning necklace. Those women who do not have a particular person to "hold" simply contribute a few skirts to each *mwagula* wearer. Every participating woman contributes some skirts for each mourning necklace, each gauging her contribution according to her relationship to the deceased. Skirts are also distributed at the *doba sagali* for reasons other than the final public payment to wearers of mourning necklaces. Skirts are given to the women who distributed skirts in the last *doba sagali*. For example, Malasi women sponsored the last *doba sagali* in 1971; therefore Lukuba women, who sponsored the *doba sagali* I witnessed in 1977, had to pay back the Malasi women for skirts they had received in 1971. This exchange is called *wai*. Skirts are also distributed to the wives and children of the sponsoring women's male kin (MB, B, MMB, and so on).[18] This payment is for the help given to their husbands and fathers in preparing food, looking after the gardens, and so on, while the men attended to activities related to the *doba sagali* and the ceremonies leading up to it.

On the morning of the *doba sagali* one is awakened by the squeal of pigs as they are slaughtered and prepared for the earth ovens. Once the butchered flesh has been placed under the hot stones to cook, the women who will participate in the skirt distribution decorate themselves and take their skirts to the central area in front of the house of the senior male member of the sponsoring *dala*. The skirts are again presented in their decorated *bubuwaga* receptacles. When all women are present, a mat is laid out in their midst. It is on this mat that the skirts are laid as each name is called. When everyone has contributed skirts to a named *mwagula* wearer, other women take the skirts to the receiver's house. After the last name is called and the last skirts have been laid on the mat to be taken away, the women retire to the background to chew the betel nut provided and smoke tobacco while their male kin move from the background to the central stage and distribute the *kaimelu* (payment) to their sisters, nieces, and mothers. Payment consists of uncooked yams and betel nut along with other, less important raw vegetables. When the *kaimelu* has been distributed to each woman who took part in the *sagali*, cooked food (yams, pig, taro, sweet potato, and so on) is then distributed again to everyone present. The communal eating marks an end to the public distribution of wealth from the deceased's kin to their affines for the latter's part in "looking after" the dead of the deceased's clan.

With the receipt of skirts from the final skirt distribution, all mourning necklaces are supposed to be buried. The wearers have been justly rewarded for their duty to others' dead kin. It remains to the wearer of the mourning necklace, however, to decide whether she or he is ready to surrender the deceased's remains altogether. With receipt of the skirts, mourning necklaces must be taken off, but wearers may decide to keep a relic in their house and not yet part with it. Should this occur, the holder of the mourning necklace periodically receives skirts, yams, and sometimes Kula shell valuables from one of the deceased's kin.[19] The woman who "holds" a particular *mwagula* wearer at the *doba sagali* usually takes on the responsibility of continuing to give to the person who retains the mourning necklace. This relationship remains until the *mwagula* holder finally takes the necklace to the grave and buries it. This done, the relationship that existed between the deceased and his or her kin to the former's affines is terminated.

CONCLUSION

With the completion of the *doba sagali* in the third phase, all public distributions and ceremonial acknowledgments to deceased members of a clan also cease. Any continuing commitments to *mwagula* holders, who have been acknowledged in a finished cycle, are maintained on a one-to-one basis between those directly involved. With the first death of a member from a *dala*/clan who has just completed the third phase of the mortuary cycle, a new cycle begins with the *yawari* (crying).

Upon marriage two groups enter into a specific exchange relationship instigated by two individuals. Each marriage opens the way for a variety of possible exchanges between these groups. Once a marriage is formally acknowledged it is inevitable (barring divorce) that both groups will enter into a final exchange relationship following the death of one of the partners (or any children to the marriage). When a death occurs the two groups are launched into the chain of events that unfold as the mortuary cycle begins anew. Only with the burial of the *mwagula* can the groups be severed.

Although mortuary observances in the Trobriand Islands can generally be said to conform to a common pattern with similar concerns, there are, nevertheless, significant differences between the various groups that diversify Trobriand culture. From a broader perspective Anne Chowning argued for a greater degree of heterogeneity between Massim societies in contrast to the more common belief that saw Massim culture as homogeneous (1978). The Trobriand Islands present this dilemma in microcosm, illustrating the diversity of groups within an area once thought to be homogeneous. A comparison of the mortuary cycle extant in the different areas partly exemplifies the diversification of these various groups.

NOTES

Acknowledgments: Fieldwork was conducted on Vakata Island during the period September 1976 to January 1978, supported by an Australian National University Scholarship and Research Grant. I gratefully acknowledge Geoffrey Mosuwadoga and the Papua New Guinea Public Museum and Art Gallery for sponsoring my research in Papua New Guinea and offering assistance during my stay there.

I am grateful for comments made on an earlier draft of this paper that was presented at the 1981 Kula Conference at the University of Virginia, Charlottesville, Virginia. In particular I wish to thank Fred Damon, Susan Montague, and Annette Weiner.

1. Women also use cooked food as an exchange commodity. Although they can cook and use for exchange men's yams, women usually harvest their own yams and other vegetables classified as "women's vegetables" (sweet potato, tapioca, certain varieties of taro, and others). On Vakuta there is a distinction made between men's yams and women's yams. There are approximately eight varieties that are said to belong to men, approximately six varieties to women.

2. Montague also notes the comparative significance of clan identity in mortuary exchanges on Kaileuna Island. (See the essay in this volume.)

3. On Vakuta Island there are at present three distinct villages: Vakuta village, the largest village on the island, population approximately 330; Okinai village, population approximately 70; and Kaulaka village, population approximately 170. Giribwa village, population approximately 30, is located at the southern tip of Kiriwina Island and is socially related to the Vakutan villages. All social events on Vakuta include the Giribwa citizens as well.

4. Previously wrist bones, jawbones, and teeth were taken (cf. Seligman 1910:718–19; Malinowski 1929:132–33; Weiner 1976:22, 81–84). Whereas Weiner writes that many people are eligible to wear relics from the deceased in northern Kiriwina, Vakutans limit that right to a spouse, a father, *or* a close kinsperson to either of these should the former be too old to take on the rigorous responsibilities of a principal mourner. A further difference between northern Kiriwinan observances and those followed on Vakuta is the insignificance of the deceased's skirt or, if the deceased is a man, his basket, as mourning relics on Vakuta (cf. Weiner 1976:82).

5. Yams, pigs, betel nut, coconut, and skirts are obtainable within the society; Kula shell valuables are not. They must be procured from outside. To fulfill their mortuary obligations toward dead kin men must form Kula partnerships outside the society so that they can obtain the shell valuables demanded internally. A man's actions in Kula must be well maintained so as not to upset the demands of the Kula "game" while attending to social obligations. (See Campbell [1983a] for a discussion of the balance needed in manipulating Kula.

6. In the past a corpse was wrapped in mats and buried. Today Vakutans construct a wooden box roughly resembling a European coffin.

7. A person does not cease to belong to her or his *dala* at death.

8. Another important feature of mortuary activities in the past was the comparatively smaller number of people involved. I was told that only the *dala* to which the deceased belongs and the affine's *dala* would be involved. Today any mortuary cycle will involve the whole island and areas farther afield. It may be that the lessening of the mourning restrictions on affines, brought about either by administrative decree or pressure by the church, had the effect of increasing the number of people who could or would take up the mourning restrictions so as to obligate the

deceased's *dala* to give the associated payments for mourning services. With the increased number of people taking on mourning restrictions the deceased's *dala* had to seek economic assistance outside their own group. This they sought from members of the same clan (but different *dala*). The whole practice has escalated until it now encompasses the entire village as well as other villages of the island so that there is a split on the island between those who mourn and receive payment for their mourning activities/restrictions and those who have to pay the mourners and sponsor the mourning ceremonies.

9. Note here that the distribution is throughout the clan and not restricted to the deceased's *dala*. As mentioned previously, the clan is more important in Vakutan mortuary transactions than in northern Kiriwinan ones, in which emphasis on *dala* solidarity seems to be the major concern (Weiner 1976, 1978).

10. The giving of Kula shell valuables as *ninaboila* or *kulututu* payments puts stress on a man's Kula because the shell valuables he has given are supposed to continue in the circulating Kula tide. If they are taken out to satisfy a mortuary commitment, a man's future participation in Kula relies on his ability to acquire a replacement, either a necklace or an arm shell. Note that in this and many other internal exchanges, the same is not returned, thus leaving the man to manipulate another exchange, usually Kula, to acquire a Kula shell valuable to redirect. For further discussion of the hazards to Kula exchange effected by internal exchanges see Campbell (1983b).

11. The present abundance of coconuts in the Trobriand Islands is a relatively new phenomenon. Prior to 1910 only a few palms existed on Kiriwina and these belonged to men of rank. In 1910 Dr. Bellamy began a coconut planting campaign, ordering all the tracks of Kiriwina Island to be lined with coconut palms (Black 1957:282). Whether Vakuta Island was more richly endowed with the palms or not, I am unable to determine. Vakutans say, however, that coconuts have always been featured as the main valuables in the *katulaguva* exchange.

12. I have been reminded that in northern Kiriwina only men handle the distribution of raw yams and other uncooked vegetables (Weiner, personal communication). In Vakutan distributions of raw vegetables, women usually distribute to themselves that which has been given to them by men. If, on the other hand, the distribution of uncooked vegetables is to the Vakutan population in general, men do the distributing. Women are the distributers of cooked vegetables. Men distribute cooked food only when the food is pig or a taro or yam pudding cooked ceremonially by men.

13. In northern Kiriwina the mortuary stage called *lisaladabu* occurs at a later stage of the cycle and approximates the Vakutan *vakakaiya* ceremony in content and aim (cf. Weiner 1976:62).

14. A *saipwala* is usually made for the death of a married adult, a fully participating member of society. Another skirt, *seburutu*, is made for the death of a child or an unmarried person. It is constructed of coconut leaf strands and only reaches the ankle of any wearer. It is less onerous to make and is not usually a communal effort. Instead the skirt is passed from woman to woman of the principal mourner's *dala* to construct. When finished, it is given to the *torikariga*. The distinction between *saipwala* and *seburutu*, however, is not hard and fast. A *seburutu* may be

made for a widow or widower if the number of women in her or his *dala* (and clan if they are willing to help) is not great in number. *Saipwala* construction is equivalent to the *sepwana* of northern Kiriwina (Weiner 1976:97–103) and that of Kaileuna.

15. The distinction between internal and external is very important in Vakutan conceptualization and is linked to color symbolism. The aging process of the human body is a prime example of the gradual change from an external to an internal focus. An infant is symbolically linked to white and is associated with innocence and the lack of power. The gradual transformation to youth and the association of red imply the power of beauty, which is completely externalized. As one's youth passes, one gradually becomes darker as the shine of beauty fades and becomes dull. Maturity is associated with the color black. Black is an internal color associated with the internalized knowledge of magic, a "power" that belongs to the aged (see Campbell 1984 for an analysis of color symbolism; also Weiner 1976).

16. *Vakapula* refers to a general payment of refreshment (cooked food, betel nut, tea, tobacco) for labor output on behalf of someone else.

17. Daughters may also give corporate help to their father's "sisters," especially if a woman's father is deceased and his clan is intending to distribute wealth to his *mwagula* wearer. The daughter, although belonging to the same clan (and probably the same *dala*) as the *mwagula* wearer, will direct her efforts to help her father's clanswomen finalize his mortuary exchanges.

18. The exchange to wives of the sponsoring women's male kinsmen is called *sigirimomova*; skirts given' to the children of their male kinsmen are called *setabula*.

19. Should Kula shell valuables be given they are of medium to low value (Campbell 1983a). A woman either receives a Kula shell valuable from a senior male in the *dala* to give to a holder of a mourning necklace or from her husband. In the latter instance, a woman's husband would be given a Kula shell valuable from one of his wife's male kinsmen in return for the one given to a *mwagula* holder.

Frederick H. Damon

The Muyuw Lo'un and the End of Marriage

• Muyuw say that the primary purpose of one of their three mortuary ceremonies, the *lo'un*, sometimes pronounced more like *lowun*, is to end the marriage between a deceased's father and mother. This is accomplished by means of an exchange called *takon*. *Takon* occur throughout the culture's most important unit of structural time, the period constituted by a marriage. The two most important *takon* are the ones that finally define the correct gender identities between a young married couple and the *lo'un* that ends their marriage upon their children's death. A second purpose of the *lo'un* is to bring back to life those survivors of the deceased who have undergone a symbolic death through mourning. This aspect of the ritual seems to correspond to the Trobriand *winelawoulo* (Weiner 1976:81), a term apparently cognate to the Muyuw *lo'un*. However, neither the Trobriand *winelawoulo* nor any of the other Trobriand mortuary practices seems to have purposes or structures designed to end a marriage. Trobriand and Muyuw cultures share many features, so it would seem that a better appreciation of their differences might derive from a precise understanding of how the Muyuw *lo'un* operates. It is, therefore, the purpose of this essay to explain how the Muyuw custom functions in the way Muyuw often assert.

To accomplish this task I first position the *lo'un* in relation to the other two mortuary ceremonies, one commonly called *ungayay*, the other *anagin tavalam*. Then I discuss what marriage in Muyuw is about. I try to show that marriage consists of the transformation of gender capacities through time. The *lo'un* is at the end point of a set of transformations of which marriage consists. Some of the data and interpretations given in this essay are drawn from another work (Damon 1983a), which focused on the forms internal to the Muyuw kinship terminology.

My concern in this essay is Muyuw social structure. By social structure I mean the forms in which and by which value is produced, circulated, transformed, and reproduced. But value in the context of this essay refers only to gender labor. A complete discussion of either a Muyuw notion of value or Muyuw social structure must entail specifying how the structures that result in the *lo'un* lead into those represented by the Kula, and how they lead back to the *lo'un*.[1] There are thus two main structures to Muyuw. Considering both, kinship and Kula, is not possible in this essay. However, it is important to position both in terms of their purposes. It is the purpose of the Kula, as Muyuw experience it, to make a name, to transform a category, "person." Although it may not be true in all of the cultures of Milne Bay Province, transforming this identity, making one's name rise, is the major goal in Muyuw life. However, the Kula neither produces nor reproduces the identities it transforms. Muyuw kinship does this. Thus, viewed from the perspective of the Kula the purpose of Muyuw kinship is the production and reproduction of the labor and social identities that the Kula then transforms. The *lo'un* plays a pivotal part in that process.

MUYUW MORTUARY CEREMONIES

In this section I provide a global account of Muyuw's three mortuary ceremonies. Several limiting factors must be known to appreciate this account. First, there is evidence, both verbal and documentary, that the culture has changed significantly over the last one hundred years. Consequently some forms of some rituals have altered, and in one or two cases others have completely disappeared. Some data also contradict other data, and I suspect that some of these contradictions result from historical processes. Footnotes aside, in this essay I incorporate into my account and interpretation neither Muyuw's history nor changes in mortuary practices. Second, many of my data are based on eastern Muyuw informants and observations. I know that there are differences among eastern, central, and western mortuary rituals. Some of these differences seem to be little more than another way of doing the same thing. Some, however, might indicate significant difference in social structure or place in the social structure. Other differences, however, I cannot yet interpret adequately. For example, eastern Muyuw call the ritual immediately following a death *ungayay*, and the next one, some two or more years later, *anagin tavalam*. Yet in central Muyuw the word *ungayay* is applied to the second ritual, although its forms and functions are identical to those of the eastern Muyuw *anagin tavalam*. I suspect the aforementioned history is partly the reason for this difference in terminology, but I will not be concerned with differences of this type here. Nor will I be concerned with the interesting point that eastern Muyuw think their *anagin tavalam*'s form involves the imposition of a non-Muyuw practice on their system. Increasingly fewer and fewer eastern Muyuw people realize this imposition; in central Muyuw, however, where the same form is called *ungayay*, most are still aware of, and disturbed by, the fact of this enforced change.

Throughout the island, *sagal* is the cover term used for all three mortuary rituals. Each has at least one other term that better describes its sense. As noted, the first in eastern Muyuw is called *ungayay*. This term may be derived from the Misima word *wun* (subclan), which Muyuw occasionally use in place of their own *dal*; and from the verb -*gayay* (to scatter): Thus "subclan scatters." Such an interpretation partly corresponds to the culture's notion of death. When a person dies all those intimately connected to the deceased are thought to have their relations with other people severed. In a sense they die too. And from one point of view almost every act by the living after a death can be interpreted as trying to bring the living back to life, trying to recut old social relationships, or facilitate the production of new ones. Death, Muyuw say, is like a tree falling across a path or over a door. The path or door must then be recut.

One of the principal activities in the *ungayay* ritual is crying at the feet of the deceased and/or his or her survivors. This task is borne most heavily by women. And after the deceased is buried they are given pork and vegetable food to compensate them for their tears. However, the more significant compensation is the pork and vegetable food distributed at the later and larger ritual, *anagin tavalam*. This term may be translated as "the fruit (*anagin*) of our (*ta*) crying (*valam*)." The *anagin tavalam* then not only follows the *ungayay* in time but is partly conceived to complete some of its consequences. It is also correlated to the *ungayay* because people say that it functions to gather together people scattered by the *ungayay*. *Katikanok* (cause to mound up) is the term sometimes heard for this process. However, the *anagin tavalam* is Muyuw's largest ritual, and its effects and purposes transcend its relationship to the *ungayay*.

Both the *ungayay* and the *anagin tavalam* should be conducted by matrilineal relatives of the deceased. Both involve symmetrical exchanges between affinally related groups. Thus any given *ungayay* or *anagin tavalam* calls for later return performances. The *lo'un* might be coupled with an *anagin tavalam*, and it is relatively small if it is so coupled, but the two rituals have distinct purposes and forms and thus need not be put on together. Although an *anagin tavalam* is part of a symmetrical pattern between affines, the *lo'un* affects the relationship between the deceased and his or her parents: It brings their relationship to a close. Hence, unlike either of the other two mortuary rituals, it does not engender a pattern of consecutive performances.

I now provide a description of these rituals. The primary purpose of the *ungayay*, the first event following a death, is to dispense with the corpse and send its *kaluwan* (soul) toward Tum (Trobriand Tuma). During my first fieldwork period many people stated that the "soul" is transformed into a *yeluw* (ancestor) and that it stays in Tum. I was told that again in 1982, but some people insisted that the *yeluw* remains around the living, where it occasionally causes trouble in various productive activities. Whatever the case, the transformed essence that goes to Tum remains there. It is never reincarnated, unlike what is reported for part of the Trobriands.

The person who puts on the *ungayay* should be a matrilineal descendent of the deceased. Because people sometimes die at a remove from their subclan mates this is not always possible, and occasionally there are minor conflicts over just who is to perform the ritual. These conflicts do not seem to be as serious as in the Goodenough area, but they are not unimportant. Burying a person on subclan land is often done to substantiate claims to that land, and conducting an *ungayay*—as it is for every other ritual—is conceived to be "work" and of a kind that allows the person performing it claims to the deceased's property. More work is involved in an *anagin tavalam* than an *ungayay*, so in fact more is at issue in its performance.

When word of a death spreads, all who can try to go to the village and house where the corpse is set up for the better part of two days, one night intervening. Attendance is not restricted to *dal* (subclan), *kum* (clan), or *sinvalam* (affinal) relationships. However, if these kinds of immediate relations cannot attend the ritual then they should hold a small crying performance in their own locales, or at some later time trek to the owner of the deceased to cry. Crying at the foot of the deceased is conceived to be a prestation, a *siwayoub* (gift). As many people as possible should do this. The deceased's affines should bring something in addition to their tears. Distant affines may bring only money, or tobacco, but closer relations should bring small pigs, anywhere from a year to two years of age. Lacking a pig a close affine may bring a *kitoum* (a personally owned Kula valuable). If neither a pig nor a *kitoum* is available the person will probably stay away from the event, "embarrassed." The gift of either a pig or a *kitoum* implements a symmetrical exchange, the context for the return being another death/*ungayay* on the part of the original giver. However, since these pigs are small, nothing happens if in fact they are not returned. The pigs are not counted as significant debts or credits necessitating a replacement by some other form of congealed wealth should the receiver default. The *kitoum* exchange here, called *lawalov*, is a little different. These *kitoum* must be returned, but it may be years before they are. One exchanged before 1970 had not been returned by 1982. This is the only occasion in Muyuw in which a Kula valuable as *kitoum* is passed from one person to another in such a way that it must later be returned as a *kitoum*.

Before these people begin arriving at the house where the deceased remains, the corpse is dressed in his or her finest clothing. As dress patterns have altered as the society has become increasingly incorporated in the modern world so has the definition of finest clothing. For women cloth skirts increasingly replace coconut leaf skirts. The corpse also has its face painted, and Kula valuables are usually draped over or hung above the body. When people arrive to cry they often wipe their tears and mucus on the body. Women tend to remain with the corpse through the night; men gradually leave the death house, forming a group just outside its door, where they sing traditional songs and United church hymns. Periodically somebody, and not necessarily a woman, goes to the corpse to sing a special song. This may be made up on the spot, and hence recall some past event pertaining to both the singer and the deceased, or it may be a song the singer knows the deceased loved. At times during the night, or just at dawn, the women inside the house perform lewd jokes or skits. These are supposed to wake people and relieve them from the tension created by their enforced somber mood. A surviving spouse, whether male or female, should remain by the corpse throughout the night's mourning.

Just after dawn the owner of the deceased should distribute small things—cups, silverware, plates, sleeping mats, lamp glasses, small bits of money, and so on—to the group of men that has sung throughout the night. Then preparations are made for burying the body. Some have money buried with them, and in central Muyuw people say that wealthy people have *kitoum* buried in place of money. The body is carefully wrapped up in sleeping mats, and even more mats are placed in the bottom of the grave and then over the corpse when it is laid to rest. Elders know that their ancestors used to practice secondary interment, but this is a very distant memory and I could learn little of it. The grave, often no more than four feet deep, is dug by men; and men are usually the ones who place the body in the grave. How the body is positioned is important, and for a number of different reasons. Before the United church began to dominate the culture, in eastern and western Muyuw, heads were set to the west, feet to the east. This is thought to be consistent with the east/west symbolism so important to the culture (Damon 1979, 1982). Now this direction is reversed. In central Muyuw people are buried sitting upright. This is called *Siguyaw*, perhaps translatable as "their chiefs." *Guyaw* is a term for high status. And this custom is practiced in central Muyuw because these people are conceived to be the culture's *guyaw*, "highest people." Muyuw liken this to the high status associated with the *Tabula* subclan, and others, in the Trobriands. But I could learn no more than that it seems to be associated with a place, rather than a ranking of subclans.[2] Presently there is no other symbolic, economic, or political manifestation of the hierarchy this burial practice symbolizes. How the body is positioned is also conceived to be important given the possible negative effects the deceased's magic can have on future gardens. If an elder who knew but did not use or pass on his or her magic dies, the situation is especially serious. It is thought that his or her powerful magic can then spread to new gardens, for years to come, to stunt growth, cause pigs or other animals to consume the crops, or exert other mystical influences. Protection from this magic can be obtained in part by laying the person on his or her side so that the face and stomach are toward the sea. That way the bad influences should be blown out to sea rather than to the gardens. But there is the chance that the corpse will accidentally be turned around, or by itself turn over, so sometimes people jam logs or stakes into the grave to keep the corpse stationary. Protection from this bad magic can also be had if some living person knows the same magic or some other magical system to counteract evil each time a new garden is cut. Much garden magic seems to be used precisely to counteract the negative influences emanating from corpses.

It is the responsibility of women to fill in the grave once the corpse is in place and the small United church service is performed over it. In western Muyuw digging the grave, carrying the corpse, and filling in the grave are all duties assigned to specific persons and compensated by specific distributions. This is not true in eastern Muyuw. Other than the gender distinction between digging the grave and filling it, these activities in eastern Muyuw receive little sociological elaboration.

After the burial a group of younger men go out to sea to net fish. When the fish are carried back into the village they are given to the women who remained through the night with the corpse. All but those affinally related to the deceased are to eat the fish. But only a few fish are brought. It is just a token. While the men are away getting the fish, the women, in eastern Muyuw only, go to some other spot along the beach, where they wash, dress themselves in their best coconut leaf skirts, and paint their faces. When ready, they parade into the village with one young woman in the lead. She bears no special relationship to the deceased or the owner of the deceased. She must be unmarried, but old enough, or almost old enough, to marry. She is more finely dressed and painted than all the others, and she should—and does—look beautiful. Every eastern Muyuw woman is supposed to do this once and only once in her life. The message of this performance may be "here is an available young woman." Why this is coupled with this ritual I have no clear idea (nor do my informants), other than the structuralist inference that it is reasonable to couple somebody's real end of existence with another's potential achievement of maturity. If this is a hint of "reproduction" lurking about this first mortuary ceremony it may be significant that the next two rituals, the *anagin tavalam* and the *lo'un*, repeat this theme and considerably embellish it. I do not know why this custom is only practiced in eastern Muyuw, and since I have not seen any initial death ceremonies in central and western Muyuw I do not know what, if anything, is analogous to it in either of those two places.

After this parade of women the pig is butchered and distributed, along with several pounds of vegetable food, to all the women attending the ritual, excepting those affinally related to the deceased. Both women and men, however, may eat this food. With this distribution the ritual is over.

In one central Muyuw village people are buried just behind the two east/west rows of houses. Most villages now have special graveyards set aside at some remove from the village. Flowers are placed over most graves, as much a traditional as a modern practice. Although some think it is Muyuw custom to keep a fire burning over a grave for some months after a death, hardly anybody does this, and quickly most graves and graveyards become insignificant.

If a deceased person has a surviving spouse or children they should not eat any garden food planted by him or her. Surviving spouses also refrain from eating certain foods the deceased particularly liked. These voluntary food restrictions last until the *lo'un* ritual, some months if not years in the future.

Almost as soon as someone dies, and sometimes before, people begin to make preparations for the next ritual. If this is to be the *lo'un* the surviving spouse may begin wearing his or her mourning dress immediately. For both genders this means taking on an unkempt appearance: men let their beards grow and wear darker colored cloth. Women knot their hair and rub dirt, twigs, and leaves into it. They also wear *seywed* (very long skirts) made from uncut, coarse coconut leaves. These should be made by matrilineal relatives of the deceased. The skirts hang down to the ground. They are so heavy that women are almost immobilized by wearing them. As is true in many places in the Massim, women also wear *mwag* (long necklaces). Neither men nor women in this state should wash, nor should they engage in sexual affairs with others. Both should cover their bodies with potblack, though now only a few women do so. If it is going to be more than a year before the *lo'un* then surviving spouses will probably wait six months or so before they take on these likenesses of death. When they assume their mourning dress a deceased's daughters, and perhaps daughters of his or her sons, will also put on mourning garb. The skirts, however, are neither as long nor as heavy as the main *seywed*. Other preparations involve raising pigs and building up vegetable food stocks. A person putting on a *lo'un* should have at least one medium-sized pig and at least one very large pig for an *anagin tavalam*. A medium-sized pig might take two or three years to produce, the larger-sized pig four or more years. Elders sometimes distribute pigs to children or nephews well in advance of their own deaths for their rituals. Over these pigs the deceased's effects are burned.

I will now separate the description of the *anagin tavalam* from that of the *lo'un*, considering the former first. It is often two or more years after the *ungayay* before the *anagin tavalam* is performed. These are the largest rituals Muyuw conduct, so much time is needed to produce or marshal the resources. There are other reasons for long time intervals between deaths and *anagin tavalams*. Between about 1950 and 1978 only three or four were conducted in central Muyuw. The main reason for this is that the necessary marshaling of resources is thought to encourage sorcery, and the central Muyuw villages during this period were in a particularly chaotic state, according to Muyuw, because of sorcery. Since 1978 their situation has become less desperate, and consequently four or five of these rituals have been performed, two between June and August 1982. Although central Muyuw people think their rituals are grander than those in the east, a point of view eastern Muyuw dispute, everybody knows that eastern Muyuw performs many more than elsewhere. During my twenty-seven months on the island ten of these rituals were conducted, one in western Muyuw, two in central Muyuw, and seven in the east. Ideally they are performed first in eastern Muyuw, beginning about May, because they necessitate yams, and eastern Muyuw people usually plant and harvest their yams before others farther to the west. This ritual season, if it can be so called, ends in the west about September or October.

Each performance requires at least two days but three or four is more common. The main consideration is how long it takes to present all the pigs, and this varies with the size of the ritual. There are, however, two main kinds of *anagin tavalam* (or *ungayay* in central Muyuw). One is called *soi-i-lau*, the other *soi-i-but* (*but* means "noise" or "fame"). The latter are always larger than the former, and for that reason alone far less frequent. Of the ten I have experienced only one was a *soi-i-but*. In it about sixty pigs were presented to the ritual owner, thirty or so of which were slaughtered and distributed. The *soi-i-lau* I saw collected at most twenty or thirty pigs, half of which were killed. The *soi-i-but*, however, is also special because it includes dancing and drumming. Only a few groups have the prerogative to do this,[3] although my informants insisted that this right had no relation to any kind of rank or hierarchical status system. I suspect that some kind of complex cyclical pattern is, or was, at the bottom of this drumming system, but I could never figure it out. For example, the right to beat the drums and dance involves a pattern of three consecutive performances at three different rituals after which the drum heads must be broken and not used again for at least, if not more than, one generation. In any case, the dancing and drumming occur at night and may start a month before the actual ritual is performed.

In its material scope and in certain of its sociological details the *anagin tavalam* resembles aspects of the Trobriand *Lisaladabu*, as described by Weiner (1976:chap. 4). In Muyuw, however, men exchange with each other, whereas in the Trobriands most exchanges are between women. Muyuw women tend to remain on the periphery of the action, the place of Trobriand men in the *Lisaladabu*. In the Trobriands women exchange skirts or banana leaf bundles, both the product of female labor. But in Muyuw pigs and vegetable food are exchanged. Although women assist in the production of each, and in the context of *takon* pig and vegetable food are considered "female things," in the *anagin tavalam* context both are chiefly considered to be male products and male things. Weiner discusses associations between the names for the female things exchanged and feminine aspects of production, or reproduction. Opposed but correlated associations exist in Muyuw. Pigs are the most important things exchanged in the *anagin tavalam*, and for this ritual what is most desired about such pigs is their "fat." Through allusion, both direct and indirect, this "fat" is associated with male sexual fluids. Among other things this ritual is a celebration of masculinity.[4]

When guests arrive at the host's site, their identities are recognized by calling out their village name and by the gift of, usually, a pot of boiled sago. This presentation recognizes their home, separates them from it, and incorporates them in the domain of the ritual. From that time on they become the responsibility of the host, who must feed them for the duration of the ritual. The next level of interaction concerns prestations of pig and vegetable food, yams, taro, packs of sago, and, increasingly, bags of flour and rice. These gifts follow *sinvalam* relationship. *Sinvalam* is a word that may be roughly translated as affine.[5] It is an asymmetrical relationship between persons tied by a marriage, a relationship that governs the direction of work in a marriage. Each person who is *sinvalam* to the host must make a gift of a pig or pigs with as much vegetable food as possible. Usually a long line forms to carry all of the things, the pigs coming first, then yams if they are carried in special containers, and after that basket upon basket of yams and taro. The woman who is the connecting link in the *sinvalam* relationship always leads the long line of people who carry the stuff to the host's house.[6] A platform will have been constructed out from its front door. The pigs are tethered below it and the yams dumped upon the platform and then moved into the house out of sight. Usually some elder related to the giver of the food makes a short speech to the host. The host is often secluded inside the house, the speech heard and answered by one of his underlings. In the largest *anagin tavalams* I saw, ones that were not considered particularly big by Muyuw standards, it took the better part of two days to make all the prestations. After these are completed the ritual enters a new stage, its climax. There are two components to this. First, while the pigs are being butchered, much of the vegetable food is lined up in evenly sized piles perpendicular to the host's house. Usually a small piece of pig fat, taken from a pig's back, is placed on each pile. These piles are then given to the name of each married woman attending the ritual just so long as she is not *sinvalam* to the host. In theory she cried for the deceased at the earlier *ungayay*, and this is her final payment. By the time this distribution is completed it is usually dark, all the pig is butchered and placed atop the host's platform, and the next stage of the distribution starts. Here pieces of pork, plus a taro or yam, are given to names of men. The host, with his assistants, decides what piece to give whom. The person's name is bellowed out from atop the platform and he is often insulted. The recipient often formally refuses the gift, shouts back his own insult, and then accepts the piece as some youth carries it to him. This distribution, usually the most joyous part of the whole affair, begins after dark and often does not end until late into the night. When it is over people begin heading back to their home villages if they are within walking distance. But the ritual does not formally end until the next morning, when a final distribution is made to each participating village as a village. This gift consists of enough vegetable food so that it may be distributed to every person or household in the community. Just as a gift to the category "village" started the ritual, so one formally ends it.

We must now look more closely at some of the sociological principles in this ritual because there are several levels involved and because there is a disjunction between the relationships between people and those between the things exchanged.[7] First of all, *sinvalam*, the term I translate by "affinity," is the principle that governs the most important exchanges. Everybody *sinvalam* to the host should bring him a pig and vegetable food. I am *sinvalam*, for example, to my wife's father and mother's brother, and every time either of them puts on one of these rituals I should bring pig and vegetable food. However, they are not *sinvalam* to me, because they are not married to me. Therefore, when I or my father or mother's brother puts on one of these rituals my in-laws need not make return prestations. They are not *sinvalam*. However, my wife is *sinvalam* to my relatives, so when we put on one of these rituals she is obligated to us. And either or both her father and mother's brother will use her obligations to cancel their debts with me. What this means is that marriage consists of two sets of asymmetrical relationships between people that affect the symmetrical exchange of things.

The things that move *beneath* the marriage relationship must be exact. If I give a male pig of a particular size the return must also be male and of the same size. If the debt is not paid the consequence is serious and will lead to the forfeit of some kind of valuable, village land, garden land, or sago or betel orchards. Sometimes *kitoum*, personally owned Kula valuables, are used to cancel these debts. In theory the same may be said of the exchange of vegetable food in these rituals; however, nobody worries much if those returns are inexact. The same holds for the climax of the ritual, the distribution of piles of vegetable food and a little pork to women and pieces of pork to the men. The pork—upper head and jaw, lower jaw, backbone, rump, stomach, and legs—given out in any *anagin tavalam* is first distributed to pay back past debts, then to all those who the host thinks will give a ritual in the near future, and finally to other men at large.[8] But this pork goes to names of men only. These individual men hold the debts, not their subclan (*dal*). Hence the returns are often inexact, or in some cases never made at all. Either situation may generate insults as the pork is being thrown off the platform, but failure to pay back these debts does not result in conversion to some other category of wealth. Although the distribution of vegetable food to women treats them as if they are identical—the piles are first set out evenly then the women's names are called—the distribution to men is effectively a distribution to "men with names," that is, those men who hold the higher status positions at the time of the ritual. However, the ritual does not make those names; it just reflects them. The names are made elsewhere, in the Kula.

We must now come to perhaps the most important point to be understood about this ritual. Although the *anagin tavalam* marshals more work than practically any other social form in the culture, Muyuw insist that it does not produce anything. When they make this kind of statement they are comparing the ritual to the Kula. The Kula produces something that is substantial. *Anagin tavalams* on the contrary, are performed and then finished. Equivalents should be exchanged. At the end all are exactly where they started at the beginning. If, as already noted, exact returns are not made, then serious changes in the control/ownership of material resources may result from these affairs. But the shuffling of land between subclans that results from *anagin tavalams* is a result not of their structure, but of their not being performed correctly. In this sense exchange in the *anagin tavalam* holds the same place in the Muyuw kinship system that the exchange of *kitoum* holds in the Kula: it relates to the reproduction of the social and material relations of production, not the purposes of production itself (Damon, 1983c:323–27). This may be stated in another way. By putting on an *anagin tavalam* the host inserts himself in the social position (literally the *kaba-* [bed]) of the deceased. The host takes over the deceased's own debt/credit networks. These may be represented in outstanding Kula or pig debts or credits, or in the deceased's claims to subclan resources. People expect to die owing at least three or four pigs. The person who replaces them, who puts on the work of their *anagin tavalam*, assumes those debts and will spend much of his life paying them off, accumulating his own in the process. But inserting oneself into a deceased's position by means of an *anagin tavalam* adds nothing new to the deceased's estate. It is just there.

Thus this ritual pertains merely to the reproduction of a social position. Inversely, of course, failure to reproduce that social position will mean, sooner or later, the loss of material resources for that estate, if not the end of the subclan itself.[9]

I now turn to the *lo'un*. If a *lo'un* is coupled with an *anagin tavalam* most of it will be performed in less than an hour's time right after the afinal prestations are made in the *anagin tavalam*, and right before the distribution first to women and then to men. The remainder of the ritual is performed in a few minutes, more or less in private, the next morning. However, the two rituals need not be performed together.

All action in the *lo'un* is conceived to occur between the *tokowadan* (deceased's mother's side) and the *tokobinin* (deceased's father's side). The deceased's mother's side conducts the ritual. It should have one or two medium- to large-sized pigs, and it collects considerable amounts of cooked and uncooked food. Many people may offer uncooked vegetable food for this affair, almost independently of their relation or nonrelation to both deceased and host. The latter, if he conducts the ritual correctly, will assemble his own pile of food from his own gardens. If the harvest has not been particularly good he may display his own food, raw, in a container in his house. This is called *aluwt kwanan* (roughly, "the spirit's burden"). It will be a conically shaped container some ten or so feet high, perhaps five feet in diameter at its base, and tapering to a point at the top. On the top he sometimes places a large piece of taro, with both the corm and the stalk attached. If the harvest has been good such containers carry a different name, *beditut*; they are outside the host's house; and there may be more than one. Although I never saw this arrangement one *lo'un* conducted in western Muyuw during my research period had four *bedituts*.[10] These are filled usually with *kuv*, a male kind of yam.

A *lo'un* should be performed whether or not the deceased is male or female, and in theory the form of the ritual should not vary according to gender. Two of the three I saw, however, were performed with a surviving woman as the deceased's spouse, and since some women still go through most of the older mortuary practices my perspective is colored by what I saw. The deceased's wife, wearing her *mwag* (neckband) and long skirt, with her body blackened, carries a basket of yams to the house that represents the deceased's father. It may take three or more men to lift this very heavy load onto her head. Then the person representing the deceased's father wipes the spouse's mouth with all different kinds of food that she stopped eating when she went into mourning. The neckband, or beard if a man, is cut by the same person. This person, or other men representing the deceased's father, places new clothes over the male mourners, and women from the deceased's father's side place new skirts that they have made over the mourning women. Publicly this ends their official mourning. However, the next morning the same officiants take each person to the seaside, where they are washed. This is called *iguwavin* for the women and *iwlot* for the men. These terms are verbalized forms of adjectives referring to Muyuw age grades, *guwavin* and *tawlot* (female and male, respectively). Both terms are the first categories applied to youths that distinguish their gender, and both imply that the persons are ready to engage in sexual affairs leading toward eventual marriage. The interpretation here is clear: from the ceremonial eating of the forbidden foods to the actual washing the persons who have undergone a symbolic death are being brought back to life so that they may remarry. In the case of the surviving spouse, however, this does not mean that he or she is no longer married to the deceased. A spouse remains formally married to the deceased until *lo'un* have been performed after their children's deaths. The deceased's relatives control the new marriage choices of the deceased's surviving spouse. Furthermore, if a dead man's (or woman's) spouse remarries her new husband technically replaces the deceased. He must now play the role of being, for example, the son of two fathers. If the new husband is from a different clan, and Muyuw insist that he must be and complain loudly if he is not, the new husband (or wife) must *po'un* the surviving spouse. This means that *kitoum*, or some other significant form of congealed wealth, must be given to the old group. If the new spouse is from the same subclan as the old one, then no *po'un* is necessary; that is why Muyuw complain.

Following the ceremonial eating and redressing of those in mourning a whole series of *takon* occur. The deceased's mother's side gives to the deceased's father's side food, "female things," in exchange for "male things," knives, axes, now money, and sometimes *kitoum*. This begins with plates of cooked food, then a pot or two of *mon* (sago or taro pudding). For the cooked food usually small pieces of change are offered, say .20 per plate. Penknives may also be used here. When these materials have been exchanged baskets of uncooked yams are transferred. A group of people will carry these from the host's house to that portion of the village that is marked off to represent the deceased's father's side (who may, of course, actually be from a completely different village). The food is set down and then practically anybody who wants it puts down some equivalent for it. A basket of yams is worth, say, an axe, a machete, or A$2.00 (2 *kina*). When a given load of food is taken away, having been "replaced" by the money or whatever, then the representative of the father's side takes it to the deceased's mother's side. There the host sees that all who gave him baskets of vegetable food receive their due. When all the vegetable food is gone the pigs are killed by the deceased's mother's side. These people begin cutting the pig in the traditional manner. However, they do not finish. Shortly after they begin cutting they carry the carcass to the deceased's father side, and those people complete the cutting and virtual selling of the individual pieces of pork. What is received from that is then returned to the other side. This ends the really public part of the *lo'un*, the distinction between father's side and mother's side followed in spirit only.

The next morning, more or less while the people who were mourners are being washed, the deceased's mother's representative, the real host, the man who constructed either the *aluwt kwanan* or the *beditut, takon* that food to the man who in fact represents the deceased's father. Here the amounts exchanged on both sides are conceived to be large. The one *aluwt kwanan* I saw *takoned* probably contained several hundreds of pounds of yams, plus the taro atop the column, and it brought its owner A$16.00, a large amount of money by Muyuw standards. In any *takon kitoum* may represent the "male things," but only in *takon* ending a *lo'un* did informants spontaneously tell me that the *kitoum* they received were large. In any case, it is this final *takon* that not only closes the *lo'un*, but is conceived to end the marriage between the deceased's father and mother.

INTERPRETATION

When viewed together a number of features distinguish the *ungayay*, the first mortuary ceremony, and the *anagin tavalam*, the second, from the *lo'un*. First, every *ungayay* and *anagin tavalam* is one moment of a continuous symmetrical relationship. By virtue of exchange rules defining the prestation of small pigs in the first ritual and larger pigs in the second, each necessitates the performance of a complementary ritual so that the debts may be cancelled. And this is a process that never ends. A *lo'un*, however, never sets up the formal conditions for another *lo'un* for its debts to be cancelled. Rather than being inserted within a structure, it would seem to define the end of a particular set of structured relationships. Second, there is an entirely different character to the agents exchanging and things exchanged in these rituals. People who are *sinvalam* (affines) exchange in the first two rituals. This relationship results from an unrelated male and female who have combined their gender labors in a marriage. They are combined in legitimated marriage before the rituals and remain so combined after the rituals are over. But they exchange things, pigs and vegetable food, that are of the same gender. This is especially so with regard to the pigs.[11] A male pig must be returned for a male pig, a female for a female. This means the genders of these things are separated. In *lo'un*, the agents are "mothers" and "fathers," in fact people who represent the mother and father of the deceased. But once the ritual is over they are no longer so related. The thing exchanged in the *lo'un takon* are "female things," pig, and vegetable food, and "male things," knives, axes, money, and sometimes *kitoum*. These male and female things usually meet in a central location. So increasingly Muyuw refer to the *takon* as a *maket* (market), as if the two different kinds of things are quantitatively identical. However, from a qualitative point of view these things are different. They are also separated from each other. The mother's side gives female things and receives male things; the father's side receives female things and gives male things. Evidently, the answer to this essay's question, how is it that the *lo'un* functions to end a marriage, derives from the differences inherent in these rituals. I can show how this is so by detailing the internal relations in Muyuw marriage as Muyuw interpret the institution from the point of view of production.[12]

From the point of view of production, marriage begins with the brother/sister relationship. A brother and sister may and often do combine their gender labors to produce things. The brother is a producer, the sister a distributor. The brother clears, constructs, and plants a garden. The sister tends and then distributes and cooks the food. But a brother and sister may not combine their gender labor to produce people. If they do one of two consequences is said to follow. Upon their marriage the woman's stomach swells and she dies, or the children they produce are sterile and consequently do not produce a third generation. To prevent this the two become separated from one another's sexuality. Muyuw young men usually leave their homes at about the age of ten, and a brother and sister should not know about the sexual affairs in which each other engages. Ideally, and often in fact, courting is done at night so that it cannot be seen.

Although a number of particular occasions go into making a young couple married two are of significance for this account, and both involve *takon*, each of which resembles a *lo'un*. The first is the first pregnancy ritual. This is called a *pak*, and in all but one or two villages it is performed in a much reduced form. In essence it involves the new mother's going into seclusion for a given time period (a few weeks in most villages, upward of a year in others).[13] Her coming out is socially elaborated. There are two main events to the occasion. First the young mother gives the first bit of excrement her infant produced to the child's father's sister or the father's mother. This gift is supposed to go to the father's sister, but in fact often the father's mother takes it. In either case the excrement is just thrown back to the sea or land. Next a small *takon* is performed. The mother's side prepares a pot or two of *mon* (taro or sago pudding), perhaps a basket or two of cooked food, yams, or taro and then often several baskets of uncooked taro. Usually no pig is employed in this affair. All the food, however, goes to the father's side in return for which the mother's side receives male things. Sometimes coconut leaf skirts are added to the female food, as female things. These the child's father's sister often takes.

The child's father may not eat this food, but all of his relatives may. The focus of this eating is usually the father's father. All of these gifts are given to celebrate and in some sense compensate the father for producing the child. In Muyuw theory women do not produce children: men do, because

87

they have produced the garden and sea food that the mother conveys to the child. This explains the gift of excrement to the father's sister. Although she is separated from her brother's capacity to produce persons, she maintains liens on his productivity. The sign of that is the gift of excrement, which is also the sign of her brother's ability to transform one thing, food, into another, the child, symbolized by its transformed food, excrement. A woman's liens on her brother's production, his ability to produce people, is stated in another way. Muyuw claim that in the absence of the father his sister has the next most important role in the control of his children. Such control is always consensual, of course, but many women adopt their brother's children, and brothers are always careful to ask for their sisters' approval if somebody else wants to adopt their children.

Although the focus of the first pregnancy ritual seems to be on the mother, the relationships being represented and elaborated concern her relationship to her sister-in-law and that woman's claims on the child. The next important marriage ritual inverts this relationship. This is called *sebuw takon* or *bulavakun*.[14] The focus of this ritual appears to be the young father, the ritual performed after he and his wife have produced several children. For this ritual the young woman's brother, invariably, produces one extremely large pig and gives this, killed and partially cut up, with skirts and several baskets of cooked and uncooked food (usually taro), to the father and his side. The exchange then is formally between brothers-in-law. Again, however, the recipient cannot eat the food. His father formally takes it and sees that it is distributed. This father also receives a special part of the pig and should try to return that with a *kitoum*. Each piece of pig, basket or pot of food, and skirt must be replaced with some male thing.

It is the purpose of this ritual to formalize the young husband's relationship to the brothers-in-law and his own children. The sign of this comes after the death of the wife. Shortly after she dies the husband must *po'un* her. This means he must give *kitoum* to his brothers-in-law, or if not to them, his children. If a man does not make the *bulavakun takon* to his sister and her husband then the latter is not required to *po'un* his wife. Informants said that such a case would be tantamount to the woman's not having any relatives, not being related to anybody. This is important. The *po'un* is supposed to "replace" the labor that the woman gave her husband. If that labor was not formally attached to a brother, this attachment symbolized by the *bulavakun*, then she has effectively not given anything to her husband. And if that is true then he need not replace anything. And this is not just anything. Sometimes people do not have *kitoum* with which to make *po'un*, so land or betel nut, sago, or coconut orchards are used in their place. But *kitoum* are what Muyuw want. These in some sense are the ultimate thing. *Kitoum* are center points of the Kula. One clear implication of the relationship between the *bulavakun takon* and the *po'un* is the transformation of a sister's labor into the structures of the Kula for her brother. From the discussion of the first pregnancy ritual I noted that a sister maintains liens on her brother's capacity to produce people. The *bulavakun/po'un* linkage demonstrates the opposite relationship, the lien a brother has on his sister's gender capacity. By being severed from her capacity to distribute things to persons, he receives a thing, a *kitoum*.

The essence of the first pregnancy and *bulavakun takon* may be illustrated by Figure 1. Every marriage, a combination of male and female gender labors, follows from the separation of gender labor in the brother/sister relationship. This pattern of separation and combination is repeated in the relationship between things exchanged in the *takon* (separated) and the persons in the marriage (combined). Although the male and female things in a *takon* appear to be exchanged for each other on the basis of culturally inscribed notions of quantitative equivalence, and although they may in fact meet in one place as the exchange is conducted, the two are qualitatively distinct and in fact separated from one another. The female things, vegetable food, pigs, skirts, are *finished products*. The male things are means of production. This distinction between finished products, or perhaps means of consumption, and means of production is important. At first glance it appears to correspond to the direction of the movement of labor. In a *takon* a brother gives to his sister and her husband female things in return for which the husband's side gives male things. But I do not think this parallelism is really the import of the transaction. On the contrary, what is important is the complementary relationship between the separation of gender labors and *uses* of the things received. The female things a brother gives his brother-in-law through his sister facilitate the realization of feminine activities on the husband's side. A woman is separated from her brother's ability to produce people and in the *takon* exchanges surrounding his marriage "she" receives the wherewithal to fulfill female activities: cook, distribute, and eat food. Separated from her brother's ability to produce food, she receives produced food. This seems particularly marked whenever pigs are given in *takon*, for before they are passed from the giver to the receiver they are killed, singed, and partly cut up; they may then only be consumed. This is in marked contrast to the exchange of pig in either of the other two mortuary ceremonies. There the pigs are always given live. The receiver then decides how he wishes to use them. Sooner or later they must be returned live, but before that moment they may be used in the ritual itself, thus killed and eaten by others; or they may be shuffled into some other circuit. Since they must eventually be returned as given, the sense of this exchange, as noted previously, is of "reproduction." In the *takon* however, since the pig may only be consumed, more or less immediately, the pig is used for production, production as defined from the feminine point of view. The same is true of the male things received through a *takon*, only there the issue is

89

Female Things

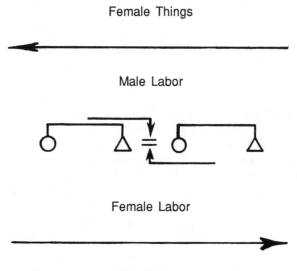

Male Labor

Female Labor

Male Things

FIGURE 1.

production from the male perspective. A man separated from his sister's capacity to distribute things receives through *takon* things he uses to realize his labor. This is not quite as clear now as it was in the past given that money is often used as a male thing. But knives of varying sizes and axes are still often given in *takon*, and in the past, aside from an occasional *kitoum*, only Suloug stone materials were used in these transactions. These are things that ideally men use to transform one thing into another, the bush into food, for example. In effect *kitoum* are no exception to this since they are means of production for the Kula.

Having situated *takon* at the level of production we may now better understand the main difference between the first pregnancy and *bulavakun takon*, and the *lo'un takon*.

The *lo'un takon* is like the other two in the sense that it operates by means of the sister's side, that is, the wife's or mother's, giving feminine things to the brother's side, the husband's, or the father's. However, it differs from the *bulavakun takon* because its pig or pigs tend to be only of medium size, and it differs from both earlier *takon* because much more vegetable food is given, and much of this food should be yams. This is significant because whenever Muyuw transact taro they always sever the taro stalk from the corm, giving only the latter. The receiver can eat the taro, but he cannot grow more taro without the stalk. Yams of course may be either eaten or saved for seed. And in the context of a *lo'un* the intent is explicit that the yams be used for seed. In the previous section I noted that there are actually two phases to the *lo'un takon*. The first is the most public. In this there is often only a nominal relationship between the people who give female things and the people who give male things. The former should be of the deceased's mother's side just as the latter should be of the deceased's father's side. Usually, however, all kinds of people join one side or the other, depending on whether they have some yams they can afford to give away for male things. Here the host of the ritual, the person who represents the mother's side, often does not even give any of his own stuff away, unless it is cooked food. Similarly the person who represents the father's side often does not participate at all, except for the pork. But both these people come to the fore during the second, more private, part of the *takon*. This usually occurs the next morning and revolves around either the *aluwt kwanan* (the container inside the host's house), or, if it has been a good harvest, the *beditut* (the larger container outside the house). It is the transfer of this food from the mother's side to the father's side, accomplished by a return of either a significant amount of money or a relatively large *kitoum*, that ends the marriage between the deceased's mother and father.

In one *aluwt kwanan* I saw the container was several feet in diameter at the bottom, and some eight to ten feet tall, tapered toward the top. The container was packed with *kuv* and *parawog*, in Muyuw terms male and female yams. Resting atop this column was an enormous taro, stalk intact. I saw this in 1974 and was told that that was the correct way to make either an *aluwt kwanan* or a *beditut*. When I returned to Muyuw in 1982 I asked another man about a *beditut* I knew he had made for a *lo'un* in late 1975. He emphatically told me he did not put a taro on top of his, but instead filled it (two actually) entirely with *kuv*. The one man, by placing a whole taro plant atop his container, was saying that not only was he giving away food: he was giving away seeds, the capacity to produce food once again. The second man's statement was identical because by his stressing *kuv* instead of *parawog* he was underlining the productive differences of each. Although one *parawog* seed produces at least two and sometimes as many as ten tubers, the way Muyuw use *parawog* as seed means that from each tuber only one planting may be made. Conversely, although from each seed only one *kuv* tuber results, people only need a slab about three or four inches long and one inch thick as a seed. Hence one large *kuv* tuber may result in many many seeds. In short the *lo'un* performed for a deceased person ends his or her father's and mother's marriage by virtue of the fact that it replaces the labor the father used to produce the child with seeds by which the father's sister's descendents may produce people again. It allows them to start a new kinship cycle all over again.[15]

CONCLUSION

In this account of Muyuw mortuary ceremonies I have employed the analytical contrast production/reproduction to answer how one ritual is conceived to end a marriage. This opposition, as most, depends upon context for its realization. From one point of view the *lo'un* might seem to concern reproduction. Its purpose is to replace the seeds a father used to produce his child. From another point of view, however, the issue here is not old production but new production. The seeds obtained through *lo'un* are conceived to end a marriage. Marriage in Muyuw is the relationship of production, its product children. It can only come to an end when those children have been transformed back into their original state, food, from which a new series of transformations can begin. It is this stress on starting over, the logical complement of ending, that suggests that the *lo'un* be viewed primarily as a matter of production. Muyuw incest notions correlate with these facts perfectly. Muyuw are not supposed to marry cross-cousins. However, the children of cross-cousins may marry. This means that only when an alternate generation has been produced may new relations of production be formed. In the last analysis it is an alternate descending generation that conducts the *lo'un* to end the marriage in the alternate ascending generation.

Although the *lo'un takon* involves the exchange of female for male things informants stressed the ending of the deceased's parent's marriage only from the point of view of the father. From their point of view it is the replacement of his labor by food and seed that ends his marriage to his wife. Socially he goes out of existence then. But what of the deceased's mother? In point of fact she seems to pass out of existence almost as soon as she dies. For then she is transformed into a *kitoum* by means of the *po'un*. Although informants state that a man remains married until the *lo'un* performed for his children, they also state, in what seems to be a contradiction, that a father has no further obligations to his wife's relatives once he has conducted a *po'un*. Rather than a contradiction, however, what is at issue here is the playing out of the different temporal consequences of gender labor emanating from the brother/sister separation. Female labor concerns finishing processes in production and so its role in the kinship system is relatively quickly completed, transformed into a *kitoum* and thus an entirely new sphere of production. Male labor concerns transforming one thing, the bush, into another, a person, and consequently is not brought to a close until its product can start its function over again. Male labor leads back into the cycles of kinship, female labor into the Kula.

NOTES

Acknowledgments: This essay is based on research conducted between July 1973 and August 1975 and from June to August 1982. The first period was partially funded by an NSF Grant (GS-39631) and an NIMH Fellowship (FolMH57337–01), the second by the Summer Grants Committee at the University of Virginia. I thank Shirley Campbell, Nancy Coble Damon, Susan Montague, and Annette B. Weiner for comments on previous versions of this paper.

1. A third social formation is represented on the island, its ties to the modern world system. Although Western involvement in the culture has been pervasive for more than one hundred years, its consequences, I think, have only been negative. Very soon it may be accurate to say that Muyuw kinship and Kula exist to produce labor for this modern world. But I do not yet believe that purpose is dominant.

2. See Damon (1983b) for a hypothesis about what the previous hierarchy on Muyuw might have entailed. But the society was once clearly far more complexly interrelated than even that model suggests.

3. Some people used the category *kum* (clan) to explain who could and who could not perform this *soi-i-but*, others the category *dal* (subclan), and still others *ven* (roughly community). Recall note 2.

4. And perhaps becoming more so. About 1978 when Dikwayas started performing these rituals again they added a new act to them. At the very end of the ritual, when what is left of the available sago and food is distributed to the different villages that have attended, one man rises on the platform, brandishes one or two bundles of sago in his hands, and usually two very large *kuv*, male yams. He calls out the names of specific men, gives each a verbal thrashing questioning his ability to produce yams of such a size, and throws the food at them. All this is greeted with great laughter and is meant to be funny. Interspersed between the throws the same man often yells at potential but unknown women who might be sorcerers. He tells them to see what fun they have all had, and if they will just refrain from sorcery they all may have this fun, perform these rituals, again.

5. The term *sinvalam* may be composed of the "companion" word *sin* and the term *valam*, the verb for "cry." The companion term is denoted by the *s*; the *i* denotes plural; and the *n* refers to the third person. If this interpretation is correct, then the literal meaning of the term, *sinvalam*, is something like "Those with whom they cry." Although this translation accurately reflects important aspects of the content of the relationship, informants speak of the term/relation more in terms of the asymmetrical flow of labor in the relationship. Elsewhere (Damon 1983a) I have glossed the concept as "working for."

6. If the prestation consists of five pigs, a unit called a *weywey*, then the male affine leads this parade. However, he puts on a coconut leaf skirt and face paint, dances up to the ritual house, and throws a "spear," a few wrapped up twigs from a tree, at the house. The spear is saved until the recipient can return a *weywey* at the giver's next *anagin tavalam*.

7. I take this notion of "disjunction" from Balibar (1975:271). Similarly the way I employ the couple production/reproduction follows closely from his work. He writes, "for Marx the conceptual pair production/reproduction contains the

definition of the structure involved in the analysis of a mode of production" (Balibar 1975:269). Relationships between levels, or exchange spheres, are discussed in greater detail elsewhere (Damon 1983a).

8. Often people discuss the initial and return pieces of pork employing terms used in the kula, *vag* and *gulugwal*. However, the correct terms, often heard in the presentation themselves, are *livabod* and *meil*.

9. About 1980 the relationship between pig debts and credits and subclan land was altered. A logging company arrived on the island and in order to disambiguate claims to large stretches of the island, for distributing logging royalties, most land was removed from this system. With government assistance subclans laid claim to large portions of the land based on subclan origin myths. Boundaries were cut to distinguish one group's land from another's. This is a major "event" in Muyuw history. Since their origin myths indicate that they are from elsewhere in Milne Bay Province, in one moment many people were effectively disenfranchised from the island's new wealth, another step toward making land a commodity was taken, the notion of subclan became substantialized, and the complex relationship between people and things, discussed later in this essay, was significantly changed.

10. In western Muyuw *buditut* are also used in *anagin tavalams*, but they are not involved in *takon*. For one *beditut* given at T1 a return must be made at T2.

11. Muyuw distinguish between male and female yams and male and female taro. In their natural cycles of production and reproduction they undergo phases of separation and combination analogous to that of people. I have noted this elsewhere (Damon 1983a). Other than the fact that male yams, *kuv*, tend to be featured more prominently in *lo'un*, these gender distinctions are not carefully followed in rituals. Availability, due to climatic differences from one year to the next, would seem to be the major reason for this.

12. Damon (1983a) discusses other aspects of the production view of Muyuw marriages, juxtaposing it to an exchange view. The exchange view concerns ranked exchange spheres. Combinations and separations of gender-defined things differentiate the hierarchies in the exchange spheres. At the bottom, when courting is at issue, combined gender-defined things interrelate separated persons.

13. She is secluded so that she turns white, as in fact she does. Whiteness is desired so that she becomes more productive.

14. *Sebuw* refers to male/female exchanges used to construct and constructed about a marriage. *Bulavakun* may be from the agglutination *bula-va-kun*. *Bula* is probably a noun classifier usually used with animals, especially pigs; *va* is a causative; and *kun* is the Muyuw pronunciation of *Kula*; thus pig-causing-Kula.

15. Conceptually *lo'un* are still very important to Muyuw. But I think, and predict, that they will become less important as the island becomes increasingly tied to the world economy. Formerly "real" wealth circulated in the *lo'un*. Now that male things are more and more just money, and now that rice and flour are increasingly replacing local foods in other rituals, much wealth is in fact leaving the island. I suspect then that fairly soon the *lo'un* will merely be symbolic, and after a while pointless.

INTERLUDE

Reflections on Massim Variability

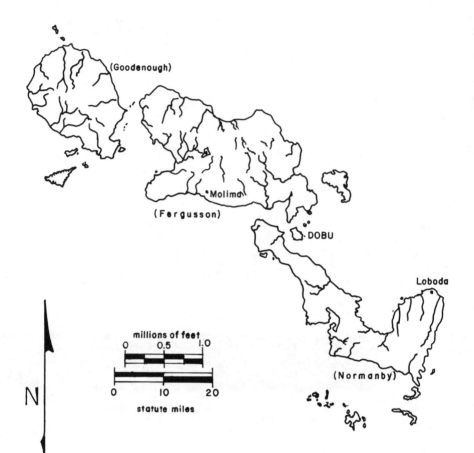

(Goodenough)

•Molima

(Fergusson)

·DOBU

Loboda

(Normanby)

millions of feet
0   0.5   1.0

0   10   20
statute miles

N

s.k. parker

Ann Chowning

Death and Kinship in Molima

INTRODUCTION

• "This is my *ova*; when I die, he will bury me." This way of introducing a very small boy, which occurred early in my first visit to the Molima of Fergusson Island, turned out to typify both their frequent and dispassionate mention of death and the classification of kin in terms of their different obligations when death occurs. The Molima regard mortuary exchanges and observances as their most important and distinctive ceremonial occasions, even though these have been altered both by missionaries, who disapproved of traditional mourning restrictions (Bromilow 1929:97–98), and government officers, who considered traditional burial practices dangerous to the health of the survivors. Wakes and funerals have altered little, and mortuary exchanges persist, so that in these cases I shall describe them as I saw them in 1957–58 and 1974–75, though for the more extreme forms of mourning I shall have to rely much more on informants' reports of what used to be done.[1]

Although their language is very closely related to Dobuan, and almost all of the kinship terms are identical, Molima social organization differs notably from that of the Dobuans. First of all, the Molima lack unilineal descent groups. In this they contrast with all other Massim societies described to date, which either have matrilineal descent groups, in the large majority of cases, or patrilineal descent groups at the eastern end, on Goodenough

Island (Young 1971) and Makaua in Bartle Bay (Seligman 1910:741).
Molima descent groups are completely cognatic.

Their kinship system has been described more fully elsewhere (Chowning
1962). In order to understand their mortuary ceremonies, it is necessary to
note a few major points. Genealogies are, by Massim standards, lengthy,
often extending for eight or nine generations, and the apical ancestors are
in no sense supernatural. Sometimes, however, they are reported to have
migrated from other parts of the D'Entrecasteaux and variations in custom
(such as tolerance of second-cousin marriage and of sororal polygyny, or
certain mortuary observances) may reflect the foreign influence. Knowledge
of genealogies is particularly important for validating claims to gardening
land, which may be used by all descendants of the putative clearer (but see
later discussion) and also determines one's behavior when a kinsman dies.
Marriage to a cognatic kinsman more remote than a second or third cousin
is strongly encouraged, partly to prevent quarrels over land, and consequently it is common for any two people to be related to each other in a
variety of ways. But rights to hamlet land, and trees planted on it, pass
through women only.[2] Since the dead used to be buried within the village,
often next to the dead person's house, and it is necessary to avoid, either
temporarily or permanently, places and food associated with dead paternal
kin, the ideal solution is marriage to a resident of another hamlet or ward
of one's village. Hamlet endogamy is forbidden. Boys commonly start
spending much time in the mother's hamlet, with a mother's brother, from
childhood, and may go to live there permanently after the father dies. The
father can ensure the boy's patrimony by planting trees for him on the boy's
mother's ground. Women usually join their husbands in virilocal residence.

While alive, kin are distinguished as "mother's family," "father's family," and "affines" (who may of course overlap with either of the first two
categories). "Blood" is inherited equally from both parents, so that the marriage of first cousins, whether cross- or parallel, is condemned because they
are "one blood." In general, relations with the mother's family apart from
actual parents are much more relaxed than with the father's. The mother's
older sister must be treated with respect, but a mutual joking relationship
exists between both mother's younger sister and mother's brother and their
sister's child. By contrast, any father's sister must be treated with respect;
though she jokes with her brother's children, they cannot reciprocate. Some
respect is shown for patrilateral parallel cousins, and the father's sister's
child, the owner of the village, has considerable authority over his mother's
brother's child, including the rights to demand food (which is not repaid) and to expel him from the hamlet if he misbehaves (Chowning
1962:96–97). Despite these distinctions, all members of Ego's personal kindred tend to feel the same kinds of responsibility for Ego. They contribute

equally to marriage exchanges, though it is common for siblings who are equally related to bride and groom to split up, one affiliating with the bride's side and one with the groom's. A person who quarrels with co-residents can always take refuge with other consanguineal kin elsewhere. Many maintain gardens on both father's and mother's land.

The kinship system is a principal reason why Molima mortuary observances differ from those described for many other Massim societies. For the Molima, there is no real distinction between one's own group and the "others" (Weiner 1983). All of those with whom one regularly interacts, including one's spouse, are likely to be consanguineal kin. As will be seen, social divisions exist: affines do form a distinct group, though their distinctness may be modified by consanguineal links; the father's side is differentiated from the mother's side; the village is composed of exogamous hamlets; and above all, death brings about a rearrangement of all kin into two unlike categories. The complexities and the distinctive features of Molima social relations are most clearly exemplified in mortuary behavior. At the same time, the whole system is clearly a Massim one, showing at some points detailed resemblances to what is found in other parts of the region, and at other points alterations of the pattern that still leave it recognizable. From the time that Fortune first opposed the "marital grouping" to the *susu* in his account of Dobu (1932:19), Massim studies have tended to focus on unilinear descent groups as if maintaining them were the central concern of their members, and sometimes individual actors seem to be totally absorbed by the structural roles they are assigned. Such absorption is epitomized in those societies in which it is stated that only "outsiders" openly mourn the dead, while their nearest kin, because of the demands of descent group membership, hide the grief they are assumed to feel. In other societies more concessions are made to the nearest kin, but even in these opposition, if not antagonism, is expressed toward the affines. Molima seems to be quite unlike many other Massim societies in treating the bereaved spouse as similar to, rather than opposed to, the siblings of the deceased in feeling and expressing grief. This assimilation, not unexpected in view of their marriage pattern, does not hold throughout the mortuary ceremonies, however. When a major ceremony (*sagali*) is planned, there develops the familiar D'Entrecasteaux division between the residents and what Fortune called "Those Resulting from Marriage" (cf. Schlesier 1970:46). Molima mortuary behavior exhibits many such contradictions, some of which probably reflect the retention of older patterns appropriate to matrilineal descent groups that have disappeared as entities but left numerous vestiges of customary behavior behind. It is precisely these that make Molima mortuary behavior look so similar to that in other Massim societies when the present rationale behind it may be quite different. Some of the comparative data will be discussed when the Molima material has been presented.

As has been noted, death produces an alteration in kin categories. Molima has a set of terms indicating that one has lost kin in any named category, although the principal terms lump together members of a number of categories. Most of these terms consist of the word used for the living relative, preceded by the negative prefix *ge-* and followed by an adjectival suffix *-na*: thus, *genowuna* (one who has lost a sibling of opposite sex: *nowu* [sibling opposite sex]). The same construction is used if an affine other than a spouse has died. But another term, *geyawuna*, which is superficially the same, does not contain a root now used as a kinship term, though *-yawu-* is presumably cognate with the term for "mother's brother/sister's child" in some other Massim languages (such as Wagawaga *aü*: Seligman 1910:481; and Bwaidoka *yau*: Young, this volume). Other terms are unanalyzable, including *wada'e* (widow), *toeda* (parent of a dead child), and *valeta* (man who has lost a brother). Since the two great categories to which all kin are assigned at death are those of *geyawuna* and *valevaleta*, the plural form of *valeta*, these terms and their range of reference will be discussed in more detail.

Valeta is the usual term of address for a man whose brother has died, used particularly by the offspring and the widow of the dead brother. The *valeta* in turn refers to the children of his dead brother as *tasi-gu vali-na* (my brother's *vali*) (or *kugwali* (orphan), if they are very young; presumably *vali-na* is related to *valeta*, despite the vowel change. But the plural form *valevaleta* has a much wider reference; it generally includes all the "sitters," those who are expected to mourn formally for the dead and to undergo restrictions on activity, dress, and eating, in contrast to the *geyawuna* (the workers and eaters), who do not mourn formally, work during and after the funeral, and in return for being feasted by the mourners, gradually lift the mourning taboos from them. For a man, the primary members of the *geyawuna*, as the quotation at the beginning of this essay suggested, are the *ova* (mother's brother/sister's child).[3] For a woman, they are the same, but only because her own children, being so closely related, are bound to mourn, whereas her sister's children (called *natu* when she was alive, like her own children) can act as *geyawuna*. The dead woman's children fall into the category of nominal *geyawuna* who are not "workers" or "eaters." The core of the *geyawuna* resemble matrilineal kin of the dead except that they do not normally include members of that person's own generation. Siblings can never be *geyawuna* (see fig. 1). Furthermore, kin who are not members of a hypothetical matriline can be considered *geyawuna*, so long as the principal tie to the dead is through a woman. The mother's cross-cousins are *geyawuna*. What the category cannot include is anyone who might also be classed as *valevaleta*. If, as so often happens, a person is related to the dead through both father and mother, or if there is a tie through any male as close as the tie through a female, it is necessary to act as *valevaleta*, helping provide, but not eating at the mortuary feasts made in honor of the dead. The parents, children, and surviving spouse are behaviorally assimilated to the *valevaleta*, though always designated by other special terms. Because the *geyawuna* are fed on prized foods such as pork at the mortuary feasts, it is highly improper for anyone not entitled to the privileged position of *geyawuna* to claim it. For those closely related to the dead, it is also dangerous to do so; *valevaleta* become sick if they eat the mortuary food, and children too young to know the relations are formally told that such food is taboo to them. Comparisons between these Molima categories and those in other Massim societies will be presented at the end of this chapter.

The basic division into *geyawuna* and *valevaleta* is partially masked by other considerations. It has been noted that primary kin are expected to mourn, and so are grandparents and grandchildren. On the other hand, some of the closest kin who are *valevaleta* usually assist the *geyawuna* in looking after the corpse and preparing it for display and subsequent burial. Furthermore, any *geyawuna* whose choose to can relinquish their privileges and go into mourning; if they do so, they are entitled to heavy payments from the true *valevaleta*. Finally, obligations to repay mourning and to provide mortuary feasts honoring one's own kin may compel a person to act as a mourner when the creditor or one of his or her close kin dies.

It is also necessary to distinguish between those who actively mourn, as by abstaining from desirable foods for lengthy periods, and those who as a sign of grief and respect for the dead simply refuse to eat *bwabwale* (mortuary feast foods), even though they are in the *geyawuna* category. Maternal uncles and aunts, and sisters' children, although they are *geyawuna* and workers, do not eat *bwabwale*; feasting is left to the more distant *geyawuna*. Furthermore, a namesake relationship creates a kind of artificial closeness (namesakes are always kin) that modifies the classification. So although it was considered proper for Peniata's mother to eat *bwabwale* for Wananadobu, Peniata himself did not because he had been named for Wananadobu's elder brother, and so was closer to the dead man than his own mother was. People also vary in the way they feel bilateral ties should extend in prohibiting eating *bwabwale*.[4]

Nowadays some people follow a "new custom" introduced by missionaries, called *ai-besobeso* (eat freely). It is held very shortly after the funeral and lifts the temporary and relatively light mourning taboos that the missionaries advocate, such as brief abandonment of the house of the deceased rather than its destruction. Nevertheless, separate food is always prepared for the *geyawuna*, who also eat apart from the other guests. Despite all the changes in mourning practice resulting from Christianity, the Molima continue to stress the distinction between *geyawuna* and *valevaleta* as strongly as in the past (see fig. 1).

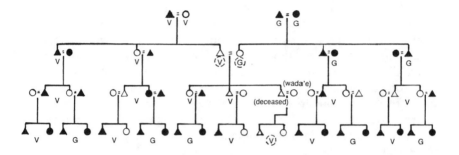

FIGURE 1. Examples of *geyawuna* (G) and *valevaleta* (V) relations.
Broken circles on the chart indicate people who could theoretically be
assigned to those categories (true parents and children) but are not.
This is the ideal case, illustrating for a deceased male the fact that
geyawuna are above all those who called him *ova*—his mother's
brother and the children of his sisters and female first cousins. For a
deceased female, the *geyawuna* are above all those who called her *sina*,
"mother," apart from her own children—the children of her sisters
and female first cousins (and also her mother's brother).

WAKE AND FUNERAL

Before further analyzing the relations involved, it is necessary to describe
behavior triggered by a death. In an unpublished manuscript comparing
death customs on Dobuan-speaking small islands with those on the mainland of Fergusson Island, Fortune says that on Fergusson, the corpse is buried immediately after death. This can happen to a baby or to the occasional
old woman who has no close kin surviving, but usually the wake and funeral occupy the best part of twenty-four hours. Word of the death must
be carried to other villages; the body must be properly arrayed and displayed; mourners must have time to come, weep, and view the body; and
decisions must be reached on such matters as the choice of burial site (in
mother's or father's village) and the nature of the mortuary rites, as well
as on who will do what. On one occasion, when the child of a prominent
family died after a very brief illness, burial was delayed for much more than
twenty-four hours, whereas if the death is not unexpected, many decisions
will have been made in advance, and the length of time between death and
burial depends on two factors. Certain rituals, notably the dispatch of the

soul to the land of the dead, and also the burial, must take place during daylight. Furthermore, the status of the dead person and the family determines the kind and number of preburial rituals as well as the need to delay the burial until kin from a distance have had a chance to view the body and weep over it.

In most cases, the close kin of the dying person have been present during the sickness, and an *ova* (mother's brother or sister's son) should be holding the body when death occurs. He lays down the corpse and straightens it out, and then starts the preparations for the funeral, sending messengers to carry the news of the death, and other men and women to collect betel nut and food for the expected mourners. All of these may be *valevaleta*, but not the closest kin of the dead. Formal mourning must not begin until the soul has been sent to Lotuma, the Trobriand Tuma, "lest tears flood the road" that it follows to the western tip of Fergusson before setting sail.[5] The closest kin of the dead—parents, children, siblings, and spouse—may be allowed to weep before this, but do so softly. Before formal mourning begins, it is necessary not only to prepare the village but also to wash and adorn the body and, usually, to set it upright. If the body is that of a headman,[6] the adornment is a lengthy ritual process, and the body may be left recumbent, only cursorily adorned, at the beginning of the mourning, but usually all arrangements are completed before those not present at the death arrive. In general, the body handlers, who also keep flexing the joints (to prevent rigidity) and waving away flies, are the *geyawuna*, led by an actual mother's brother or sister's son, if the latter is old enough to know proper procedure. The others present can, if they wish, devote themselves wholeheartedly to mourning, but in fact the closest kin are likely to want to maintain contact with the corpse, and they often help with the body handling. They do, however, often break off just to weep, whereas the *geyawuna*, although they weep on set occasions (on first arriving after news of the death, for example), do not mourn ostentatiously.

The adornment includes painting the face, if necessary shaving the beard and sideburns, cutting the hair, and putting new clothes and a variety of ornaments on the corpse. A sort of chair is constructed of spears and poles, and the corpse is seated on this, chin resting on a horizontal piece and hands propped up at shoulder level. (I saw nothing like the "huge logs" that Fortune describes for Dobu [1932:10].) The body is usually displayed either on the veranda of a house, usually that in which the death occurred, or in front of it, where the body can be easily seen and touched by the mourners. Over and around it are draped and strung additional ornaments and objects of wealth: arm shells, shell and tusk necklaces, pearl shells, flowers, beaded belts, cassowary plumes, ornamental baskets, and nowadays, paper money. (See Chowning 1983 for a description of wealth.) Kin lend many of these

103

valuables to enhance the appearance of the corpse and to demonstrate the wealth and importance of the family, but some should be buried with the corpse.

When the body has been prepared, a *geyawuna* who knows the formula strikes the house with a stick and tells the ghost to depart for Lotuma. He then blows a conch shell, and the *valevaleta* burst into loud wails, punctuated with sung or hummed dirges and with reproaches to the dead for leaving: "And now who will do what you would have done for me? Why did you abandon me?" As visitors arrive singly, they go to the corpse, weep (always producing tears), and then retreat to sit together. When a whole group arrives from a distant village, especially if the deceased was an important man, they may rush in aggressively, throwing spears, slashing at trees and houses, and sometimes constituting a real threat to the residents and their property. They are said to be expressing anger at the local people for not averting the death (as by neglect, including failure to pay for curing ceremonies). They can be bought off by payments of valuables, *guba* (see Chowning 1983), but more often simply make a gesture and then begin to weep. Not going to weep over dead kin is considered highly reprehensible; if the offender is a woman, she may be suspected of witchcraft, particularly because corpses are thought sometimes to open their eyes and look at the killer.[7] Children are not, however, expected to weep much, though they may be dragged forward to view the corpse. The general atmosphere at a wake, for those not in the immediate vicinity of the corpse, tends to be matter-of-fact, with general conversation and even occasional joking. Food is produced at intervals for the visitors, and if the wake is lengthy, men nowadays often play cards. When most weeping has ended, the *geyawuna* again handle the corpse and flex the limbs.

In the case of a headman, full decoration is delayed until the ingredients can be ritually prepared and the process carried out by men who know the proper spells, called *le'i*. I only saw this done once, and it started very late at night. To the accompaniment of the chants, which are of the type used for love and trade magic, but with a different tune on this occasion, the performers slowly crushed aromatic leaves, broke open a coconut, scraped it, heated the leaves and coconut oil with a hot stone, prepared face paint, and then concealed the corpse while they adorned it to the tune of further verses that accompanied the perfuming, face painting, and arranging the hair. Ideally the initial *le'i* should be the one the dead man used to procure his wife, but if the singers do not know it, another one may be substituted. On the occasion I saw, a principal performer, who not only is skilled in magic but possesses a particularly fine voice, was the dead man's son-in-law; here as elsewhere the *geyawuna* may be helped by *valevaleta*.

At intervals during the wake, women of the *geyawuna* sing the special female dirge, the *'ewabamu*. This describes the voyage to Lotuma, the corpse being depicted as a trader in full regalia (appropriate in this case, but used even when the corpse is female or a child), but with many references to the mourning. As they sing, they dance and flourish food and objects associated with the dead: personal property and, in the case of a headman, armshells. I was told that the women sometimes perform naked, especially if they are pregnant, but I do not know the reason (but see Weiner 1976:92–93).

Other mourners continue to come, and some people weep more than once, especially if they leave and then return. Meetings may be held at intervals; in these, the father's kin and mother's kin, or in the case of a woman, her husband's kin and hers, come together to decide on such matters as the disposal of the dead person's property, including which goods are to be put in the grave; the nature and timing of the mortuary ceremonies; and, if not already decided, the location of the grave. (Women are often buried in their own villages.) Occasionally such discussions lead to fierce quarrels. At the very least, they take up much time; Molima of both sexes are notable orators. Some of the speeches are likely to concern and be directed at the witches considered responsible for the death.

Meanwhile some of the *geyawuna*, often aided by other volunteers, are digging the grave. Traditionally this was an open shaft, at the bottom of which the body was seated in the same position in which it was displayed. A large circular capstone was put on top, but the body was not covered with earth. Often several members of the same family were put into one grave, bones simply being moved aside (after a spell is recited to invalidate any harmful magic their possessor may have known) in order to make room for the new burial. The Australian administration insisted that graves be located outside the villages and also filled in. The Molima report that they long resisted the former command, for fear that witches would interfere with the bodies if the graves were not guarded,[8] but after repeated jailings, turned to the present practice of burying in abandoned villages. (In recent times, most interior villages have shifted to the coast, so there are many old village sites in the hinterland.) It is still common to reuse old graves. To prevent earth from touching the body, it is either put into a coffin (usually made of an old canoe) or a chamber excavated at the side of the shaft and closed off by a fence. The face must be left uncovered so that it can "see."[9]

When the grave is finished, the gravediggers return to the village. This is the signal for renewed wailing, and some of the mourners will return to touch the corpse and bid it farewell. The gravediggers may also weep again. Then parents, siblings, spouse, and grown children are led away from the corpse (or sometimes dragged away) by the *geyawuna*, laid face down on the ground, and covered with mats or leaves. They lie weeping bitterly as the corpse, bundled up in leaves or a mat or put into a coffin, is carried to the grave. It is considered appropriate for children to take a farewell look at the dead person, and a man's children are usually the only members of the *valevaleta* to go to the grave, though occasionally another member will help carry some of the paraphernalia to be buried with the corpse. Otherwise the burial party consists of *geyawuna*.

At the grave, the body is placed inside and if a missionary is present, a Christian service (in Dobuan) will be read at this point. Then, if divination is to be used, the grave is covered for a few minutes with leaves or thatch, before being examined for signs of the cause of death. These may be objects put into the grave by the witch, such as a fish bone or a possum tooth, or discolorations on the body, particularly the arms. I only once witnessed such an examination, and nothing was found on that occasion, but the divination was reported to be successful at other burials that took place during my stays. Then one of the *geyawuna* waves a sprig of an aromatic plant much used in magic, under the nose of the corpse and calls the person's various names. The namesakes who are present answer and take bits of the plant. The names are now transferred to the *geyawuna*, who alone may say them; they are temporarily or permanently taboo to the *valevaleta*. (See later discussion.)

Valuables are put into the grave, including not only some of the jewelry worn by the corpse but additional prized possessions such as a large lime gourd or a carved walking stick, and wealth ranging from large arm shells to paper money. A stake set up beside the grave holds a peeled yam, which is said to be food for the dead. Nowadays crosses covered with flowers are also likely to be set up by the grave. Dirt is put into the shaft, the grave is covered, and the surrounding area is cleaned. The gravediggers then depart to bathe, using magical herbs to purify themselves. Objects that have been in contact with the corpse, such as the arm shells hung near it and the wooden dish used for washing, must also be washed, but this can be done by the *valevaleta*. The *geyawuna* who had charge of the body, and those who buried it, abstain from work for several days afterward, but true mourning is the duty of the *valevaleta*. All who actually touch the body must abstain from gardening for a period of several weeks, or the yams would die or fail to sprout. Those who simply dig the grave are not affected. If a death occurs during yam planting, some *geyawuna* who would be willing to handle the body may be instructed by others to abstain, so that they can plant yams for those who are under taboo.

Despite the bathing and the taboo on planting, I never received the impression that burying the dead was regarded as a profoundly onerous and contaminating task, as it seems to be in some other Massim societies (discussed later). In Molima, although the people who buried the corpse do receive constant gifts of food, the reason seems to be rather that they worked at a variety of tasks while the *valevaleta* were left free to mourn.

THE DISPOSAL OF PROPERTY

During the wake, and immediately after the funeral, any property of the dead that was not buried is divided among the two sets of heirs, used to pay the dead person's debts, or destroyed. The house should be burned as well; the surviving spouse is not incarcerated in it, because continued contact with it would be dangerous to health. Indeed, the surviving spouse never again approaches the house site. The house is called *vanua lulube*, a term that Fortune (unpublished manuscript) reports as being widely used on Fergusson for such houses. In Molima, all personal property closely associated with the dead is also called *lulube*.[10] This includes clothing, bedding, betel-chewing equipment, cooking and eating utensils (but not large pots used for cooking feast foods), contents of the yam house and garden, fruit of any tree planted by the dead person, and tools, including fishing canoes (but not overseas trading canoes). Contact with these is dangerous for anyone but the *geyawuna*; the *valevaleta* would sicken and die if they took these things.[11] Items in this category that no one wants are destroyed, usually by burning. When the *geyawuna* take the utensils, they give the surviving spouse replacements needed for survival, but receive much more than they give back. A man may keep his father's pigs but will use them to make death feasts for the father. (Although mortuary feasts in Molima are intended to compensate the workers, the fact that the compensation is in cooked food puts the "work" into the category of aid, such as that given workers who help plant a garden or thatch a house, rather than a service that demands payment in valuables or even raw food [Chowning 1983].)

The taboos on eating food belonging to the dead person apply to different members of the *valevaleta* for varying periods of time. The surviving spouse can never eat this, nor will a widow eat any food cooked in the dead husband's village for fear it may contain oil from some of his coconuts. (Women do not plant coconuts.) A person also permanently abstains from eating from trees planted in the dead father's village, but can in time, if the proper ceremonies are carried out, eat from trees that the father planted elsewhere. Children of the dead can also enter the garden to gather from it, though they will not eat the food, whereas the surviving spouse never reenters the garden.

Gwegwe (wealth) should be used first to settle any outstanding debts left by the dead person, especially those associated with his or her marriage. All marriage exchanges should be balanced at a death (Chowning 1983), and some "mourners" state that they are going to a wake primarily to collect debts. Some of the rest of the wealth, particularly overseas trading canoes, may be used temporarily by the *geyawuna* while the heirs are still in deep mourning, but will be returned when the heirs have made one of the mortuary feasts. The usual heir for wealth is the son (or sons) of the dead, although a dead man's brother may hold the property, or a considerable part of it, for his lifetime. If there are no sons, a sister's son takes precedence over a brother's son, so that *geyawuna* may inherit wealth as well as *lulube*. It is, however, permissible to dispose of personal wealth, especially before one's death, as one wishes, providing that one's sons are not disinherited, and some of this may be passed to women.

At a funeral, wealth such as an arm shell may also be given to any mourner who came from a distance. Acceptance obligates the recipient to make a *bwabwale* (mortuary feast) for the dead person. The donor is one of the close kin who will also be making *bwabwale*, and he is, in effect, hiring someone to help with the job of feasting the *geyawuna*. This "gift" is called *guba*, a term that usually refers to compensation, but mourners do not expect to be paid (except when they are collecting old debts).

MOURNING

Traditional mourning was very similar for widow or widower, as the Molima report it, but my strong impression is that it was more arduous for the widow, and descriptions tend to focus on her. I shall accordingly do the same, noting where relevant the comparisons with the widower's behavior.

The whole mourning complex was called *mwagula*, which is also the name for material worn around the neck by the widow and widower. Hers was made of barkcloth (see photograph of the "widow's neck tie" in Fortune 1932:Pl.II), whereas his was made of shredded vine with cowrie shells and pearl shells dangling from it and rattling when he walked. Relics of the dead person were not incorporated into the mourning costume. The widow also wore a contraption of rattan that partly covered her breasts, a long skirt of undyed leaves, a barkcloth head covering, and a barkcloth cloak. None of these was reported for the widower. Both sexes shaved their heads and blackened the head, face, and limbs, and the widower let his beard grow. Neither bathed during the period, of weeks or months, spent in seclusion. This costume was the same for any man or woman who went into deep mourning, such as the parents of a dead child or a sibling of the dead. (The costume is no longer worn, except for a long plain skirt for women, but mourners cut their hair short and men still let their beards grow.)

Mourning typically has three stages or, if a *sagali* is made, four, with the end of each signaled by the provision of feasts, generically called *bwabwale*, for the *geyawuna*, who then formally lift particular taboos.[12] For example, when one man died before the yam harvest, residents of his village such as his daughter-in-law were unable to eat yams until the *geyawuna* had been feasted and had lifted the taboo by walking through the village holding a steaming piece of cooked yam. So many *bwabwale* feasts are produced that everyone needs to be alert to relationships with all the recently dead, in order to know whether to eat of any food that is brought back to the village by the *geyawuna*, or to allow one's children to eat it. Really remote kin, whether *geyawuna* or not, can share such food without causing offense, but it is always taboo not only for the close *valevaleta*, but also for anyone in a *bwabwale* debt relationship. That is, if your father abstained from eating *bwabwale* when my father died, then I should not eat the *bwabwale* for your father, and similarly for the other close kin. As has been noted, some *geyawuna* refuse to eat *bwabwale* as a sign of grief for the death, even if they do not undertake full mourning; abstention is particularly characteristic of those most closely related to the dead, even though they are also most likely to have "worked" at the funeral.

There is a gap of a few days between the burial and the first feast, called *vegabu* or *gabugabu*. During this period, the mourners prepare the mourning costume and abstain from eating any but roasted foods; they drink only heated coconut milk. Some of the mourners fish or hunt and then cook a small feast including the fish or game for the *geyawuna*. These in turn bring soup, which they give to the *valevaleta*, making it possible for them to eat coconut cream. The *geyawuna* put the costume on the principal mourners, who then go into seclusion. The house of the dead person is burned at this time (*gabu* means "to burn," as well as "to roast"). The widow goes to stay near a brother of the dead husband, whereas the widower can remain in any part of his own village that is distant from where his wife died. Uxorilocal residence is uncommon in Molima, and he would not be expected to live in the wife's natal village.

Other kin, such as the deceased's sister, may go into seclusion together with the widow or widower. During the seclusion period, the mourner stays in the house during the day but crawls out at night to defecate or urinate, with coconut shells under the hands to protect them from the ground. Within the house, it is necessary to walk slowly, and speak only in a whisper.[13] Food is brought by the *geyawuna*; when they knock and whisper that it is there, the mourner raises the door covering slightly and pulls it in. Diet is very heavily restricted, but not so much as in the days before additional starchy foods such as manioc and sweet potatoes (both introduced by Europeans) reached the area. Taro, "good" yams, and animal protein are all forbidden.

At the end of the period of intense mourning, determined by the family of the spouse in the case of widow or widower, the *valevaleta* who are not in seclusion put on a large feast, and the house is opened by the *geyawuna* joined by those sisters of the dead spouse who have not secluded themselves. The release ceremony is called *ve'enovila*. For a widow, food, including pudding cooked with coconut cream, is brought, along with jewelry (arm shells, necklaces, and pearl shell ornaments). The visitors open the door, two of them enter and take the mourner by each arm, and all three crawl out together. As he or she emerges, they all weep together, and then the mourner is escorted around the village to look at all the places from which he or she has been shut away. The escort typically includes the secluded person's own kin. A widow then sits down with her husband's sister and weeps with her, and all the women present may perform an 'ewabamu at some point. Food offerings are piled around the mourner but the jewelry, which was brought just to cheer him or her up, is taken back. The food can be eaten by the widow's children, but otherwise is given to the geyawuna proper.

During the period of seclusion, the widow's sons and the geyawuna will have made a new garden for her, and she can now work in it but will still have to observe food restrictions, particularly those on taro and animal protein. She can collect firewood and gather greens (many of which are wild). The widower can also work, but in the past would ask a son or nephew to climb trees for him, for fear of damaging his mourning regalia. The widow and widower could chew the leaves of various trees, but betel chewing is forbidden until the next ceremony.

After the ve'enovila, formal mourning is ended for everyone except the widow and widower. They remain under restrictions until the ve'alaupa. At this ceremony, the geyawuna cut off the mwagula and, for a widow, shorten her long skirt. They squeeze coconut cream over her, paint her face, and put arm shells and a shell necklace on her. (I assume that she is also bathed before being decorated, but did not inquire.) The release from mourning is similar for the widower. He can now resume normal life, but the widow is still expected to stay in her husband's village, and not to remarry, until a sagali ceremony is made for her husband. She is given a pig to rear that would be killed for this sagali. She should remain chaste and also avoid the part of the village in which she and her husband had lived and his grave site. She can chew betel nut and eat anything except the fruit of trees in her husband's village.

A widow who has fulfilled all her mourning obligations and thus proved herself to be a proper wife is a particularly desirable marriage partner, but also an expensive one, since the new husband has to pay her dead husband's kin as well as her own. If she does remarry, the kin of her dead husband, blowing conch shells, escort her and seat her in the lap of her new husband, saying "Here is your widow." The family of the dead wife are similarly involved in the remarriage of a widower, and the marriage of a widow to a widower is more elaborate than any other sort of marriage. It is the geyawuna of the dead who receive most of the marriage payments.

THE AFTERMATH

Until missionaries forbade the practice, the most extreme form of mourning was the lopping of a finger joint. This could be done by any of the *valevaleta*. It is said to have been voluntary. If done by someone who was not a spouse or a very close kinsman, it constituted the strongest claim to a portion of the dead person's property, usually land or fruit trees. Denied such claims, the creditor would display the mutilated finger, and the sight should silence any objections. Finger lopping was particularly common after the death of a headman, and women were most likely to lose a joint.

Even today, the death of an adult permanently alters the status and behavior of certain kin of the dead: not only the surviving spouse, but above all the children of a man who has died. As has been noted, while both parents are alive, there are differences in behavior toward kin on the mother's side and those on the father's side, but the actual parents are treated alike, and no particular respect is shown to the father's brother. Once the father has died, not only is his brother addressed as *valeta*, but his name is avoided, and he is treated with special respect. The *valeta* can command the labor of his dead brother's children.

The children also permanently avoid the dead father's name. I was not told that it was offensive to say that name in his child's presence, but among the worst curses are such phrases as "Your father's grave" and "Your father's skull," and perhaps the worst is "Your father stinks" (*mwawulu* [to putrefy]). This avoidance of the name of the dead paternal kin is immensely important. Repeatedly, Molima expressed shock that foreigners—other Papua New Guineans as well as Europeans—"even say the name of a dead father!" Years of being asked the father's name by government officers have only slightly weakened this taboo.[14] In addition to the name, the grave and trees planted near it are permanently avoided, though if a *sagali* is held for the dead person, his paternal kin can eventually eat from other trees in his hamlet. Garden sites and fruit trees outside the village are similarly not used until a *sagali* has been made.

All of these restrictions apply, in somewhat more attenuated form, to all dead kin on the father's side, of his own or ascending generations. For other kin, taboos on names of the dead are lifted when the *geyawuna* are fed pork at a special feast, usually held many years after the death, and in return "call the name in the open." The *geyawuna* have always been able to say the name.

After they themselves are released from mourning, the closest kin of the dead may still have the task of compensating remote kin or *geyawuna* for mourning and helping with *bwabwale*, as well as refusing to eat it, thus demonstrating exceptional grief. In one case I saw, such a *geyawuna* was

111

cooked a special pot of food by the dead man's son, who also ritually cleaned him because of his contact with the "juices" from the corpse, which he had embraced, and he was also given a pig to dispose of as he wished. If this had not been done, the geyawuna and his descendants would have "bossed" the land that would normally go to the dead man's heir. Failure to repay bwabwale made by close kin who are themselves valevaleta may also lead to loss of land rights. In one case, a man was disinherited by his second cousins because when his father died, the father's first cousin made a bwabwale that the son did not repay when the first cousin died. I have heard many complaints of improper behavior and disputes over debts and property rights resulting from the failure to settle mourning obligations sometimes incurred a generation earlier.

Other kin of the mourners may also be feasted. One woman told me that after she had finished mourning the death of her child, she provided a small feast for her own kin who had looked after her and helped soften her grief. (These people were geyawuna but too closely related to the dead to eat bwabwale.)

Finally, part of the aftermath of a death is the possibility of giving some prestigeful object, such as a canoe or a large lime gourd, a name such as tamageva (fatherless). Such an act keeps others aware of one's loss. I was told that if a man commemorated a dead sister by the name he gave his lime gourd, he would not allow those who had living sisters to take lime from it.

My data from Molima do not suggest that mortuary rituals following the dispatch of the soul to Lotuma are in any way directed toward the dead. I also never heard any stories about life in the land of the dead or ideas about the fate of the soul, even though encounters with ghosts are sometimes reported. Speaking the name of the dead or having contact with the personal possessions, where these are thought to cause sickness, is nevertheless not said to be a consequence of any act by the ghost or any other spiritual being. Some Molima do believe that reincarnation may occur; if a child is born within the same family shortly after an older one died, any similar character traits may be attributed to its being the replacement of the dead child, though it is considered dangerous to give it the same name until it is well grown.[15] But apart from a few suggestions that some spiritual essence may remain (as in keeping dirt from the eyes of the corpse), concern is centered on what happens to the flesh of the corpse. It is perhaps significant that the Molima, in contrast to so many people in the Massim, had no tradition of secondary burial or of removing bones as mementoes of the dead. The corpse should be guarded against cannibalistic witches, and the proper recitation of spells while it is decorated will also prevent insects from eating it. Decay is, however, normal, and when an old grave is opened, the bones

112

are handled and discussed in a matter-of-fact way, though direct contact with them is regarded as somewhat dangerous.

But though the soul is safely in Lotuma and the body is properly interred, the thoughts of the principal mourners remain centered on the person they have lost. Avoidance of places associated with the dead is not just a duty; the sight of them may evoke unbearable grief. Burning a whole hamlet to the ground, and moving far away, is the extreme expression of such grief, but even the quick disposal of personal possessions may indicate desire to avoid reminders of the dead as much as worry about contamination or conformity to custom. Grief can, however, be assuaged by observing mourning and by carrying out the mortuary rituals.

During the period of formal mourning, ended by *bwabwale* that frees the bereaved spouse, those most concerned, whether as *valevaleta* or as *geyawuna*, are largely self-recruited from the bilateral personal kindred of the dead, including the closest affines. Admittedly some roles are ascribed: a true mother's brother or sister's son, if capable, can hardly choose not to play a major role in the mortuary rituals, and the widow/widower is automatically the chief mourner. To a great extent, however, those who choose to observe mourning taboos and to make *bwabwale* for the dead, and also those who feed and generally care for the mourners, are those who felt close to the dead person, regardless of genealogical distance. (In one case, the stepbrother of the mother of the deceased was a leading member of the *geyawuna*, along with the mother's first cross-cousin, who had helped the dead son care for his widowed mother.) Admittedly in the case of a dead child, sympathy for the bereaved rather than grief for the dead may be the primary motive, but the same people are likely to feel both of these emotions. The implications of the degree to which individuals choose their mortuary behavior, rather than having it forced on them as in some other Massim societies, will be discussed later.

SAGALI

At least in the past, it seems that some sort of *bwabwale* would always be put on for any dead person who was mourned, and it was the obligation of the principal male mourner other than the former spouse to sponsor it. No prestige accrued to this sponsor; he would simply be condemned if he did not carry out his duty. He could, however, acquire prestige, and sometimes wealth, by putting on *bwabwale* for remote kin for whom he was not naturally a principal mourner. But sponsoring a *bwabwale*, or even a number of them, will not create the kind of reputation an aspiring headman wants. Such a man must sponsor a *sagali*, and it does not matter which of his dead kin, including affines, he chooses to honor. Although the dead person and the *geyawuna* are not forgotten, the focus shifts to the sponsor, his kin and coresidents, and their affines. Affinal exchanges, *po'ala*, are the dominant transactions until the end of the *sagali*, and so the *sagali* cannot be understood as just another kind of *bwabwale*. The social relations involved are quite different.

The major mortuary ceremonies, classed together as *sagali*, should only be attempted by actual or aspiring headmen. If the latter, they should be closely related, as son, nephew, or grandson, to a previous headman who could instruct them in all the intricacies of putting on a proper *sagali*. Anyone who has not been so instructed is likely to be publicly derided if he attempts to make a *sagali*. (On the other hand, those who should know better may perform badly; these are usually criticized behind their backs rather than publicly.)

There are various types of *sagali*, of which the *dayo* and the *sagali* associated with the construction of a new canoe are the most prestigious (Chowning 1960; Young 1983a). It is the *dayo*, characterized by an elaborate women's dance as well as dances by men, that the Molima consider particularly characteristic of themselves and the people most like them linguistically and culturally, the inhabitants of the Salakahadi-'Ebadidi region in the interior of Fergusson. The Molima do, however, say that the *dayo* has only recently spread from the interior, so that it is not equally well known in all coastal villages. Aspects of the *dayo* are described in Chowning 1983, so that here I shall focus on matters not previously discussed.

When a *sagali* is contemplated, the sponsor first begins to raise pigs, possibly beginning with those inherited from the dead man as the start of his herd. If internal quarrels have split his village, he also tries to bring about a reconciliation; it is useless to undertake a *sagali* without the cooperation of numerous kin. He then gives two feasts, one to announce the *sagali* and one to allocate land for special yam gardens. Kin living elsewhere may move back to his village temporarily, but he also depends on the families of women from his village who have married out of it. These constitute the core of affines who turn much of the *sagali* into a kind of affinal exchange (Chowning 1983). Pig rearing is intensified, and *gwala* (taboos) may be placed on reefs, streams, or coconuts so that a supply of food may be built up for the interim feasts.

In order to understand affinal relations, it is necessary to know more about marriage patterns. As has been noted, it is considered ideal to marry someone from the other hamlet of one's own village, but the small population of hamlets makes it unlikely that many such marriages can take place. Furthermore, many headmen of the past were polygynists—as some still are—and although some Molima approve of sororal polygyny, others do not. A headman is likely to identify at least one quite different village as *'asa-vaivai* (affine's village) (*vai* [to marry]), and other villages may be *'asa-*

vaivai to coresidents of the headman. The relations between '*asa-vaivai* should involve constant donations of raw food, including major catches of game and fish, going back and forth so that "the path is open," not choked by weeds as it would be if the exchanges were neglected. Initial marital exchanges are organized not by the parents of the spouses, who should not concern themselves with economic transactions involving their children, but by other kin, and frequently incipient or actual headmen will undertake this task, which provides an opportunity to display ability to marshal resources and also to behave aggressively in a semihumorous attempt to shame the opposing group. Tension between affines is expected[16] but usually repressed, particularly in the case of brothers-in-law, but it can be vented freely in the context of affinal exchanges, especially during a *sagali*, though always in a joking manner. The managers of these exchanges, if they are aspiring headmen, must be careful not to antagonize the affines whose cooperation is essential if a *sagali* is to succeed, and no one can become a headman without sponsoring a *sagali*. To do so, he must begin by demonstrating both that his own kin and coresidents accept him as a leader and that his (and their) affines will profit by cooperating with him. The relations between leader and follower are as significant as those between affines in determining the success of a *sagali*, and so the character and ability of the individual leader influence the outcome more strongly than do any formal relations between villages.

Once the yam gardens are ready for harvest, '*au'ona* begin and may continue for months. These are visits from the villages of the affines to the village of the sponsor in which the visiting men sing and drum and the women dance, to be fed and given quantities of raw food and betel nut to take home. Special pots for the *geyawuna* should also be cooked on each of these occasions. The affines, who are given such valued foods as pigs and dogs, will in time bring yams to be displayed during the *sagali*. The sponsor may also construct a *mwadale* (special elaborate yam house) (cf. Róheim 1950:178ff.), which his close kin help fill, and later dispense yams from this to those who help him with the *sagali*. Most sagali include displays of yams (*Dioscorea alata* only) in a variety of special containers: ground-based '*udila*, made of vertical slats; baskets decorated with flowers and placed on the verandas of houses; small yam racks that, like the *mwadale*, have a carved miniature canoe under the base; and the enormous rack with compartments for separate contributions of each host and affine that dominates every large *sagali*. This last is decorated with foodstuffs including sugarcane and taro complete with leaves, as well as bunches of betel nut. The smaller racks and *mwadale* are often adorned with particularly large yams painted and dressed like men and women.[17]

The *talaboo* (main yam rack) contains yams for the *geyawuna*; those destined for the affines are put into the smaller containers, set up near the *talaboo.* When the *yehena,* the affinal kin of the women from the sponsor's village, bring their contributions, they blow conch shells, clown, praise or deride their affines (as by repeating criticisms the latter have made of them), handle the local residents roughly (as by pouring ashes over them), and despoil their houses. The observers find the occasion hilarious and repay the treatment at a return *sagali.*[18] As the yam racks are filled, kin of the sponsor from other villages may also enhance the occasion—"decorate the village"—by clowning and dancing in front of the rack. Meanwhile the men of the affinal villages, and, in the case of a *dayo,* the female kin of the dead, have been rehearsing their dances that will precede the *'une* (distribution) of the *sagali* food. Except in a *dayo,* men do the principal dancing, either singly or in groups of three, while women do simple steps in place; for the *dayo,* a long line of women dance, with three of them performing elaborate steps and figures. The female dancers are both kin of the dead person and coresidents of the village of the sponsor. All dancers are fully adorned, wearing dance skirts, face paint, feather headdresses, arm shells, and a variety of other jewelry and clenching a circular boar's tusk mounted in fiber between the teeth. A great deal of magic precedes these performances; special taboos are observed, spells are recited over the ornaments before they are put on, and more spells accompany bathing, hair combing, and face painting. Some of the magic is directed at the dispensers of the food, the men especially hoping to receive large amounts of pork, and some is love magic aimed at the general spectators. The female dancers do not receive food intended for the *geyawuna* but may receive some of that contributed by the affines. (Prior to the ceremony, the sponsor recites spells over the yams in an effort to ensure that there will be enough to make the bellies of all the guests bulge, while still leaving some for him and his coresidents.)

A high platform (though nothing like forty feet high; cf. Young 1971:233) is constructed next to the yam rack to hold the butchered pigs and the speech makers. The actual performance begins with the women's dance, a very simple one, to the tune of drums and singing from local men, if the performance is not a *dayo.* The women then climb onto the yam platform and throw betel nuts into the crowd, whereupon the groups of male dancers burst into the plaza and begin to perform, either in succession or simultaneously. The sponsor and, if he is not the same, the boss of the marriage exchanges, will then summon people to receive pork, which the male dancers carry from the platform, and yams, which the female dancers take to the recipients. The fact that the largest amount of food goes to the *geyawuna* of the person in whose name the *sagali* is made constitutes almost the only evidence that the whole complex and joyful ceremony has any relation to death. Nevertheless, the Molima say that only the making of a *sagali* truly ends grief for the dead.

What else does the *sagali* accomplish? Most conspicuously, it enhances the reputation of the sponsor and places various recipients of pork and yams under an obligation to him. In time, he should be repaid, but if he is not, his reputation is the greater. He has, in fact, sponsored a competitive Melanesian feast-cum-ceremony of the classic type (Brown 1970:115); it is not uncommon in Melanesia for these to be nominally in honor of the dead (Goodenough 1955). It bears the same name as ceremonies held elsewhere in the Massim, but how similar is it in fact? Almost peripherally, the *sagali* makes it possible for the *valevaleta* (particularly the children and siblings of a dead man, if they have sponsored the *sagali*) to regain many of the privileges denied them in the years since the death, notably the use of certain real property. (If the dead person was female, she had less real property and her children could use it much sooner.) They will never, however, regain all of the privileges they had before the death. A man who has lost a brother, or a person who has lost a father, is permanently in the *valeta* category and in a new relation to his dead brother's children. Less obviously, the same point applies to a bereaved spouse. Remarriage is possible, so that the title of widow or widower is lost, but avoidance of the hamlet of the dead, including food cooked with coconut from the trees, is permanent. But the surviving parent is not separated from his or her children, and Molima do not usually depict avoidance of the hamlet of the dead as a burden; often, it is a natural expression of grief. By contrast, it is also necessary to avoid the hamlet of a divorced spouse, and children of divorce sometimes pass permanently to the care of only one parent (Chowning 1983). This taboo can cause more pain than staying away from the place where one's spouse lived and was buried.

Neither the *sagali* nor the *bwabwale* can restore relations to what they were previously. Permanent imbalance and deprivation remain, particularly if the dead person was a father. In Molima, although one is related to both parents in the same way (by shared "blood"), relations with the father's side differ basically from those with the mother's side, and death emphasizes the difference. The asymmetry found here differs from the stress in affinal (and foreign) exchanges on precise balance and exact equivalence, including in both cases the exchange of identical objects. In contrast with many other Melanesian societies, here there is no difference in the objects given by the groom's side and the bride's side, or by individual men and women (Chowning 1983).[19] This shift from the one-sided *bwabwale*, which echoes the general dominance of the father's sister's child over the mother's brother's child, to the *sagali* centering around balanced affinal relations, is also a shift from being, to a great extent, caught in an ascribed position, the product of one's genealogy, to the relative autonomy of marriage. In contrast to Young (see essay, this volume), I would argue that the Molima see all deaths as very much alike, in that they should trigger the same observances, whereas marriages tend to differ (except for the now rare ones following formal betrothal). Molima marriages usually result from the desires of the couple, who have many opportunities to influence the course that they take. Social pressures can of course be exerted against marriages that displease the kin of either spouse, but the weakness of these pressures is indicated by the existence of several matches generally regarded as incestuous, including one in 1974 involving a full brother and sister who had borne a child and were living together. To be approved, however, rather than merely tolerated, one manipulates the rivalry with affines so that these people are ultimately kept content, well fed, and properly recompensed for what they have given. Minor strains can be harmlessly released in the licensed joking of the *sagali*. The sponsor, while honoring the dead, solidifies the ties that bind his affines to him and so to his children, whom they will care for when he dies and the children go into mourning. The *sagali* is also the occasion for the creation of new ties between the residents of different villages, as a result both of the spontaneous affairs that result from frequent visiting and night dances and of the love magic practiced by the performers in the *sagali*. (Admittedly these new ties sometimes lead to the dissolution of old marriages.) The Molima say that a person adorned for the dance regains lost youth. Participation in a *sagali* is almost wholly pleasurable; even those who complain do so privately rather than disrupt the festivities. The sponsor can believe, at least temporarily, that he has achieved the ideal of simultaneously pleasing his kin and his guests, including his rivals. Young refers to the Goodenough *sagali*, which they have imported from Fergusson Island, as festivals and "entertainments" with "no explicit connection with a death" (Young 1971:232); the outside observer of a Molima (or Salakahadi) *sagali* might easily view them in the same way. The competitiveness that underlies these exchanges, and that drives a headman to demonstrate his organizational abilities, is muted. In a society that says that their leader should be "playful, like a child," it is not extraordinary that the most important ceremony he sponsors should so stress enjoyment, regardless of its inspiration. It is also pertinent that in a society that lacks exclusive descent groups, the *sagali* should be viewed as the accomplishment of an individual rather than a group.

MOLIMA MORTUARY BEHAVIOR IN THE MASSIM CONTEXT

Molima culture is in most aspects typically Massim (Chowning 1978), and mortuary behavior shows many detailed similarities to that recorded for other parts of the area. What is distinctively Molima can only be appreciated when it is understood how much the Molima resemble their neighbors. At first glance, Molima custom looks like an uneasy amalgamation of bits and pieces imported from elsewhere, perhaps reflecting the varied origins recorded in some genealogies, joined with retentions from a time when descent groups were matrilineal. Probably part of the initial picture is accurate, but two points should be kept in mind. First, the Molima themselves view their behavior as a reasonably coherent whole, while acknowledging different family traditions. Second, many of the variations in such matters as property claims and assignment of roles to the bereaved are recorded for other Massim societies that, by virtue of possessing unilineal descent systems, have sometimes been depicted as rarely if ever departing from the expectations raised (in the outsider) by descent group membership. Weiner's correction of Malinowski's description of normal Trobriand residence patterns (Weiner 1976:154) should remind us that Fortune found Dobuan practice in teaching the same magic to son and sister's son and in a man's passing garden land to both "horrifying" and "subversive to the general lean of the law in favour of the susu," while acknowledging that the Dobuan in no way shared his attitude (1932:15,18). Even if Molima descent groups were still unilineal, we should not have to expect all social behavior to reflect descent group membership.

This said, it must nevertheless be noted that terms cognate with *geyawuna*, in particular, seem in at least one other Massim society, Wagawaga, to designate only members of the dead person's matrilineal descent group who act as gravediggers and then are called by this term. In Bartle Bay the term designates the gravediggers "who may be the *varina* (brothers and cousins) or *au* (sisters' children) of the deceased, assisted by the dead man's *kimta* mates, or failing these any members of his clan" (Seligman 1910:615–16; *kimta* are men who were initiated together). According to Seligman, in Tubetube *gariauuna* are the dead man's sister's children, so-called when and after they act as grave-diggers (1920:613–14). What emerges from Seligman's description is the suggestion that the term actually designates those kin, at least partially self-selected, who bury the dead, but that the core of these will be his sister's sons. Presumably sister's sons who do not join the gravediggers are not called *gariauuna*. Macintyre presents a completely different picture in which the death plays no part in the distribution of these groups: "the social organisation of Tubetube is constructed around totemic groups, with paired matrilineages of the same totem living in contiguous hamlets; they are called *yanasa* or *galiauna*" (*sic*). The *yanasa/galiauna* are nevertheless obliged to carry out all the activities connected with burial (Macintyre, this volume), and it may be that the terms (or *galiauna* at least), are used only with regard to mortuary observances.

Some of Seligman's data suggest that *gariauuna* and cognate terms refer only to those who assume a special role, particularly that of digging the grave at a funeral, and that although the principal gravediggers are expected to be the sister's sons of the dead man, the term does not actually designate

119

a category of kin of the dead. Macintyre's material would not support such an interpretation, and neither would that from Molima. It may be that Seligman misunderstood the range of reference of the term. It also may be that the Molima form has been altered, by folk etymology, to accord with their usage. I do not know that the *gari-/gali-* prefix is a negative or expresses loss,[20] whereas Molima *ge-* certainly is. Given that the Molima term is parallel in construction to a whole series designating those who have lost kin in a particular category (as discussed previously), it seems reasonable to assume that at least in Molima *geyawuna* designates a category defined in terms of how people were related to the dead person, and not how they behaved after the death. If *valevaleta* help dig the grave, they do not become transformed into *geyawuna*.

Although *geyawuna* seems on linguistic grounds to be clearly related to terms used in parts of the Massim to the south of Molima, the entire system of special designations for various kin of the dead is more characteristic of a different region, notably the Trobriands.[21] By contrast, in parts of the southern Massim such as Dobu and Tubetube, death brings about a shift in the way of applying the standard kin terms used for the living (from Iroquois to Crow terminology), so that the children of a dead man begin calling all male members of the father's lineage by the term for father, and so on (Fortune 1932:37–38; Macintyre, this volume).[22] In the Trobriands, as in Molima, there is a complete set of what Leach calls necronyms, and it includes the term *valeta* (Leach 1978:16). Seligman notes that these terms are only used during mourning (1910:720).

Usage, however, seems to differ from one island to another. For Vakuta, Campbell (personal communication) says that it designates a person whose sibling of either sex has died, but with reference to Kaduwaga, Montague says (n.d.:144) that *valeta* include "MB/ZC" as well as "siblings", and "instead of going into mourning, they must *sagali* to pay the *kakau* (widow/er) and *makapus* (*ina* and *tama*) for the extended mourning" (*Ina* include mother and mother's sister, *tama* father and father's brother). By contrast, as I have noted, the Molima *valevaleta* do not include the mother's brother, do go into mourning, and make *sagali* to pay the *geyawuna* who have worked while they have mourned and who then release them from mourning. The *valeta* term is also recorded for Goodenough, but there *valevaleta* refers to the most intensive mourning taboos, which are observed by those "who addressed the dead man as 'brother'" (Young, this volume). In both Goodenough, with patrilineal descent, and the Trobriands, with matrilineal, the *valeta* or *valevaleta* include members of the dead person's lineage, but not all of them. The comparative data do not suggest that the Molima either borrowed or inherited terms that originally distinguished members of the lineage of the dead, who took one role in mourning, from those of another lineage, such as that of the surviving spouse, which was assigned another role. Because reported mourning behavior in many Massim societies reflects this division precisely (as discussed later), such an assumption is not implausible, but the totality of evidence despite variations from one society to another suggests a different interpretation. This is that regardless of the descent system, siblings of the dead (possibly called *valeta*) were expected to play a different role after the death from that of the sister's child (and perhaps mother's brother), who might be called something like *gariauna* or *geyawuna*. Furthermore, throughout much of the southern Massim it is these latter who are the first choice to bury the corpse, taking on a role that excludes them from the most rigorous mourning. Such is the case among the matrilineal Wagawaga and Dobuans (Fortune 1932:193), the cognatic Molima, and the patrilineal Bwaidoka. Molima divisions of the kin of the dead may, then, have little relation to their distinctive descent system but be part of a much wider Massim pattern.

If this is so, what constitutes the pattern? Above all, it involves a distinction between workers and mourners, and one of the prime tasks of the former is to dig the grave and bury the corpse. Also, a series of mortuary feasts is held in connection with the lifting of taboos from the mourners; these may constitute the whole of what could be termed mortuary exchanges or there may be others. A fundamental distinction between societies lies in ideas of which people suffer because of a particular aspect of the mortuary observances and so deserve compensation. Is it the "workers" in general, who toil while the mourners just "sit," or is it particularly the body handlers, who risk pollution by close contact with the dead? Or is it the mourners, who suffer privations while others enjoy freedom? Major differences in the direction in which payments, including feast foods, pass reflect some of these variations in attitude, as well as, in some cases, at least the covert suspicion that one category of kin or affine might have been responsible for the death.

In some areas, the matrilineal kin of the dead abstain from conspicuous mourning and form the core of the workers; in time, in return for gifts of food from the mourners, they release the latter from their taboos. Three different explanations have been given for this division, which has tended to astonish outside observers. One is that the matrilineal descent group is so much a unit that its members "do not mourn, because their body is one with the deceased; they cannot mourn for themselves" (Róheim 1950:203). A second explanation is that, at least in demanding *bwabwale* (Dobu *bwobwore*), the lineage of the dead are demonstrating their dominance over the mourners: "the point of the marriage grouping's subservience to the *susu* group is reinforced" (Fortune 1932:195). Especially in the Trobriands, Dobu, and Normanby, it is also suggested that the mourners were actually responsible for the death (Malinowski 1929:150; Weiner 1976:65). Not only must they grieve ostentatiously in order to reduce suspicion of complicity, but what they give the matrilineal kin is regarded as either a bribe to free them from suspicion (Campbell, this volume) or "a kind of fine or ransom . . . to the aggrieved party" (Róheim 1950:204). On Normanby, it is the *bwabwale* that serves as this "ransom," whereas in the Trobriands an additional special gift of valuables is needed "to allay sorcery accusations" (Campbell, this volume). As can be seen from the quotations from Róheim, these explanations are not mutually exclusive, nor are all invoked for each society.

None of these seems pertinent to Molima practice. As has been noted, the membership of the *geyawuna* does not correspond to a matrilineal descent group, and ideally affines should also be cognatic kin. Although there is some opposition between affinal groups, it is not a situation in which one side dominates the other. As regards witchcraft, it is not expected within the hamlet, and although it is true that a failure to mourn by remote affines can arouse suspicion, that would not be a reason for expecting a spouse or children to express grief. The Molima custom of buying off aggrieved mourners who come from outside the village can be viewed as a sort of ransom, but these outsiders do not form the core of the *geyawuna*, who tend to be present at the death.

A more interesting comparison with Molima can be found in the pattern described by Thune for Loboda, and Seligman and Macintyre for Tubetube. In both places there are paired matrilineages, and it is the responsibility of those people defined as matrilineal kin but not the closest consanguineal kin of the dead to act as workers, while the others are free to mourn. Thune is particularly explicit about this: what he calls "immediate *susu* mates of the deceased" not only wail and assume mourning attire but "cannot share in the yams and pork distributed in the course of the mortuary feasts though . . . for the feasts immediately following death yams and pork formally derive from the immediate *susu* mates of the deceased to be presented to distant *susu* mates and *bukuna*" (members of the paired matrilineages, which may be associated through a shared totem, former coresidence, or other means) (Thune, this volume).[23] In Tubetube the *galiauna* (or *yanasa*) of the other matrilineage bury the dead and carry out other rituals while the bereaved spouse and the members of the *susu* of the deceased all mourn (Macintyre, this volume). A similar pattern seems to have existed in Wagawaga, where a dying man was "tended by the inhabitants of one particular hamlet, viz. that which subsequently eats the funeral feasts known as *banavihi*," and "at the *banavihi* half the food is deposited in one heap for the *gariauuna* of the deceased; the other half goes to one hamlet of the dead man's totem" (Seligman 1910:609,621). The *gariauuna*, who dig the grave and observe food taboos until the *banavihi*, are simply said to be "sister's children or . . . men of his clan" (of the deceased) (Seligman 1910:610), but clearly there are similarities to the division described for Loboda and

Tubetube (as well as to "food exchanging partnerships" in Kalauna [Young 1971:69]).

If we assume that many aspects of Molima social organization reflect the former presence of matrilineal descent groups that have been replaced by cognatic ones, and furthermore that mourning behavior was once closer to that of Loboda and Tubetube than to that of Dobu and the Trobriands, then the composition of the *geyawuna* becomes more intelligible. The functioning ones, as opposed to those so classified who are allowed to mourn, are the equivalents of the more distant matrilineal kin, perhaps primarily those of a paired lineage of the same totem, who bury the dead and are exempt from formal mourning in Loboda and Tubetube. It may well be that at one time the usual two hamlets of a single Molima village consisted of linked matrilineages; to this day each long-established village has a single associated taboo bird that should not be eaten within its boundaries. Nowadays, with the threat of warfare gone and outsiders' encouraging a shift from the interior to the coast, villages have split apart and many hamlets are on new sites, but in the past, when paired hamlets intermarried, a man's sister's child might indeed have lived in the other hamlet of his village. Within living memory, however, hamlets have not contained anything that could be equated with a matrilineage. Although men might return to the mother's hamlet and assert privileges as "owners," such "owners" are not necessarily linked by direct matrilineal ties. A mother's village was where one's mother was born or grew up, and given the normal pattern of virilocal residence, that was likely to be her father's village, whether he was living with his own father or his maternal uncle. The hamlet could not, then, be the property of a single lineage, as in Dobu. The absence of exclusive exogamous descent groups in Molima also means that whatever the formal similarities in observances and exchanges when they are compared with those of Loboda and Tubetube, Molima mortuary behavior differs in aim; there is no corporate group that tries to reconstitute itself in the face of death (cf. Macintyre and Thune).

As regards the system of taboos associated with the dead father and his kin, however, the Molima resemble matrilineal societies throughout the Massim. Seligman was much struck by this behavior in the Massim societies he examined (1910:14); it typically included avoidance of the name of the dead father, insult resulting from a reference to his death, and the grave, house site, and food planted near either of these. This pattern is peculiarly and distinctively Massim, in contrast with the infliction of heavy mourning restrictions on the widow, which is found throughout Melanesia, and of course in many other parts of the world. (Dobu seems to be unique in making mourning as heavy for the widower as for the widow.) The similarities between Molima and some other Massim societies should not, however, be attributed wholly to retentions of former matrilineality, since there are also strong resemblances between Molima and Bwaidoka. Patrilineality seems, from all reports, to be the common pattern in the societies west of Molima, in the so-called Northern D'Entrecasteaux, and it seems reasonable to assume that influence from the west may have helped produce the apparently unique Molima descent system. Aspects of the mortuary ceremonies may also have come from the west, though I have no direct evidence (whereas Young reports borrowing by Goodenough Islanders of ceremonies from Fergusson [1971:259]).

Molima is like Bwaidoka in traditionally lacking exhumation and special treatment of the bones of the dead, although exhumation was practiced elsewhere on Goodenough (Jenness and Ballantyne 1920:119–20); treatment of the corpse in both societies must necessarily have lacked the symbolism that Macintyre reports for Tubetube. A more impressive resemblance is the expectation that those observing mourning taboos will be the bilateral kin of the deceased, especially those of his generation, and the labeling of the mourners as *valevaleta*. Although the term is found in the Trobriands, the associated behavior is not. In Bwaidoka, too, much of the personal property of the dead is "given to the MBs (whether or not they bury), since it does not have to be repaid" (Young, this volume). Young does not mention the possibility that it would be supernaturally dangerous for the *valevaleta* to keep these things, as it would be in Molima, though he does mention supernatural sanctions enforcing other mortuary taboos, particularly the need for the widow to avoid the hamlet of her dead husband. I have noted elsewhere (Chowning 1962:99) that a division of property into that which must go to the matrilineal kin of the deceased and that, especially arm shells, which a man is allowed to give to his sons is found in several other Massim societies, including Tubetube (Seligman 1910:441); throughout the Massim, inheritance patterns tend not to follow strict unilineality.

Where the Bwaidoka specifically resemble the Molima is in the degree to which greed for property actually intrudes on mourning behavior. Although the Molima do not so openly compete to obtain property as do the Bwaidoka, just as Molima feasts never become so aggressive as Kalauna *abutu* (Young 1971), yet similar attitudes can be discerned. In Molima, the sons of the dead must feast the *geyawuna* who help provide *bwabwale* and do not eat it, or such *geyawuna* could claim their garden land and trees (and this is typically the man, the father's sister's son, who is already entitled to their father's village trees). A woman has her finger lopped when her brother dies so her children can claim the dead man's land (this point was repeatedly made when a woman's mutilated hand was shown to me in 1974). Attendance at a funeral may be motivated as much by the desire to claim debts or demand compensation for the death as by grief. These actions are taken by individuals, however, and not by the groups that, however constituted, seem to act in a more unified fashion in other Massim societies (cf.

Thune, this volume, on Loboda reactions to individualistic behavior). It may be that here, too, the absence of strongly corporate descent groups permits more individual decisions as to how one should behave after a death, even though in Molima as in other Massim societies supernatural sanctions help keep individualism within bounds. On the other hand, Bwaidoka, which does have unilineal descent groups, seems to permit individuals as much latitude as does Molima, and mourners are recruited bilaterally.

As has been noted, the contrast between Molima and other Massim societies often lies as much in rationale as in overt behavior. Just as they carry out observances similar to those elsewhere without the same concern for how their behavior may affect the soul of the deceased and consider burial a special task without regarding it as one requiring great rewards,[24] so the Molima mourn and commemorate the dead in ways that are found throughout the Massim, but with a different object. Elsewhere the deceased seems to be regarded primarily as a member of a descent group, except when an exceptional person such as a powerful magician receives special treatment (Weiner 1976:67–70; Young, this volume). In Molima what is mourned is the loss of an individual—at most the member of a social category, a dead sister or father, but not a member of a group. The difference is of course not absolute, but one of emphasis; the widespread Massim practice of forbidding the name of the dead or words similar to it (Seligman 1910:629–31; Schlesier 1970:53) shows that indeed individuals are, probably everywhere, to a certain extent mourned in their own right. But lacking the exclusive corporate groups found elsewhere, the Molima naturally focus to a greater degree on the single person.

If Molima mourning customs up to and including the *bwabwale* resemble those elsewhere in the Massim more in form than in function, the opposite could be said of the *sagali*. These concluding ceremonies seem to differ greatly from one society to another, as various essays in this volume indicate. It is nevertheless interesting that Lepowsky, for example, notes that the Sudest *zagaya*, along with its other special functions, not only enables the host to "build his or her reputation" but also enables many people to come together and form new relationships "or deepen existing relationships in ways that may have nothing to do directly with the ritual demands of the *zagaya*" (Lepowsky, this volume). Although Weiner concentrates on the degree to which the Kiriwina *sagali* "reconstitute(s) the social network that the deceased created and maintained" (1976:84), she also makes it clear that it affords opportunities for many other relationships, which have little connection to the deceased, to be strengthened, modified, or established for the first time. Throughout the Massim, the *sagali* (by whatever name) seems usually to have been not only the principal way in which an individual sponsor could acquire or increase his prestige,[25] but the focus for the display, strengthening, and reestablishment of the complex of social relationships, involving the dead as well as the living, most important to that society. That these major mortuary ceremonies have been retained, despite alterations in content, in the face of many acculturative pressures is proof enough of their significance to the people. The type of *sagali* that the Molima now put on is tending to alter,[26] as overseas trading canoes are no longer made, pig numbers have been reduced so that cash crops can flourish unmolested, and the rehearsals necessary for the *dayo* have become too time-consuming, but *sagali* are held as often as in the past and the enthusiasm of the participants is undiminished.

Throughout the Massim, there exist both more variety and more uniformity than appear on the surface. The use of cognate terms throughout the region at first conceals the differences in application. A Molima *kaiwabu* is not a Kalauna *kaiwabu*; Molima *po'ala* is not the same as Kiriwina *pokala*; and by the same token *bwabwale* and *sagali* do not have the same content and functions wherever they are found as names for mortuary rites. Nevertheless, the differences between them are largely variations on a few themes—such as the distinction between a dead man's children and his sister's children, and the special taboos associated with a dead father—that are distinctively, even if not exclusively, Massim. Each society manifests its own elaborations and emphases, but many recognizable cross-cultural resemblances remain. Recent detailed accounts (for example, those by Campbell and Thune, this volume) even make it look as if both expressions of grief (at least initially) by all the closest kin, and tolerance of departures from the roles assigned to group members, are found just as frequently as rigid separations of those roles. Themselves proudly individualistic and resistant to coercion of any kind,[27] able to shift residence and to affiliate easily with a new set of cognatic kin rather than being tied for eternity to a single group, usually concerned with a bilateral network of other independent human beings rather than with groups or with the spirit world, but still respectful of ancestral ways of mourning and honoring the dead and of acquiring prestige—the Molima, for all their distinctive characteristics, are nevertheless clearly Massim, and never more so than in their mortuary observances.

NOTES

Acknowledgments: My first period of research was supported by a National Science Foundation Postdoctoral Fellowship, and my second by the University of Papua New Guinea.

1. Time in the field was twelve months in 1957–1958 and two months in 1974–1975. During that period more than a dozen deaths occurred in the vil-

lage in which I lived, and I attended at least some of the mortuary ceremonies for each.

2. The Molima offer no explanation for this situation, which is one of several clues pointing to the earlier existence of matrilineal descent groups (Chowning 1962).

3. In Molima kinship terminology is Iroquois, with bifurcate merging terms for ascending and descending generations, and classification of parallel cousins with siblings. Cross-cousins may be classed together as *nibai-*, or distinguished as *toni'asa* (Owner of the Village, father's sister's child) and *labalaba* (Boundary Man, mother's brother's child), to use Fortune's translation of the identical terms in Dobu (Fortune 1932:14).

4. Peniata (and others) criticized Lobati for eating the *bwabwale* of Bagita, Lobati's mother's brother's daughter's son, and Peniata said he would not eat if the child of his father's sister's daughter, Didioni, died. He considered this child potential *geyawuna*, the equivalent of Bagita to Lobati. Figure 2 gives actual cases of *geyawuna* relationships, one set involving a dead man (Wananadobu) and one including the potential *geyawuna* of Peniata. In addition to what is shown, it should be noted that Peniata, like his mother, was *geyawuna* to Wananadobu and actually helped dig his grave.

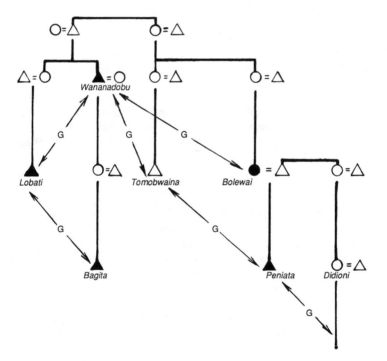

FIGURE 2. *Geyawuna* relationships.

5. Although most Molima speak of Lotuma as the destination of the dead, others refer to Bwebweso, the site on Normanby to which Dobuans go, and still others assume that the dead go to a site in the interior of Fergusson. I have heard all three sites mentioned in the songs at a single funeral. When questioned, people usually answer that the location of the land of the dead depends on the location of one's village, so that those from western villages go to Lotuma, those from eastern ones to Bwebweso, and those from mountain villages to the interior.

6. The Molima *kaiwabu* is a headman whose position is semihereditary; once he is awarded the title, which depends on a combination of wealth, knowledge, and achievement in sponsoring *sagali*, the title is his permanently. Compare the use of the same title on Goodenough (Young 1971:76).

7. Some deaths are not attributed to human agency, but of those that are, only female witches are blamed. They may have a variety of motives, and only if the witch is thought to be offended because the victim failed to share food with her will divination reveal the cause of death. The identification of a witch usually depends on dreams.

8. The Molima do not think that witches actually dig up bodies, but summon them magically to the surface. They will not do this if there are spectators (Róheim 1950:214).

9. It is, however, insisted that the person is not present in the grave. The *le'i* summons other ghosts, but not the dead person himself.

10. This term seems to correspond in meaning to Bwaidoka *laova*, though not cognate with it (Young, this volume).

11. Sometimes the *geyawuna* also fear contact with property of the recently dead, especially if there have been several deaths in recent succession or if the household of the *geyawuna* contains a vulnerable baby.

12. It is also possible to substitute a single feast called *obayau*, made long after the death when yams had been grown and pigs raised for it, for the three-stage *bwabwale*. The *geyawuna* receive both cooked and raw food at this ceremony.

13. This stress on silence during mourning is also characteristic of Kaduwaga (Montague, personal communication).

14. People who quarrel may sever relations by referring to the dead kin of an opponent. Mentioning the dead father is a particularly drastic act, and when the quarrel is finally settled, compensation must be given to his *geyawuna*.

15. The reincarnated child need not be born to the same parents as the dead person; in one case, it was assumed that a woman's granddaughter was the reincarnation of her husband's son by a previous wife.

16. Bad luck in fishing or other endeavors may be attributed to criticism voiced by one's affines, which is mystically harmful.

17. Although the term for coconut cream, *niula weto-na*, also denotes semen, food in Molima does not seem to have sexual associations. Personified yams are explicitly of both sexes, "fighting" as well as "giving birth" in the gardens at night (compare Damon 1983:325).

18. See Fortune (1932:198–200) for an account of similar rowdy joking at a Dobu *sagali*.

19. It is probably significant that the other Papua New Guinea society I know that shares the feature also has cognatic descent (the Sengseng of West New Britain).

20. It is tempting to relate it either to the Proto-Oceanic *kali (dig, bury) or to the first syllables of the widespread Milne Bay word for "die" represented by Vakutan *kariga*, but if either etymology were correct, one would not expect the derivative to begin with /g/.

21. It also occurs outside the Massim, as Iamo's 1981 paper on Aroma (this volume) demonstrates.

22. As another variant, in Me'udana the father's brother, formerly called *madia*, is addressed as *tama* (father) after his brother dies (Schlesier 1970:61).

23. The Molima say that *bu'una* (=*bukuna*) is Dobuan for Molima *susu*, which for them designates the descendants of a kinswoman, usually one who married outside Molima. This *susu*, in line with general Molima kin reckoning, may include her descendants through men as well as women.

24. Here Molima contrasts with what Fortune reports for Dobu, where not only are the "sextons" paid but if valuables are not available, a child may be passed over, in the case mentioned by a widow delivering her daughter to her husband's *susu* (Fortune 1932:194). This sounds much like what Young reports for Bwaidoka, where a pig is given by the widower's kin to those who bury a woman, and, failing such a pig, a child may be passed to the dead woman's side (Young, this volume).

25. In Molima, by contrast with Sudest and Kiriwina, a woman can only acquire this sort of prestige as an adjunct to her husband.

26. There have always been various alternative forms available, like *sagali* based on fresh-water foods such as eels and sago.

27. Here I refer primarily to the pre-Christian situation, before the introduction of a hell-fire religion made people fearful of the consequences of many acts. The absence of male sorcerers was probably one factor which permitted the relatively free expression of opposition to others, and the absence of exclusive corporate groups meant that a person could always find supporters. Molima men glory in jail records resulting from assault on labor supervisors who treated them badly, and a frequent statement in village meetings is, "I'm not a pig or a dog to be given orders."

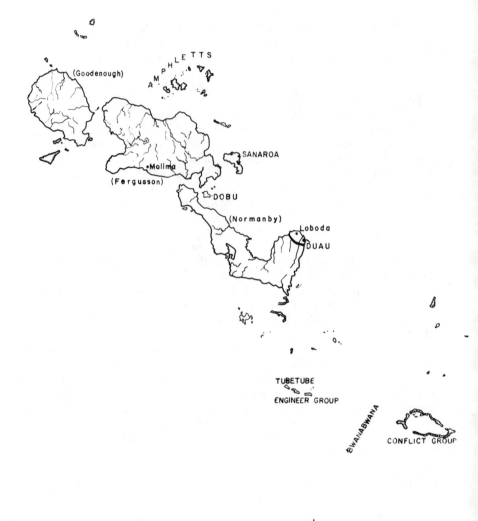

(Goodenough)

AMPHLETTS

SANAROA

•Molima

(Fergusson)

DOBU

(Normanby)

Loboda

DUAU

TUBETUBE

ENGINEER GROUP

BWANABWANA

CONFLICT GROUP

N

millions of feet
0   0.5   1.0

0   10   20
statute miles

PART TWO

The Southern Massim

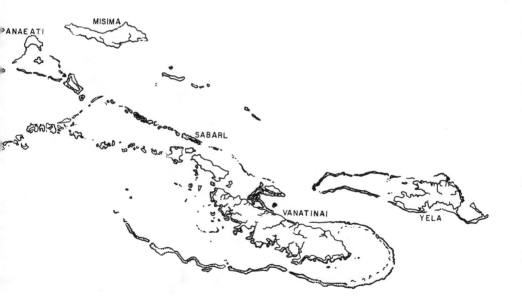

Martha Macintyre

The Triumph of the *Susu*

Mortuary Exchanges on Tubetube

◆ In this essay I shall examine the structure and sequence of mortuary rituals in the Bwanabwana region. The research on which this essay is based was undertaken on Tubetube Island during 1980–81. There were several deaths on Tubetube during this time and I observed all the mortuary rituals described in this paper. I attended *soi* feasts on the neighboring island of Kwaraiwa and on Ole in the Laseine Group. The Bwanabwana region is linguistically and culturally homogeneous, so that the mortuary practices on Tubetube are present throughout the whole region. The social organization of Tubetube is essentially similar to that of Dobu and Duau (Normanby Island) with the primary group for all exchanges being the *susu* (matrilineage).

The ceremonies themselves reflect an ideology of the inviolability of the *susu* and the ephemeral nature of all social relationships other than those consanguineal matrilineal bonds with the *susu*. Mortuary rituals serve not only to dispose of the dead and ensure the passage of the deceased's soul to the world beyond, but to dispose also of all the decedent's socially constructed relationships—particularly those resulting from marriage.

In the first section I shall outline the system of social organization and the relationships established by marriage. Affinal links beyond the *susu* are precisely those that construct the problematic that has then to be resolved in the ritual sequence following death. In the second section I shall set down the sequence of mortuary rites, showing how they symbolically represent the relationship that exists between the widow/widower and the *susu* of the deceased person. The corpse and the surviving spouse no longer have any place in the *susu*, and just as the body of the deceased is gradually transformed from a *susu* member to an ancestor, from a rotting corpse in the village to a basket of bones in a remote ancestral cave, so the widow/widower is transformed from an affine within the hamlet to a marriageable person outside the village. The secondary treatment of the dead described in this section is no longer practiced on Tubetube nor are the bereaved spouses subjected to the same taboos and rites of exclusion. Mourning customs and procedures are abbreviated, but the succeeding feasts and exchanges still bear the names describing these practices, and the rites that today structure the mortuary sequence still reflect the dual problem that besets the *susu*: the removal of the dead person from the realm of the living and the removal of the spouse from the hamlet.

In the third section I have focused on the ceremonies and exchanges as they are still practiced within the region. The transactions that occur after the death are structured around the problematic established by marriage. Mortuary exchanges continue to express and resolve the social contradictions inherent in the strong matrilineal ideology that informs social structure and defines social identity. The particular contradiction that I explore here is that of the husband and wife relationship, where in-marrying spouses are necessary for the continuation of the *susu* but must be excluded in order that the *susu* maintain its identity. My analysis of the transactions at each stage of the mortuary ceremonies is sociological, and I have based this on the metaphors of space and paths that Tubetube people themselves use to represent concepts of social distance and obligation.

SUSU

In the Bwanabwana region the primary social group is the *susu*, hereafter *lineage*. Tubetube people define the lineage genealogically as those descendants of a woman three generations distant; there is rarely any historical depth, and the name of the ancestress is seldom recalled. Lineage identity and name are locationally determined, the name of a hamlet being used to designate a matrilineage and its land. Each lineage has a bird totem, *man*. The totemic classification is, however, not unique to each lineage and the social organization of Tubetube is constructed around totemic groups, with paired matrilineages of the same totem living in contiguous hamlets; they are called *yanasa* or *galiauna*.

Brother/sister solidarity is the basis for hamlet ownership, inheritance, and residence. The *tanawagao* (hamlet owners) consist of men and their sisters and their sisters' children. In-marrying spouses are designated *tovelam* or *sinevelam* (in-marrying man and woman, respectively); they are *laolaoma* ("strangers," literally "people who come here") throughout their periods of residence in the hamlet. Children of in-marrying women are called *natunatuleia* and have no rights over their father's land or property.

The kinship system is identical to that described by Fortune for Dobu ([1932] 1963:43ff.), and as on Dobu the peripheral status of in-marrying spouses is periodically reaffirmed throughout the marriage by alternating residence between the wife's and husband's hamlets. Tubetube customs of changing residence no longer operate rigidly after the first four years of marriage, and the long-term patterns of residence are now predominantly uxori-local.

As on Dobu, kinship terminology for patrilateral relatives alters after a man's death (Fortune 1962:37), so the gulf that ideally exists between a man's children and his sister's children is explicitly reflected in kinship terms. The man's children then refer to their father's heirs as *tamagu* (my father) and *yayagu* (my father's sister). This designation serves to stress the generational divisions within the lineage while it alienates all those who are *natunatuleia* by collapsing the generational categories of all in-marrying persons so that social distance is exaggerated.

The integrity of the lineage is symbolically reconstructed at death. The mortuary sequence abounds with metaphorical enactments of closure, exclusion, and severance of social links beyond the hamlet. Not surprisingly, the widow or widower is the focus for those rituals of exclusion. As burial must occur within the decedent's own hamlet, the bereaved spouse is the archetypal "stranger," utterly isolated, all links to the hamlet having been severed by death. In the case of a widow, her children, strangers in their father's hamlet, sometimes choose to remain there, but they are subject to similar taboos and share their mother's peripheral status during the period of deep mourning. For the duration of the mourning the bereaved spouse is referred to as *-ala sibauwa* (our widow/widower), the possessive pronoun *ala* being the one applied to objects. (All kin terms are constructed with possessive suffixes that indicate inalienability.) From the moment of death the bereaved spouse loses status as a person until he or she is redeemed by his/her natal lineage. The corpse, however, suffers no loss of personhood; indeed all funeral chants consist of repeated choruses in which the mourners summon and remonstrate with their deceased kin, calling him/her by the kinship term used during life.

THE CORPSE AND THE WIDOW: SECONDARY TREATMENT OF THE DEAD ON TUBETUBE

There are four stages in the mortuary sequence: *Wali* (singing), which is the period of mourning over the body; *Buga/Mayaumate* (the death of the fire), which is the ritual of burial within the village and the feast for the

135

people who bury the body; *Ligaliga boaboa* (the Stinking feast), the first feast given by affines of the decedent, lifts the taboos of deep mourning; and *Ligaliga oloolo* (feast of sweet smelling coconut oil), which is the second feast by affines, freeing the bereaved spouse from all mourning obligations and restoring him/her to his/her original *susu*.[1]

Until about fifty years ago widows in deep mourning were subjected to a wide range of taboos. These were seen by missionaries as so severe that they interpreted them as a form of draconian punishment of the widow for having outlived her husband. The widow would blacken her body with putrescent substances from the corpse mixed with coconut ash, and from the time of death until the final feast she would not wash. During this time she could not eat any food classified as *kan* (yams, or food in general); she had to eat only those things recognized as edible, but not cultivated as staples. She could not eat from the gardens of her husband's lineage, nor could she eat with his family. She was confined to a small house, sometimes specially constructed, within their hamlet, but she was forbidden to participate in any social activities there. Occasionally siblings of the deceased voluntarily assume the role of a person in mourning and blacken the body or confine themselves to poor foods, but this was done as an expression of grief and was not obligatory. The missionaries opposed these practices as part of their campaign for health and hygiene, and so initiated alternative or substitute mourning practices that, over a period of thirty years, gradually gained acceptance. They gave black clothes to converts to wear instead of blackening their bodies. They encouraged people to restrict their food, tabooing only one or two foodstuffs, rather than wasting away on the extremely limited diet formerly prescribed. They preached against the incarceration of widows for the period between the burial and the first feast, and they introduced various Christian elements into the ceremonies associated with burial.

The missionaries did not campaign against the secondary treatment of the corpse in mortuary ceremonies; colonial government officers were the force behind the abandonment of these practices. They imprisoned men for burying bodies in shallow graves within the hamlet and for disinterring skeletons. Two men still living on Tubetube had been imprisoned for these offenses, and it would appear that the demise of customs of secondary disposal of the corpse occurred within the last thirty years. Beliefs in the afterlife, in spirits and ghosts, and in the influence of the ancestors on living people have altered dramatically now that the people have become Christian. No longer are the corpse itself and its disembodied spirit the focus of ritual elaboration once the burial has taken place. Ritual divination to determine responsibility for the death is not practiced, and the passage to the afterlife is not deemed hazardous, nor can it be obstructed by actions of the living. Formerly breaches of mourning taboos were thought to jeopardize the spirit's safe passage to *Bwebweso* (the land of the dead), but now they are spoken of only as "disrespectful." Previously, failure to fulfill mortuary obligations and pay debts was thought to provoke the wrath of the deceased's ghost, who might carry off a child as retribution. Now the only sanctions come from the living, who claim compensation in the form of pigs and shell valuables.

In spite of all these changes, the mortuary ceremonies still follow the same sequential pattern that was formerly structured around the secondary treatment of the corpse. The gradual transformation of the deceased from corpse within the village to ancestor in the cave is still implicit in all the ceremonies that focus on the widow. The metaphorical relationship between the widow and the corpse remains central in all the rituals, and the widow,

NAME OF CEREMONY	TREATMENT OF CORPSE	TREATMENT OF SURVIVING SPOUSE
Wali	Corpse is washed, oiled, shaved, painted, dressed in new clothes, displayed with shell valuables on arms and around neck.	Widow/widower is blackened, coarse twine armlets and long mourning necklace put on; widows wear long skirt of coarse fiber. Food taboos and taboos on washing begin; the person is incarcerated in a small house.
Buga/ Mayaumate	Body is wrapped in mats, covered with gifts and flowers, and placed in a shallow grave in hamlet; the head is covered by a pot. A small house is built over the grave and a fire lit inside it.	Widow/widower lives in hamlet, confined to house, not allowed to garden, cook, or eat normal food. Taboos on washing, shaving, cutting hair. The whole body is regularly blackened with ash and oil mixture.
Ligaliga Boaboa	Body is unearthed, bones washed clean and stored in a basket in a house.	Widow's skirt is cut to calf length. Widower changes clothing. Taboo on leaving house is lifted, but the person is not allowed to walk on paths or attend any feasts.
Ligaliga Olo-olo	Bones are whitened, the skull put into a small round basket, with other bones in a large wooden platter, and taken up to be placed in a cave with bones of previously deceased *susu members*.	Widow/widower's hair is cut, face shaved. Body is washed and covered in sweet-smelling oil. Mourning necklace and armlets are removed, person dressed in fine new clothes, decorated with flowers. Person is fed portions of all previously tabooed food and restored to natal *susu*.

perhaps even more than in the premission era, is the focus for all negative connotations of death. In the past, when the body rotted in a centrally located grave within the village and was then disinterred and the cleaned bones kept in a basket inside a house, the material remains were a concrete reminder that the widow was not *really* "like a corpse." Nowadays, the widow's mourning garb is the only sign that death is in the hamlet. The complete parallel between the rites for the deceased and the rites that gradually allowed the widow to be reintegrated into her natal lineage was a clear representation of the twofold concern of the bereaved hamlet. Now that the soul is thought to be immediately taken to a Christian heaven, the ambiguous status of the widow is highlighted. However, the lineage affected by death still has to reconstitute itself as a corporate whole. This regenerative process was formerly symbolically represented in the treatment of the corpse as it changed from something black and stinking into a bundle of pure white bones. This process was a concrete expression of the lineage's triumph over death. The cave of whitened bones testified to the lineage's control over its own regeneration and continuity, for the bones were believed to have been formed by *susu* breastmilk.[2] The flesh and blood, now vanished, were produced by foods and "paternal substance," their disintegration proclaiming the ephemeral nature of the affinal relationship.

Today, the widow's person alone bears the burden of this symbolic representation of the transformations wrought by death. But a brief description of the earlier practices[3] reveals the symbolic transferences that resolve the dual problematic posed by death, now only implied in practice.

BUGA /MAYUMATE: THE BURIAL AND THE FEAST OF THE DYING FIRE

This is the way it goes. Suppose that in a village someone dies—then they cut down trees there, they chop down coconuts, they create havoc, everything in disarray, spoiled. The place looks terrible. The people would be sitting there, their faces distorted with grief, and someone comes and says, "Why are you sad?" Then they reveal their grief and we say, "Oh! Death is in your village! We'll chop down their trees, we'll spoil this place, change it around just as your old man has been transformed by death. There, look at your faces; they are not normal, your faces changed by your sadness, just like his death, so you too must sit quietly out of grief. We, we your clanspeople will damage your village so that it matches your grief-stricken faces. We'll spoil it; we'll turn it upside down, according to the customs of our ancestors." . . . Then we make *Mayaumate* for the place, we make *liga-liga*. We make *liga-liga* and then the village is turned over again, set to rights. Only then are paths straight; people regain their strength, and we are all happy. Everybody is the same again.

Thus Panetan, a respected elder of Tubetube, described their customs of death. In fact such a scenario would never occur; this was a hypothetical situation constructed so that I might understand the apparently wanton destruction in a bereaved village. On Tubetube the death of an old person rarely comes as a surprise to anyone on the island, for most of them have already spent a day or two sitting by the sick person, waiting for the death. When death occurs, those in the house begin to wail; clansmen of the deceased person begin their devastation, as news is carried to relatives in other hamlets or on nearby islands. On Tubetube, the taboos of death mean that no fires are lit in the open; no lamps burn; the hamlets, normally swept each day, must be left dirty; no man can go fishing and no garden produce can be carried on the head. Voices are subdued as most adults make their way to the hamlet of the dead person.

The task of *kabui* (turning over) the village so that life is restored to normal cannot be performed by members of the dead person's own matrilineage. Nor can they be performed by *any* "clanspeople" of the deceased; rather, the obligations to bury the dead and ritually restore the village to normal life in the face of bereavement, and the taboos they create, fall on a single group of fellow clanspeople: the *yanasa* or *galiauna* of the deceased. The *yanasa* consist of members of a second, paired matrilineage; each pair of matrilineages, joint "owners of the village," usually are co-resident in the same hamlet and have reciprocal responsibilities to one another. Mortuary rituals are an enactment and dramatization of the relationship—asymmetrical in regard to any particular death, but in the long run reciprocal and symmetrical—between such paired matrilineages, each in a *yanasa* relation to the other.

When a death occurs, whether expected or not, members of the *yanasa* lineage immediately take on the tasks of burial. They send a messenger to other islands to summon the relatives; no one but *yanasa* can name the dead or mention the fact that someone has died in the village. The bereaved spouse and children sit and wail with members of the decedent's lineage. In the case of a man's death, his children, being of a different lineage, are treated differently from the other mourners. They are led into the house by one of the *yanasa*, who then directs them so that each child prostrates himself/herself across the body of the father. They lie thus, crying and chanting for about an hour, after which they are led away by the *yanasa* and the lineage members sit around the body.

As the mourners come into the village—their passage obstructed by the tabooing of all exits and entrances across which coconut trees have been felled—they sit in a hastily constructed shelter outside the house where the body lies. While the close relatives sit beside the body, keening and crying, those outside begin a vigil of hymn singing, which usually continues for two days and nights. Unlike in all other hamlets, lamps blaze all night, for the night is the main period of mourning. The chanting of the chief mourners, each one repeating the term of address he or she used for the dead person, blends with the various harmonies of Wesleyan hymns as more and more mourners arrive, stumbling through the bush without any light to guide them.

Meanwhile the *yanasa* prepare the grave, clear weeds and flowers from the ground, and fell trees or lop branches from the huge nut trees or frangipanis around the hamlet.

On the second or third day the funeral and burial take place. A procession of men and women from the person's lineage and those who have married into it enters the village, the young men bearing pigs tied to platforms decorated with betel nut garlands, other relatives carrying baskets of yams on their heads. The same keening and wailing continue as they deposit the mortuary offerings outside the house. The widowed person and the children of the deceased remain inside as the relatives file in and place the gifts of *mulolo* or *lowalowa* on the body, now wrapped in mats in preparation for burial; these mats are also *mulolo*, gifts of love that are placed in the grave. Money, shell valuables, bundles of cloth, dishes, and wooden platters are placed on the body, most to be buried, some to be retained by the bereaved relatives. An opening is made in the wall opposite the door and the body carried to the grave between rows of mourners. It is at this time that young children attend, carrying wands of frangipani and hibiscus made by stringing the blooms on the spones of coconut leaves. The path to the grave is lined with people, all holding garlands, wreaths, or bunches of flowers that have been made by young women. The widowed person remains in the house with his or her children.

The body is placed in the grave—six feet deep and at least fifty yards from the nearest house, in accordance with government regulations—and the Christian burial service is read by the pastor. A senior man or woman then gives the funeral oration, and each person steps forward and places flowers in the grave. Usually at this time several more mats are placed in the grave by friends and relatives: these are also *mulolo*. The visiting mourners disperse, the people of the *susu* return to the hamlet, and their *yanasa* fill in the grave and build a small hut over it. Inside this hut a fire is lit.

The burial takes place in the early morning; by midday the fire on the grave has gone out. *Mayaumate* (fire dies), the first in a series of mortuary feasts, begins. The food that has been brought in the morning is arranged in heaps of twenty or so yams inside the house in the place where the body lay. Outside the slaughtered pigs are butchered and the cuts of meat sorted out into piles and arranged for display on new mats of green coconut leaves. The work of the *yanasa* is completed, and rituals associated with the feast of *Mayaumate* begin.

A young man from the deceased person's village is sent out to fish in a canoe; as he paddles around he can be seen by people in other hamlets, and this is the signal that the taboo on fishing is lifted. Later the catch, one token fish, is strung up on a pole that is carried from hamlet to hamlet, children following and chanting a nonsense rhyme. Fires are lit in the open, hamlets are swept, and women proceed to their gardens for food.

In the bereaved village work for the feast proceeds in earnest. The bereaved spouse remains shut in the house while the lineage members and their affines clean the village and prepare the food. Normal domestic cooking is done in a small hut; feasts are prepared, ostentatiously, in the open on the beach. Newly woven mats and windbreaks are set up and large wooden platters are piled with carefully peeled yams. Men prepare two special dishes, *silibwala* (a broth of blood and coconut milk in which the offal is boiled, with banana dumplings) and *mone* (sago dumplings boiled in coconut milk). Women place the yams and cuts of meat in huge new feasting pots that form part of the gifts to their *yanasa*, and then as the food cooks the mourning ceases.

At this point the ritual of *talawasi* begins. This is a cathartic ritual, its purpose always to lift the sorrow of the people gathered. *Talawasi* means "to joke," and, in its ceremonial form, it consists of mimes and stories performed by senior men and women. One old woman, usually the sister of the dead person, seats herself in the center of the cleared ground and starts to tell funny stories about events long past. As people begin to laugh, women and children deck them with flowers and rub grated coconut on their hair; the mourning taboo on washing is lifted. By the time this uproarious activity has stopped, the food is cooked, and people carry it to the houses of their *yanasa*. As night falls all signs of the day's work are cleared away, and people return to their hamlets to eat their evening meal. "Only then are things straight: people regain their strength and we are all happy. Everything is the same again."

LIGALIGA: FEASTS FOR THE REMOVAL OF TABOOS

But all is not quite the same. The bereaved spouse remains in mourning, wearing dark clothes, avoiding foods eaten by the spouse prior to death. The house in which the person died is sealed; inside, the deceased's personal possessions are bundled together, as *boboloi* (tabooed objects), awaiting ritual burning at the feasts that occur about six months or a year after the funeral. These feasts, called *ligaliga*, are primarily concerned with the release of the widow/widower from mourning taboos. There are, in times of plenty, two *ligaliga*. The first, *ligaliga boaboa* ("the stinking feast"), consists of a small feast of yams and a pig, which are given by the widowed person's

141

lineage to the lineage of the deceased. These allow the person to return to his or her normal appearance. The "stink" alludes to the fact that in earlier times the widow or widower was covered in ash and coconut oil and was not allowed to bathe. A widow wore very long grass skirts and cut her hair short; a widower wore a number of armbands of twine and could neither shave nor cut his hair. At *ligaliga boaboa* the person would be rubbed clean with coconut oil; a man would have his armbands removed; a woman would have her skirt cut to midcalf length. Today these customs are practiced only in very limited areas of the Bwanabwana region; they have not been part of mourning on Tubetube for about forty years. Instead, the second feast, *ligaliga oloolo* ("the feast of scented coconut oil"), has become the occasion for the removal of all taboos associated with death of a spouse.

The decision to make *ligaliga oloolo* depends on the availability of pigs and yams, so the feasts tend to occur in the months following the yam harvest, from August to December. The feast takes place in the village where the person died. This is usually the village hamlet of his or her *susu*, but if the person died in another village, then the relevant clans gather there. The widow's or widower's lineage members and their affines assemble together some distance from the village with baskets of yams. Several young men load the pig for the feast, tied to a decorated platform, onto a canoe and paddle around to this place. They signal their progress with conch shell blasts as they pass each hamlet. When they go ashore, the procession moves slowly to the village, where the lineage members of the deceased's clan and their *yanasa* are seated in the clearing in front of the house where the person died. The pig is killed, and then the *boboloi* (the personal possessions of the deceased) are taken from the house and put into the fire that is made to singe the hair off the pig. The *boboloi* pig is then butchered and the meat and yams are placed in a decorative fashion on freshly woven mats in front of the house. Some members of the clan sit inside, weeping and wailing; the people who have brought the feast foods remain outside, a few of them standing by the walls sobbing and keening. The widow or widower sits inside with her/his affines and the visiting feast givers cook the food. When it is ready, he or she is led out and seated in the clearing. The person always displays great reluctance during this procedure, indicating that he or she is still grief-stricken. A widower is then shaved, his hair is cut, and sweet-smelling coconut oil is rubbed on his head and body; he is then dressed in new clothes by one of the *yanasa* of the deceased. In former times a widow's mourning skirt would be cut to knee length, indicating her marriageability; now she is rubbed with oil and decorated with flowers. Throughout these proceedings the person sits solemn and silent. When the decorating is completed, the sister or brother of the deceased steps forward with a small plate of yams, fish, and pork—*kanisikote* ("abhorrent food"). This is held up before the widow or widower by the senior person in the decedent's lineage and the person holding the food shouts, "Polo ukwan!" ("Eat your pork!"); as the person takes a bite the assembled crowd shouts, "O! Polo ikanikan!" ("Oh! He/she is eating pork!") This same procedure is repeated as each type of food is tasted. Finally, the person stands and there is jubilation as he or she is reclaimed by his or her clan. People dance, making the person dance with them as if he or she were young and unmarried. The food is divided between the *susu* and *yanasa* of the village, and the others depart with their reclaimed member, now freed from all mourning taboos and obligations.

SOI: THE MEMORIAL FEAST

Soi is the final ceremony in the cycle of mortuary rituals. It is not associated with a particular death and so must be seen as structurally separate from the previous ceremonies I have discussed. The *Soi* is a huge memorial feast, involving the consumption of cooked food, but primarily concerned with the distribution of raw food and pigs. *Soi* are organized by the people of one corporate matrilineage to commemorate their dead. A feast is held in honor of several specified people, who usually constitute all the members of one generation of a particular *susu*. The timing of the feast varies with respect to the death of one generation; sometimes a group of siblings will die over a period of twenty or more years, so these feasts are comparatively rare. Unlike *Mayaumate* and *Ligaliga*, the lineage is under no obligation to make a *Soi* for its dead members, and it is claimed that these feasts are held less frequently than in former times. However, Seligman (unpublished diaries) wrote that *Soi* feasts occurred every five or ten years, and oral evidence indicates that on Tubetube there have been three *Soi* feasts in the past twenty-seven years, so the "decline" may be imaginary.

A *Soi* requires at least a year's preparation, as special yam gardens must be planted and many trips made to trade partners in search of pigs. In the week or so prior to the feast a *nakanaka* (special ritual platform) is constructed; on the day before the *Soi* it is elaborately decorated with branches and garlands of betel nut and yams tied up like parcels. Across the top of the *nakanaka*, hanging from a pole, are numerous *mwali*. All night drums play, groups of young men and women dance, and singers go through their repertoires. The following morning the hosts load the platform with yams and place freshly cut coconut branches on the ground beneath the *nakanaka*. When all these preparations are completed, people sit and the *Soi*, the distribution, begins. A procession of men carrying pigs enters the clearing in front of the *nakanaka*. As each one is brought in, the person who is giving the pig gives a declamatory speech to the "owner of the feast" instructing him/her to kill the animal. Then the feast givers themselves lead in their pigs one by one. The pigs are speared and butchered; the meat is placed in piles beneath the *nakanaka*. This extremely noisy and bloody business can take up most of the day, as up to sixty or seventy pigs may be slaughtered.

Finally, the feast givers mount the platform and call out names. As each person is called, someone runs forth and collects his/her portion and delivers it to the named guest. The "runners" are the young men and women of the host lineage, dressed in their finery, their bodies glowing with scented coconut oil (and exertion!). As the young women run back and forth bearing dishes of yams and slabs of meat, there is the constant clinking of their families' *bagi*, dangling down their backs. The distribution continues until everything has been given out, and then the cooking begins. The drums are brought out again and all the women present dance; those whose families gave five pigs carry a mango branch, some carrying three. The branches are tokens, and the success of a *Soi* is judged and recalled in terms of the number of mango branches women carried.

At this point, some sociological clarification is needed. The *Soi* is being given by members of a single corporate matrilineage. Members of this group, whom I shall refer to as *feast givers*, will have spent many months accumulating resources by raising pigs, growing yams, and obtaining pigs and valuables by purchasing them and initiating exchanges; they will also have called in outstanding obligations from their trading partners and other debtors. The period before a *Soi* is marked by this concentrated trading and accumulation. Note, however, that the initial procession of men carrying pigs into the clearing and the men and women who give the declamatory speeches are not the feast givers themselves; it is only after these pigs have been brought in and *presented to* the feast givers that the latter bring in their pigs and the *Soi* actually begins.

Those who present pigs to the feast givers constitute "honored guests"; they are not members of the lineage whose loss of a generation is being commemorated. They fall into several categories, and those in each category will be guided by different strategies and obligations in making contributions of pigs to the feast givers. However, when the butchered pork is distributed, the portions—of pigs contributed by feast givers and by honored guests—go to the latter. All guests are classified according to their relationship to the feast givers:

Yanasa: Those members of the paired matrilineage who have performed the rites of burial for each of the deceased. Their interests in contributing pigs to the *Soi* given by the paired *susu* lie in their long-term symmetrical and reciprocal relationship: in the short run, these prestations of pigs assert prestige and confirm reciprocal obligation; in the long run they are exactly reciprocated.

Sinevelam and Tovelam: Women and men, respectively, who have married into the village of the feast givers.

Eliam: "Friends" of the dead who had special (nonkinship) bonds to them, which are acknowledged in the presentation of special food portions. These prestations, in creating no future obligation, dramatize the fact that friendship and personal closeness, however important, are ephemeral.

Taumana: Visitors, those who had no special relationship to the deceased persons but have come to honor them. People in this group, forming at least half of the "audience," are given one or two yams each and are fed, but their participation is peripheral and creates no obligations.

Feasting and dancing continue until dawn, when the feast givers bring forth another pig and spear it; this meat is distributed to those who sang, danced, and drummed. The dancers are showered with small gifts of betel nut and other items as *dasi* (payment for services). As the day dawns, visitors load meat and yams into their boats, leaving their hosts to take off their finery and clean the village. Finally, the *mwali* are taken down from the pole and returned to their owners. A generation has been laid to rest.

PATHS OF EXCHANGE

At this point we need to look more closely at the ways people on Tubetube conceptualize the networks created and maintained by exchange, in mortuary ritual and in other contexts, and then to look, in terms of this model, at categories of transactions and the social relationships to which they are appropriate.

The structure and sequence of mortuary exchanges reflect an ideology of social relationships and obligations created and maintained by the exchange of shell valuables, pigs, and food. The language of mortuary exchange is the same as that of *kune* (*kula*) and marriage. The metaphors are spatial, of places linked by *kamwasa* (roads). As with *kune*, roads between affines are made and maintained by use, by flow of goods between one village hamlet and another. The language of affinal exchange is that of "road maintenance." Ideally, all roads should be "straight," and all traffic should be orderly, proceeding according to "rule." If people neglect their affinal obligations the roads become "overgrown." If they refuse to fulfil their obligations it is said "they have 'closed' or 'blocked' the road" (*kamwasa sipei kausi*). If, at a *Soi*, affines choose to give prestations that constitute an exact repayment of debts then it is said that "the path has died" (*kamwasa iboita*).

The paths radiate from a central point, the *yanua* (village hamlet) of one specific matrilineage. The closest people are the *yanasa* (those of the neighboring matrilineage). Other paths extend beyond the village and surrounding garden land to the villages of affines. The places and the distances between reflect an ideological rather than empirical model, for these people who marry and live in the village are seen as "strangers" or "migrants," more distant relatives than *yanasa*, who may in fact live on another island. Children of men who are *natunatuleia* (owners of the village) remain "strangers" throughout their lives. Regardless of residential arrangements, they are obliged to maintain those paths into the village of their fathers, which were initially created by their mothers' marriages, by regular prestations of pigs, food, and valuables.

Other paths are made between individuals on distant islands for the purposes of trade. These are the roads along which things—pigs, boats, food, mats, baskets, pots, and shell valuables—travel. The people are *enaki* ("foreigners"), but once the path is established, they become *muli* (partners).

The concept of social distance, then, is expressed in the image of paths that lead out of the village, first to affines, then beyond the island to trade partners. The mortuary ritual sequence also expresses this notion of distance in temporal terms, each mortuary exchange incorporating people at a greater distance from the *yanua*.

The first gifts come from the closest relatives, those of the same *susu*. These are *mulolo* ("gifts of love"); they are not displayed. Produced and used within the lineage, they are tokens of altruistic relations between members of the lineage. They do not move beyond the village; they create no paths and no debts. The second gifts, *lowa-lowa*, come from affines; these are gifts on behalf of *natunatuleia* (children who are patrilaterally related to the deceased). The third funerary prestation is also called *mulolo* and usually consists of mats that are placed in the grave. These come from trade partners, distant friends, and people who have no kin ties but whose relationship with the deceased was affectionate and lasting.

The first mortuary feast, *Buga Mayaumate*, is for the *yanasa* (those of the same totem who are joint owners of the village of the bereaved lineage). *Yanasa* address each other as consanguineal kin and are responsible for care during any time when a lineage is in a tabooed state, on any occasion when a household is affected by birth or death. The second mortuary feast, *ligaliga*, occurs months later and involves both *yanasa* and affines. The mortuary feast, *Soi*, which is held years later, incorporates all people who have any social or economic relationship whatever with the village of the feast givers. The visitors often travel great distances, from Murua (Muyuw) and the Louisades. Their attendance reflects Tubetube's status as a trading community.

This descriptive model, of people and villages connected by paths, is used by Tubetube people themselves. The designation of the bereaved lineage as the "feast givers" does, however, give the false impression that goods flow in one direction at death. In fact, the mortuary feasting periods are occasions for heavy traffic in both directions on all these paths. The *mwali*, yams, and pigs are constantly spoken of as if they were produced and owned by the feast givers, but in fact they are not. The display is not simply of *affluence* but of *influence*. Most of the pigs are acquired in *kune*, and preparation for a *Soi* plunges each member of the lineage into numerous *kune* debts with partners on Ware, Duau, and islands in the Bwanabwana region. Many of the *mwali* hanging on the platform are on loan for the duration of the *Soi*, borrowed from neighbors, relatives, and visitors. They testify to the deceased people's influence as *kune* traders over a wide area, each *mwali* representing a link beyond the village. The *tanalele* (display pole) declares their prowess in *kune*, as every *mwali* displayed has at one time traveled on a "path to that village." Their actual wealth, in the form of *kitomwa* (shell valuables owned by people of the lineage), is worn by the women, the *bagi* around the neck, the *mwali* on the arms, the constant clinking of the decorations and the cries of trussed pigs proclaiming the prosperity of the lineage.

Similarly, the piles of yams on the ritual platform are always spoken of as if they were the produce of the large *Soi* gardens planted by the lineage. About two-thirds of the yams are indeed produced by the *susu*, but the rest are given by *yanasa* and affinal relatives.

So, in all exchanges there are three types of prestation, and mortuary feasts provide the opportunity for debtors and creditors to conclude or reestablish exchange relationships. The three types of gift are *mulolo, yaga*, and *maisa*. *Mulolo* is the gift par excellence, freely given as a token of love, ideally offered without thought or expectation of repayment and carrying no obligation or debt. The archetypal *mulolo* gifts are those buried with the corpse; they are not displayed, simply placed on the body just prior to burial. They are given by members of the deceased's lineage so they are not repaid: nobody counts the gifts or notes what was given. This word was chosen by the first missionary in the area as the word signifying God's love. It is familiar throughout the area where the Methodist missions were established, and its meaning has now been extended so that it not only means "a gift of love" but, by extension, blessing, grace, devotion, and charity. Usually *mulolo* gifts are not repaid; indeed it would be offensive to imply that something was repayment for *mulolo*. The existence of the concept of *mulolo* allows for the rhetorical use of the term in a wide range of other

147

transactions that really do entail indebtedness. The ideology of affinal relations demands that all initial gifts be presented as *mulolo*, but of course nobody would really accept them as such.

The second type of prestation is called *yaga* (a gift that creates a debt). This is the "opening gift" that clears the path between transactors. The return prestation, the final or clinching gift, is termed *maisa* (payment). Although the opening gift in an affinal exchange is ostentatiously given as *mulolo*, the recipients carefully note it as *yaga*, and at a subsequent exchange they will be equally pointed in their terminology, referring to the initial gift as *yauya* (a neutral term meaning "something given"), and insisting that their prestation is *maisa* (settling the debt). If for any reason the transactors want to maintain their relationship, to keep the paths open, then their prestation would be larger or smaller than the first gift, so that the relationship of indebtedness continues.

So, for example, *lowalowa* refers to the mortuary gifts of shell valuables that affines place on the body and are retained by members of the bereaved *susu*. *Lowalowa* can be *maisa* or *yaga*, but it is usual for *lowalowa* to be *yaga* when it is paid at the funeral so that it creates a debt. The valuables given must be *kitomwa* (personal possessions of the donor and unencumbered by debt). Once given, they become the *kitomwa* of the recipients. Shell valuables for *lowalowa* must always be of the highest class; arm shells in this category are called *mwalikau*, necklaces *bagiliku*. When these are placed on the corpse, a short statement denoting their significance as tokens of love and grief is made. However, their economic function as *yaga* or *maisa* is crucial, in that it is on the basis of these prestations that affinal links are maintained, severed, or restricted.

Lowalowa keeps a path open that might otherwise have been closed by the death of a linking affine. Gifts usually come from the lineage of a woman who is married into the bereaved lineage, and they are the main way of securing patrifilial inheritance. By giving *lowalowa*, the woman's lineage secures for her children rights of usufruct over some part of their father's land. The people who receive the prestation have then to cancel the claim at some later date by giving the return payment, *maisa*, in the form of shell valuables or pigs. They cannot use the same items that they were originally given, but must give arm shells or necklaces that are *bagiliku* or *mwalikau* or pigs that are of sufficient size to be equivalent in value to the debt.

Lowalowa transactions are extremely complex as they can extend over many years and the debts can be built up or settled at *any* funeral in either of the corporate matrilineages involved. They are further complicated by the ways in which their economic functions are never referred to in any public way, so that two matrilineages can exchange *lowalowa* at successive funerals, offering them as tokens of sorrow, and a debt has been made and cancelled without any mention or claim being made about land. It is only when one group cannot repay that the land becomes an issue. As *lowalowa* is usually made on behalf of children, and the land is tabooed until the second mortuary feast, many years can elapse before usufructory rights are claimed by them and land that was claimed on their behalf might be redeemed before they are old enough to assert their rights.

At a funeral for an old man that took place in February 1981, the wife of the decedent's sister's son had one large arm shell as *lowalowa*. This was given on behalf of her children, who are *natunatuleia* in their father's village, the village of the bereaved lineage. These children are now very young, but this *lowalowa* constitutes the first in a series of *yaga* payments that, when their father dies, become the basis for their claims for usufructory rights over his land. If at any stage the father's lineage wants to prevent these claims from being made, they must repay the initial *lowalowa* at a funeral for one of their affines from this marriage. This payment would then constitute *maisa*. On both occasions, however, the valuable would be offered as *mulolo*, without any reference to the underlying economic nature of the transaction. The dual significance of *lowalowa*, as a token of the affinal bond and the altruism that forms it and as a claim for patrilateral rights over property, is a clear example of the tensions inherent in affinal relationships.

However, the economic functions of *lowalowa* cannot be claimed as primary in the majority of cases, even though they are latent in all *lowalowa* prestations. Transfer of property rights after death occurs very rarely. The ideology of the inalienability of *susu* land is usually respected in all affinal relationships, to the extent that most *lowalowa* payments seem to be carefully calculated with respect for the affinal lineage's capacity to repay.

All mortuary prestations and the rituals associated with death are not only overt displays of wealth and occasions for the redistribution of this wealth but displays of emotions: the participants dramatize, through their demeanor, the ideology and morality underlying all social relations. In stressing the economic elements in the mortuary exchanges on Tubetube I have perhaps failed to convey the other social aspects, the emotional and dramatic impacts of these rituals on all participants.

For the people concerned, the most important issues at a mortuary feast are dramatizations of grief and bereavement and *yakasisi* (displays of respect). Failure to fulfill mortuary obligations is viewed first as a gross insult to the dead and second as a breach of an essentially economic contract. There are powerful sanctions against those who do not pay debts or do not perform the correct mortuary rituals, and the economic element, although significant, is certainly not viewed as the central issue at stake. In the final section I shall briefly describe the two institutionalized sanctions imposed on those who do not pay mortuary debts.

KAMIASIO AND *KIYO*: RITUAL FOR SHAMING AND DEMANDING COMPENSATION

Kamiasio means "we sit down," an exact description of the practice. If any group of, say, *yanasa* or *enaena* considers that they have not been adequately repaid, they simply sit in the village clearing and refuse to move until the debt is honored. Throughout the "sit-in" the senior members of the *susu* harangue the village owners, accusing them of insulting their own dead and of being people of no substance or influence. Exchanges such as *ligaliga*, in which balanced reciprocity is important, are the occasion for such disputes. Similarly, the *yanasa* people can insist on a certain number of pigs as *maisa* and simply keep stoking the fire on the grave so that the bereaved lineage remains in a tabooed state for days until they manage to find another pig as payment. The *kamiasio* seems to be mainly concerned with getting payment; however, in the event the lineage simply may not be able to pay, and after a short period of time, the people leave, having won a moral victory. A *kamiasio* is seen as shameful, and in order to avoid the indignity the village owners try to negotiate a settlement, forfeiting a small area of their land.

Failure to fulfill mortuary obligations associated with the lifting of mourning taboos is viewed as a serious breach of custom and a gross insult to the dead person and his or her lineage. In fact it is very rare for a person to renege on these responsibilities, so that *kiyo* (the shaming ceremony) has only been performed on Tubetube once in the last thirty years. On this occasion, in June 1980, a man remarried before he had made *ligaliga* for the family of his first wife. He owned a motor vessel that was worth several thousand *kina*, and this valuable property made his neglect of the *ligaliga* prestations appear to be deliberately disrespectful rather than due to an inability to pay. In normal circumstances the boat itself would have been tabooed until after *ligaliga*. When the people of the dead woman's *susu* discovered that "their widower" was living openly with a new wife, and her family were sailing about in his boat, they decided to demand compensation for the insult to their sister and repayment of all debts, and so a *kiyo* was organized. All members of the aggrieved family assembled some distance from the village where the man had settled, and then, in procession behind the senior man and woman of the lineage, they advanced on the hamlet, chanting their demands for compensation. The man and woman of the dead wife's lineage gave long and dramatic speeches demanding necklaces, arm shells, and pigs and—for the first time—money, as compensation. At first, a pig and a *gaeba* (large platter), exact repayments of outstanding *lowalowa* debts, were thrown on behalf of the husband at the feet of the aggrieved man and his sister. Then two necklaces, three arm shells, and another large pig were added. The angry visitors refused to be placated and continued to shout abuse and demand money until the family of the man's new wife handed over K.137 in cash. After this they left, dividing the wealth among members of the lineage and their *natunatuleia*. This was accepted as payment in spite of the fact that it did not match the amounts of money given by the wife's family to pay off the loan for the boat. This money had been given throughout the twenty years of marriage, even when the wife's relatives had no access to the boat, which was based on Madang. Later, in discussing the *kiyo*, it was explained that the payment constituted adequate compensation for the insult and the outstanding *lowalowa* debt. Realizing that there was no way that the debt of money contributed for the boat could be paid without selling the boat, the dead woman's lineage had decided to "write it off" as an irretrievable loss. However, they were not prepared to capitulate on the issue of *lowalowa* and compensation for the insult to their sister. The repayment of *lowalowa* was demanded not because of the economic element, but as a gesture that effectively cut off all relations between the two groups. Economically it was to their disadvantage to close this exchange path, since it was on the basis of their *lowalowa* that children from the man's marriage could have claimed rights over the boat or their father's land.

Mortuary ceremonies are the only formal rituals regularly performed by Tubetube people today. *Kula* exchanges no longer involve elaborate or ritualized social interaction—indeed the *Kula* valuables are more likely to be taken home to Tubetube in a rice bag on a motor vessel than paraded on a display pole. Marriage exchanges are now informal, and the alternating residence of young couples occurs without any procession or exchange of food, the woman merely entering her husband's village with a token bundle of firewood to indicate that she has come to stay. However, the persistence of mortuary exchanges and the sanctions that are imposed on those who do not fulfill all their obligations are an indication of the persistence of the social forces and structures that are reified in the ceremonies. Mortuary exchanges are a focus for *all* social relations and the exchanges that mediate them, both within Tubetube society and beyond.

In this essay I have attempted to describe briefly the rituals themselves and the patterns of social relations on which they are structured. Panetan concluded his description of the rationale behind mortuary exchange in this way:

> Before we had more feasts; there were more people and they knew all about *kune* (*kula*) with pigs and canoes and *mwali* and *bagi*. Marriages were different, pigs, *mwali*, *bagi*, and yams going up and down the paths between villages. Sometimes you think it is all finished, but when a person dies then you see that all the paths are really still there and the essential [*yaina* (trunk)] things remain the same. But now only *ligaliga* and *soi*: at these times we find our boundaries, we find our

boundary markers, and we stop all the disrespect for boundaries. As I said before, it's all about paths—you have to make them straight every now and then. At death we do this.

NOTES

Acknowledgments: I am particularly grateful to the following people, who assisted me in formulating this description: Panetan and Din of Bwasikaene village, Tubetube; Edith of Tewalai village, Naluwaluwali; Pansi of Lobiu village, Naluwaluwali; and John Wesley of Maimaibeia, Tubetube.

1. I shall assume throughout this section that the deceased person is male and refer to his "widow." As the mourning procedures are the same for both sexes the gender terms can be juxtaposed without affecting the description or argument.

2. The transformation of the corpse to pure "generative substance" is clearly expressed by the double meaning of the Tubetube word *maiamaiale* (white). Reduplication of the first syllables indicates intensity when the word is an adjective. When the term is used verbally, reduplication indicates continuous action in the present. The verb *maiale* means "to burst into flame," "to glow," and, by extension, "to generate," as "a fire generates heat." So the phrase "*tuatuao simaiamaiale*" means "the bones are white" and "the bones are generating."

3. Only a few people on Tubetube recall in detail former mortuary practices and beliefs in the afterlife. I have reconstructed the sequence from the writings of early missionaries and from informants' descriptions.

Carl E. Thune

Death and Matrilineal Reincorporation on Normanby Island

This is our grandparents' custom. Our customs are like this. We are living and perhaps our sisters or our brothers or perhaps our other relatives are dying and we feel sad. We are thinking all the time about making a *sagali* for them. I feed my pigs and when they are first rate, we make a *Gwala*. We make the *Gwala* and our affine come and they dance with drums. They dance and we make a feast. We make a feast and give the *Walisipwa* feast. When it is finished we wait a year and then we make a *Lokarai* feast. We make the *Lokarai* feast and when it is finished, we plant again. We raise a lot of food and we make the *sagali*. We make a big *sagali*. We build many *sagali* houses. We finish them and our affines come and cover the houses with yams. They cover them with yams and they dance. They make a lot of *hwahwa* soup and we are happy. We make the *sagali* distribution and we remember our dead. We do this and it is finished and we sit quietly. That is enough of our ancestors' customs.[1]

INTRODUCTION

• For the people of northeast Normanby Island located in the Milne Bay Province of Papua New Guinea, death is a supremely threatening event. Structurally, death lies midway between birth, which reproduces the matrilineage and, hence, indirectly, matrilineage solidarity, and the final feast of the mortuary sequence, which recreates and reaffirms that solidarity. Indeed, dying represents the most extreme movement that people make

153

in the direction of individual autonomy and independence from their matrilineage.

On the one hand, death isolates a person from his or her own matrilineal relatives and, indeed, more generally, from the matrilineage as an ideal, abstract, ahistorical essence. On the other hand, through death, a person is precluded from playing the historical, active, and creative role of matrilineage representative to his or her spouse and spouse's relatives. In a society in which an essentially inward-looking matrilineal embeddedness and a corollary outward-looking matrilineal representativeness are stressed above all, to die is to commit a fundamentally antisocial act.

However, as with marriage (which in this matrilineal society is, in many ways, also an antisocial act), death is ritualized and socialized. When properly ritualized, a person's death disappears as a historical, individualistic, socially destructive event. And, properly socialized, it precipitates a reaffirmation of the solidarity, homogeneity, and ahistoricity of the deceased's matrilineage.

However, the matrilineage is not reconstituted directly. Rather this is achieved indirectly through the invocation of the geographical landscape as a second, ideally more real, unchallengeable, and natural sphere that can, at times, be taken to stand behind and naturalize it. Landscape and matrilineality, as a pair of complementary idioms for representing social relations, are used to naturalize and legitimize one another. The mortuary sequence consists of a series of structurally different kinds of exchange transactions. Each kind reaffirms a different dimension of threatened matrilineally grounded social relations by refracting it through the unproblematic, natural landscape.

THE STRUCTURE OF THE PERSON

Blood, Marriage, and Expanding Sociality

At birth each northeast Normanby Island person arrives in the world sharing *lala* (common blood) with his or her mother and the remainder of her *susu* (matrilineage). Indeed, when asked to describe the matrilineage, northeast Normanby Island people stress the fundamental identity of all matrilineage mates that reflects their common blood. Indeed, this common blood implies a matrilineal homogeneity that can be violated only with a violation of the natural order of things. Matrilineality, as such, provides no means by which relations can be established with those outside the matrilineage. The matrilineage, ideally, then, is an ahistorical, unchanging, indivisible unity that stands outside time. It should, ideally, require no dependence upon or even relationship to nonmembers.

Yet, given the prohibition of marrying those identical to oneself, the matrilineage can, in the world of history, reproduce itself only through births deriving from marriages with outsiders.[2] Consequently, every child has a father to whom he or she has an essentially affinal relationship. This is a relation that, being transactional, is created and not natural. And, given the fact that the child receives things from his or her father that can never be repaid, paternity implies a relation in which a permanent indebtedness is inevitable (cf. Thune 1980).

This embedding of a person's persona within other matrilineages is necessarily doubled at marriage. Indeed, the longer a person lives, the more his or her identity becomes estranged from the matrilineage to become tied up with those of friends, affines, Kula partners, and today, employers and teachers from other parts of Papua New Guinea. Nevertheless, however much people may complain of this estrangement, all also recognize that matrilineage fame and renown within northeast Normanby Island and, more widely, throughout the Massim, is dependent upon members' returning to their matrilineage bearing fame derived from accomplishments beyond it.

Body, Spirit, and the Nature of Death

Most northeast Normanby Island people agree that each *tomotai* (person)[3] possesses *nuwanuwa* (a mind or intelligence) and a *yaluwaluwa* or, sometimes, *makamakayaow* (spirit or soul or shade) that is the source of their intelligence, will, and self-motivation. But a "person" also possesses *bwalana* (literally skin but generically body), the most important element of which is its blood, which gives it matrilineage identity. The "body," then, represents that part of the person that participates in and bears the a-historical essence of the matrilineage. By contrast, the "mind" and "spirit" are the parts of the person that are historical and situated in the mundane world. "Mind" and "spirit," rather than body, are responsible for the creative (but also disruptive) activities that draw a person away from his or her matrilineage.[4] In this sense, they are the essentially "unnatural" part of the person.

Ideally, at death, the "body" is buried in the deceased's matrilineage-owned hamlet. With time his or her name and particularities will be forgotten and he or she will become one of the anonymous ancestors. By contrast, the "spirit" of a deceased person is regarded as a potential nuisance that would prefer to continue social relations with its living matrilineage mates. On occasion, particularly if the deceased was willful and ill-tempered (that is, had a "mind" that disregarded his or her matrilineally derived obligations), a "spirit" can be vaguely dangerous. Hence, it is encouraged (and sometimes coerced) to depart from the hamlet of the living as quickly as possible.[5]

Death itself is not an original feature of the natural world but a product of the actions of specific people in the past. The story of Kekewageihi, for example, describes the origin of death on Normanby Island.

> Kekewageihi told her daughter and grandchildren that she would go to Bwebweso [the land of the dead for the people of Normanby and Dobu Islands] after she died but then would return to the world of the living. When she returned, they were to wash her body with hot water to wash away the cadaverous appearance that her body had acquired in the grave. Then she would continue to live normally with them once more.
>
> She died. However, when she returned, her grandchildren, frightened by her ghastly appearance, thought she was some kind of witch. Kekewageihi was hurt by her matrilineage mates' rejection. As a result, she returned to Bwebweso after telling her grandchildren that death would now be final. She now lives there, sitting with her back to us.[6]

Had the children followed their grandmother's instructions, that is, had they played their proper rules as matrilineage members rather than acting as independent, assertive individuals, death would not have its present finality. In other words, had the children recognized and acted upon their biological identity with Kekewageihi rather than upon the creative vagaries of their "minds," they would not have been offended by her appearance upon arising, worm-eaten, from the grave.

After telling this story, Lasaro, the storyteller, went on to suggest that each of the homes of the dead[7] had its own Kekewageihi—*Kekewageihi* is used as both a proper and a generic name—whose rejection by her matrilineage mates led to the present finality of death for her ethnic group. Lasaro was, in effect, arguing that in the real, historical world, the events of a story analogous to that of Kekewageihi inevitably occur. People, because they possess a self-assertive "mind" and a "body" that can only reproduce itself through an alliance with other matrilineages, inevitably, it would seem, will forget their ties to their matrilineage mates.

All northeast Normanby Islanders recognize that there is a real threat to matrilineage integrity when a person refuses to marry because of loyalty based on bodily identity with his or her matrilineage mates. At once, no younger members are introduced into the matrilineage, and the matrilineage has little hope of garnering renown through sponsoring affinally based feasts. Yet it is precisely the rebellious self-interested "mind" necessary to reproduce the matrilineage that brought death into the world.[8]

Both mortuary and marital exchange activities focus upon attempts to resolve the contradiction between the motivations deriving from the "body" and those deriving from the "mind," between the given matrilineal and the created affinal, and, more abstractly, between the ahistorical and the historical. In both cases the goal is to recover the "body" for the matrilineage and

156

discard the "mind" while still retaining though collectivizing the fame of its accomplishments.

Like the good marriage, the good death leads to a reproduction of the natural and the given. For both, the desired end can only be accomplished by removing all historically created individuality from the centrally involved people (the bride, groom, or deceased), who must become again, first and foremost, members of their own matrilineages.

The bad death, like the bad marriage, results in the departure or expulsion of the person from his or her matrilineage. In death he or she becomes an enemy of and predator upon the matrilineage mates; at marriage he or she becomes a member of a marital pair existing independently of the matrilineage and the matrilineage of his or her spouse.[9] With both the bad death and the bad marriage, the overdeveloped "spirit" has not only rendered the accomplishments of the "body" inaccessible to appropriation by the matrilineage but removed the body from its natural embeddedness within the matrilineage.

THE STRUCTURE OF THE LANDSCAPE[10]

Each matrilineage owns at least one "true" *kasa* (hamlet), at the formal center of which is the *bolu* (a low stone platform). The stone platform and the ground and the products of plants surrounding it are reserved for the use of members of the owning matrilineage. More than this, they are dangerous to members of other, especially affinally related, matrilineages. On formal occasions, the owning matrilineage distributes pork from the stone platform to affinally related recipients, thus reinforcing the opposition of it as a matrilineal center to its affines.

Usually a number of graves of deceased matrilineage mates will be located around the stone platform. Most commonly these are graves of old, probably widowed, women or young children, that is, of people whose external affiliations had least estranged them from their matrilineage. Indeed, many suggest that a merely convenient stone platform becomes a true *bolu* embodying matrilineage identity as deceased members are buried around it. In sum, the stone platform is a visible concretization of matrilineage identity and history.

Surrounding the stone platform is the *katamana* (an open grassy area that is the center for hamlet, as opposed to matrilineage, activities). Around the edges of this area are the hamlet houses. Ideally, living in each house is *toni kasa* (a member of the owning matrilineage), his or her spouse, and their children. Hence, the ring of houses is the zone in which another matrilineage is intrusively represented within the hamlet. It is also a zone in which members of another matrilineage may become estranged from their own matrilineages to support local activities. And, more threateningly, it is a

157

zone in which matrilineage mates themselves may be coopted to support activities of other matrilineages.

The stone platform is formally public, unproblematic, unchanging, and ahistorical. It embodies the ideal of the matrilineal world. By contrast, the house is private and, in fact, off limits to all but household residents. Given the embodiment in the household of all of the worst of the world of obligatory affinal relationships, it is not surprising that the household is unstable, problematic, radically historical, and threatening to the ideal of matrilineality. Hence, there is a dramatic juxtaposition of matrilineality and affinity, ahistoricity and historicity, ideal and actual, inscribed on the landscape of the hamlet itself.

From a broader perspective, the hamlet, and the matrilineage concretized in the stone platform, is opposed to other hamlets owned by matrilineages to which it has affinal links. Although this formal opposition of hamlet to hamlet is not particularly important or developed, its existence does define a third, residual geographical sphere that encompasses all land that the matrilineage does not own and that does not belong to matrilineages to which it has affinal ties. Lacking a genealogical basis for organization, this residual zone is spoken of in geographical rather than social structural terms. It is the realm of the alien, the unknown, and the uncontrolled, and the source of power and efficacy. More importantly, however, it is the zone from which fame and renown can be acquired, but also the zone in which, if a matrilineage is to possess renown, there must be recognition of its accomplishments.

However, this zone of the geographically alien is more than simply an outside that is opposed to an inside.[11] It is the zone in which the idealized, ahistorical, unchanging matrilineage can act within the historical world without forming affinally based alliances that would compromise its integrity as a discrete and independent unit. In contrast, the hamlets, and particularly the stone platforms of affinally related matrilineages, are distinctly dangerous. Although they exist within a zone in which the matrilineage may act in the historical world, it cannot do so without compromising itself by embedding a portion of itself within the destiny of other matrilineages.

Finally, this residual geographical zone is an area where people, if they are anything other than anonymous representatives of a geographical district, are only the relatively anonymous representatives of their matrilineages. Hence, in general, action within this sphere is less individualizing than is action within the sphere of affinal relations. And, hence, in general, it is easier for an individual to act individualistically while still personifying his or her matrilineage in this zone than it is in the world closer to home. Thus, it is not surprising that this residual geographical realm is where *Kula* traders seek fame through trading and seek to spread the fame of their matrilineages through their travels.

THE MORTUARY SEQUENCE

The northeast Normanby Island mortuary sequence consists of four distinct phases. Each is characterized by a unique structure of exchange activities. And each is built around a distinct opposition of what appears to be natural and what is taken to be most problematic and in need of being reaffirmed. Finally, each refracts social relations through a different pair of geographical zones.

Death and Burial: Internal Matrilineal Transactions

Burial takes place in a *kerikeri* (deep grave) generally in or near the local hamlet of the deceased's matrilineage.[12] Between death and burial the immediate matrilineal mates of the deceased remain close to the body. They sit together, emotionally distraught, visibly detached from the day-to-day world in which the body must be buried and in which the appropriate exchange transactions following burial must be organized.

These mundane affairs are the responsibility of the deceased's more distant matrilineal mates, who are self-controlled, competent, highly visible, and seemingly emotionally unaffected by the death. They are supported by their *bukuna* (members of closely associated matrilineages that, for formal purposes, are taken to be structurally identical to their own).

Immediate affines of the deceased—his or her spouse and/or father—are invisible. They are either totally absent or hidden inside a house with no role to play.

The deceased's immediate matrilineal mates are proscribed from eating the yams and pork that they pay for the "work" required to prepare and bury the body. Hence, they formally assign the role of principal gravedigger to a favored, more distant matrilineal mate or member of an associated matrilineage. Doing so assures that the body will receive the respect and concern that can only be expected from a matrilineal mate or close associate. Equally importantly, many point out, the practice keeps the yams and pork used for the "payment" within the deceased's matrilineage.

After the burial, the deceased's matrilineage stages a small distribution of yams and, after the death of an important person, possibly pork. Yams and possibly a pig are provided by the immediate matrilineal mates of the deceased. These are augmented by yams contributed by affines of the deceased's immediate matrilineal mates and other interested people. This food is distributed to the principal gravedigger, distant matrilineal mates, members of associated matrilineages, and others having an intimate relation to the deceased or the deceased's matrilineage. The recipients of yams act as representatives of their own affines, with whom they share the food they receive. This latter sharing, like the movement of yams and pigs from affines to the deceased's immediate relatives as the prestation is created, is informal and not publicly accounted.

This feast, and indeed all feasts associated with this phase of the mortuary sequence, is a two-party event conducted within rather than between matrilineages. The matrilineage is split into two divisions, each of which absorbs its affines so completely that they are invisible.

As in any northeast Normanby Island exchange transaction, the explicit recipient of the major prestation—here the principal gravedigger—is expected to repay it in a structurally similar context in which roles of giver and receiver are reversed. Hence, the principal gravedigger is expected subsequently to appoint one of the deceased's immediate matrilineal mates as principal gravedigger when one of his own immediate matrilineal mates dies.

From the perspective of internal matrilineal politics and organization the decision to appoint a principal gravedigger is an important strategic move with long-term implications. For example, those seeking to consolidate their centrality within a large, dispersed matrilineage may use the appointment as an opportunity to strengthen ties with more distant matrilineal mates. However, formally, the mere occurrence of exchange (rather than sharing [cf. Thune 1983]) within the matrilineage underscores the fact that death provokes a fragmentation of a natural unit that, by its very nature, should be indivisible.[13]

On the day following the burial feast, the *Basa* (a somewhat larger feast of the same underlying structure) is held (fig. 1). Again yams and pork are distributed by the deceased's immediate matrilineal mates to the principal gravedigger, members of associated matrilineages, and other people having some special relation to the deceased or the deceased's matrilineage. Cooked yams, *mona* (a sago, yam, or taro pudding), and *hwahwa* (a mashed yam soup) are also served to these people.

During the *Basa* distant matrilineal mates and members of associated matrilineages cook yams for the deceased's immediate matrilineal mates and their supporting affines. We see here the pattern of a prestation countered by a *maisa* (acknowledgment gift) that is found in all exchanges between matrilineages. Again the depth of the division within the matrilineage is analogous to that normally found between affinally related matrilineages.

As a part of the *Basa* young men of associated matrilineages build a small screened-off enclosure in which they make the *duguma* house (a model, traditionally styled saddle-backed house). Near the end of the day, women of associated matrilineages, each with a dish of yams on her head, stand before the enclosure and sing one of the women's mourning laments. Although the lament is in a little understood, archaic form of the contemporary northeast

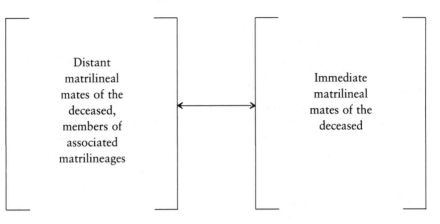

FIGURE 1.   The structure of the *Basa* mortuary feast.

Normanby Island language, people say it recollects the existence and accomplishments of the deceased.

Just before the end of the lament, the young men, with loud shouts, burst through the walls of the enclosure carrying the *duguma* house and scattering the women. The women burst into a loud, uncontrolled wail similar to the wail of visitors when they first see the body of the deceased. Once the young men have disrupted the women's lament, transforming it into hysterical wailing, they quietly and informally carry the *duguma* house to the deceased's grave to place it on top of his or her grave house.[14]

In many ways, the *duguma* house stands as a substitute, now anonymous, for the body of the deceased.[15] Its presence reflects a reunification of the matrilineal unit as immediate relatives, distant relatives, and members of associated matrilineages once again act upon their common identity and collectively cry for the deceased. The grave and *duguma* house become both a focus of attention and a concrete representation of the now unified matrilineage. This interpretation is supported by the fact that traditionally burial took place next to the deceased's matrilineage's stone platform.

The unified matrilineage of the deceased remains isolated from normal society after the *basa*. Nonmembers should show their respect for the deceased and his or her matrilineal mates by not visiting the deceased's hamlet or engaging in conventional informal intercourse with its members.

These restrictions are relieved after matrilineal mates and members of associated matrilineages make a festive trip through the deceased's hamlet cluster and often through adjacent hamlet clusters in which the deceased had relatives or close associates. Omitting only the hamlets owned by the matrilineages of the deceased's father and spouse, the party formally presents betel nuts and tobacco to the people whom they meet. They also symbolically oil and clean the people they encounter by squeezing a few drops of coconut oil on each of them.

At each hamlet, the residents in turn provide the party with small gifts—plates, perhaps a few coins, betel nuts, baskets, and the like—in compensation for the loss that they experienced and in payment for their having lifted the villagewide mourning restrictions. With this, social relations, marked symbolically by the freedom of nonaffines to ask members of the deceased's matrilineage for tobacco and betel, are reestablished.

Frequently a day or so later, the members and affines of the deceased's matrilineage organize a *dalauwa*[16] (group fishing expedition) to recognize the importance of the deceased as a fisher publicly. The largest fish are saved for the immediate matrilineage mates of the deceased. The remainder are informally distributed among other residents, especially affines, of the village. After this distribution, people are freed from the prohibition on fishing that they were expected to follow out of respect for the deceased.

Some say that the real importance of this event is that it is the last public occasion on which the deceased's name is formally called out in a public feasting context. In other words, this is the last time that the deceased acts as an individual, named member of his or her matrilineage in any transactional exchange activity. Henceforth, the deceased's name should never be used by any but matrilineal mates.

By the end of the first phase of the mortuary sequence the deceased has disappeared as a distinct individual. His or her body has been metaphorized as the publicly visible but anonymous *duguma* house and his or her name has been retired from public use. The matrilineage has reestablished its integrity and solidarity. It is united by the fact that the deceased's name is theirs alone to use and by the fact that the *duguma* house now serves as an evocative presence for all, no matter how distant, members.

In other words, the abnormal genealogically based division between immediate and distant matrilineal mates of the deceased has disappeared. This done, no further two-party transactions within the matrilineage are possible. Burial is really not ridding the living of an unneeded body. Rather it is reconsecrating the land around the stone platform to reaffirm the essential integrity of the owning matrilineage. Precisely because the land is unchanging, because it contains the bones of the ancestors and hence the essence of the matrilineage, the image of the land is uniquely suited to evoke its reconstitution.

This recreated internal integrity is only possible because externally the matrilineage now collectively opposes the deceased's affines, who remain under a variety of severe mourning restrictions. At the same time that the deceased's matrilineage recovers its unity through the grave site and the stone platform, it must verify and demonstrate this unity through reestablishing a facsimile of affinal relationships to other matrilineages that death disrupted. By freeing all nonmatrilineal members except those of affinally related matrilineages from formal mourning restrictions, attention is tightly focused on affinal connections between the deceased and other matrilineages.

In many ways an idealized predeath status quo is now created. The deceased's only public presence is as an anonymous matrilineage member having external affinal ties marked by a relation of mutual indebtedness but not emotional or intellectual attachment. Certainly this anonymity is an improvement over the more threatening affinal relationships in which both partners are alive and partially detached from their respective matrilineages. However, the deceased's matrilineage remains implicated with the matrilineages of his or her father and/or spouse until their mutual indebtedness is erased.

The Bwabwali Sequence

The second phase of the mortuary sequence consists of a series of feasts culminating in the final *Bwabwali* feast (fig. 2). With it the presumably negligent affines of the deceased compensate the deceased's matrilineal mates for their loss. During the same feast the deceased's matrilineage compensates the deceased's affines for their mourning privations. By the end of the *Bwabwali* the entanglement of the deceased's matrilineage and the matrilineages of his or her spouse and/or father may be severed because the debt of each to the other has been largely erased.[17]

At death the deceased's spouse and father are expected to assume a formal mourning demeanor and attire. These include wearing old, dirty, dark clothing, refraining from public bathing, avoiding certain desirable foods, following special rules regarding how they may walk and carry loads in the vicinity of the deceased's hamlet, and withdrawing from participation in the pleasures of day-to-day social life. To a lesser extent, all of the deceased's affines and all affines of the deceased's matrilineal mates are expected to follow these rules. Although mission and government pressure has reduced some of the more extreme privations imposed by these mourning rules,[18] their spirit is still assumed by affinally related mourners and is still enforced by the deceased's matrilineage.

These restrictions take effect immediately after death. However, they are not publicly visible until the end of the first mortuary phase when the deceased's matrilineage has been reunified. From that time until the *Bwabwali* they serve to reinforce the formal opposition between the new, clean, controlled, and competent matrilineal mates of the deceased, whose

THE MOURNER'S SIDE   THE SURVIVOR'S SIDE

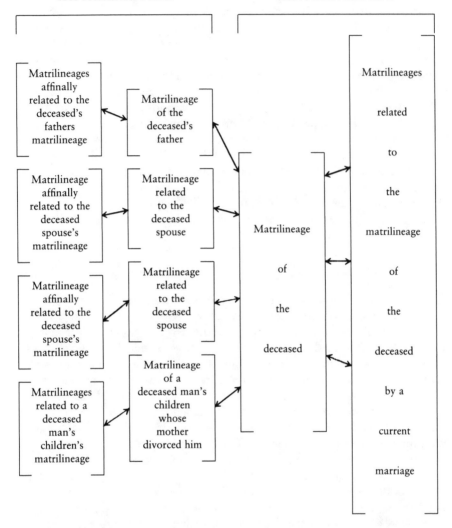

FIGURE 2.   The structure of the *Bwabwali* mortuary feast.

demeanor no longer identifies them with the deceased, and the mourning affines, who, being physically and structurally like the dead, are set apart from the society of the living.

The series of feasts culminating in the *Bwabwali* feast have a four-party structure similar to that of other marriage-related feasts. Matrilineages affinally related to the matrilineage of the deceased organize prestations of yams, pork, and such feast-quality delicacies as bananas, sugarcane, and specially cooked foods. These are informally given to the matrilineage of the deceased, who add yams and pork of their own. The entire prestation is then formally presented to the matrilineages of the deceased's father and/or spouse.[19] From there it is informally distributed among the recipient's affinally related matrilineages. A smaller counterprestation, the *maisa* (literally, payment or price), simultaneously moves in the opposite direction. Formally, as in marital feasts, the gifts move from the deceased's matrilineage to the position of the deceased. From there it moves to the surviving spouse and/or father (or, if he or she is already dead, to his or her empty structural position) and finally to his or her matrilineal mates.

At the final *Bwabwali* feast each of the deceased's maritally or paternally related matrilineages presents a massive conical heap of large yams known as the *Bwabwali* to the matrilineage of the deceased. At the end of the feast, after the affines have all gone home, the *Bwabwali* yams are divided among all matrilineal mates and members of associated matrilineages, including those immediate relatives of the deceased who are allowed to receive but not to consume them. Notably, no distinction in the number or quality of yams received is made among immediate matrilineal mates, distant matrilineal mates, and members of associated matrilineages. Many of these *Bwabwali* yams will move on to the recipients' own affines.

In repayment, the deceased's matrilineage and associated matrilineages formally present a fairly sizable though smaller quantity of small, ordinary yams to the widow or widower or, if there is no widow or widower, to the matrilineage making the *Bwabwali* prestation. To this are added bowls of cooked luxury foods, large bunches of overripe betel nuts, dried fish, and perhaps other delicacies such as sugarcane, cooked yams or rice, and tinned fish. These are shared equally among the members of the deceased's spouse and/or father's matrilineages and their own affines. All of the people who contribute yams and other goods to the *Bwabwali* should receive a portion of the yams that the matrilineage of the deceased provide.

As people speak of the *Bwabwali*, they stress that its primary "work" consists of the formal "cleaning" of the deceased's matrilineage's affines and most especially of the deceased's spouse and/or father. The beards of male affines are shaved; their hair is cut; their bodies are cleaned and oiled with coconut oil; and they may receive new clothing. Female affines have their long mourning grass skirts cut to the normal length; receive new, festively

165

dyed and decorated grass skirts; and have their hair cut and combed. Often both men and women are dusted with scented talcum powder and sprinkled with trade store perfume. The actual exchange of yams and pork is spoken of as supporting the cleaning and return to society of those who have mourned.

On the day of the *Bwabwali* the surviving spouse is led by one or two of the older women of the deceased's matrilineage from his or her own hamlet into the center of the deceased's hamlet. He or she is seated next to the conical piles of *Bwabwali* yams.

The widow or widower should affect a senile, decrepit, passive, confused, and all but helpless appearance as he or she is led into the hamlet. As he or she appears, the deceased's matrilineage mates burst into wails. The surviving spouse, like the *duguma* house earlier, serves to evoke and personify the deceased. He or she is as close to being a barely living body without mind or spirit, to being one of the dead rather than one of the living, as possible. Indeed, at the moment when a person plays this role he or she is more dramatically present as a detached, isolated, mindless body than at any other point in life.

During the entire process of being cleaned, dressed, and returned to the world of society and the living, the widow or widower should remain passive, unaware of the circumstances of the cleaning, and unconscious of what is being done. He or she should be unaware of being the center of attention.

Finally the newly cleaned but still humble and "shy" widow or widower is helped into the center of a circle of the former spouse's matrilineal mates, members of associated matrilineages, and other persons taking a close interest in the affairs of the matrilineage. The men of this circle each carry a *pwanikahu* (long yam) cradled in their arms, and the women each carry a similar yam balanced on their heads as they surround the surviving spouse and sing several of the men's mourning songs. However, in contrast to other occasions on which these songs are sung, this occasion is sad and frequently punctuated by contagious waves of wailing that leave but few actually singing. There is a real feeling of loss as the matrilineage is about to give up a portion of its historical presence by severing its association with its former affines. With the last of these songs the widow or widower is led away from the former spouse's hamlet for the last time.

By the end of the *Bwabwali* the affines, including the surviving spouse, have all departed for their respective hamlets and the *Bwabwali* prestation has been equally divided among members of the deceased's matrilineage and its associated matrilineages. The matrilineage stands solitary, homogeneous, and independent of other matrilineages.

Thus, the body of the surviving spouse provides a focus for articulating the second phase of the mourning activities in much the same way as did the *duguma* house during the first phase. Yet, whereas the *duguma* house served as a substitute for the body of the deceased in its role as member of an ahistorical matrilineage, the surviving spouse represents the last vestige of the deceased's individuality (derived from his or her "mind") embedded within the historical world of affinally based intermatrilineal affairs. In other words, by the time of the *Bwabwali*, if matrilineal mates want to recall the deceased's presence as a distinct person, they can only do so indirectly by invoking that remaining historical part of his or her identity still incarnate within the body of the surviving spouse. With the final departure of the surviving spouse, the last of the deceased's historical aspect is removed from the matrilineage.

A body is still the point of articulation, but it is a body that is made complementary to the body that the matrilineage lost. Not surprisingly, whereas the body of the deceased is honored, the thrust of the *Bwabwali* sequence is to devalue until the very last moment the body of the surviving spouse. The deceased's body is reincorporated into the ahistorical matrilineage by honoring it during the wake preceding burial and by decorating it to resemble the deceased in his or her most dramatically attired moment.[20] The spouse's body is expelled from the deceased's matrilineage by rendering it as close to death in terms of social persona and physical appearance as possible. But for each body there is a final reversal: the decorations are removed from the body of the deceased before it is buried; the pollution is removed from the surviving spouse as his or her body is decorated immediately prior to being expelled from the deceased's hamlet.

The decoration of the deceased's body is individualizing, historical, and nonessential. Hence, at the final moment, it is reversed. Devaluing and polluting the body of the surviving spouse mark his or her continued relation to the deceased's matrilineage (he or she would have deliberately underdressed as a matter of respect in the presence of matrilineal elders even during the life of the deceased). Decorating the body of the surviving spouse, even highlighting the temporary historical aspect of his or her appearance with trade store–purchased hair oil or baby powder, is the most appropriate way to sever his or her relation to the deceased's matrilineage. The deceased is left pure body, the "spirit" having departed; the surviving spouse is left pure historically created appearance, the essence of his or her body now invisible from the perspective of the deceased's matrilineage.

Yet, though the deceased's matrilineage has eliminated the portion of the deceased's identity that was implicated in the historical world of intermatrilineal relations, it has not addressed the portion of the deceased's identity embodying anonymous matrilineal identity in a positive fashion. It is the task of the third phase of mortuary activities to reembed the deceased within his or her matrilineage and to honor his or her anonymous identity as a matrilineage member.[21]

The *Sagali* Mortuary Sequence

Mortuary activities of the *sagali* mortuary phase (fig. 3) involve the matrilineage's acting as a united, homogeneous unit existing apart from and independent of all other matrilineages. These feasts honor not specific historically placed individuals but anonymous matrilineal members who no longer have any public, which is to say, affinal, presence. Most honor not a single person but all of those who have died since the last *sagali* occurred.

Given this role of honoring a matrilineage as a whole rather than specific individuals, of asserting the uncompromised matrilineage after years of being compromised by death (and marriage), and, indeed, of spreading fame (again, of a matrilineage rather than of an individual) as widely as possible, it is not surprising that the *sagali* does not reflect any variation upon the marriage feasting structure. Marriage feasts reflect the presence of the matrilineage within a historical world. Although they may honor a marriage between matrilineages or even honor a person, they cannot honor a single matrilineage as a discrete, unified, independent, ahistorical whole.

Sagali and related feasts allow a matrilineage to recognize and honor itself by using a transactional structure built upon geographical rather than

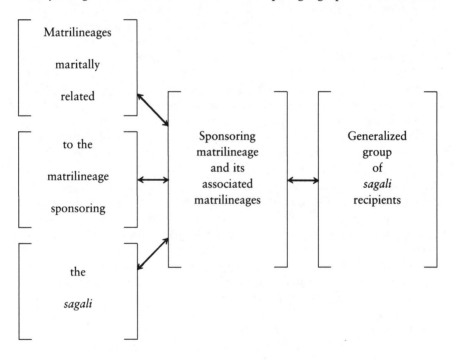

FIGURE 3. The structure of the *sagali* mortuary feast.

matrilineal relationships. These feasts produce a euphoria that results in the temporary spread of the matrilineage's fame far beyond geneological lines to extend throughout Normanby Island and, beyond, to neighboring islands. But this invocation of geography rather than matrilineality is always risky: the uncontrolled euphoria, the bringing together of people who have no matrilineal basis to control their social relations, inevitably results in squabbles and even open fights that occur more frequently than on any other occasion.[22]

Sagali and *gwala* are infrequently held. The *sagali* is performed by a matrilineage only every twenty years or so. It is the culmination of a two- to three-year sequence of increasingly large all-night dances and feasts. *Gwala*, a small version of the *sagali*, is held more frequently, perhaps every five to ten years.[23]

As with other feasts, the matrilineage sponsoring a *gwala* or *sagali* is supported by its affines, who provide the bulk of the required yams, pigs, and labor. However, unlike in the earlier mortuary feasts, the magnitude of the efforts of affinally related matrilineages in a *sagali* requires explicit accounting and recognition of their contribution. Indeed, each affinally related matrilineage along with its own supporters acts as a distinct, unified group rather than an anonymous member of a group composed of all the sponsoring matrilineage's affines.

Each of the affinal matrilineages is responsible for constructing "its" own *kabiboi* (a traditionally styled saddle-backed house) on the perimeter of the sponsoring matrilineage's *katamana* (central front yard). These houses are decorated and partially filled with massive amounts of large yams. Each affinal matrilineage also provides pigs, that, along with the yams and pigs provided by the sponsoring matrilineage, are distributed from a *bwaima* (massive distribution platform) to one side of the *katamana*.[24]

The relative discreteness of each affinal matrilineage partially individualizes the member of the sponsoring matrilineage to whom it has a marital connection. All of these individuals simultaneously and visibly embody their matrilineage by providing a link between it and a supporting affinal matrilineage. Uniquely, in the *sagali* all married matrilineage mates simultaneously play this concretizing, fame-generating, apparently individualizing role.

The recipients of pork, yams, and other goods distributed at the *sagali* are structurally anonymous individuals, not specifically situated within a matrilineal field. *Sagali* attract people from a number of villages and districts and even other islands. Many come because of curiosity and hope for excitement rather than any special relation to the sponsoring matrilineage.

Indeed, the distribution of food at a *sagali* is, in part, territorially rather than social structurally based. Frequently, a live pig is given, not to a matrilineally defined unit, but to the people of a whole village or district. As in other feasts a certain amount of yams and pork is formally presented to specific individuals. However, a considerable amount is frenetically distributed en masse among groups of anonymous, otherwise unknown individuals associated solely because they happen to be seated or standing together.

The visitors are anonymous representatives of a wider geographical domain juxtaposed to the hamlet of the sponsoring matrilineage. However, because the visitors are thus geographically situated as opposites without themselves being concretized in any specific location such as an analogue to the sponsoring matrilineage's distribution platform or the affine's *sagali* houses, they remain very much of an incoherent, negatively constructed group.

Indeed, unlike in other feasts, the sponsoring matrilineage defines the whole social universe as recipients, not so much to define itself in relationship to a dyadic other as to assert its presence in and of itself. And, unlike in all other contexts, giving here, by being geographically focused, denies rather than creates or demonstrates social relations.

One of the clearest marks of this positive, concretized definition of the giver and diffuse, negative definition of the recipient is the fact that the recipients of yams and pork distributed during the *sagali* do not simultaneously return an acknowledgment "gift." With the exception of certain formalized giving to the local church, this is the only context in which an acknowledgment gift is not given when a prestation is received. The sponsoring matrilineage stands alone, able to embed portions of itself in the external world beyond itself but unwilling to allow that world to reciprocate.

In contrast to the pattern of other feasts, the excitement of the *sagali* overcomes any attempt to account for or even recollect the movements of goods in the course of the formal distribution. A wholly unique apparent largesse and uncaring generosity replace the usual pragmatic concern with defining relations of indebtedness between one's matrilineage and other matrilineages.

Finally, the *sagali* is the one context in which a variety of men simultaneously seek fame through organizing their affines in support of their matrilineage's activities. Hence, it demonstrates, ideally, that it is possible to achieve personal fame without threatening the matrilineage as a whole or individual members within it. This is a collectivized personal fame that should not anger matrilineal witches who feel responsible for defending the indivisibility of their matrilineage even if it requires killing overly ambitious (and hence overly self-centered) matrilineal mates. And, also ideally, it demonstrates that a collectivized personal accomplishment is possible without offense to sorcerers who, being individualistic and self-interested, are willing to kill any upstart, even a matrilineal mate, who threatens to eclipse their power.

170

The Final Matrilineage-Centered Feast

Some months after the *sagali*, the sponsoring matrilineage holds a small party attended only by its members. A few undistributed yams that were deliberately left on the tops of the *sagali* house display racks are quietly cooked and eaten at this party.

During the party there are no formal transactions and no attempt by individuals to distinguish themselves. If the *sagali* is a dramatic statement of the matrilineage's internal strength, solidarity, and homogeneity that is presented to the external world, this final party suggests that even this external demonstration is no longer necessary.[25]

Like the *sagali*, this party with its private, nontransactional structure, is anomalous within the overall pattern of northeast Normanby Island feasting. Indeed, the only similar northeast Normanby Island event is a small private party that matrilineage members occasionally hold to cook and eat feast-quality bananas or an elephant taro that had been raised near their stone platform. Food served at this party is dangerous to all but members of the owning matrilineage because it is so intimately linked with their land.

In contrast to that of other feasts, the message carried by these parties is not "about" the relation of the sponsoring matrilineage to other matrilineages as created and expressed through formal exchange. Rather, sharing food within the matrilineage demonstrates the identity of all members with their collective ancestors in the final mortuary feast and to their hamlet land consecrated by their ancestors' graves in the hamlet party.[26]

In other words, in both kinds of parties internal sharing provides the idiom in which to express unity and homogeneity. With both parties, sharing can only be formally demonstrated through being articulated by the formal use of food. In the case of the hamlet party the food used is grown near and hence embodies the matrilineal ancestors. In the case of the final mortuary party the food is consecrated to the ancestors by being assembled for but not given during the *sagali*. Food, land, and ancestors are formally identical. However, although all three are used in each of the four phases of the mortuary sequence, only by the final, dramatically contrastive and unusual formal sharing rather than the more common formal exchange of food is this identity finally overtly expressed.

ONE-, TWO-, THREE-, AND FOUR-PARTY EXCHANGE STRUCTURES

Events of the first mortuary phase are built around an underlying two-party structure in which the immediate matrilineage mates of the deceased face an opposed group of distant matrilineage mates and members of associated matrilineages. Two-party transactions are not unknown in northeast

Normanby Island.[27] However, their infrequency and the fact that the transactions of this phase occur within a matrilineage underscore the extent of
the threat to matrilineal solidarity that death offers.

During the second phase, transactional activity reflects the typical four-
party structure found during affinal feasting. In addition to the two central
matrilineages that formally exchange goods, there are two outside matrilineages, one providing and the other receiving the majority of these goods.
Like all four-party transactions, these display the matrilineage in its fully
developed historical role based on a variety of historically created and hence
historically dissolvable affinal ties to other matrilineages. As such, these
feasts reflect the historical component of matrilineality, forcing matrilineage
mates to recognize and act upon that aspect of their identity that is embedded within other matrilineages, if only so that their own matrilineage can
gain local fame and reproduce itself.

Sagali-type mortuary feasts are three-party events in which the third, recipient party is a generalized nonmatrilineally defined residual collectivity.
However, the real productive power of *sagali* type feasts derives from the
division of the feasting universe along geographical rather than genealogical
lines. Consequently, *sagali* can mark that idealized ahistorical aspect of matrilineal identity. They transcend the contradictions within matrilineality requiring external marital and paternal ties and a search for fame in the historical world.

Formally, the final, one-party party involving only matrilineal members
is the structural opposite of the three-party *sagali*. If the *sagali* reflects the
accomplishments of the ahistorical matrilineage within a geographically defined but still historical world with all the temporal vagaries that it implies,
the final party moves outside the historical world altogether to a realm of
motionless matrilineal essence. It is a static celebration of the matrilineage's
existence in and of itself, outside time and outside the external social world.

Thus, there are two mirror movements in transactional form. The first,
focusing upon and deriving from the death of a specific person, consists of
the movement from a two-party event within a matrilineage reflecting the
challenge to matrilineality itself to a four-party event between matrilineages
that recreates and then breaks the deceased's full complex of affinal relations. In doing so, it allows the deceased to disengage himself or herself from
his or her historically created relations to return to anonymous matrilineage
membership. The second and complementary movement focusing upon the
matrilineage as a whole moves from the three-party *sagali* creating fame
within the historical and explicitly geographically structured world to the
final one-party party revealing essence within the ahistorical world.

Underlying both the idiom of geography and the idiom of matrilineality
are a series of oppositions—the natural and the cultural, the given and the

created (or derived), the physiological and the acquired, the consanguineal and the affinal, the shared and the exchanged, the maternal and the paternal, even the "body" and the "spirit"—that are always problematic. Northeast Normanby Island mortuary ceremonies do not resolve or mediate these oppositions. Nor do they serve simply to maintain and codify belief in the formal priority and naturalness of the matrilineage in some naively functional sense, though, for a moment, they may seem to achieve this goal.

Rather, by refracting the matrilineage when threatened by death through the natural, ahistorical landscape, the mortuary cycle articulates various different dimensions of these unresolvable contradictions. It points to the impossibility and yet the necessity of trying to enact the ahistorical within a world of history, an enactment that must be repeated in each generation if the matrilineage is to reproduce itself. If anything, it is the tension of the historical and the ahistorical, the creative and the static, that makes the collective representation of death—the division of "body" and "spirit"—and life—their conjoining and consequent conflict—the key to the underlying problematic of northeast Normanby Island life.

NOTES

Acknowledgments: This essay is based on field research conducted in Loboda village located on Normanby Island in the Milne Bay Province, Papua New Guinea, from September 1975 to May 1977. It was supported by the National Institute of Mental Health (Grant Number 1 F31 MOH5340). An earlier draft of it was presented at the 1981 Conference on the Kula at the University of Virginia. Discussion of the essay with the participants at the conference and detailed comments on a later draft by Fred Damon and Susan Montague helped me clarify and develop many of the issues that it raises.

I gratefully acknowledge the help and encouragement that I received from Bunsa Taukwaelo, Toni Lemunaiya, Lasaro, Malaipa, and Manuweli, who were my principal consultants as I sought to understand Loboda Village mortuary practices.

1. This description of the northeast Normanby Island mortuary sequence was given to me during a *Basa* mortuary feast that I attended several days after arriving in Loboda Village.

2. Northeast Normanby Island people argue that intramatrilineal marriage should be avoided because the normal kinds of exchange between affinally related matrilineages are impossible within a matrilineage. Given the feeling that there is a homogeneity and essential physiological identity of all matrilineage members, no structural basis exists for defining two opposed sides that can transact with one another. See Fortune (1962) for a discussion of marriage within the matrilineage.

3. The category of *tomotai* includes not only all human beings in the conventional western sense but also a variety of beings such as *tokwatokwai* (dwarfs),

tonitonibakwa (elves), and *welabana* (witches) that live in the *welabana mitowaiya* (deep bush), *welabana gaula* (rock caves), or *galaboi* (ocean). *Bebai* variety yams are also *tomotai*, and as such possess a "mind." This accounts for their independence and self-will and for the respect with which they are regarded by the careful gardener (cf. Fortune 1962).

Many suggest that all normal animals, both domesticated and wild, possess a "spirit" that accounts for their manifest intelligence. By contrast, the automatons like familiars of witches, *diyadiya* (certain bats), and *mwalikwakwakwa* (a flying stone) that are controlled solely by their owners, lack a "spirit" and are described as consequently *hwohwa* (mindless, foolish, or idiotic), a term that can be applied to humans, particularly children, not displaying normal or reasonably expectable intelligence.

4. In a close parallel to the principles underlying this division of the person into "body" and "spirit," *welabana* (witches) are believed to be motivated by matrilineal concerns, killing those who fail to share properly within their matrilineage. By contrast, *barahu* (sorcerers) are motivated by individualistic concerns, killing those outside their matrilineage who compete for prestige with them or who otherwise offend their unpredictable sensibilities (cf. Thune 1980). Witches do not derive their power from a voluntary decision but are initiated by their mothers. Sorcerers make a conscious decision to acquire their knowledge, which is strictly technological. Some speculate that it is the witch's "spirit" that travels about at night as her body sleeps in her house.

5. But many people suggest that some sort of human spirit may remain resident within or around the hamlet in which the body was buried. Some argue that those people who were troublesome in life leave the *yaluwaluwa biti* (a bad spirit), that may drift about the hamlet as a general nuisance, frightening people, preventing babies from sleeping, and the like. Or such a spirit may walk about the village at dusk carrying the fruits of its bad deeds—for example, a stolen pig or betel nuts were the deceased a thief.

The general consensus is that before missionization, most "spirits" of Normanby Island dead went to Bwebweso, a desolate geologically disturbed area roughly northeast of Sewa Bay. There they maintained a social existence with other "spirits" that was analogous to that of ordinary living people.

Today the status of Bwebweso is considerably more confused, for Christian notions of heaven and, to a degree, hell are at least vaguely known and accepted. One theory has it that with missionization the Christian God "stirred up" the ground at Bwebweso and took all of the then-resident "spirits" to heaven. Today, according to many, "spirits" go directly to the Christian heaven or hell without going to Bwebweso first. Other theories suggest that Bwebweso may be a way station where "spirits" await God's decision regarding them, that perhaps it is a sort of purgatory, or even that some "spirits" go there and others go to heaven.

An additional uncoordinated belief is that "spirits" of victims of cannibal feasts went, apparently automatically, to Budibudi. There they were condemned eternally to gather wood each morning to build a fire on which they would immolate themselves each afternoon. Presumably they continue to do so today.

174

6. This is a condensation of an approximately thousand-word story told by Lasaro of Loboda village.

7. *Bwebweso* is both a generic term for any home of the dead and a specific name for the Normanby Island site tenanted by "spirits" of Normanby, Dobu, and east Fergusson islands. Hence, both Tuma, where the Trobriand dead are said to go, and wherever the dead of America or Europe presumably go would also be termed *Bwebweso*. Sharing a common Bwebweso is a mark of a relatively unified cultural and ethnic group.

People avoid Bwebweso or, at least, pass through the area only by day. There is no cult or even propitiation of the dead analogous to that found in the Trobriands.

At least in cultural, if not psychological, terms Róheim was correct when he noted that alongside this hostility of the dead to the living there is a complementary hostility of the living to the dead engendered by their feelings of abandonment. Many spontaneous mourning wails and laments could be read as reflecting both a sadness and an anger about the passing of a relative upon whom they were dependent (Róheim 1950).

8. Almost all northeast Normanby Islanders are at least nominal Christians. Hence Normanby Islanders have a variety of not clearly formulated Christian-derived beliefs about the soul and the nature of death that exist alongside the more traditional theory presented here. I do not deal with these beliefs because they are not articulated with the overall understanding of social relations or with the normal mortuary sequence.

9. Hence, the typical sorcerer is a man sufficiently absorbed into his own marriage that he lives an isolated life within a detached nuclear family. Although such a sorcerer rarely kills his own matrilineal mates, his unwillingness to submit to any form of social control makes him an object of fear by all.

10. See Thune (1980) for a more detailed treatment of the northeast Normanby Island conceptualization of the geographical world.

11. This is not to suggest that the movement from one's hamlet to hamlets of affinally related matrilineages and then to the residual geographical world is merely a measurement of increasing geographical distance from one's stone platform. An unrelated hamlet immediately adjacent to one's matrilineage's hamlet may be formally far more distant than a hamlet owned by a branch of one's matrilineage in southern Normanby Island or even on another island.

12. In the past people were buried in the center of their hamlet near the stone platform. As a result of government and mission pressure, today most are buried on the *mwaumwau* (outskirts) of their hamlets or, more infrequently, in the matrilineage-owned section of a hamlet cluster cemetery.

However, even today very young children and very old women who have long lived in, cared for, looked after, and "loved" their hamlet may be buried near their stone platform. Structurally these are people who are most central to their matrilineage because they are least alienated from it through their external ties. Even should a person be buried on the outskirts of his or her hamlet, he or she hopes to be buried in the mother's grave, in effect returning to the solidarity that he or she had with her and her ancestors before she died. By contrast, troublesome or diffi-cult people or those who deliberately isolate themselves from their matrilineage may be buried in the bush far away from the living.

13. The only other time a matrilineage might be divided in this fashion would be after an "incestuous" marriage within it. Under such circumstances the ma-trilineage temporarily splits in half for marriage transactional purposes. Notably, both death and improper marriage reflect an extreme dissociation of an individual from at least part of his or her matrilineage.

14. Each grave is surrounded and protected by a low thatched roofed grave house. The grave house is created for purely mundane reasons: it helps keep pigs and dogs away from the grave. Some suggest that the *duguma* house serves to mark the grave house so visitors will not confuse it with the play houses children fre-quently construct.

15. Some suggest that the *duguma* house is placed on the grave house in order to distract the attention of cannibalistic witches. Witches planning on stealing the body take the *duguma* house instead.

16. In bush areas where people do not fish, a hunting expedition may be or-ganized instead.

17. In fact even after the *Bwabwali* the deceased's matrilineal mates continue to have a certain portion of their identity embedded within the deceased's spouse. Throughout the life of the surviving spouse he or she will be referred to as *ida kwabula* (our widow) or *ida sibouwa* (our widower).

A widow or widower can never enter the hamlet of the deceased spouse. How-ever, the surviving matrilineage mates continue to have an interest in their widows and widowers as possible opposites who may be juxtaposed against them. Should a surviving spouse remarry, that person's new spouse becomes structurally identical to the deceased. As such, this person automatically becomes a *hesuwai* or *gatu* (liter-ally "appearance"), a quasi-adopted member of the deceased's matrilineage who can participate in its formal exchange activities, has access to its gardening land, and can even be buried in its graveyard. The deceased's matrilineal mates acquire similar rights to act as formal members of the matrilineage of their *gatu*. The extent to which these privileges are activated varies considerably on the basis of idiosyncratic factors such as personality and self-interest.

18. See Fortune (1962) for a good summary of the traditional mourning re-strictions in the Dobu–northeast Normanby area.

19. In the *Bwabwali* the structural identity of marriage and paternity is visibly manifest. A father and father's matrilineage play a role identical to that of a spouse and spouse's matrilineage. For a child the father and father's matrilineage and its affines would provide the sole formal mourners. For an adult, they would formally mourn and participate in the *Bwabwali* alongside the deceased's spouse, if still alive, and/or his or her matrilineage, albeit usually on a lesser scale.

20. During the wake, the body is oiled with coconut oil, ostentatiously dis-played in the best quality clothing available (for example, thick new grass skirts for women), and often surrounded by Kula valuables and large yams. Rarely if ever would a person so dramatically decorate himself or herself during life.

21. The preceding discussion is based on the assumption that a married adult

died leaving a surviving spouse. This is the ideal form used by northeast Normanby Island people as they discuss their mortuary customs.

After the death of a widow or widower the structure of the activity is the same, but there is no visible surviving spouse to play the role of central mourner. Events proceed as when there is a surviving spouse, with people simply working around the actual absence of a living person in this structural position. It, however, still serves as a focus for the entire sequence of activities. After the death of a never married person, the father and father's matrilineage take on essentially the same role as that of the surviving spouse. When a person had multiple spouses, what are essentially separate but simultaneous *Bwabwali* are held between the deceased's matrilineage and each of the deceased's spouses, if surviving, and his or her matrilineage.

Note that *Bwabwali* are always paired. When a surviving spouse or father dies the matrilineage of the deceased receives a *Bwabwali* from the matrilineage to which it earlier presented one.

22. Northeast Normanby Island people suggest that *sagali* feasting has expanded in scale since government "pacification" because there is now an external power capable of maintaining the peace between unrelated people who otherwise would quickly revert to the kind of violence that stories from the past graphically describe.

On the other hand, others argue that with the press of garden work, cash cropping, government and mission projects, *sagali* and related feasts have become less frequent than they were in the past.

23. There are also a number of variations on the basic *sagali* such as the *waganeihaneiha* (literally "canoe paddling"; cf. Fortune 1962) made at the completion of a major new canoe. These are structurally identical to it, though of varying scale and complexity.

24. The hamlet as reconstructed for the *sagali* resembles a dramatically idealized version of the ordinary hamlet. The distribution platform is structurally identical to a hamlet's stone platform. Each *sagali* house represents an affinally related matrilineage and its supporters, just as an ordinary dwelling less dramatically represents the presence of an alien matrilineage.

Other feasts are characterized by the elaboration of the familiar—for example, a basket or food storage rack—to provide the focus for the transaction. However, only *sagali* and *gwala* elaborate a piece of territory embodying affinal relations. The other feasts simply elaborate those things such as baskets that are used to present gifts of food to affines on informal day-to-day occasions.

25. Until about twenty years ago the bones, especially the skull and long bones, were exhumed for secondary burial in a small matrilineage-owned cave or hole in the coral rocks along the coast. This reburial was done privately with a minimum of public display and knowledge, by a few of the matrilineage's male elders. After the reburial there was a small private feast or party for matrilineage mates alone.

26. See Thune (1980, 1983) for a discussion of the contrast of exchange and sharing. The only other contexts in which formal sharing occurs are during certain church-sponsored functions such as a wedding or ordination party and during

going-away parties for anomalous outsiders such as teachers (and anthropologists). In both cases, these parties reflect a unity within a geographical area—a hamlet cluster or village—that has no structural integrity within the matrilineal ordering of things and that was only partially successfully created as a conceptual unit through the efforts of the mission and colonial systems.

27. Perhaps the most familiar examples of two-party exchanges are Kula transactions (cf. Thune 1983).

Michael W. Young

"Eating the Dead"

Mortuary Transactions in Bwaidoka, Goodenough Island

◆   In what is a relatively homogeneous culture, the mortuary practices of Goodenough Island are remarkably diverse, probably more so than any other institutional complex. For this reason it is difficult to present a concise account of general validity. The two communities I have studied in depth on several visits over a period of fourteen years, Kalauna and Bwaidoka, make an appropriate paired contrast, since details of their mortuary practices differ in ways that can be related to features of their social organization and respective cultural adaptations to hill and coastal environments and, not least, to their different histories of missionization. But even a controlled comparison such as this would have been scarcely manageable in an essay of this length, and for the purposes of a broader, Massim-wide comparison, an overly schematic picture would be less useful than a bread-and-butter account of the ethnographic findings from a single community on Goodenough. Accordingly, I have selected Bwaidoka since its representative status is probably somewhat greater than Kalauna's and it conforms more readily to conventional notions of Massim societies.

I use *Bwaidoka* in the current sense to refer to the large local government council ward of that name, which comprises four "villages" and a United church (previously Methodist) mission station, situated on the southern shores of a tranquil double bay in southeast Goodenough. At the time of effective European contact about 1900, when the mission was established, there were three villages: Kabune, Bwaidoga, and Ukuna. Although they sometimes fought one another, these villages claim a common ancestry and share a common dialect. Bwaidoga has given its name to the "language" of Goodenough as a whole, and because it was disseminated widely by the Methodist mission it became the standard dialect of the island, orthographically as well as phonologically.

The three original villages have expanded greatly during the last four decades, necessitating local migration.[1] Kabune people have crossed the bay and established a few small settlements there; Ukuna people have moved farther into the hills behind the bay. But Bwaidoga village, hemmed in on either side by Kabune and Ukuna hamlets, expanded across the inner bay until it had virtually reproduced itself in a village called Banada. Old Bwaidoga came to be known as Melala (which means simply "village") as mission and administration appropriated the name for the district, though it is nowadays spelled *Bwaidoka*. Each village is composed of a number of named clans internally divided into subclans and *unuma* (patrilineages). Banada, of course, shares its clan names with its "mother" village, Melala. The *unuma* is the local land-owning and minimal corporate group. Villages tend to be endogamous (approximately 80 percent) though Melala and Banada, understandably, intermarry more frequently with one another.

Jenness and Ballantyne (1920:chap. 9) gave a general account of death and burial in Bwaidoga for the period shortly after contact (1911–12). Their description rings true as far as it goes, but they had little understanding of the categories of kin involved in mortuary tasks, and they seem to have greatly underestimated the complexity of the sequences. (It is a more reasonable inference, I think, that they did not investigate mortuary exchanges with any thoroughness than that the latter have developed such complexity since 1912). I shall be concerned here mainly with the *transactions* that follow a man's death, that is, with the system of exchanges and the politics of burial. I give scant attention to the finer details of mortuary "custom" and the observed behavior of mourning; I do not discuss eschatology, beliefs in sorcery, ghosts, souls, necromancy, or the deprivation of widowhood. Death itself gets short shrift, and I deal only with the practical ways—typically Melanesian in their scope—by which Bwaidokans put death to social and political use.

TAVUNA: BURIAL

All deaths are more or less dissimilar; all marriages are more or less alike. But in Bwaidoka, just as every marriage is linked through the exchange system to several other marriages, so is every death linked to many other deaths. When a death in the family occurs, the first problem facing the survivors is not how or where to dispose of the body, but precisely who shall

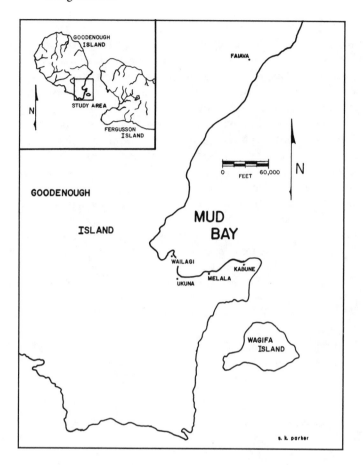

dispose of it. Choosing the *tomotavuna* (gravedigger(s), whom I shall call "burier(s)" is a decision not lightly made. In almost all cases this decision has to be made by a close male agnate (father, brother, son) of the deceased; he is *toinavuvuna* ("root man"), though I shall refer to him as the "owner," and the members of his patrilineage or subclan as the "owners." They are in local parlance *tonimelala* (owners of the village), and hence *tonialika* (owners of the dead one).

As news of the death spreads through the villages kinsmen go to ask the owner if they can bury. These kinsmen may be distant patrilateral relatives from another subclan; they may be matrilateral relatives, particularly from the deceased's mother's group; or they may be no relation at all, but are sent by a big man in another village who wishes to stress his own link to the deceased. Between ten and twenty men may bury (women also bury in

181

some Goodenough communities, but rarely in Bwaidoka), with the result that there is room for all categories of kinsmen to participate. But unless it has been decided already by the testament of the dead man, the important choice for the owner to make is the group identity of the buriers; this is represented by the man the owner nominates as the chief burier, for he in turn chooses most of the other buriers.

Broadly speaking, the owner has two options. He can declare that his own group will bury, which means he will nominate several young men from his own (the dead person's) hamlet. One of these will assume the role of leader and recruit other buriers from his mother's group and his father's sisters' sons' (FZS) group, until the burial team has a suitably mixed and wide-ranging social composition. But the fact remains that agnates are burying their own. The other option is the one fraught with most difficulties, yet all else being equal it is the one most attractive to an ambitious man. This is to nominate the dead man's "mother's group" as chief buriers.[2] Actual genealogical reckoning may not be important here, for the actors think in terms of categories. Hence "mother's group" might be "mother's mother's group," and it is easier to determine the relationship from the point of view of the would-be burier who is pressing to bury his *tubuga* (sister's child [ZC], FZC, or FFZC). For simplicity's sake, however, I shall follow Bwaidokan usage in speaking of "mother's group" and "*tubuga*" even when the actual relationships concerned are more distant, as in figure 1.

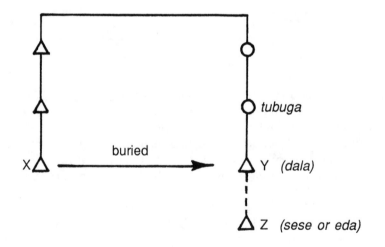

FIGURE 1.

Two generations ago a woman of X's lineage in Bwaidoka married a Faiava man from the far side of Mud Bay; this lineage called her child *tubuga*, a term colloquially applied to *her* children too, including Y. Strictly speaking, however, *tubuga*'s child is *dala*, and there is a series of other terms for subsequent generations, until kinship through the linking female is said to "finish" after five generations, after which marriage is possible between them. I have indicated Z by *sese* (bridge) or *eda* (road), generic terms for this way of tracing kinship through women who marry out of the subclan or lineage. In this particular case, X went to Faiava with a number of his agnates and was permitted to bury Y. X spoke of Y as his *tubuga* and Y's kinsmen spoke of X and his "brothers" as Y's "mother's group," though some at least were aware that strictly speaking it was not. In the burial payments that followed, all the goods flowed from Y's group to X's group, except the last, which was repaid by X. The crucial item of information to make this illustration intelligible (for why should the owner give the burial task to a group from another village?) is that an ancestress (Y's grandmother [GM]) was buried by her Faiava husband's group. From this perspective, then, X was permitted to bury Y in an explicit reciprocation called *daima ana fata* (paying back the digging stick). In similar ways are all deaths and marriages linked over the generations.

Sometimes *tubuga* ask to bury their mother's brothers (MBs), but this is considered to be bad form unless special circumstances prevail (for example, adoption by MB). The reason is that ZSs should not put themselves into the position where MBs are obligated to them. Burial is a supremely "dirty" task in which one becomes contaminated with the body dirt of the corpse—to the extent that a burier may never roll a cigarette for the widow for the rest of his life. It therefore connotes a menial task, albeit one willingly undertaken, which must be massively compensated. In essence, to bury someone is *a veveola* ("asking for food"), which as I have shown elsewhere is tantamount to a challenge as well as a form of soliciting (Young 1983a). As "wife-receivers" the patrilineal group of which ZS is a member should show more respect to their MBs, the "wife-givers." Given this principle of fundamental inequality, it is entirely appropriate that a member of the woman-transferring group should bury a member of the woman-receiving group, if what is at issue is the direction of the flow of wealth and food. One Bwaidoka man put it simply:

Because my mother came from that place—that is why my brother will give the digging stick to them when I die. My father gave them brideprice before I was born. Then he gave them presents at my birth. I gave them money and wealth when I came back from working abroad. They will bury me when I die, and my brothers will give them my wealth and gardens. Then it is finished. Someone else will bury my brothers.

This man also refers to a subsidiary principle: MBs bury only one ZC of a sibling set, ideally the firstborn (a tokenism that applies in other domains of the culture). None of this means that *tubuga* may never bury MBs, for it sometimes happens that the owner of a dead man will invite one to do so, or that a MB, nominated to bury by the owner, may select the deceased's *tubuga* for his own reasons (for example, his father's sister's daughter's son [FZDS]). Indeed, the broadest principle of all—notwithstanding the group identity pinned onto the burial group through the relationship of the leading burier to the dead man—is that the buriers should represent the widest spectrum of the dead man's kindred, the *makakaudiga*. This effectively ensures that the food and wealth that flow after a death trickle into the farthest corners of Bwaidoka along the channels of kinship.

It is the relative weighting, therefore, of matrilateral to patrilateral kinsmen in the burial group that allows people to declare that the "mother's group" is burying or that they are "burying themselves." Much hinges on this distinction, so much in fact, that the dead can be forgotten while the issue is decided. I have seen groups of men argue for an entire day over who is to bury, while the corpse lies neglected and unmourned, stiffly awaiting the outcome. The issue is simply this: if MBs are permitted to bury, then the owners have a hard year ahead of them, straining their resources to the utmost to meet the customary obligations to repay the "mother's group" for its services. Far less work is involved, on the other hand, if the owners bury for themselves, together with a few token members of other groups. Hence the issue slides toward the competitive vein of Goodenough culture: the challenge of the gardens and the taunts of being "afraid" (of hard work, of being unable to match the efforts of others). The issue is magnified if the death was that of a big man or a *tobakula* (garden man); then it is almost incumbent on the owners to let MBs bury him. Only in this way would his memory be honored by the work done on his behalf. When MBs bury it is *faisewa vitana* (heavy work, in both its current English senses). When agnates bury, it is *faisewa meyameyagina* (easy, carefree work), tantamount to a private burial with few social repercussions and little investment of social labor. Small wonder that the corpse must wait while the matter is thrashed out.

If it is too late to bury on the day of death there is a wake, attended by "sons" and "brothers" from both sides of the family. Throughout the night a sister warms her hands and rubs the joints and smooths the face of the corpse to delay their stiffening, though she must be careful to avoid touching the widow after performing this duty. The brothers turn the corpse on its mat periodically. There is still no weeping or keening, only the muffled cries of the widow from another house.

The weeping begins in earnest next day, after the body has been laid out for display and after the gravediggers have almost completed their task. If mourning begins before the digging, it is said that the work will be impeded by stones and roots. The hole is deep (Jenness and Ballantyne say eight feet, which is very hard to credit, but I measured one of five feet), and there is a recess or chamber at the bottom to accommodate the body. Sometimes one of the buriers will lie in it to take its measure. This is an act of bravado that the owners must reward at the conclusion of the mortuary sequence. The keening reaches a crescendo as the buriers lift the body, wrap it in one or two new pandanus mats, and carry it to the grave.

Graves are dug on the outskirts of the hamlet, a few feet from the path. There are few if any grave goods: a personal ornament perhaps, a cooked yam "for the journey," or a "Christian ticket," which certifies that the deceased had been baptized and can enter Heaven. Other grave goods are at the whim of the mourners. I once saw a bereaved brother strip himself of the new shorts and jacket he was wearing and tread them into the partly filled grave (though the jacket was retrieved by another man as soon as the brother turned his back). The same man unaccountably sprinkled a box of matches into the grave.

The keening continues while a lay missionary helper reads a short burial service; his dress invariably consists of white shirt and trousers, dark tie, and spectacles. As he reads the dust-to-dust litany the buriers wait alongside or in the grave ready to fill it, and they hold a mat pressed against the wall of stout planks that they fasten to seal the chamber. If the dead man had been a garden sorcerer of notoriety, certain prophylactic rites should be performed before he is lowered into the grave. There are also postburial rites for renowned garden magicians, rites designed to dispel the ancestral spirits who are believed to attend the deaths of such men. These spirits are a threat to the gardens, but they are "blinded" and dispersed by the smoke from magical roots, ritually burned a few days after the burial. Until this is done no one should plant.

MATAILUWANA: "FOOD FOR TEARS"

The ground has been trampled down, the grave marked by a rectangular pile of jagged lumps of coral, and a croton planted at its side. The widow or widower has been carried bodily from the grave side where she or he lay prostrated, now to disappear from the public gaze for weeks, eating "rubbish food" and conveying respect for the dead spouse by looking as pitiable as possible. For the rest of their lives they must avoid the deceased's subclan's property: its food, leaves, land, firewood, canoes, mats, betel nut, pots, eating utensils, stone sitting circle, pigs, reefs, baskets, ornaments, paints. A widow's taboos, particularly, define the composition of a subclan. She risks blindness if she breaches them, and nothing could be more calculated to remind her of her loss than the vigilance required to maintain this total severance from all the "things" she used and lived with while her husband was alive.

Immediately after the burial the gravediggers plunge into the sea and scrub themselves and their implements. When they return a meeting gets under way in the owners' hamlet. As one man defined the purpose of this meeting: "People talk to the dead man's group and ask for things." It might be the first of several meetings, but it is usually the most important. The principal issues to be discussed are (1) the disbursement of funeral gifts called *luwana*, (2) the plans for subsequent mortuary arrangements, (3) the cause of death if circumstances are particularly suspicious (in Kalauna they are invariably suspicious, and all postburial meetings in that village are greatly preoccupied with identifying the source and type of sorcery). All the leaders and prominent men speak and every interest is aired. Such meetings are wonderfully cathartic occasions, and feelings often run high as men review the current state of relations between different sections of the community; they detail previous deaths and their mortuary arrangements, and they review genealogical connections and sundry gardening reputations. Countless grievances surface. The rhetoric veers from pagan images to Christian pieties and back again.

During the meeting the owners' wives put out pots of plain cooked food, and before the crowd disperses at dusk, the owners will have distributed to every household representative who attended (or every representative of each subclan if they are more distant) a gift of uncooked bananas, yams, and sweet potato. This is called *matailuwana*, for those who "cried," and it is not repaid. Some *matailuwana*, however, may be sent to an "enemy" in another village for which an equal quantity of food is immediately returned. This repayment is called *lumaimaiwa* and is said to be for the widow or widower, who, of course, cannot eat any of the owners' food.

LUWANA: FUNERAL GIFTS

Some of the speakers at the meeting are, in effect, "asking for food" in the form of *luwana*, that is, a pig and an appropriate amount of vegetable food to accompany it. They are likely to be distant kinsmen of the dead man, or just good friends in whose houses he had eaten or with whom he regularly went fishing. Some of them may remind the owners about *luwana* pigs given to the dead man at previous burials many years before, for *luwana* must be repaid in time. The owner will have decided already, even before hearing the death rattle, who should get the dead man's pigs and one or two other pigs available in the hamlet. Nevertheless, unexpected claims are invariably made, usually for the repayment of old *luwana* debts that the owner had forgotten or been ignorant of, and the owner is constrained to refuse some of these demands.

There is an exception to the rule that *luwana* must be repaid. If a woman is buried in her husband's hamlet by his group (including her sons), they will also give a *luwana* pig to her own agnates; this is called *vavine luwanidi* (wife's *luwana*). Even if her own group bury her, it can expect to receive the pig she had been rearing when she died, though if she had had no children her agnates would be given wealth items only. This payment is conceived of as "finishing" the marriage, the last installment on her brideprice, as it were, especially deserved if it had been a fruitful union. It used to be the custom that if the husband's family had no pigs to give her group, the latter could claim a child, a ZS preferably, who would then live with his mother's brothers. The child was spoken of as *ana luwana* (the father's *luwana* for his dead wife). This is clearly indicative of the element of "childwealth" in the *luwana* pig given on a woman's death, and more generally indicative of the role of pigs in substituting for humans in Goodenough culture. In this connection it is interesting to note that Jenness and Ballantyne defined *luwana* as "payment for an injury, especially blood-price" (1928:402); they do not mention that it was given as a funeral payment, and it is conceivable that it has evolved as such since 1912.

One or two other pigs might be given at the postburial meeting; these are called *inagetutubuna* ("the insides soothed") and they need not be repaid. The owner gives these in consideration of the feelings of the men—especially the dead man's MBs—whom he had refused permission to bury. Hence, the pig to "soothe the insides" is a form of compensation for the disappointed right to bury a kinsman.

Pigs and vegetable food are not the only things to be disbursed as *luwana* at this meeting. Almost everyone who goes to cry at a burial has good, kinship-justified reasons for being there; likewise, practically everyone has a right to be given *luwana*. These lesser claims the owners meet by the distribution of pots, plates, utensils, shell valuables (rarely given nowadays except to repay old debts), and cash: one or two *kina* here and there. Some of these articles will have belonged to the dead man, in which case they are designated *laova*. This is usually given to MBs, whether or not they bury, since it does not have to be repaid. But many goods and most of the cash will be brought out of the owners' houses. They "help" with *luwana* payments in this fashion and can expect to be repaid at the funerals of others. In contradistinction to *lokoloko laova* (the dead man's wealth), that given by his agnates is designated *lokoloko yawaiyawa* ("wealth of the living").

The right of the "mother's group" to appear on the doorstep of their dead *tubuga's* house and demand some of his wealth, particularly if he is the firstborn, must be reconciled with normative patrilineal inheritance. In practice, fathers take anticipatory evasive action by passing on their baskets of valuables to their eldest sons long before they expect to die; it is an acknowledged part of the retirement process, paralleled by the assumption of land control by mature sons who are said to "take their father's place" even while he is still alive. At his death the eldest son may at his own discretion give one or two pieces of wealth—an arm shell or boar's tusk pendant—to the insistent "mother's group" who are poking about the house in search of things to "remember" their *tubuga* by. Given by the son, however, these items are *luwana* or *lokoloko yawaiyawa* and not *laova*, so they must be repaid, and in fact the identical items are often returned when the son, in his turn, goes to cry at a death in the other's group.

VENIMAIKOLA: "TO WASH THE HANDS"

Throughout the day of burial the owners have been supervising the events, weeping, plotting, orating at the meeting that overflows the hamlet, and worrying about their food supplies. The younger men, if not involved in the burial as gravediggers, will have been dispatched to the gardens to fetch the *matailuwana* food or directed to seize and secure the *luwana* pigs. When not keening over the corpse, the women of the hamlet will have spent their time preparing and cooking the food for the buriers and visitors. This food is plain fare, the first of weeks if not months of boiled vegetables conspicuously unflavored by coconut cream. The prohibition on "squeezed" food (that is, creamed with coconut oil) affects everyone in any way associated with the death. The distribution of this cooked food during the postburial meeting is called *lalau* (literally "hot water"). But it is with a real bowl of hot water that the owner washes the knees, elbows, and shoulder joints of the buriers lest they shiver with the chill of death and their own joints stiffen. They are also given warmed green coconuts to drink.

After the *matailuwana* has been distributed and most of the visitors have gone home, the owners can now think of their own needs. Their exchange partners should have already brought them food and coconuts from their gardens. This gift is called *venimaikola* ("washing the hands"), denoting the service performed for the owners by the exchange partners. Before they sit down to eat, the exchange partners douse the owners with warm water and wipe their hands and faces, which are said to have been "spoiled by tears."

ENOVEKUVEKUBAMA: "SLEEP IN THE DEAD MAN'S PLACE"

Sometimes the hamlet does not empty as dusk descends, and a few of the visitors prepare to stay and camp there for a night or two. These are kinsmen or special friends of the dead man who wish to show respect, especially if the man they mourn had been a big man who had fed them well during life. To "make *kubama*" for him indicates that they are "taking his place" and, however inadequately, filling the void left by his death. Magical notions are involved as well as the idea of comforting the bereaved owners, but *kubama* is a difficult concept to grasp, since it applies also to objects that are lost, misplaced, or left elsewhere than in their "proper" place overnight. A threat to the gardens is invited by the failure to perform *kubama*.

Yet other visitors who may stay overnight actually sleep in the dead man's house; these are the dead man's brothers-in-law (sister's husband [ZHus]). They accompany their wives (Wi) (whose duty as sisters keeps them in their natal hamlet for a day or two) and spread their sleeping mats in the house. This is called *kilelunou* ("to roll up a sleeping mat"), and the men who perform this solicitude can expect to be given food and perhaps a pig on their departure next day. It is the only mortuary gift given to a dead man's affines as such, and it has to be earned in this fashion. (Obviously, brothers-in-law in the category of "wife-givers" [WiB] do not perform *kilelunou*, and the only material benefit they can expect to receive after the death of a ZHus is bride-price if and when their sister remarries.) Pigs given to a ZHus for *kilelunou* are to be repaid in similar circumstances; the practice, in other words, is yet another way of "asking for food."

TOWATOWA: "SWIMMING / WASHING"

A few days after the burial the men of the deceased's village go fishing in their canoes; the women meanwhile collect shellfish on the reefs or in the mangrove swamps. These activities are referred to as *towatowa*. The men deploy their canoes cooperatively and sweep the reefs with their nets and fish spears; they also *towa* (wash) by diving into the sea. Their entire catch is delivered to the owners' hamlet, where it is cooked in pots with vegetable food and the shellfish gathered by the women. This is preparation for another form of *lalau* distribution (the food is not flavored with coconut cream), though it only appears to be done if the owners themselves buried. Unless they are kinsmen—members of the dead man's kindred and their spouses—people from other villages do not attend, since the meeting that follows the distribution of food on this occasion concerns the dead man's village only. Each family will have cooked its own pot of food and fish, and at dusk the pots are pooled and exchanged indiscriminately. Only the chief owner cannot eat of any of them; he is likened to the *kaiwabu* who conspicuously abstains at a feast (see Young 1971:248–53).

For the buriers, however, there are two special pots of banana pudding, succulently saturated in coconut oil. These pots are called *kumakumaga* (hermit crab), and the payment is said to chase away the hermit crabs that are nibbling the corpse. Coconut oil is skimmed from one of the pots and rubbed into the buriers' shoulders, "because they carried the dead man."

VEWAWANA AND *VALEVALETA*: MOURNING TABOOS

The pots of banana pudding given to the buriers signalize that they are henceforth under no obligation to observe food taboos for the dead man: they can "eat anyhow." This contrasts with the situation of the owners and other mourners. After the day of burial, all members of the kindred of the dead man, plus other men in his village of his own generation, are expected to observe a number of prohibitions called *vewawana*. They deny themselves coconut creamed food and betel nut, and they neglect their personal appearance by neither shaving nor combing their hair, and by eschewing all body decoration including new clothes. These *vewawana* prohibitions are so general, however, that I was frequently in doubt as to whether people were taking them seriously. At fairly distant removes from the dead person only one member of each sibling set would do *vewawana*, such that, for example, two brothers would say they could "eat" and one brother would say he could not.

The *vewawana* prohibitions are intensified and compounded by members of the close kindred who observe *valevaleta* taboos. Those who do *valevaleta* are spoken of as the "root" of the kindred, whereas those who do *vewawana* are said to be the "branches." However, I found numerous examples of *valevaleta* who were at some considerable remove from the dead man (for example, MFBSS, MZDS, and, on the father's side, FFBSS and FZSS), so the notion of "root" is a rather elastic one. The principle of *valevaleta* selection is expressed as "elder sibling, younger sibling," and it is the men and women who addressed the dead man as "brother" who adopt this role of principal mourners. Their number may be supplemented by "sons" or "fathers" if the dead man is very old or very young, or if there are few "brothers" in the village. Between ten and twenty persons are *valevaleta* for any death.[3]

The meeting held by the owners and others of the dead man's kindred following the *towatowa* cooked food exchange is to decide what additional foods shall be tabooed to the *valevaleta* and—for a shorter period—the *vewawana*. Traditionally, each clan had its own crop to taboo under such circumstances: a type of yam, a class of bananas, a species of fish. Nowadays such niceties are disregarded, though it is common to taboo a food because it is especially associated with the dead person. A man renowned for his yam magic was commemorated at his death by making all yams taboo to the *valevaleta*; another man who died in Samarai while working in the

190

Burns Philp store had tea, sugar, and biscuits tabooed for him. All such taboos are lifted from all categories of mourners at the *alakuku* ceremony, held about a month after the burial. A general taboo is also placed on the coconut groves of the entire village; this ensures the availability of hundreds of coconuts for the creamed food of the *alakuku*.

In addition to the *vewawana* prohibitions on dress, rich foods, and foods specifically tabooed by the owners, the *valevaleta* must avoid the dead man's things. They should not ride on his canoe, catch fish on his reef, take firewood from his land, nor, least of all, eat food from his gardens or fruit from his trees. As if this were not enough, the *valevaleta* cannot eat from each other's gardens or even their own. This taboo, the supernatural sanction for which is deafness and bad breath, causes much petty inconvenience, for men have to exchange food from their gardens with their children or friends who are not *valevaleta*, and their wives often have to cook two pots each night.

GUFA: "FRESH WATER"

A few weeks after the burial another major payment is made to the buriers. *Gufa* is a mixed payment comprising the *lokoloko laova* (remaining wealth) of the dead man and *lokoloko yawaiyawa* (a great deal more wealth contributed by the owners and their helpers). The items include shell valuables, tools, plates, pots, utensils, clothes, and cash. They are placed in two piles according to category and distributed to the buriers so that each man gets something from both piles. As in the case of *luwana* payments, *laova* may be kept without repayment but *yawaiyawa* must be repaid. The former is said to be "cooked" and the latter "raw"; it is the "raw" that is repaid a few days later.

Within days there may be another payment, this time of uncooked food only, which is designed to complement the *gufa*. This prestation, called *lifi* ("to cover"), consists of the same categories of "dead" and "living," "cooked" and "raw," as the *gufa*. And as before, the "raw" *yawaiyawa* pile of food must be repaid, and the buriers and their helpers try to manage to repay it a few days later. Their measured return is called *nimatutagona* ("stepping/pressing on the hand").

GUFAIYAFI: "WATER SPRINKLE"

Some time during the month that follows the burial, the owners provide a few pots of food for their exchange partners, the ones who performed the service of "hand washing" on the day of burial. *Gufaiyafi* is an explicit reciprocation of this service and the food that accompanied it. The owners take the greasy leaves used as pot lids and shake them over the heads of their exchange partners. This lifts the taboo they had been observing since the burial of not accepting food, betel nut, or tobacco from the owners.

ALAKUKU: "SPITTING OUT"

The first new moon after the burial is said to "blow the dirt off the skin." It signals preparation for one of the largest—and certainly the gayest—transactions of the mortuary sequence. If the "mother's group" had not buried then it is common to end the sequence with *alakuku*, for once the *vewawana* have been released from their prohibitions and allowed to eat normally again, the only observances that remain are those of *valevaleta* and the immediate family of the deceased, and the only subsequent feasts or ceremonies are of a private rather than public or villagewide nature.

Every household in the village cooks for *alakuku*, as do kinsmen of the deceased in other villages. The coconut trees are stripped, and men accumulate betel nut and tobacco; they fish for days before, and women collect shellfish from hitherto tabooed beaches. As in the *towatowa* exchange, the pots of food are chalked for easy identification, then pooled and distributed almost randomly. It is up to the recipient to complain if he has been given one belonging to someone whose things are taboo to him, or if it is much smaller than the one he contributed.

Before the distribution of pots, however, the *vewawana* people have their taboos lifted by one of the owners. He offers them food from a pot containing *laova* food from the dead man's gardens. Every person takes a morsel, chews it for a second, spits it out, then takes another mouthful and swallows it. The same ceremony occurs with a second pot, this time of the vegetable water or broth in which the *laova* food was cooked. While this is happening the owner walks among the *vewawana* and brushes their shoulders with a greasy banana leaf from one of the *laova* pots. This completes the lifting of their taboos, and they may now eat anything from anyone's gardens, shave their beards, or trim their skirts. There is a festive atmosphere as the pots are exchanged, and later that evening after a rich and satisfying meal, singing and dancing—though not in the owners' hamlet—continue till dawn.

In the owners' hamlet another meeting of the kindred is held. This time it is to discuss the strategy for completing the "work" for the dead man. If the "mother's group" did not bury, then the only work left to do is to release the *valevaleta* and the owners from their remaining taboos. This must be done at a second, smaller *alakuku* that concerns only the "root" of the kindred.

If the "mother's group" did bury, however, then a number of strategies are possible for making them the final, massive payment.

BWABWALE: "BLACK HOLE"

Bwabwale should take place about a year after the *alakuku* for the *vewawana*. It is often more rushed than this nowadays and may occur a month or two later; men have other things to do than work tirelessly for their leading owner, and the *valevaleta* become impatient with the taboos still upon them. They all complain quite openly about having to work and wait so long for something that, providing the pigs can be found, could be finished in a matter of weeks.

The several ways of paying *bwabwale* are described as "long" or "short," according to their complexity. I list them in order of increasing length:

1. The owners and their helpers, including *valevaleta*, of course, amass raw food and two or three pigs and give them directly to the buriers. This is the basic form of the *bwabwale*. The food is displayed in two large food frames: one designated *laova* (dead man's food) and the other *fayawaiyawa* (gardens of the living). The pigs are similarly categorized. Although the buriers take everything and redistribute it among their own kindreds—so that after a *bwabwale* the whole of Bwaidoka eats—they must repay the "raw" *fayawaiyawa* food frame and 'pigs of the living'. Conscientious buriers recognize that these repayable gifts (which amount to somewhat more than the non-repayable *laova*) are their *niune*, which means they should be passed on to their exchange partners for distribution (see Young 1983a). If this happens the exchange partners repay on the following day in measured quantities; only then can the buriers eat it. Days or perhaps weeks later, the buriers make their repayment to the owners, who redistribute it to all those who contributed to the burier's *yawaiyawa*. This transaction is the last one to involve the buriers as a group, and through them the particular social configuration or network of recipients and donors.

2. Everything takes place as in (1), except that instead of passing on the *fayawaiyawa* food and pigs to the chief burier's exchange partners, he invites his traditional enemy from some village beyond Bwaidoka to come and take it. If this happens, the food ends up in the bellies of the traditional enemy's exchange partners and its (preferably incremented) repayment returns to the buriers by the same route.

3. After the *alakuku* the owners take their still unshaven beards to a village beyond Bwaidoka, preferably traditional enemies, and challenge

them to a competitive food exchange or *abutu* (Young 1971). The owners' whiskers are said to "ask for food." Other villages are wary of mourners, men with beards, for the beards signify that they have well-stocked gardens under taboo, so they may be "afraid" and refuse the challenge. If, on the other hand, they have dead of their own they wish to commemorate or buriers they wish to pay with sumptuous food, then a deal may be struck. The *abutu* food that comes back from the enemy can then be (a) given directly to the buriers as *bwabwale* or (b) rerouted through exchange partners so that it is the Bwaidoka payback that furnishes the *bwabwale*. This is a "long way" that, although it is meant to increment the final prestation to the buriers, can result in misunderstandings, quarrels, and a good deal of bad feeling. Fractiousness is an exponential function of the number of stages in a ceremonial exchange and the numbers of people involved in carrying them through.

This strategy also involves the buriers' giving some of their own food and pigs to the owners for their trouble in fighting an enemy with "the dead man's food"—for there is no doubt that the *abutu* is challenged in the name of the dead man, and his yams are given pride of place in the displays. The buriers' compensation to the owners is called *kamoita* ("see stomach").

4. An even longer way to pay *bwabwale* is what every ambitious owner dreams of doing, though, alas, he is almost invariably defeated by the inertia of his less inspired and less energetic followers, and by the prospect of other calls on his hamlet's food wealth. The last time this "way" was followed in Bwaidoka was in the midfifties.

After *alakuku* the owners sponsor a *Modawa* (drum) or *Fakili* (comb) festival, or a version of the type of *Sagali* found throughout west Fergusson Island (Young 1971:Chapter 11). These festivals, lasting a year or more, honor the dead man by regular nightly entertainment: singing, dancing, and food distributions. They also give scope for an entirely different range of auxiliary exchanges and are major feats of organization and enterprise.

When the pigs are mature or the owners for other reasons need to end the festival, they can either give their amassed food and several pigs to the buriers directly as *bwabwale* or first seek *abutu* with an enemy as in option (3).

A variant of this procedure, and one that more readily ensures an *abutu* contest with a neighbouring village at the end, is to set various taboos on the village, thereby "closing" it; and when innocent visitors unwittingly transgress they are bullied into making *abutu*. This is a type of *kwala* (compare the *gwala* or *gwara* of Dobu and elsewhere), though strictly speaking *kwala* is the taboo that is placed on the dead man's stone sitting circle, and it is the deliberate breach of this taboo by an "invading" village that challenges *abutu*, thereby "opening the village." As indicated previously, however, any *abutu* food derived by these strategies is passed to the buriers as *bwabwale*.

INUWA ("REMEMBERING") OR EBANUADUDU ("MEMORIAL FEAST")

Some years after the burial the owners and other close kinsmen of the dead man may provide themselves with a modest commemorative feast. This does not concern the buriers, for whom the death was "finished" with *bwabwale*. Such feasts are an indulgence for the owners, all of whom—except the chief owner, who should provide the pig—may eat. He will have kept a relic of the dead man for *inuwa*: a shirt, walking stick, lime gourd or spatula, fingernail or lock of hair. This relic will be ceremonially burned while the pig is being butchered for distribution. One man kept the radio of his dead brother, dismantled it for the memorial feast, and burned the pieces. In 1977 I left a shirt in Melala with which to wrap the body of my "father," who was then very close to death; when I returned in 1980 I provided a pig for an *inuwa* feast that people referred to as "shirt." Nowadays there may be one more memorial feast if a relatively wealthy owner decides to lay a cement block on the grave; "cement" is acknowledged to be a European custom, however.

SIDAMANENA: "MISTAKES"

No account of Bwaidoka mortuary transactions would be complete without a mention of the blunders that occur in every sequence. On my first field trip, with only fragments of a given sequence to observe, I attributed the quarrels that arose over the "proper" way of doing things to a kind of bumbling ignorance of customs long since subverted by the mission. Informants who were unsure of the correct procedure themselves blamed the mission: "Our fathers did not teach us properly"; "We have forgotten how to do this." Although it may be true that some of the "long" sequences are so infrequently followed that procedural rules have indeed been forgotten, I now believe that charges of "making mistakes" are instances of political rhetoric in circumstances in which the options are legion.

A list of common "mistakes" in the mortuary practices would be out of place here, although, as might be expected, genuine confusion frequently arises over who should get what in the distributions, and whether or not the transactions should be repaid. Misunderstandings often arise over the *laova* (cooked) and *yawaiyawa* (raw) distinction, and the wealth and food in each category get mixed up so that arguments arise over precisely what is to be repaid. (I hardly need mention my own confusion at their confusion when it came to sorting out bunches of bananas and baskets of yams on the ground.)

There are also innovations, though for the most part these are branded as "mistakes" too, for political reasons as well as conservative resistance to change. In 1973 a Banada big man was in Port Moresby with his Melala sister's husband when the latter died. The big man paid for the body to be flown home, then decided to take on the role of owner, though he delegated the task of choosing the actual buriers to the president of the local government council, another Banada man. He mollified public opinion by recruiting eighteen young men representing a wide spectrum of the dead man's kindred. Nevertheless, it was an unprecedented presumption to abrogate the rule that agnates are owners and to take charge of a brother-in-law's mortuary arrangements. (One of the big man's motives was to divert suspicion from himself in case he was suspected of practicing sorcery against the dead man in Port Moresby.)

According to some Ukuna kinsmen who aired their complaints during the postburial meeting for another death months later, the big man compounded his "mistakes" by (1) giving *luwana* pigs to the real owners instead of nonrepayable *inagetutubuna*; (2) making a "party" of the *alakuku*, with tables for communal eating so that the *vewawana* were mixed with others and improperly released from their taboos; (3) insulting the dead man ("eating his bones") by turning the *alakuku* into a kind of welcoming party ("as if he was coming back from Moresby alive"); and (4) confusing Ukuna village by giving them an undesignated pig, so they did not know whose *niune* it was and who should repay it. These were serious charges, and the Banada leader was hard put to answer them, though he affected colossal indignation at their looking gift horses in the mouth, especially since his generous prestations had been made at a time of drought and local food scarcity.

"A MAN DIES AND YOU TALK ABOUT MARRIAGE!"

Such was the big man's retort to the protest that he had no right to bury his brother-in-law. Such too would be many an anthropologist's observation on listening to the oratory at any of the postburial meetings in Bwaidoka. But marriages are predictable and can be ordered in ways that death cannot. Deaths, moreover, are dissimilar: men's and women's, children's and grandparents', rubbish men's and big men's. There are also the *gilai* (violent, sudden deaths), which mock the culture's capacity to order death and provide for smooth continuity. There are multiple deaths, too, that demand contingent arrangements, such as occurred in 1973 when three deaths in as many weeks shook one Ukuna clan. The result was a paring down of some of the ceremonies, a joint *alakuku*, and a splendid *bwabwale* ingeniously managed to pay all three sets of buriers at once. Although there was ample scope for "mistakes" here, there were surprisingly few, but another death at this time would have brought havoc to the careful planning.

More generally, too, do mortuary transactions interlock and create a network of reciprocities in time and space through the exchange of food, wealth, and services. In this manner they parallel, echo, and extrapolate marriage transactions; for death must be paid for as life is paid for. There is balance in duration, perhaps, but from the urgent perspective of the present there are only uncertainties, and the business of politics is the interminable attempt to guarantee a future for the play of self-interest, reputation, and name and the unbroken line of descendants.

Death is for Others, whatever the dead man's spear might say when it "asks for food" in an enemy's village. The Bwaidoka mortuary sequence provides a series of optional courses, but to avoid the charge of being "weak" and "afraid" of hard gardening, the owners can be provoked into taking the more strenuous ones. *Waka gi ota* ("the canoe is fleeing"), it is said of a dying man; and it is as if a corpse were like a new canoe, providing the pretext to dare to go abroad and "ask for food." Death is a matter of "heavy work" for the owners as they strive to meet the expectations of those who have buried. They must demonstrate the strength and worth of their dead if he was himself a notable *tobakula* (gardening man).

The logical consequence of this worldly, materialistic, and competitive ethos is that a big man may plan for his own death by providing a premortuary feast: a coercive, anticipatory payment. Thus Abela, a Kabune man with few sons and brothers, killed a pig in 1973 and presented it to his mother's group. He called it his *bwabwale*, his own *laova*, which would not have to be repaid and which thereby committed his mother's brothers to bury him with a flourish when he died. Or again, bearing in mind that MBs are inclined to bury their *tubuga* only once in a while, a big man may prevent their burying one of his brothers in case his own chances of being buried by them are prejudiced. In this scheme, then, I have detected a concern with "reciprocity" rather than "reproduction" (Weiner 1980), and there were times when it seemed that death was just an excuse for shunting food around the village.

Finally, however, despite the politicking about death and big men's endeavors to make social virtues of its necessity, and despite the "mistakes" in procedure that affect only the living (notwithstanding the mystifying pretense that they insult by "eating the dead man's bones"), there is a covert symbolic attempt by the living to overcome the dead. At this level the mortuary sequence is about learning to "eat" the dead man, to absorb and assimilate him until he has disappeared without trace. (As cannibals in the past,

Bwaidokans used to grind to powder the bones and teeth of their victims in order to ingest them utterly.) The last people to come to terms with his death are those who mourn him most, the *valevaleta* at the "root" of the kindred. By the time they are released from their taboos, the food from the deceased's gardens—the *laova* that is said to be "cooked"—has been wholly dispersed and eaten by others; the *laova* wealth too has been "eaten" by the buriers. And if the buriers were "mother's brothers," as is appropriate, they will have ingested most of their *tubuga*'s things: his gardens, his pigs, and his wealth.

It is tempting to see in this pattern an inversion of the structure found in many, if not most, of the matrilineal societies of the Massim. Burial in these societies involves the symbolic reconstruction of the dead person through substitutions of food, pigs, or wealth, and there is a "reclamation" of personhood by the owning matrilineage. The pattern is less clear-cut in Bwaidoka, though there is a sense in which the bones (apt symbols of agnatic continuity) are retained by the owning patrilineage while all other remains are incorporated by other patrilineages. Ideally, in the exemplary case of the firstborn, it is the mother's patrilineage that claims these symbolic components of personhood. It is as if the mother's brothers were redeeming the loss of their sister and her procreative power, an interpretation that gains some support from the fact that *tubuga* also means "to be born" and "to grow/increase." The burial of *tubuga* confirms the right to "eat" him. The imagery of cannibalism may seem fanciful or fortuitous, but it is consistent with an embarrassing ethnographic secret of Bwaidoka. They believe that before Europeans came, and indeed before pigs were in general use, mother's brothers used to kill, cook, and eat their sister's firstborn child as brideprice. This is the final clue to what may have been the pagan ideology of Bwaidoka: kinship, marriage, and mortuary meet in the belly.

NOTES

1. The total population of Bwaidoka in 1980 was 1,447. Constituent villages were as follows: Kabune (270), Ukuna (408), Melala (287), Banada (405), and Wailagi Mission (76).

2. *Tamadiyavo* is the most common usage for mother's brothers, though it refers also to father's brothers. *Yaudiyavo* is pedantically correct, but like *yau-* for MB/ZC, it is rarely heard. *Susu* for mother's group is occasionally used, though it is frowned upon by purists, who recognize it as a borrowing from Dobuan.

3. Bwaidokans are aware that *valevaleta* is also a Molima term, though they are ignorant of its somewhat different usage there.

Maria Lepowsky

Death and Exchange

Mortuary Ritual on Vanatinai (Sudest Island)

♦ In a small-scale society where almost all deaths are believed due to sorcery or witchcraft, a death generates fear and mutual suspicion among surviving kin and neighbors. On Vanatinai (Sudest Island), an elaborate mortuary ritual sequence forces key members of the deceased's social network into a continuing exchange relationship with one another despite the death of the nodal figure and suspicions of supernatural foul play. These rituals are a formal enactment of harmonious social relations among the living and between the living and the dead. They include the payment of compensation, in the form of ceremonial valuables and other goods, to the heirs of the deceased by affinal mourners and their supporters. Mortuary ritual not only preserves but intensifies the deceased's social ties by the moral pressure to honor the dead through exchange and through ritual expressions of interdependence and peaceful intentions.

Individuals on Vanatinai choose hamlet coresidents and exchange partners from a wide social field of possibilities. During the crisis of death, threats of sorcery can rupture ties of coresidence, affinity, and kinship. In other forms of intrahamlet conflict, the aggrieved individual or faction often moves to another location where at least one person has land rights. The death of a hamlet member forces surviving spouses, who are sometimes suspected of causing or willing the death, to remain in the deceased's hamlet until the end of the long mortuary ritual sequence, fulfilling mourning obligations and contributing labor and valuables toward each mortuary feast. If conflicts follow a death, other residents may move away, but they too must contribute to mortuary feasts. Their failure to do so would constitute an open breach of peaceful social relations.

Death on Vanatinai forces a renegotiation of existing social contracts through mortuary ritual exchanges involving the kin, affines, patrilateral connections, neighbors, and exchange partners of the deceased. It is also the occasion for renegotiating the contract between the living and the dead. All human good fortune is believed due to the favor and goodwill of ancestor spirits. Failure to honor the spirit of the deceased risks the anger of not only this spirit but all ancestor spirits, who might retaliate by causing crop failures, drought, sickness, and death. In the exchange between the living and the dead, the living preserve and honor the memory of the deceased by observing mourning taboos and exchanging with one another the goods and valuables consecrated to the deceased and symbolizing fertility and rebirth. The ancestor spirits reciprocate by bestowing future good fortune upon the living.

Mortuary ritual events are a major arena for the formation of new social ties among all participants. New primary relationships are often formed between individuals who were previously connected only by ties to the deceased. Participants may arrange future exchanges of goods or valuables that are completely unrelated to the current mortuary sequence. Many local marriages trace their origins to a meeting at a mortuary feast. The opportunity these feasts provide for courtship is critical in a region of low population density and settlement by small, dispersed hamlets consisting largely of kinfolk.

The ongoing demands of the mortuary ritual sequence generate the production of a surplus of foodstuffs and household goods that are also used in a wide range of intra- and inter-island exchanges between individuals. They are the primary stimulus for these individual exchanges, which are the local equivalent of Kula (Lepowsky 1983). Mortuary ritual provides an avenue to prestige for individual men and women who choose to host mortuary feasts or to contribute more heavily to them than the minimum demanded by custom. The temporary accumulation of one's own surplus production plus that of others followed by the public distribution of goods to heirs of the deceased at a mortuary feast earn an individual the coveted title of *gia* (literally "giver"), the local term meaning both "big man" and "big woman" (Lepowsky 1989a and 1989b). Mortuary ritual reflects the relative equality of the sexes found on Vanatinai. Women as well as men may choose to compete in the same arena of prestige, accumulating and giving away the same kinds of valuables. Vanatinai mortuary ritual also reflects the tension between individual autonomy and power as a cultural ideal and the pressure to cooperate with and be generous to others, a pressure that may take the form of magical coercion.

Each mortuary ritual event mirrors the ongoing dynamics of Vanatinai social life. Each is an attempt at conflict resolution involving a unique set of individuals and potential social schisms to be mended through the public exchange of valuables. This often leads to a disparity between the cultural ideal of how mortuary ritual should be conducted and how a particular individual's ritual sequence is structured and implemented.

The people of Vanatinai take conscious pride in the fact that they are more culturally conservative and adhere more closely to traditional customs than their neighbors to the northwest, particularly the peoples of the Misima language group. They call these customs *taubwaragha* (the way of the ancestors).

The island called Sudest or Tagula (its Misima language name) on maps and charts is known as Vanatinai (motherland) to its inhabitants. Fifty miles long and eight to fifteen miles wide, it is the largest piece of land for over two hundred miles. In the late 1970s it was home to 2,075 people who spoke nine different dialects of the island's unwritten language. The islanders are swidden horticulturalists who plant yam, sweet potato, taro, manioc, banana, and pineapple in their gardens. Sago is a major staple, and, along with betel nut and yams, exported by sailing canoe to the coralline islands of the Calvados Chain and as far away as Ware Island. Pigs and the shell-disk necklaces known as *bagi* are also major exports to these islands and to Misima. Vanatinai people also fish and collect shellfish on the reef and in the streams; hunt wild pig, monitor lizard, crocodile, possum, and fruit bats; and collect a variety of wild vegetable foods in the rain forest. Per capita cash income is well under twenty dollars per year. There are no hereditary chiefs or officeholders. The society is matrilineal, and women own and inherit garden land, pigs, and ceremonial valuables. Postmarital residence is bilocal, with couples often shifting residence during the year between the hamlets of the two spouses.

DEATH AND THE AFTERLIFE

Almost every death on Vanatinai is attributed to sorcery or witchcraft. The death therefore arouses strong emotions not only of grief but of anger, fear, and guilt directed toward known individuals. It is these dangerous and potentially socially disruptive emotions that mortuary ritual practices channel and assuage.

A sorcerer is called *ribiroi* (literally poison). Although sorcerers do know plant poisons, descriptions of sorcery that I heard during my residence on the island were all of forms of magical attack, also called *ribiroi*, such as the supernatural firing of a projectile into the victim's body or the bespelling of personal leavings. A sorcerer's destructive power is obtained through contact with ancestor spirits and other supernaturals. Most, but not all, sorcerers are male. *Wadawada* (witchcraft) is said not to be indigenous to Vanatinai but to originate on Misima Island. Most, but not all, witches are female. A witch's power is normally inherited at birth, but a number of Vanatinai men and women are said to have learned to be witches. Witches' spirits generally leave their bodies when they are sleeping or dozing and fly to the victim's house, where they magically attack the entrails, causing weakness and lethargy and later sickness and death. Chronic and wasting illnesses and mental illness are usually attributed to witchcraft. Deaths and illnesses on Vanatinai can be blamed on a witch from Misima or the Calvados Chain islands.

Witches often attack their own kin as well as affines, neighbors, and seemingly unconnected individuals. Sorcerers may also attack close associates, but many deaths on Vanatinai are attributed to a sorcerer living in another hamlet on the island. The local sorcerer may be implicated in a death by the belief that his permission must be obtained before another sorcerer may kill someone in the former's hamlet or district, said to be under his supernatural protection. The killer then owes his colleague a death from his own area, a supernatural form of exchange. Witches exchange, too, taking turns at killing and presenting victim's spirits at supernatural cannibal feasts. Most of the powerful men and women described as *giagia* (givers) are believed to know sorcery or witchcraft, but it is said that some of them have not used their deadly skills for years except to protect their kin and neighbors against the attacks of others (Lepowsky 1981: 423–68 and n.d.).

Occasionally deaths on Vanatinai are attributed to taboo violation. Certain sections of reef or stream and certain mountain peaks or rock formations are *silava* (sacred).[1] They are guarded by place spirits that often take the shape of a snake or giant octopus. Some must be completely avoided on pain of death or illness. Fish and shellfish from *silava* places can cause death, and *silava* in the sea may cause shipwrecks (Lepowsky 1981: 380–85 and n.d.). Violation of postpartum sex taboos or of food taboos may cause the death of a young child (Lepowsky 1985, 1987, n.d.). Failure to adhere to mourning taboos attaching to persons or places may also lead to death. Failure to respond immediately to the crying of an infant may cause its death, as people say it would "become angry and leave us."

The death of a man in his eighties was the only one during my residence on the island attributed to natural causes, specifically to old age. People said he had lived so long because he had never worked sorcery on anyone else and thus fallen victim to a retaliatory attack.

The verb *mare* (to die) is also used when someone faints or is unconscious. Upon hearing news of a death, one must not literally say "He/She is dead," for this indicates that the speaker killed the person through sorcery. Instead the euphemisms "He/She has left us," "He/She is sleeping," or even, "The tree has speared its leg" are used. To inform kinspeople of a death, one may pluck a leaf of the dead person's totem tree and cast it silently at their feet. Most deaths are announced by the wailing of members of the deceased's household.

In traditional Vanatinai belief Rodyo, the creator spirit, sends his sailing canoe to pick up the spirit of the newly dead. His canoe is called Maigoigo (noisy, a reference to the bones of the deceased) or Matawikenu ("eyes are sleeping" in the Misima language). The canoe stops first at an uninhabited point on the south coast called Tevaiwo, where the "bones" are reformed into a human image, then sails clockwise around the island. The spirit is said to walk inland from near Araida on the north coast carrying a white sleeping mat and white basket. It may be seen by mortals. It pauses at a big rock called Egina, where there is a fine view of the island and lagoon, to weep for family left behind among the living, to gaze at the view, and to rest. Here it is met by the spirits of dead kin, who tell the new spirit not to weep as it is moving on to another life and lead it to the summit of Mt. Rio, which is the highest peak on Vanatinai.

Formerly when someone died the kin would climb onto the roof of their house holding a spear and call the name of the deceased. If they heard a voice in return, it would indicate that the spirit of the newly dead one had arrived at the top of Mt. Rio. This custom was stopped by missionaries about 1950.

The spirit of a dead person is called *kaka*. Spirits are said to reside with Rodyo and other supernaturals on Mt. Rio, a distinctive triangular peak frequently shrouded in clouds.[2] They have spirit gardens, pigs, and coconuts, which look like wild vegetation and animals to mortals. If one sleeps in certain sacred caves below the summit, one may hear the spirits whispering to each other, "Be quiet; our friends are sleeping." Spirits communicate with the living in dreams, through magic and ritual involving the use of relics of the dead, and through animal familiars such as the bird called *manuwijiwiji*. Since World War II, many older people have believed that America too is the land of the dead and that whites coming to the island may be returning spirits of dead islanders (Lepowsky 1989c).

MODERN BURIAL PRACTICES

In the early twentieth century the Australian government required all inhabitants of Papua living in areas under government control to bury their dead only in specially designated cemeteries on the outskirts of the settlement (see Lepowsky 1981:204–10 for a discussion of precolonial burial practices). On Vanatinai today most people are buried in individual graves just outside the hamlets in which they lived and not in official cemetery areas. This is closer to the traditional practice of burying the dead under the houses and near their living descendants. Married couples are frequently buried in adjoining areas.

The deceased is laid out on a pandanus mat and dressed in his or her best clothes. If any white cloth garments are available, the corpse may be dressed in these, or they may be draped over the body. The color white is associated with death. People come from all over the island to weep for the dead and attend the burial. Those who come and cry for a dead person are entitled to eat pork at the *zagaya* (the final memorial feast) held several years hence or at a special feast called *vearada* (crying) sometimes held to feed pork and vegetable food to those who cried at the burial. People unable to attend the burial may come and cry for the deceased months or even years later at the time of their first visit to the hamlet where the death took place. They normally spend about fifteen minutes in ritual wailing before engaging in a visit with the survivors.

If the person who caused the death through sorcery approached the corpse, its eyes would fly open. The absence from the burial of a suspected sorcerer who lived close enough to attend would cause comment.

Women and men cry over the corpse, addressing it by the appropriate kin term, real or fictive. Close relations may hold tender private conversations with the deceased. The widowed spouse or other affines care for the body, washing, dressing, and decorating it; remain with it; and keep flies off it with coconut-rib broom or a branch of croton leaves. Croton is associated with death and planted near graves. The red in the leaf is said to be the corpse's blood and the yellow the liquid of putrefaction that exudes from a corpse.

During the usual night and day before a corpse is buried or at a later time, close kin may discreetly obtain a *muramura* (relic) from the body. These are pieces of human bone, tooth, or hair. Their mere possession is illegal, for they are considered evidence of sorcery practice by government officials as well as being violations of burial regulations. But relics are more often used by the living to request different forms of aid from spirits of the dead, such as success in gardening, hunting, fishing, love, exchange, or curing illness. When a parent, uncle, or other close relative dies, an individual may go privately to where the corpse is laid out and speak to it, asking permission to remove a tooth or later to obtain another bone, such as a jawbone or a piece of skull, and request the future aid of the deceased. A tooth would be pulled out before burial, but other bones would be secured months later by secretly digging up the grave at night. This is done with special "digging magic," which makes the ground soft and the body easy to uncover, as the grave will open of its own accord with minimum digging.

Relics are also obtained by digging up bones believed to be those of long-dead heroes who were known as particularly successful warriors, lovers, or traders. Those wishing to gain power or destroy the power or health of others may secretly visit century-old battlegrounds or grave sites such as shallow caves to obtain relics. They are sometimes secretly exchanged by such individuals. Relics are so powerful they make the house where they are stored extremely "hot" and supernaturally dangerous. Their presence alone may make children or adults fall ill. They may therefore be hidden in secret locations in the forest. A few people carry them around in the soft woven coconut-leaf baskets used for betel nut paraphernalia, combs, and other possessions.

Shortly before burial a corpse is rubbed with scented coconut oil and its face is painted to make it beautiful for its journey to meet the other spirits, just as the living beautify themselves before entering the hamlet of an exchange partner or before attending a feast. It is decorated with flowers and scented leaves. *Daveri* (shell currency pieces), or occasionally two kina banknotes, and *bagi* (shell-disk necklaces) are placed in its hands and on its forehead and chest. Just before burial these valuables are removed and given to those who have helped care for the deceased during life. The essence of the valuables is said to remain with the spirit "like a photograph." It is said that if a corpse is not so decorated with valuables, its spirit will be refused admission to the land of the dead on Mt. Rio by the other spirits. Decorating the corpse with ceremonial valuables is said to be part of an exchange between the living and the dead. The living honor the deceased with valuables so that the spirit can make a good showing in front of the other spirits, and in return the spirit offers supernatural aid in future to those who have decorated it.

A myth relates that in early times the living could travel to Mt. Rio and exchange directly with the dead, for all mortuary ritual events were held in the community of the dead with the spirits participating. But Mwajemwaje, the supernatural patron of various types of food magic now living in an unspecified location in the rain forest, once became angry with his mother for refusing him a small bunch of choice bananas and closed the "door" to the land of the dead, a stone called Varidamo.

Rodyo, the creator spirit who is the "owner" of the dead and lives with the ancestor spirits on (or inside, some say) the rock summit of Mt. Rio, formerly had the shape of a snake. If the spirit of a newly deceased human arrives at the mountain and its nose and ears are not pierced, Rodyo will pierce them himself with his tail in order to make the spirit "like a snake," so that it will not be turned back and prevented from joining the other spirits. Snakes on Vanatinai symbolize the immortality of the spirit.

Green coconuts are placed in the grave for the spirit to drink on its journey, and sometimes pieces of ripe coconut meat, vegetable food, or sago roasted with grated coconut are also buried along with the corpse as food for the passage to the spirit world. The actual burial is carried out by matrilineal kinsmen and the patrilateral cross-cousins of the deceased. The mourning coverings worn by the spouse and other affinal mourners, normally a fine coconut-leaf basket worn inverted over the hair and a woman's new coconut-leaf skirt or piece of cloth worn around the shoulders, are given to the kin of the deceased after the burial.

Sometimes small shelters of bush timbers and dried coconut fronds are erected over graves, and decorative plants such as croton and cordylline, also planted in food gardens and used in ritual, may be planted nearby. Some graves are completely unmarked. Graves are generally neither visited nor avoided, although people may be afraid to go near them at night because the spirit is said to be aware of visitors. Children are particularly fearful of grave sites, even though spirits do not normally harm the living.

Burial customs are little affected by the Christian beliefs of some islanders. In one of two burials that I witnessed there was no Christian ritual at all, even though some of the principals consider themselves to be United church members (Methodists). In the other, a United church pastor from Vanatinai was present. He conducted a short prayer service before the burial and delegated people to nail together a cross of wood, which was covered with red hibiscus flowers and placed first in the house near the body and then by the grave. A small card with a prayer printed on it in the Dobu language was placed in the corpse's right hand. The pastor also supervised the application of scented coconut oil and facepaint to the corpse and saw to it that pieces of ripe coconut meat and roasted sago and coconut pancakes threaded on a piece of bush cord were tossed into the grave.

The length of time the spirit lingers near the hamlet is unclear. Rodyo is supposed to send his sailing canoe to pick it up immediately after death, but the idea that "only bones" travel in it until they are reconstituted at Tevaiwo suggests the passage of time during which the corpse decomposes. In precolonial times a fire was kept burning on top of the grave, under the deceased's house, "to keep the spirit warm." The fire would be small in the daytime and large at night, when family members would sleep beside it to prevent the spirit from feeling lonely. The fire was kept burning on top of the grave until the entire mortuary feast sequence had been completed and sometimes afterward. Completing the feast sequence today assures survivors that the spirit will be properly respected by other spirits on Mt. Rio and fully willing and able to help its descendants. The spirit is said to observe and influence the actions of the living before, during, and after mortuary rites.

Hertz's (1960) idea that local treatment of the corpse, specifically temporary and secondary burial, reflects ideas about the fate of the soul is suggestive in the Vanatinai case. Secondary burial was practiced in precolonial Vanatinai, as was the now extinct custom of smoking some corpses over a fire and hanging them in certain large trees so that they would be incorporated over time into the growing tree. People say that skulls of both kin and enemies were formerly kept in houses or caves as relics.[3] Bracelets consisting of the mandible and collarbone were worn by the living in 1849 (Huxley 1935:191–92), Macgillivray 1852:215–16). The continuing custom of taking relics from the deceased and the former custom of secondary burial of at least some individuals suggest that particular stages of the present-day mortuary ritual sequence were originally correlated with specific manipulations of remains, including secondary burial.[4]

THE MORTUARY FEAST SEQUENCE

There are three to four feasts held on Vanatinai after the death of an individual, a sequence that influences every aspect of the island's traditional social, economic, political, and religious life. The first feast is held several weeks after the burial and is called *jivia* (literally, break), referring to the ceremonial breaking and mutual feeding of pieces of cooked sago during the ritual. The second, called *velaloga* ("for walking"), is only held when the deceased is survived by a spouse. It lifts the taboo that enjoins the widow or widower to remain in seclusion inside the house and is normally held a month or two after the death. The third feast, *ghanrakerake* (literally "food goes out") "clears" the taboo against storing, cooking, or consuming food inside a house that has been "closed" in memory of the deceased. It takes place two to six months after a death. The final and most elaborate feast is called *zagaya* (the generic term for feast); *bigibigi* (things), referring to the valuables that are exchanged; or *mwaguvajo* (*mwagu* goes over"). Its central ritual is the *mwagumwagu*, where valuables are publicly transferred to the heirs of the deceased, ending the mourning period. There is normally a hiatus of anywhere from one year to a whole generation in mortuary ritual activity following the completion of the preliminary feasts and before the *zagaya* is held to lift the remaining taboos on individuals and communities resulting from a death.

Table 1 summarizes the memorial feast sequence, the nature and direction of the principal exchanges within each feast, and the functions of the different feasts in removing specific taboos (Lepowsky 1981:186–370). Only the final feast, the *zagaya*, will be discussed in detail in this chapter.

The valuables publicly presented by mourning affines and their kin at memorial feasts are regarded as compensation to the kin of the deceased for the death. But the idea that giving away valuables is a sacrifice and a form of compensation is contradicted by the cultural principle that by giving away valuables one becomes known as a wealthy and important person. The hoarder of valuables is criticized, and the ostentatiously generous person is admired. The display and presentation of wealth to others at

TABLE 1
The Memorial Feast Sequence on Vanatinai

Feast Name	Time after Death	Valuables Exchanged	Direction of Exchange	Taboos Lifted (Affinal Mourners)	Taboos Lifted (Community)
Jivia	3 days– 2 weeks	Daveri (shell pieces) Gile (pearl shell) Tobotobo (axe blades) Plates Mirror Sago Garden produce	Tau, kin → affines Affines → kin, tau	May feed self May leave hamlet (not spouse) May eat animal foods	May exchange pigs and valuables May store, prepare, eat food in deceased's house if pig killed
Velaloga	2 weeks– 2 months	Tobotobo Daveri Sago Garden produce	Affines → kin, tau	May leave hamlet (spouse) May bathe (spouse) May shave (spouse)	None
Ghanrakerake	2 weeks– 6 months	Tobotobo Daveri Ceremonial lime sticks Sago Garden produce	Affines → kin, tau	None	May store, prepare, eat food in house
Vearada (Optional)	1 year	Pigs Sago Garden produce	Kin → community	None	None
Zagaya (Bigibigi, Mwaguvajo)	1–25 years	Bagi Tobotobo Ceremonial lime sticks Daveri Pigs Sago Yams, garden produce Skirts Clay pots Mats Baskets Trade store plates, silverware, fabric	Affines →kin Kin → affines Kin + affines → tau Tau → spouse	May wash, cut hair, decorate body, wear new clothes May dance, travel, court May remarry May leave spouse's hamlet May eat father's pigs, sago, coconuts, betel, garden produce	May drum, sing, dance

mortuary feasts enrich one by putting others in one's debt, a subordinate state, in a fashion similar to that of the potlatches of the American Indians of the Pacific Northwest. The balance is redressed only when there is a death in the affinal lineage and the roles of kin to the deceased and mourning affines are reversed.

MOURNING CUSTOMS AND SOCIAL STRUCTURE

On Vanatinai the bulk of mourning restrictions fall not upon matrilineal kin but the surviving spouse and other affines such as sons- and daughters-in-law and the spouses of the deceased's uterine nieces and nephews. Marriage unites not just two individuals but two matrilineages. Spouse and kin aid affines with labor, food, or ceremonial valuables on a wide variety of occasions. Affinal exchanges are roughly equivalent during the lifetime of the marriage partners, but the death of one means that the survivor and kin must compensate the kin and the *tau* (patrilateral heir) (discussed later) of the deceased with large quantities of valuables to demonstrate publicly that they did not cause the death and that they will not benefit from it materially through an end to their affinal obligations. Mortuary ritual is therefore a culmination of the series of affinal exchanges begun at the marriage of the deceased. When the widow/widower dies, valuables flow in the opposite direction. Through mortuary ritual, the surviving spouse and other affines affirm publicly that they wish to preserve the exchange link between lineages despite the death. Furthermore, the custom of compensating a patrilateral heir of the deceased, normally a father's sister's child, means that exchange links formed between lineages by the marriage of the deceased's parents are also publicly affirmed and reinforced despite the crisis of death.

Relationships between living affines are characterized by respect and avoidance. They never call each other by name but instead employ teknonyms or terms such as "in-law" or "that man there"/"that woman there."

Immediately after a death, the surviving spouse and other affines must remain in their houses, blacken their bodies with burnt coconut husk, and refrain from washing and from cutting their hair or beard. These acts symbolize and communicate the mourner's renunciation of normal social and sexual relations. Mourners wear old clothes and cannot decorate their bodies with armlet, leglet, facepaint, flowers, or scented plants. Women wear the *yogeyoge* (the coarse, ankle-length mourning skirt). Until the *jivia* (the first feast) mourners leave the house only to eliminate, accompanied by a kinsperson of the deceased, their bodies covered by pandanus leaf sleeping mats or coconut-leaf skirts slung over their shoulders, a coconut-leaf basket over their hair, walking slowly with eyes down and arms crossed over their chests. Mourners are forbidden to feed themselves during this period or to touch their hands to their mouths. They must be fed by the kin of the deceased, who place mouthfuls of food to their lips. The matrilineal kin of the deceased therefore literally hold the life of a surviving spouse in their hands during the tense period immediately following a death, for it is only they who can feed the mourner, in a relationship reminiscent of that between parent and infant, and they who hold the power, in theory, to withhold food or to poison a spouse believed guilty of causing the death.

The central act of the *jivia* itself is the ritual feeding of affines by kin of the deceased and of kin by affines. The sharing of food is an intimate act on Vanatinai. Unrelated people do not normally eat together, and affines avoid doing so, except spouses. A couple is considered married when the man stays in the morning to eat the food the woman has cooked, rather than departing discreetly before dawn. To share food is a mark of trust, for sorcerers may poison it or bespell it. The ritual feeding and sharing of food are remarkable as reversals of normal practice. At the *jivia*, affines feign placing choice mouthfuls of roasted sago loaf and sago pudding to their own lips and then deny themselves, giving away food and hand-feeding the kin of the deceased. Kin and affines alike ritually emphasize their enduring mutually dependent and trusting relationship despite the death.

The rigorous mourning enjoined upon a surviving spouse indicates the ritual pollution resulting from close contact with death (cf. Hertz 1960:38). The survivor endures stringent restrictions for one to twenty or more years after the spouse's death to demonstrate that she or he did not cause the death by means of sorcery or witchcraft or benefit from the death. People say privately that certain widows/widowers did in fact kill their spouses and that their mourning is a sham, but in most cases public opinion attaches blame for the death to other parties.

Several people said that in early times an individual's death meant that the surviving spouse's family had to kill someone and present the body of the homicide to the kinspeople of the deceased, who held a feast at which the body was eaten. Nowadays pigs are substituted. Again the implication is that the survivor is responsible for the spouse's death, and the human or pig's body is compensation.[5]

To demonstrate grief and lack of complicity, a widow/widower must undergo a form of social death and later rebirth. He or she withdraws from normal social life, being first confined to the house and then to the hamlet and nearby garden. The widow/widower remains with the deceased's kin, under their authority, until the final mortuary feast. They then publicly release the spouse from all mourning restrictions through bathing, dressing, and decorating the mourner and leading him or her to dance before the feast guests, after which the spouse may resume normal social relations and remarry. Vanatinai mortuary rites and mourning customs conform closely to the pattern proposed by Van Gennep (1960:11) for all rites of passage, consisting of rites of separation, transition, and incorporation. The Vanatinai term for the liminal period of mourning is *ghabubu* (taboo, sacred, or closed).

When a father or one of his matrilineal kin dies, his children may not eat food from garden lands belonging to him or his matrilineage; sago, betel nut, or coconuts from his palms or those of his matrilineage; or pork from any pig belonging to him or his kin. These taboos are not lifted until the final mortuary feast, when children present substantial quantities of ceremonial valuables, vegetable food, sago, and pig to the *tau* (their father's matrilineal heir). A father's children do not usually blacken their bodies and undergo the other mourning restrictions upon his death. This burden is borne by their spouses. Formerly daughters- and sons-in-law went into mourning when any member of the father-in-law's matrilineage died, but nowadays they only ritually mourn the father-in-law himself. Children may blacken their bodies and daughters wear the mourning skirt when they undertake exchange journeys in quest of valuables to present at a mortuary feast. They are expected to make major contributions to the father's mortuary feasts, which go to his kin and patrilateral heir, because they excreted upon him as infants, and he uncomplainingly cleaned up after them (cf. Malinowski 1929:156–57). Maternal care is not so explained and compensated because such intimate care is a cultural given between close matrilineage members. In many ways children are structurally and ritually treated as affines of their father.

After a death the house where the deceased normally lived is placed under a special taboo. No food may be stored, cooked, or eaten within it until the *ghanrakerake* (a special feast) is held. The entire hamlet where the deceased lived or died may also be placed under taboo by surviving kin so that it is forbidden to drum, sing, dance, or, nowadays, play guitar there until the last mortuary feast is held. Taboo persons or places are also called *ghabubu*.

MALE AND FEMALE ROLES IN MORTUARY RITUAL

The deaths of men and women on Vanatinai are marked by equally elaborate mourning and by the identical sequence of memorial feasts. Both *wabwi* (widows) and *sibawa* (widowers) blacken their bodies, wear mourning garb, and refrain from washing or cutting and combing hair. Widowers grow a beard. Both remain in seclusion until the *velaloga* (second mortuary feast), and they do not travel away from the hamlet except to work in the gardens to accumulate food for feasts or to travel on exchange journeys in search of valuables for the final feast. They may not dance or take lovers. Widowed spouses generally begin to bathe again after the second feast.

211

Although technically they blacken their bodies until the final feast, they usually do so only sporadically after the second feast when there are visitors in the hamlet, when they travel on exchange journeys, or when they are feeling particularly sad. Full mourning regalia is put on again for the final feast.

People say "there must be a woman to sit down" at the *mwagumwagu* (the key ritual of the final feast), when valuables are transferred to the deceased's heirs. Those who "sit down" at the *mwagumwagu* are also ceremonially handed over to the heirs, who will then lead them to the stream to be bathed, decorated, and liberated from all mourning taboos. They always include a surviving spouse.

These mourners represent their entire matrilineages and their economic contributions to the mortuary feasts. Although mourning taboos and obligations are onerous, following them diligently and making substantial contributions of valuables are primary means of increasing personal prestige and that of the matrilineage. When a death occurs, the surviving kin and affines meet separately and decide who besides the widowed spouse will follow mourning restrictions and who will host particular feasts in the mortuary series. Big men and big women achieve their status mainly by hosting or making substantial contributions to feasts after the death of kin or affines. The hosts and contributors to feasts are regarded as working to liberate themselves, their kin, or their exchange partners from mourning restrictions. At least one woman will have to follow all mourning taboos for a period of years on behalf of her matrilineage. This may be the widow or a sister or other kinswoman of the widower. Although an outsider might regard the stringent mourning restrictions for this woman as evidence of lower female status, the people of Vanatinai say that only a woman may represent her kin group in this essential ritual process and thereby bring honor to it. Her matrilineage and its exchange partners generously contribute labor and possessions to show proper respect for the deceased.

Women as well as men may host mortuary feasts, usually, as with men, in honor of their fathers or deceased affines. The majority of feasts are hosted by men, but even so the active participation of their wives, sisters, mothers, and other female associates is crucial. Women are called "the owners of the garden," and they always decide whether there is an adequate surplus of garden produce, particularly yams, to hold a feast or whether it must be postponed for another year.

Women are expected to contribute ceremonial valuables as well as pigs, sago, and garden produce to feasts. They may go on exchange journeys in quest of valuables, traveling the length of Vanatinai and sometimes visiting other islands by sailing canoe. They have personal exchange partners and act as individuals, seeking contributions on the basis of the closeness of their relationship to the deceased or to the host of the future feast. Their husbands sometimes *muyai* ("follow" them) to assist with their obligations. In most other parts of the Massim, women generally do not participate in the exchange of ceremonial valuables such as shell-disk necklaces or greenstone axe blades in *kula* and related forms of customary exchange. Instead they have a separate arena of exchange featuring less durable valuables that they have produced themselves, such as banana-leaf skirts in the Trobriand Islands (Weiner 1976) and fine yams on Panaeati Island (Berde 1974). On Vanatinai women and men compete for prestige in the same arena of exchange for the same valuables. Although exchanges of women's skirts and of yams are an essential element of Vanatinai mortuary ritual, these exchanges are far less elaborate, and they accompany the exchange of ceremonial valuables (discussed later).

Some Vanatinai men say that women are not expected to make as large or elaborate a contribution to feasts as men because they do not know as much powerful exchange magic, but certain women surpass the exchange activity and the volume of contributions to feasts of most men. Women are also frequently the recipients of valuables presented at feasts, for they may stand in the patrilateral relationship called *tau* (heir) to the deceased.

INHERITANCE AND MORTUARY FEASTS

A few days after a death, the deceased's matrilineal kin meet privately to discuss who will inherit the dead person's property and to distribute these goods. Any last wishes of the deceased concerning who should receive certain valuables are respected. Debts in ceremonial valuables incurred by the deceased are inherited too and must be paid in full at this point or during one of the mortuary feasts by descendants, or they fall under the threat of sorcery by the deceased's creditors.

Ceremonial valuables, pigs, and rights to garden land are inherited equally by the men and women of a matrilineage. Individuals who inherit the bulk of the deceased's wealth are under the strongest obligation to host or contribute substantially to mortuary feasts. In this manner goods inherited immediately after a death may flow later to affines and patrilateral relatives of the deceased. Either the actual pigs and ceremonial valuables of the deceased or their equivalents may be contributed to a later feast. Inheritance on Vanatinai is therefore a complex procedure taking years after a death to complete and binding together the various members of the social network of the deceased in exchange relationships.

Matrilineal kin also meet during the weeks following the death with the deceased's patrilateral relatives to agree upon who will host each of the feasts in the ritual sequence and who will receive the valuables contributed. The principal recipient of valuables at a feast is the *ighan zagaya* (the person who "eats the feast") or *ighan ghunoi* (person who "eats the fruit"). The "fruit" refers both to the corpse of the deceased and to the valuables, including the mourning spouse, which are publicly exchanged to commemorate the death and which represent the corpse.

This recipient is ideally a patrilateral cross-cousin of the deceased who was chosen during the latter's infancy by the father from his own matrilineal kin to stand in a special exchange and inheritance relationship to his child. This person is called *tau*, a reciprocal term. *Tau* also address each other as "my father" and "my child," even if the *tau* is a woman. *Tau* are chosen without regard to gender. *Tau* relationships are a series of patrilateral links among matrilineages.

The importance of the *tau* is in many ways parallel to that of the matrilateral kin such as the mother's brother in exchange relations in patrilineal societies elsewhere in Papua New Guinea and in other parts of the world. A good *tau* is supposed to contribute food, pigs, ceremonial valuables, and trade store goods upon request by the "child" throughout the latter's lifetime without as strong an expectation of return of equivalent items as from normal exchange partners. For when the "child" dies, the *tau* should "eat the feast" and receive the bulk of the valuables contributed in the "child's" memory. Paradoxically, the custom of patrilateral cross-cousin inheritance at the final mortuary feast strengthens and supports the principle of matrilineal inheritance. It is perceived as compensation to the father's matrilineal heirs for valuables the father gave his children during his lifetime as well as for what the cross-cousin has given to the mother's brother's child.

The *tau* relationship not only binds members of a matrilineage to the offspring of their male members, who are collectively their "children," and these "children's" kin but also maintains social and economic relationships between members of matrilineages that were originally brought into an exchange relationship by a marriage in the grandparental generation. The matrilineage of the father's father must be compensated by means of valuables presented to the father's *tau* upon his death. People say that by presenting valuables to the deceased's *tau*, "we are thanking their lineage for marrying his [deceased's] mother." Figure 1 illustrates the relationship among the matrilineages of the *zagaya tanuwagai* (feast host), the deceased, and the *tau* of the deceased at the death of a man; figure 2, that at the death of a woman.

If the *tau* dies before his or her child, as often happens as the *tau* is generally several years or even a generation older, a new one is chosen from among the father's matrilineal kin. A father's sibling or more distant kinsperson may be appointed. Sometimes kin request to be the *tau* of a child as a mark of their special affection or respect for the father, and there may be several claimants to the honor, a situation that must be handled tactfully by the father.

Some people contribute much more to their "child" as *tau* than others.

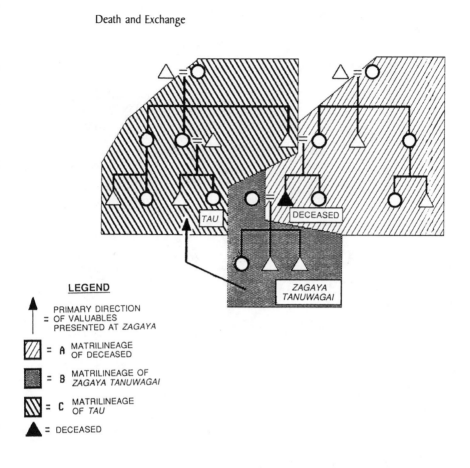

FIGURE 1.   Flow of valuables at the *zagaya* of a man.

If a *tau* has generously given all manner of goods and valuables for many years, she or he has an undisputed right to "eat the feast." But if the *tau* never or rarely aided the "child," she or he may not receive any valuables at all at the feast, although she or he may be compensated with valuables privately beforehand.

In some cases a powerful matrilineal kinsperson of the deceased makes it publicly known that she or he expects to "eat" a particular feast or the entire feast sequence as compensation for a lifetime of aiding the deceased in finding the valuables to fulfill the latter's ritual obligations. This custom in which kin "eat the feast" is called *vowo*. Such a claim may be made either just after the death or many years later, shortly before or during the final feast, causing consternation and fear among the feast organizers. Defiance

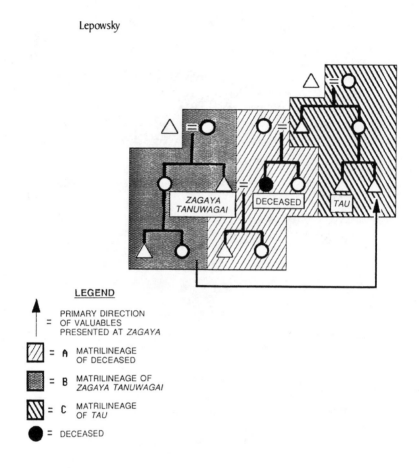

LEGEND

↑ = PRIMARY DIRECTION
OF VALUABLES
PRESENTED AT *ZAGAYA*

▨ = A MATRILINEAGE
OF DECEASED

▦ = B MATRILINEAGE OF
ZAGAYA TANUWAGAI

◪ = C MATRILINEAGE
OF *TAU*

● = DECEASED

FIGURE 2. Flow of valuables at the *zagaya* of a woman.

of the demand would put the associate of the deceased at risk of being killed
by the sorcery of the claimant, for those who demand to "eat the feast"
of their matrilineal kin almost always are known as powerful sorcerers. If
the claim is made early enough, the other kin and affines who are organizing
the feast sequence arrange to obtain enough valuables to give in memory
for the deceased to each individual with a valid claim, often including both
the *tau* and the matrilineal kinsperson of the deceased. Some of these claims
are disposed of by arranging for valuables to be given to the kinsperson at
one of the earlier feasts, but this strategy may backfire as the claimant demands further compensation at the upcoming *zagaya*. Last-minute claims
by kin may cause a feast to be postponed or its conclusion delayed while
the host lineages frantically try to obtain more ceremonial valuables from

their personal exchange partners. If they refuse to do this or are unsuccessful, the claimant is likely to boycott the feast and brood at home, placing a cloud of fear over the *zagaya*, for the participants recognize that such an open breach in social relations may lead in the near future to sorcery attempts by the claimant.

People sometimes say of occasions when a matrilineal kinsperson of the deceased "eats the feast" that the organizers are "making a mistake" and not following Vanatinai custom, but such instances are in fact quite common on the island. Table 2 shows the relationship of those who "ate the feast" to the deceased at *zagaya* that were held on Vanatinai during 1978–79 and shows the types and numbers of valuables exchanged. Of nineteen feasts, the principal recipient of valuables was a patrilateral relation or *tau* of the deceased in only nine cases. The recipient came from the matrilineage of the deceased in seven cases, from the deceased's husband's matrilineage in two cases, from the deceased's brother's wife's matrilineage in one. Less than half the *zagaya* followed what people describe as the custom that a patrilateral cross-cousin or other patrilateral relative of the deceased should "eat the feast" at the final and most elaborate mortuary event.

In its ideal form, mortuary ritual exhibits an orderly series of cross-cutting ties among matrilineages linked by marriage, but an examination of the details of each real event reveals inter- and intralineage competition and the individual power struggles that are inevitable in an egalitarian society precisely because there are no systems of ascribed status. This competition illustrates the tension between the ethic of respect for the autonomy of individuals, which is based in part upon fear of their potential destructive power, and the ethic of cooperation, sharing, and exchange that is necessary for survival in a small-scale subsistence society. Each mortuary event is a map of ongoing social relations, reflecting a history of individual choices made by key participants, including the deceased, about the establishment and maintenance of ties validated by the exchange of goods.

ZAGAYA

Zagaya take place anywhere from one to twenty-five years after the deaths they commemorate, depending upon the ability of surviving kin and affines to accumulate adequate quantities of garden produce, sago, pigs, and ceremonial valuables for presentation to the heirs of the deceased during the feast. They are normally held about three to five years after a death.

The host is called *zagaya tanuwagai* (the owner of the feast). The host must have enough prestige and exchange partners to mobilize sufficient amounts of the goods necessary to discharge group obligations to the dead. When sibling sets host a feast after a father's death the oldest or most

TABLE 2

Valuables Presented at Vanatinai Zagaya in 1978–79 (Excluding Pigs, Foodstuffs, Personal and Household Goods, and Cash)

Zagaya Tanuwagai's (Host's) Relation to Deceased	Sex of Deceased	Loghan Zagaya's (Heir's) Relation to Deceased	Zimwagu's (Mourner's) Relation to Deceased	Total of Valuables Presented to Loghan Zagaya	Bagi	Tobotobo	Lime sticks	Daveri
S	M	B	W, WZ(2), WZD, BW	50	2	30	2	16
WMZS	M	FZD (tau)	W, WZD, D	21	1	11	1	8
WFWB	M	FZD (tau)	W, WFW	20	2	13	1	4
ZH	M	FZD (tau)	ZH, ZHZ	18	2	9	1	4
ZH	M	"B"	D	30	1	15	1	8
ZS	M	FZS (tau)	S	17	0	9	1	7
W	M	"B"	W	31	1	17	2	11
W	M	BS	W	36	1	22	0	13
BS	M	"B"	W	18	0	10	1	7
BS	M	"B"	W	14	1	6	1	6
BS	M	"B"	W	8	1	4	0	3
B	F	FZS (tau)	SW	23	1	9	2	11
B	M	FZS (tau)	BW	17	1	8	1	7
"B"	F	H	"BD"	14	0	8	1	5
DH	F	S	DHZD	14	0	8	1	5
H	F	FZS (tau)	4 women (?)	56	2	28	2	24
S	F	HZS	3 women (?)	18	1	17	1	8
S	F	FZS (tau)	1 woman (?)	30	1	12	1	16
F	M	FZD (tau)	D, FZ, DHZ	14 + ?	1	13	?	?

dominant sibling is described as the host. Sometimes the feasts of several deceased individuals who are all kin or affines to the host are combined and held at the same time, with separate ceremonial presentations of valuables for each individual.

A "strong" or wealthy individual may relieve his or her kin and affines of the burden of holding a *zagaya* by hosting one himself or herself during life. This custom is called *ighan ghunogu* ("he or she eats my fruit") and takes place very rarely.

Preparations for a *zagaya* begin years in advance. Pigs must be fattened to an imposing size. Often the prospective host places a *ghive* (taboo sign) on the hamlet outskirts to notify others that the pigs and ceremonial valuables of all hamlet residents are reserved for the *zagaya*. Large tracts of extra garden land must be cleared and planted to provide food for feast visitors, many of whom will remain in the hamlet for weeks before, during, and after the feast. Enormous quantities of sago starch must be processed to feed guests and to be used during the rituals. Sometimes additional houses must be built for feast guests. The closest kin, affines, and friends of the host gather in the hamlet to help with the final weeks of preparation.

The network of exchange links activated by *zagaya* preparations often extends to distant islands, and it is thus difficult to separate "internal" from "external" exchange on Vanatinai. Would-be contributors to the feast, women and men alike, travel on foot or by canoe to the other districts of Vanatinai to call in old debts of pig or ceremonial valuables or to initiate new exchanges by requesting a specific item to present at the feast. They may also sail to other islands of the Louisiade Archipelago. Feast hosts and their associates frequently travel down the Calvados Chain islands requesting valuables from exchange partners, then visit Panaeati and even Misima Island. Rossel Island is more rarely visited than a generation ago, and most, but not all, visits across the treacherous passage between Sudest Lagoon and Rossel Lagoon are made by securing rides on small government or trading boats. Some of the most ambitious feast givers travel by sailing canoe as far as Ware, Tubetube, and Normanby islands. After *ghiva* (extended expedition) people bring back as many as fifty valuables, mostly *bagi* (shell-disk necklaces) and *tobotobo* (polished greenstone axe blades) (Lepowsky 1983). Not all of these will actually be contributed at the feast. They also receive promises from exchange partners to appear with pigs or additional ceremonial valuables at the feast itself. Since promising valuables later but failing to deliver is a frequent practice in exchange, such promises introduce additional tension and uncertainty to the host's plans for a good showing at the feast.

Success in obtaining valuables is attributed to the power of one's exchange magic, such as bespelled scented coconut oil, which has been boiled with a human relic, sometimes that of the deceased for whom the feast will be held. Wearing this oil and otherwise beautifying oneself make exchange partners of either sex "dizzy with desire" and unable to prevent themselves from giving away their valuables. Ancestor spirits in this way are believed to participate directly in feast preparations.

Several dozen *zagaya* are held every year in the Vanatinai-East Calvados region. Often one does not take place until others have been completed, as a major contributor expects to "eat the feast" at one and present some of the valuables received later at another. Many ceremonial valuables thus pass through numerous hands at feasts held in communities throughout the region in the space of a few weeks or months.

Zagaya are generally held during the season following the annual yam harvest in July and the planting of new yam gardens, allowing time for lengthy feast preparations. On Vanatinai in 1978–79, they were held from September to as late as April, with none from May to August, despite a regulation passed by the Louisiade Local Government Council that all feasts in the archipelago must take place in December.

The year in which a feast is held depends on when sufficient quantities of goods and ceremonial valuables have been stockpiled. But some big men or big women who could host the final feast a few months after a death delay it several years to avoid shaming their affines, who might not be ready with their return gifts of valuables and who might not be able to host a feast as mourning affines after some future death on such an accelerated schedule.

Every feast guest is expected to contribute valuables, or at minimum a basket of garden produce or bundles of sago, even those who "eat the feast." Each visitor, except the latter and close associates, expects to work hard at the innumerable tasks connected with feeding hundreds of people several times a day and organizing the ritual. Close kin, affines, and friends of the host who have not obtained ceremonial valuables or pigs for the feast often do not attend, as they are ashamed to appear with nothing more than a basket of food.

Zagaya last anywhere from two days to two weeks, with much of the time in longer feasts spent waiting for guests to assemble from distant hamlets and islands. The host must feed them well during the waiting period.[7] A food magician (either male or female) is appointed to look after all food resources and items such as firewood and leaves for building the stone oven. These are bespelled to make them last a long time. They make guests feel full after only a few bites and thus not deplete all the stores. The central clearing of the hamlet is not swept until the feast is over, or it will spoil this magic. The food magician receives ceremonial valuables from the host at the end of the feast.

Public affinal presentations of valuables to a host at the start of the feast are called *muli*, a term which is both a noun and a verb referring to the act of presentation.[8] No host could make a successful feast without major contributions of labor, food, pigs, and ceremonial valuables from the matrilineages to which she or he is related by marriage. The affines must support the host or face public shame. Generous affinal contributions build the reputation of the entire lineage as *giagia* (givers). Affines can expect the same degree of support in future when roles are reversed and it is their turn to host a feast. Those unwilling or unable to work hard to make affinal presentations at feasts are advised against marrying the close kin of *giagia*, individuals who have built their reputations by hosting many feasts through the years.

Muli presentations are thus another round of the exchanges between affines that began with bride wealth payments and counterpayments and continue well beyond the lifetimes of married individuals at their mortuary feasts. A presentation of large quantities of fine valuables and foodstuffs during the *muli* is a public testament to the industry and generosity of both male and female members of the affinal lineage. A good showing enhances the desirability of members of their matrilineage as potential marriage partners, for it shows that they are a kin group who will work hard to support their affines.

There is a competitive flavor to *muli* presentations that is not normally acknowledged publicly. Affinal matrilineages strive to outdo the *muli* they received when hosting a previous feast. The whole *muli* procession accompanied by the blowing of conch shell is a public display of the affines' wealth and generosity reminiscent of the competitive food exchanges of Goodenough Island in the northwestern Massim, a society where feasting is not traditionally connected with death but where ceremonial exchanges stress interlineage or affinal competition in displays of wealth and power (Young 1971). Elsewhere in the Massim, affinal exchanges with a competitive edge are a major feature of mortuary feasts in the Trobriand Islands (Weiner 1976:61–120), Dobu (Fortune 1962:195–200), Normanby Island (Róheim 1946:760), the Bartle Bay area north of Milne Bay (Seligman 1910:635–36), Wagawaga on Milne Bay (Seligman 1910:624–25), and Panaeati Island in the Misima language area (Berde 1974:169–75).

Privately, Vanatinai people say that *muli* is "like a fight" but one not carried to the same extreme as with East Calvados and Misima peoples, in which affines perform a triumphant, warlike dance on board their sailing canoe and ritually spear the house of the feast host if they have succeeded in bringing five pigs to a feast. The reason, they say, is that affines who in this manner boasted of their wealth and strength would be struck down by wrathful and insulted Vanatinai sorcerers. But the prideful challenge of *muli* was especially obvious at one Vanatinai feast where the host's affines presented a huge boar carried by four men on two crossed poles. Two youths stood on the beast's belly, one blowing a conch shell, as it was carried into the hamlet, preceded and followed by a line of men and women carrying sago, baskets of garden produce, and several smaller pigs. Vanatinai, and perhaps all Massim, mortuary ritual averts social conflict through ceremonial exchange, but it does so by channeling and ritualizing aggressive behavior.[9]

The feast host receives visitors inside a house, where some guests present valuables that the host will later distribute publicly to the deceased's heirs. The host organizes valuables for the presentation and also carries out preliminary exchanges, called *ghayawa* ("to take to a feast") or *ziravagavile* ("they exchange equivalent valuables"). A visitor may exchange a shell-disk necklace, greenstone axe blade, or other valuable with a virtually identical one belonging to the host, who contributes the newly acquired one at the feast. It is against custom to give a valuable to the person from whom one has obtained it or his or her kinsperson. By exchanging valuables privately, the host is usually able to contribute the "new" valuable without worrying about its recent ownership. Those who participate are said to be "feeding" valuables to the host and "helping" him or her, even though there is no net gain in the number of valuables in the hands of the host and the exchanger usually carries the host's former valuable home.

These exchanges of like for like emphasize that it is the maintenance of the exchange relationships and social ties between individuals and matrilineages—rather than a net gain of valuables by one side or the other—that is the primary goal of mortuary ritual. Similarly, individuals take baskets of produce to a feast and leave bearing baskets of produce given them by the host from the feast storehouse. Some people travel long distances taking a pig to a feast and return home bearing an equivalent pig from the host's own herd or from those donated by the host's exchange partners to the feast.

MWAGUMWAGU

The *mwagumwagu* (public ritual presentation of mourners and ceremonial valuables to the heir of the deceased) is the central act of the *zagaya*, the culmination of years of work and the last stage in the observance of mourning taboos. The widowed spouse and other affinal mourners, wearing full mourning regalia, their bodies blackened with burnt coconut husk, sit silently in the central clearing of the hamlet, their heads down. As the assembled guests watch silently, the host and other contributors drape the mourners one by one with ceremonial valuables. They place shell-disk necklaces around their necks, lean greenstone axe blades in carved wooden handles against their backs and sides, and slip ceremonial lime sticks of tortoiseshell or wood in their armlet. They pin *daveri* (shell currency pieces)[10] in woven pouches to the baskets worn inverted over the mourners' hair, slip them under the baskets, and lay them on the seed yam placed in front of the mourners before the ritual began and along the line of additional greenstone axe blades accumulating in a line in front of the mourners. Some people step unexpectedly out of the crowd to add their valuables. Then the person who "eats the feast" replaces an axe blade, necklace, or lime stick on the widow's/widower's body with one she or he has brought. The heir swiftly collects the presented valuables, including the new coconut-leaf skirts covering the mourners' shoulders, placing the smaller items in the baskets that covered the mourners' hair. The valuables are lined on a mat or on the skirts just taken from the mourners, their number counted aloud and the total announced to the waiting crowd. The totals in 1978–79 *zagaya* ranged from eight to fifty-six (Table 2).[11] The valuables are then gathered up and taken inside. Creditors of the heir take this opportunity to request repayment, and many valuables are redistributed within hours.

Raw pork and cooked vegetables are given by the host to family groups and eaten in the various households crowded with guests. Clay pots of sago and green coconut pudding are privately exchanged by the mourning affines and the person who "eats the feast," who ritually feed each other as in the *jivia* mortuary feast that closely followed the death.

The affinal mourners are said to have been physically given to the deceased's heir along with the ceremonial valuables. They and the valuables represent the corpse of the deceased and are offered in exchange. In theory the heir can either kill the mourners or restore them to full social life. Later that day or the following day, the heir takes the mourners to a stream or to the sea and assists them in bathing and washing off their black mourning pigment. The women's mourning skirts are covered with fine new skirts provided by the heir, and all the skirts are cut at the knee with a trade store knife. Male mourners are given new clothes or a new piece of cloth. The mourners' hair is cut and beards are shaved. Both men and women are then rubbed with scented coconut oil, their faces are painted, and they are decorated with flowers and scented leaves stuck in their hair and their new armlets by the heir or attendants of the same sex belonging to the heir's lineage. The mourners are then led back to the hamlet to dance for the guests. They are now cleared of all mourning taboos, and they are free to remarry.

There often are traditional dancing, drumming, and singing all night during a feast, particularly in the style called *rausi*, said to have originated on Normanby Island. Musicians and dancers receive gifts such as skirts, clay pots, sleeping mats, and even greenstone axe blades for key players for having "helped" the host. These dances celebrate the lifting of mourning taboos on the hamlet and honor the deceased while indicating the renewal of normal social relations. Appropriately they are a prime arena for courtship and for lovers' rendezvous. Many marriages, and thus many new sets of affinal exchange links, originate from meetings at feasts.[12]

The spirit of the deceased and other ancestor spirits are said to be watching every aspect of a mortuary feast. If the deceased has been properly honored by the observance of mourning taboos and by appropriate exchanges of valuables at each feast, the spirits will in exchange help the living to maintain health and prosperity.

On Vanatinai sago rather than yams takes the central place in ritual food exchanges. In most of the southern Massim, formal presentation of yams by mourning affines is a key aspect of mortuary ritual, for example on Dobu (Fortune 1963:199–200), Panaeati (Berde 1974:170–71), and the rest of the Misima and West and East Calvados regions. Although the yam exchange element in Massim mortuary ritual is not highly elaborated on Vanatinai, it is still retained. During the Vanatinai *mwagumwagu* it is customary for each affinal mourner who "sits down" in the formal ritual presentation to the heir of the deceased to be accompanied by one seed yam placed on the ground near him or her. This yam is not fresh and perfect as in the Misima-area *hagali* yam presentations but is often old and moldy. If possible, it is a yam that came from the garden or the garden lands of the deceased. The yams are presented along with the mourners, the ceremonial valuables, and other goods to the deceased's heir and, ideally, cross-cousin and are said to represent a transfer of generative power and fertility from one lineage to another.

Another element of Vanatinai mortuary ritual that is more highly elaborated elsewhere in the Massim is the exchange of women's skirts. Before the final feast, female mourners and their associates must manufacture fine new coconut-leaf skirts. Each mourning woman will drape a new skirt that she or a kinswoman has made over her shoulders as a cloak during the *mwagumwagu* ritual. (Some mourning men also drape their shoulders with skirts made by kinswomen; others cover themselves with pandanus-leaf sleeping mats, also made by women.) These skirts, like the mourners themselves and the other goods laid out during the ritual, are presented to the deceased's heir. Later the heir and kin bathe the mourners and provide the women with equally fine new skirts that the heir's kinswomen have made for the occasion.[13] The exchange of fine new skirts between women of different matrilineages represents the alliance between their kin groups and their willingness despite the death to continue exchanging men with one another through exogamous marriages, thereby ensuring the continuing fecundity of each matrilineage.

In the Trobriand Islands large numbers of banana-leaf skirts are manufactured and exchanged by women affines during mortuary rituals (Weiner 1976:94–120), and skirts are women's wealth items and their avenue to prestige just as yams and Kula valuables are men's.[14] On Vanatinai, where both women and men are expected to contribute Kula-type ceremonial valuables, yams, pigs, and other goods at mortuary feasts, the skirts exchanged at feasts are ritually essential items of wealth generated by the labor of women, but they are one among many kinds of goods exchanged during the event.

MORTUARY EXCHANGES AND THE INDIVIDUAL

A reputation as a big man or big woman is not gained by any one act of generosity in exchange or by hosting of one feast. There is a developmental cycle of personal exchange activities as an individual matures and takes on new social responsibilities. Young people begin their exchange careers by producing foodstuffs and household goods—yams and garden produce, sago, pigs, mats, baskets, and skirts—for use at feasts, for less spectacular exchange purposes dictated by lineage needs, and for home consumption, thus gaining a reputation as hard workers and desirable marriage partners. The unmarried young are also expected to work hard at the many tasks of the feast itself and may even be rewarded by the host by presentation of a ceremonial valuable.

By their twenties, many people contribute ceremonial valuables as well as foodstuffs to feasts as individuals. They are already developing their personal networks of exchange partners, usually beginning with kin, father's kin, and favorite exchange partners of their elders.

Not all adults feel compelled to participate even minimally in exchange, although most people honor their basic kin and affinal obligations and contribute foodstuffs or valuables to mortuary ritual. Some men and women choose to exceed the minimum demands of custom and become well known throughout the region for their wealth, industry, and generosity. They develop large exchange networks, host mortuary feasts or contribute substantially to them, make big gardens, and raise numbers of large pigs. These people are the *giagia* (givers). Both sexes on Vanatinai have the opportunity to build their personal reputations as *giagia* through exchange activities. But it is up to the individual to decide whether the effort is worth the reward of areawide renown and the risk of the sorcery attempts of envious neighbors.

CONCLUSION

The death of every adult threatens to obliterate the social ties that the deceased has formed over a lifetime. These ties are a form of capital created by individuals that may in theory be transformed as needed into the assistance of others in the form of "gifts" of labor, foodstuffs, or ceremonial valuables. In a small-scale society like Vanatinai, connectedness has a high social

225

value. The individual with the greatest number of ties to others has more social options, the greatest potential for survival in case of disaster, and more power and influence through the ability to control the labor and surplus production of others. The loss of these ties through the death of a contracting party is therefore counter to the interests of the deceased's closest associates.

Mortuary ritual reinforces and even intensifies the social ties of the deceased, bringing members of the deceased's social network together in an evanescent group. It focuses particularly upon exchanges between individuals connected to one another through the marriage of the deceased and the marriage of the deceased's parents. Affines are expected to be each other's most reliable exchange partners, providing goods and services uncomplainingly as requested in a reciprocal relationship. But affines are outsiders, not kin, and their demands may conflict with those of matrilineage members. The affinal relationship is characterized by outward respect and avoidance behavior and by covert tension and competition. This tension becomes more open at the death of a spouse, when the surviving spouse and kin must compensate the kin and heirs of the deceased for years through mourning observances and presentations of valuables. Failure to compensate affines for a death changes the affinal alliance to enmity (cf. Leach 1982:171–72). Mortuary ritual is a peacemaking ceremony (cf. Fortune 1963:207, 209 on Kula and peacemaking) and a mechanism for conflict resolution. It preserves the affinal exchange ties generated by the marriages of the deceased and deceased's parents. Afterward the principal survivors have a choice of continuing or abandoning their exchange relationship. In most cases the relationship is maintained. Mortuary ritual thus transforms and reassigns the most significant exchange relationships of the deceased. The expression *"Ighan ghunoi"* ("She or He eats its fruit") refers to the public acceptance of valuables, including the person of the surviving spouse, presented to the deceased's heir at the final feast. All of these are said to be the "fruit" of the corpse. The exchange ties in which the deceased participated are also "fruit" of the corpse consumed and reincorporated by the heirs of the deceased.

Although the *zagaya* is held as the result of a death, paradoxically it is mainly a happy event and a celebration (cf. Huntington and Metcalf 1979). It signals the end of mourning restrictions and the social rebirth of not only the widowed spouse but the deceased's hamlet. It is the means through which proper respect is paid to the spirit of the deceased and through it to all ancestor spirits. It is thus the primary means through which the living can petition the ancestor spirits for continuing health, fecundity, and prosperity.

The *zagaya* is sacred, and it has solemn and emotional moments such as the *mwagumwagu* ritual, when participants sometimes cry spontaneously as they remember the person they have lost to death. It is also the scene of ritual competition between affinal lineages. Individual quarrels over valuables may erupt during its course with serious potential consequences of sorcery attempts or of permanent breaches in social relations. Extreme anger at the sorcerer alleged to have caused the death being mourned, who is sometimes present at the feast, may be voiced among those attending. The atmosphere at certain feasts is particularly tense because of such conflicts. But the prevailing emotional tone at most of these highly charged events is one of pleasure and excitement. Through the *zagaya*, potentially destructive individual emotions of grief, anger, fear, and guilt that arise at a death are generally sublimated and ritualized into proud displays of generosity and exchange of symbols of fertility, abundance, and rebirth. The *zagaya* reaffirms life itself. It is a hopeful ritual evocation of the peaceful exchange relations among the living and between the living and the dead on which human survival and good fortune depend.

NOTES

Acknowledgments: The field research on which this chapter is based was conducted primarily from January 1978 to February 1979 on Vanatinai (Sudest Island), Papua New Guinea. Archival research was carried out in Port Moresby, Papua New Guinea, in December 1977 and March 1979. This research was funded by a National Science Foundation Pre-Doctoral Research Grant and by the Chancellor's Patent Fund and the Department of Anthropology of the University of California, Berkeley. I returned to Vanatinai in April and May of 1981 and from June to August 1987. Transportation to Papua New Guinea in 1981 was financed by the Papua New Guinea Institute of Applied Social and Economic Research. Support for my 1987 field research and during revisions of this chapter was provided by a National Institutes of Health National Research Service Award held through the National Institute of Child Health and Human Development, by the Wenner-Gren Foundation, and by the Graduate School of the University of Wisconsin, Madison. All of this financial support is gratefully acknowledged.

1. *Silava* are similar to the *yaba* (sacred places), and their guardian spirits, of nearby Rossel Island (Armstrong 1928).

2. Spirits from the small, Saisai-speaking (East Calvados language) islands of Panaman and Yeina (Piron), adjacent to Vanatinai, are also said to go to Mt. Rio. Spirits from Nimowa and Panatinani (Joannet) islands go to the easternmost point on Panatinani, which is called Bwebweso, the name of the mountain that is home to the dead on Normanby Island (cf. Fortune 1963:187, Róheim 1946:223). Spirits from the other East Calvados islands go by canoe to Hanhiewa, a sandy beach on the uninhabited island of Hemenehai across the channel from Sabara Island (Sabarl). Spirits from Kuanak and from the Misima-speaking islands of the West Calvados go to the summit of Mt. Oyatau, the tallest peak on Misima, or to a cave called *Bwanagum*, near Hinauta at the eastern tip of Misima.

3. Decorated skulls of enemies were exchanged for ceremonial valuables in precolonial Vanatinai as well as the East Calvados and Misima-Panaeati areas (Lepowsky 1981:171–79). *Bagi*, the shell-disk necklace used in Vanatinai mortuary ritual and in Kula exchanges, may have originated as decorated skulls. Vanatinai and East Calvados people say that in early times the *bubugera* (the conch shell piece still called the "head" of the bagi and from which pearl shell pendants are strung) used to be a human skull.

4. Armstrong (1928:114) mentions the *wili* feast of Rossel Island, where bones are removed from the grave and placed on a platform and the skull and collarbones cleaned and placed in the widow's/widower's house or exposed in the village.

5. Róheim (1937:50) reports a similar custom for precolonial Normanby Island. On Vanatinai at least one *bagi* should also be presented at the final mortuary feast by affines. Since the *bagi* are locally said to have been decorated human skulls, they too may substitute for affinal compensation through homicide.

6. A similar mechanism of exchanges with matrilineal kin of the deceased's father operates in the *hagali* of the Misima language area islands (cf. Berde 1974).

7. The host often makes a ritual speech exhorting guests to eat as much as they want and urging them to feel free to climb his or her coconut and areca palms to obtain drinking coconuts and betel nut (cf. Lepowsky 1982).

8. Berde (1974:25) notes that on Panaeati Island *mulimuli* means "in-law presentations." Fortune (1963:197–200) defines the Dobu Island term *murimuri* as "members of . . . villages connected with the village of the dead by intermarriage" and describes the ritual presentations of the *murimuri* to the village of the deceased during the Dobu mortuary feast sequence.

9. Another example of the element of challenge and competition inherent in feast exchanges is the custom called *uraura*. This is a ritual speech during which a public challenge is delivered to an exchange partner, affine, or kinsperson, who may or may not be within earshot, to present the speaker with a particular desired valuable or with an especially large *muli*. It is often made just prior to or during a *zagaya* (Lepowsky 1981:334–36).

10. *Daveri* is the same as the *ndap* (shell money) of Rossel Island (Armstrong 1928).

11. People say that in late precolonial times endemic warfare made it impossible to hold a *zagaya*, an ancient ritual, after each death and that skull exchanges were the principal occasions when ceremonial valuables were exchanged. Since pacification (a gradual process lasting from 1888 to 1942), the size and lavishness of mortuary feasts have increased, and there has been substantial inflation in the number of valuables considered necessary to exchange at a *zagaya*. In early precolonial times two to five valuables were sufficient (Lepowsky 1981:171–81 and 1983).

12. Feast participants may also sing traditional Vanatinai mourning songs such as the type called *nuaroru* until late into the night. These songs are accompanied by the rhythmic tapping of a lime stick upon a gourd lime pot. People say that when singing *nuaroru*, "*la va wozinga woye kaka*" ("we are singing with the spirit").

228

13. Berde (1974:174) reports the custom of "cutting the mourning skirt" after a *hagali* presentation on Panaeati Island, where a woman from the clan of the deceased bathes and dresses female affinal mourners in three new skirts, presumably manufactured by kinswomen of the deceased. There is apparently no presentation of comparable skirts by female mourners to kinswomen of the deceased during the Panaeati *hagali* and thus no exchange of skirts.

14. Although Kula valuables are primarily male forms of wealth in the islands of the "Kula ring," Damon (1980:275) and Scoditti (1983:255–56) note the participation of a Kitava Island woman in an important *kula* relationship, and Macintyre (personal communication 1981) has observed that Tubetube Island women are active in Kula and other exchanges involving ceremonial valuables.

John Liep

The Day of Reckoning
on Rossel Island

• This essay describes death, the funeral, and the mortuary feast on Rossel Island (Yela). The mortuary feast culminates in a series of exchanges between various categories of relatives of the deceased. My main focus is an analysis of these exchanges. I attempt to make them intelligible by placing them in two contexts. At one level I see death on Rossel as a moment in the cycle of social reproduction. Schematically this cycle takes its beginning at marriage, goes on through the lives and deaths of the partners of the marriage, and comes to an end at the deaths of children to this marriage. The mortuary prestations gain significance from this perspective, where they are seen as part of a range of other exchanges concerning people as kinsmen and affines. At another level I have sought to view mortuary exchanges on Rossel in a wider perspective comparing them with other Massim exchange structures. I cannot do this on an island-to-island basis. Instead, I have chosen to view the way that Rossel mortuary exchanges relate to a theme that seems to me relevant to the whole Massim region—that of social hierarchy—or, to be more accurate, its absence, which is generally the case in the region, except in northern Kiriwina of the Trobriand Islands. This may sound rather cryptic but will become more meaningful, I hope, in the course of the argument.

I, therefore, begin with a discussion of the problem of hierarchy in the Massim.[1]

SOCIAL HIERARCHY IN THE MASSIM

Two "traditional" nexuses of social reproduction stand out in the Massim, as well as in most of Melanesia. On one hand, people engage in subsistence activities at home, in local production and consumption of staple food. On the other, they are involved in a nexus of specialized production and trade that ties the local community into a wider regional network of relations. From these nexuses emerge two basic and opposed forms of social wealth and sources of power. On one hand, the "staff of life," the produce of ancestral soil. On the other, "exotic" goods, valuables (and today money), derived from the external circulation. The two nexuses presuppose each other. A surplus of food sustains trading and visiting expeditions and maintains communities specialized in craft production and sailing. External wealth enters into the regulation of local kinship relations through social exchange.

This duality of reproduction engages every community in a contradiction between local and external involvement that the internal social relations have had to absorb. Through continual processes of cultural interpretation the Massim peoples have sought to reconcile the external-internal opposition with other social oppositions, such as male/female, wife-taker/wife-giver and senior/junior. One solution, which is more or less developed in parts of the Massim, combines these oppositions in a clear-cut structure of complementary, asymmetrical exchange. The two categories of wealth are separated in affinal exchanges. Male valuables are contrasted with female food, so that valuables pass from wife-takers to wife-givers and subsistence produce the other way. (This corresponds with the descent structure found in most of the Massim, which associates land transmission with the female line.)

Such asymmetric marriage exchanges bear evidence of a spectre that haunts the Massim: social hierarchy. In historical time a hierarchically organized society has existed only in northern Kiriwina. The system involves rank differentiation among *dala* (land-owning-matrilineal subclans), chieftainship, permanently asymmetrical marriage exchanges, superiority of wife-takers to wife-givers, and elaborate mortuary rituals with potlatch-type distributions. The political hierarchy is based on the chiefs' polygyny and a structure of marriage exchanges in which centrally distributed external valuables (axe blades and shell ornaments) flow through marriage alliances downward and outward from the center from wife-takers to wife-givers. (In Kiriwina this flow was augmented and now is partly replaced by locally produced female wealth in the form of banana leaf bundles and skirts.) In the opposite direction pass yam harvest gifts and labor service from wife-givers to wife-takers. The male valuables may be used to acquire rights of use to land, which become permanent if counterprestations of

231

valuables are not forthcoming from the landowning descent group at the death of the lessee (Weiner 1976:157ff).

The Kiriwinan hierarchy is usually regarded as an isolated development in the Massim. It might also be seen as a representative of once more wide-spread tendencies. Societies with ranked descent groups and some form of chieftainship are found in pockets in several places in northern and eastern Melanesia. It has been suggested that stratified formations based on asymmetrical exchange and monopoly over "prestige goods" derived from long-distance trade were once of wide distribution in island Melanesia (Friedman 1981; Rathje 1978). Hierarchies based on distribution of foreign prestige goods seem to be a common legacy of Austronesian peoples. In Fiji Sahlins has described a structure in which chiefs stand as foreign conquerors from the sea, wife-takers and providers of valuables in relation to the indigenous people of the land (1976, 1981).

Apart from the hierarchy in northern Kiriwina the societies of the northern Massim (the Trobriands, Marshall Bennetts, and Muyuw) are linguistically and culturally closely related. But cultural affinities extend farther in the region. Chowning (1978) has called attention to traces of hereditary leadership in several places in the Massim, often associated with the word *guyau* (leader or chief). Large competitive food distributions connected to mortuary celebrations are characteristic of the region all the way to Sudest.[2]

This might indicate that societies throughout the Massim have earlier been articulated to a more encompassing hierarchical system. We need not at all assume that the whole area once was a unified chiefdom—only that local societies were connected by trade, and possibly marriage alliances, to one, or several, centers of long-distance seafaring monopolists of prestige goods (such as stone axes, obsidian, pottery, or shell valuables) with a ranked social structure.

As I have already mentioned, several Massim societies posit the affinal relationship as asymmetric and complementary: wife-takers supply external valuables against food prestations from wife-givers. (This form is more or less strongly present in Kiriwina, Muyuw, Dobu, and Panaeati.) In a hierarchical prestige goods system such asymmetry sustains a rank differentiation in which wife-takers hold superior rank and wife-givers inferior. (This is reflected in Crow cousin terminologies that are frequent in the Massim. Here cross-cousins on the wife-taking side are assigned to a senior position and on the wife-giving side to a junior position.) Only in Kiriwina is this structure fully realized in a hierarchical political system. Elsewhere it appears in various states of decomposition. Maybe this is less due to a "failure" of development of hierarchy than to successful efforts toward its subversion.

Clastres has argued that acephalous societies were "societies against the state" (1977). They were deliberately constituted to negate the development of inequality and political centralization. Although his thesis as a whole is too extreme, he makes the point that social stratification may not arise as a response to a general need of "society." It may well be resented and opposed by at least some of the people.

The integration of subsistence-based local communities into larger regional systems characterized by a differentiation of functions enables individuals and groups to acquire control over the movement of people, goods, and information between the internal and external sectors. Such control can be used to enhance their status and to dominate other people. We should, however, expect that other individuals and groups will resist the attempts of some to come out "on top of" the rest of the people. Throughout the ages local structures and institutions of the Massim have taken shape through such struggles.

In each Massim society the problem of hierarchy has been dealt with in a process of cultural interpretation according to elements of preexisting cultural codes, the society's position in the regional network of trade, specific historical conjunctures, and other factors. The solutions vary from island to island. They are the result of complex transformational processes and many of the determinants belong to an unknown past. Yet, I argue that a perspective that takes account of the struggle for hierarchy will allow for fruitful comparative interpretations of social forms in the Massim.

THE NEUTRALIZATION OF HIERARCHY

The basic problem that local societies have confronted is how far asymmetrical marriage exchange should be allowed to develop into a manifestation of rank inequality. How is a tendency toward permanent indebtedness and rank differentiation counteracted? In Kiriwina affinal exchanges remain asymmetrical throughout the lifetime of a marriage. The chiefly hierarchy depends on a renewal of marriage alliances between chiefly and satellite lineages. If these alliances are reestablished the flow of asymmetrical prestations is perpetuated through the generations—a regular wife-taker/wife-giver relation is reproduced. Note that this conforms to the structure of *matrilateral* marriage. Dependent headmen give "sisters" to the paramount chief. The chief's sons eventually return to their "mother's brother's" villages and succeed to subclan leadership. A subclan "sister" goes to renew the marriage alliance to the successor of the paramount chief (his sister's son), who accordingly marries a "mother's brother's daughter" (Powell 1969:197; Eyde 1976:243). This is generalized exchange in one sense of Lévi-Strauss's formula, but it does not conform to the pure model of a "circulating connubium." In Kiriwina there are permanent rank inequalities between subclans, but the hierarchy is not completely stable. At each level of rank there is rivalry about relative positions. A compromise solution is then to reverse the wife-taker/wife-giver relationship in the next generation (cf. Powell 1969:196). Accordingly the conscious model of the most suitable marriage is patrilateral.

In other societies of the Massim an asymmetrical definition of marriage is allowed at its inception but is thereafter overlaid with delayed reciprocal exchanges, such as the *kula* between affines in Muyuw (Damon, this volume). Asymmetry is more radically negated in the Dobu model, which involves alternating residence and a corresponding reversal of the marriage prestations and counterprestations (Fortune 1963). Another solution dissolves the male/female categorization of wealth and prescribes that affines should assist each other currently with feast contributions of both kinds of wealth (valuables *and* food). The outcome is a delayed exchange of like for like and no formal asymmetry is maintained. This is the case on Sudest (Lepowsky, this volume) and on Rossel.

We have hitherto been concerned with the qualitative aspect of the exchange relation between parties to a marriage. But the quantity of the mutual prestations is also of consequence. The balance of debts between affines may influence the residential status of married couples, it may have repercussions for the transfer of land rights, or it may determine ritual manifestations of prestige, such as the burial site of deceased spouses.

When one of the partners dies, a critical stage in the marriage cycle occurs. At this moment the mortuary payments between the relatives of the spouses may indicate a continuation or a restructuring of the relationship between these two groups of affines. If the mortuary exchanges maintain a qualitative difference between prestations of the male and of the female side, an asymmetrical relationship is carried on into the next generation. If, on the other hand, prestations are identical for both sexes and reversed at the death of the surviving spouse, a symmetrical and equal relationship is expressed in the mortuary sphere. In most Massim societies the last situation seems to prevail.

Other mortuary prestations are concerned with the marriage of the deceased's parents. In all Massim societies children are involved in exchanges with respect to both their mother's and their father's groups. The relationship engendered by a marriage must thus last for two generations. Some societies seem to hold that it should last no longer. They stress that certain prestations at the mortuary feast sever the relation between the two groups of the deceased's parents. Such is the case at least on Muyuw and Rossel. This expresses the cancellation of any formal debt relationship between the groups and renders them equal and independent. Even in Kiriwina asymmetry is contested during the mortuary exchanges. Important payments of male and female valuables (the *kalakeyala kapu*: Weiner 1976:112ff.) from the deceased's to the deceased's father's *dala* constitute a counterweight to the flow of valuables during the deceased's parents' marriage. They probably represent an effort to square the former unequal relationship between wife-givers and wife-takers (Mosko 1985:221ff).

Let me summarize the argument. Hierarchy lurks on the horizon of Massim societies. It is present as a possibility in a structure of exchange between providers of overseas wealth and yielders of women and fruits of the land. It is present as a reality based on this structure in Kiriwina. If it is to be kept at bay, something must actively be done about it and this is what other Massim societies have been busy doing. It is done by confusing the distinction between male and female prestations, by counterpoising any imbalance in kind in affinal exchanges during a marriage, or at least at the critical moment of death, and, finally, by formally cancelling the marriage alliance at the termination of the second generation.

We shall now see how the hierarchical problem is handled on Rossel Island.

MORTUARY PRACTICES ON ROSSEL ISLAND[3]

Compared to those of other Massim societies the mortuary proceedings on Rossel are of limited scope. The mortuary feast is held a week after the funeral. There are no further large-scale mortuary celebrations on Rossel today.[4] Mourning restrictions mainly concern widows. The exchanges that take place at the mortuary feast consist only of payments of "shell money" and other valuables. There is nothing like the large prestations of raw or prepared food that are so conspicuous at other Massim feasts. As the mortuary feast on Rossel is held so shortly after the death it does not give scope for long-term planning and marshaling of wealth. Compared to other exchanges, such as bridewealth and the pig feast, the amount of valuables is rather limited. Thus the mortuary feast on Rossel is not the important institution it is in most other Massim societies. It is not a major event in the buildup of big man status. Yet, several features of the mortuary complex on Rossel are similar to those of mortuary practices on other islands of the Louisiade Archipelago. It seems likely that much of the form of the mortuary complex has been imported from the west.

The more restricted scope of Rossel mortuary feasting and the absence of large food distributions in this connection, then, call for an explanation. One should here note that Rossel, in distinction to the other Louisiade islands, is not part of an extensive trading system that involves ecological interdependency of large and small islands (Liep 1981). The former trade between Rossel and Sudest consisted solely of luxury items. Both islands are large and rich in food resources. On Rossel there was thus no engagement in trade that would tend to intensify food production for export and make agricultural resources the object of competition. Land is, on the whole, not

scarce on Rossel. It is probable, therefore, that the long-term mortuary celebrations and food prestations, which on the other islands are directly connected to the areal exchange system, did not develop on Rossel.

Before I enter upon a description of Rossel mortuary practices the social
background, in terms of kinship structure and exchange procedures, must
be summarily presented.

KINSHIP AND EXCHANGE ON ROSSEL

The social universe on Rossel is structured in terms of matrilineal descent
categories. There are altogether fifteen *pū* (named clans). The clan is a dispersed group and does not operate as a unit. Clans are segmented into *ghi*
(branches), which I call subclans. A subclan is named after the land area
(or some feature of it) with which it is associated. Subclans are exogamous,
as are most clans. Subclans are also dispersed groups. The descent groups
established in a given area may be termed local subclan sections. (There is
no Rossel word for lineage.) The subclan or its local sections do not function
as corporate bodies. They are neither corporate land-managing groups nor
political units. The subclan does, on the other hand, constitute a focus of
solidarity in terms of mutual support and hospitality. Subclan members do
cooperate in social exchange, and this cooperation is more sustained and
frequent among members of the local section.

Subclans acknowledge ties of kinship to the other subclans of their clan,
which are utilized in exchange cooperation. (This is especially so if they are
coexogamous.) But in addition they also claim consanguinial relations to
one or more subclans of other clans.[5] Such *linked subclans* share exogamy
and their members cooperate in exchange. This fictive kinship bond exists
between individual subclans and does not extend to the other subclans of
their respective clans.

A subclan's members also maintain a close relationship with their *tpū*
("children"), or filiates: the children of men of the subclan. A clan possesses
a stock of names that men of the clan give to their children.[6] A man often
names his own children after his mother's brother's children. Thus a person
is immediately identifiable by his or her name as the "child" of a certain
clan. Such cofiliates apply sibling terms to each other, they may be namesakes, and they draw on each other's support in exchanges.

At any given kinship exchange occasion—for example, a bridewealth
payment or a mortuary payment—one finds the participants aligned in at
least two opposed parties, or *yo* ("sides"), as the Yela say. One side collects
the prestation and transfers it to the other side, who redistributes it. Each
side constitutes a cluster of categories of persons defined in relation to the
individual, who is in focus as the giver or recipient of the prestation. At
the core of each side are the adult members of the individual's own local

236

subclan section, who most regularly combine to amass prestations. Fanning out from this core come the subclan members of other local sections, members of the other subclans of the same clan, members of linked subclans, and filiates of these descent groups. Finally, the core group relies on support from its affines too. When support is drawn from so wide a spectrum it is not surprising that individuals often appear on both sides in a transaction, given a tendency toward local endogamy.

Having set out the structural framework for exchange cooperation, I shall now briefly describe the exchange situation between affines as it unfolds through the course of a marriage.

On Rossel marriage is established through a genuine bridewealth. The payment of bridewealth involves several stages, and there is some variation between parts of the island, but this need not concern us here. Suffice it to say that the bridewealth is a large transfer of *ndap* and *kö* (shell money) from bride-takers to bride-givers (roughly six hundred to eight hundred *ndap* and fifty to sixty *kö*.) The bride's side should provide cooked food, which is redistributed by the groom's side to the contributors of high-rank shell money, but this is a normal procedure in connection with other payments (for example, for pigs, houses, or canoes) and cannot be interpreted as signifying a future lien on the garden produce of the wife's relatives. People say that the bridewealth recompenses the wife's relatives for the care and food they have spent raising the girl. Instead of seeing the unilateral prestation of bridewealth as establishing rights over the production of the bride-givers, I, therefore, regard it as concerned with rights over the *person* of the bride only. The wife usually moves to her husband's place of residence, which is most often in his father's hamlet. Most of her labor is transferred to her new household and her husband's relatives. There are no regular harvest prestations between affines. Bridewealth may also be seen as establishing partial rights over the children of the couple by the husband and his relatives. This double affiliation of children is well expressed in the bridewealth exchange. Both the groom's father's and mother's sides contribute to the payment, and both the bride's father's and mother's sides receive it.

Although the flow of bridewealth is thus definitively asymmetrical, it does not inaugurate an enduring asymmetrical relationship between wife-takers and wife-givers. During a marriage affines are expected to assist each other. They provide labor services and contributions of food for feasting. They contribute to the payments that persons on each side are undertaking— such as bridewealth; payments for pigs, houses, or canoes; and mortuary payments—and they partake of the redistribution of payments received. It is a relationship of delayed reciprocity, and at least not a markedly lopsided one. This symmetrical relationship between affines, after the payment of bridewealth, is also, as we shall see, expressed in the mortuary exchanges.

237

In another way bridewealth is separated from mortuary exchanges. This is related to the restrictions on the circulation of the various forms of valuables in Rossel exchanges. One group of valuables are the external, imported valuables—*chumo* or *vyape* (axe blades), *kpuwo* (foreign shell necklaces), and *ngga* (ceremonial lime spatulae)—together with the *wuluwulu* (locally made necklaces) or—in the rest of the Massim—*bagi* that were formerly the dominant export item from Rossel. All valuables in this group tend to move together. On the other hand, there is the Rossel shell money, the *ndap* and *kö*. Some *ndap* were earlier imported from Sudest, where *ndap* shells are also wealth items, but the majority were, and still are, made on Rossel. *Kö* are only made and used on Rossel; thus they are strictly internal valuables. *Ndap* straddle the two poles and are employed in all Rossel exchanges. Now, whereas in bridewealth (and most traditional pig feasts) only *ndap* and *kö* are used, the external valuables figure conspicuously in the mortuary payments, but *kö* are excluded. In other payments (such as those for houses and canoes) valuables from all categories go together. Cash has entered into this exchange group and also into pig exchanges but, significantly, is excluded from bridewealth and from the most important mortuary exchanges concerned with the relationship between affines. The picture that emerges is not very clear-cut, and I can offer no exhaustive explanation of the various combinations and separations. It seems significant, however, that bridewealth, which is concerned with rights over women's lives, is protected from intrusion by external wealth, whereas mortuary payments, which concern both sexes and other aspects of interpersonal relationships, allow foreign valuables. The exclusion of *kö* (and high-rank *ndap* as well) from mortuary exchanges allows for the inheritance of these valuables, which would otherwise tend to disperse at death.

Figure 1 indicates roughly the areas of circulation of the various kinds of valuables and of cash.

DEATH AND THE FUNERAL

On Rossel Island death causes grief, but it also provokes anger. Both emotions color the mortuary practices, but although grief and anger may result in apparently uncontrolled outbursts just after a death, their expression becomes more formalized and well structured at the funeral and especially at the subsequent mortuary feast.

At death, while grief is expressed in wailing, especially by women, relatives often turn against each other in anger. I have not been present at any death, but I have been told that people are beaten up on this occasion. It is generally the deceased's brothers or other close relatives who vent their rage against the deceased's spouse or children, but feelings run so high that brother may even strike brother.

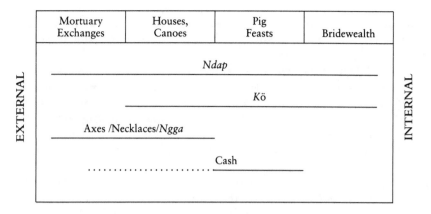

FIGURE 1.   Simplified scheme of circulation of Rossel valuables.

In a way death becomes the moment of truth on Rossel. In ordinary life the Yela are quite restrained people, who avoid showing strong emotions or hostile behavior. Public quarrels, not to speak of scuffles, very rarely take place. At death violence breaks through. Although the hostility and aggression displayed at the mortuary feast are more tempered, the contrast to normal behavior on Rossel is striking.

The funeral takes place at the latest on the day after the death. People from the surrounding area collect at the village of the deceased. As the burial is so soon after the death there is not time for people from farther away to attend. At the two funerals I witnessed the dead man was laid out under the house where he lived. Female relatives surrounded the body, wailing and whisking away flies with *cordyline* branches. Upon arriving visitors went straight to the corpse and cried, before they settled in groups around the house of the deceased. Soon some elderly man among the visitors rose and opened a public inquiry about the death, which would be taken up again at the mortuary feast. This *yaaka* (argument) has the character of an inquest in which the circumstances surrounding the death and its possible causes are reviewed.[7] We shall return to it in the section on the mortuary feast.

Meanwhile, the work of preparing the grave site is in progress. Two teams of about five younger men each are working. One team is the gravediggers. The *kpö* (grave) is usually made in an L shape, with a chamber at the side of the shaft. The body is placed into the chamber behind a partition of sago frond sheaths, so that no dirt touches the corpse. (The burial practice is similar on Goodenough and in Molima; see Young and Chowning, this volume.) The other team of workers erects a small house over the grave, presumably to protect it from pigs. Formerly the gravediggers should have

239

been young men of the deceased's father's subclan (such as male cross-cousins), but now any young man of the locality can participate in the two teams.

When all the visitors have wailed at the body, and the preliminary inquiry into the circumstances of the death has ebbed out, the corpse is shrouded in bedsheets, sprinkled with baby powder, and wrapped in mats. Both funerals I saw were of Catholics. When the corpse had been wrapped and the work at the grave site accomplished, the priest said Mass. The body was then carried to the cemetery by the team of men, who also built the grave house. At this stage the funeral changed from a public to a very private event. Only one or two close relatives followed the deceased to the grave.

When the *ghötmi* (spirit) leaves the body at death, it travels to Yeme, the mountain of the dead, a peak at the western end of Rossel. According to another belief, mentioned by Armstrong, the spirits of the dead go to *Teme*, the Rossel underworld and retreat of the deities of old.[8] *Teme* is probably a cognate of *Tuma*, the Kiriwinan underworld and destination of Northern Massim and D'Entrecasteaux dead.

Mbwe (ghosts) are not greatly feared on Rossel but may annoy the living some time after death. The cry of an owl in the night in the village or a firefly circling around a person's head is taken as the presence of a ghost.

EARLIER MORTUARY PRACTICES

The mortuary complex was considerably curtailed by government interference during the early part of this century. Formerly bodies were sometimes kept some time after death beside a fire, so that visitors arriving from far could see the dead. The practices of interment varied (Armstrong 1928:103–4). Usually the corpse was buried in a shallow grave under the house, sometimes in a sitting position. After a couple of months the body was exhumed. According to my information the cleaning of the bones was performed by close female relatives of the deceased (his or her father's sister's daughters and sister's daughters). These women received a large payment of shell money and other valuables (axe blades, and so on). The skull and a few of the larger bones were placed on a shelf or plate in the village or in the house. After some time—probably many years—the remains were transferred to a rock shelter in the bush.

The mortuary feast for an important big man was earlier associated with cannibalism. When a big man died a victim had to be procured for the mortuary feast. (There was a similar custom on Sudest; see Lepowsky, this volume.) Usually the deceased's relatives made strong allegations of sorcery, most often against affines of the deceased. To avoid being slain the suspected sorcerer must kill somebody else and take the body to the deceased's village. The compensation paid to the victim's relatives constituted the largest

240

prestation in the Rossel prestige economy and involved the highest-ranking *ndap* shells and other valuables. The soliciting of valuables for the payment resulted in debts and replacements that probably took years to settle.

THE CONTEMPORARY MORTUARY FEAST

The *kpakpa* (mortuary feast) is held about a week after the death.[9] Visitors from a wider area than those who attended the funeral now flock to the village of the deceased. Guests from the same locality arrive together and file in, led by their big men. Those who did not attend the funeral walk straight to the cemetery and wail at the grave.

In the village the atmosphere is strained. Close male relatives and affines of the deceased, and men of the locality, sit gravely under the deceased's house, the house of death that will be abandoned to rot and fall down. Whatever strife divided them at the hour of death, they now confront the world together. Entering the village the guests often show hostility by cutting down trees and by striking local men. Male visitors group themselves facing the men under the deceased's house. The women (local and visitors) are in a more peripheral position at the back of the house. Some of the local women are busy cooking food to be served for the guests later. If the deceased was a married man the *kungö* (widow) is at the back of the house, screened off by an enclosure of palm leaves. It is most important that she be concealed from the deceased's brothers. She remains in seclusion for several weeks. A *nangö* (widower) is not subjected to isolation.[10]

The "inquest" that began at the funeral is now reopened in the wider forum of the mortuary feast. The visitors are here opposed to the men who were socially and spatially close to the deceased, as accusers to defenders. It is implicit that the deceased died from sorcery. Suspicions concentrate on the latter group. On one hand, they were the ones responsible for taking care of the deceased. On the other, local troubles are the most likely to have led to malevolent designs on him or her. The visitors thus act the part of the concerned public. Supported by rhythmic handclaps, elders from this party rise and harangue the local men for not having "looked after" the deceased well. Veiled or open accusations of sorcery are put forward. The local elders, similarly backed by their group, deny any complicity in causing the death. In the search for causes, all sorts of recent local conflicts are reviewed. If the deceased was an important figure, or the death sudden, the argument may become very vehement.

The dispute is often interrupted by a stylized kind of unequal contest between members of the two parties. Men among the visitors demand that some of the defenders come out into the open and then *tele* (bombard) them with missiles (such as pieces of banana stem or firewood), which their targets attempt to *ngmaa* (dodge). Whereas the argument and the subsequent

241

exchanges are wholly dominated by elder males, the hitting and throwing things offer young men a singular opportunity to molest and even ridicule elders, who are otherwise shown much respect.

The "inquest" may last from less than a half hour (a case of an old widow) to several hours. The character of the illness may indicate the kind of sorcery that killed the deceased. But the inquiry does usually not result in the public determination of guilt of specific persons. First, local strifes, which could lead to sorcery, may be difficult to connect unambiguously to the deceased and the death. Second, it seems that people hesitate to provoke a suspected sorcerer by naming him openly, lest "somebody soon would die again." Therefore, only elderly men speak at the "inquest" because they are experienced in the art of veiled discourse.

THE MORTUARY EXCHANGES

The "inquest" opposed people who, by kinship or residence, were close to the deceased to the wider public. Now the organization of the event is transformed. The two groups of males coalesce, and a *ndang* (circle) of elders from both groups forms under the deceased's house. Younger men and women collect at the periphery. (If the deceased was a woman, there are some separate exchanges conducted between women at a different site from that of the main exchanges.)

On the ground inside the circle of men the valuables of the basic section of the mortuary exchanges are now arranged. The mortuary exchanges separate and oppose three parties or "sides," centering on the three descent categories involved in the deceased's own marriage and the deceased's parents' marriage. Further, the two teams of men who performed funeral services appear in the exchanges.

In the basic section *ndap* shells and other valuables are laid out in a formal arrangement that concerns the three "sides" and the team of gravediggers (fig. 2).

Four rows of *ndap* are arranged on the ground: a short row of five *ndap* followed by three rows of ten *ndap* each. Subsequently other valuables (stone axes, necklaces) are added to the last two rows.

The typical unit of *ndap* payment is a *ndaptii* (*ndap* line), a set of usually ten *ndap* that represents a range of ranking, from lower to higher rank. In Figure 3 *ndap* sequences are represented by letters: from *a*, a piece of lowest rank, equivalent to, say, 5 to 10 *toea*, up to *f*; a medium-rank piece, equivalent to, say, 1.50 to 2 *kina*. Ndap of about this rank are the highest pieces still circulating. As will be seen from the figure, the *ndap* in each row ascend in rank from left to right, and the rows ascend in compound rank from bottom to top. The arrangement has a fixed mnemonic form that is repeated at all mortuary feasts for married people.

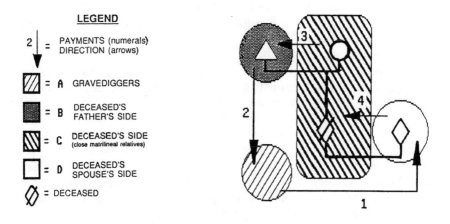

LEGEND

2 ↓ = PAYMENTS (numerals) / DIRECTION (arrows)

▨ = A GRAVEDIGGERS

■ = B DECEASED'S FATHER'S SIDE

▧ = C DECEASED'S SIDE (close matrilineal relatives)

□ = D DECEASED'S SPOUSE'S SIDE

◇ = DECEASED

FIGURE 2. The social categories involved in the basic section of the mortuary exchanges.

4. *b c c d d d d e e f* + 2–3 axes and 4–12 necklaces *(tpi tomũ)*
3. *b b c c d d d d e e* + 1–2 axes and 1–2 necklaces
2. *a b b c c d d d d e* + 2–6 kina (in Jinjo area)
1.   *a b b c c*

FIGURE 3. The basic arrangement of valuables at the mortuary exchanges. Small letters refer to *ndap* pieces. The *ndap* sequences shown here are an ideal representation constructed on the basis of observed exchanges. The letters indicate approximate *ndap* rank levels, not actual *ndap categories*. The number of *ndap* categories involved in any actual mortuary exchange would be considerably larger.

1. *Kiyã pü dyuu*[11] Five *ndap* given by the gravediggers. A solicitory gift similar to others presented at the mortuary feast (see below). It is taken by the deceased's spouse's side.[12]

2. *Kpö chiye kpaatii*[13] Given by the deceased's father's side. Taken by the gravediggers. (In the Jinjo area this set is supplemented by cash: 2–6 kina.)

3. *Yiyem kpaatii*[14] Given by the deceased's side. Taken by the deceased's father's side. This set is supplemented by a few other valuables (1–2 stone blades and a valuable necklace or two).

243

4. *Taaka tii*[15]   Given by the deceased's spouse's side. Taken by the deceased's side. This set is supplemented by a payment of other valuables called *tpi tomũ* consisting of several stone blades and necklaces (and occasionally ceremonial lime spatulae).

The arrangement so far described is only the beginning of the mortuary exchanges. It is supplemented by further prestations. Additional rows of *ndap* are laid out adjacent to the basic arrangement (below row 1 or above row 4) or at nearby sites. Still further sets of *ndap* and also other valuables (stone blades, necklaces) may be collected and given away informally. All these additions may possibly represent an expansion of the mortuary payments from the basic form. All the rows of *ndap* of the basic arrangement, and the other valuables that accompany them, are distributed among several recipients, mainly in the subclan section forming the core of the respective side. *Ndap* sets in the additional prestations are each taken by one recipient only. All these sets are just called *kpaatii* (mortuary line, in the following called "ordinary sets"). Their compound rank corresponds with, or is lower than, row 2 of the basic arrangement. People announce a claim to a payment by presenting single solicitory *ndap* pieces of low rank called *kiyã pü* (compare row 1) or *ndap u tpye* (mother of *ndap*).[16]

The additional prestations may be divided into the following categories:

5. A number of ordinary sets given by the deceased's spouse's side. Taken by the deceased's side. Other valuables (stone blades, necklaces) may be added. A supplement to the *taaka tii* (row 4).

6. A number of ordinary sets given by the deceased's close relatives (mainly members of deceased's subclan section). Taken by more remote relatives on deceased's side (for example, members of other sections of deceased's subclan, clanspeople from other subclans, members of linked subclans, or filiates) or by exchange friends of deceased. If the deceased was a woman, close female relatives of her give away some ordinary sets to other of her kinswomen.

7. A number of ordinary sets and some stone blades/necklaces given by the deceased's side to repay prestations received by deceased at former mortuary feasts.

The total number of ordinary sets of all categories varies between ten and twenty (100–200 *ndap*).

8. *Tpodotii*[17]   Given by the deceased's side. Taken by the team who built the grave house and carried the body. Consists of one or two rows of *ndap*. (In the Jinjo area supplemented by cash: 2–6 *kina*.) This payment corresponds to the *kpö chiye kpaatii* (row 2) but is often somewhat larger.

In summary, the deceased's own side and his or her father's side each pays for a part of the funeral services (payments 2 and 8). There is a unilateral payment from the deceased's side to his or her father's side (payment 3). The spouse's side makes relatively large payments to the deceased's side (payments 4 and 5), which are taken mainly by the deceased's close matrilineal relatives. These people themselves make payments to more remote relatives and exchange friends of the deceased (payment 6). They also repay people (or their heirs) who earlier gave the deceased mortuary payments (payment 7) (Figure 4).[18]

At the "inquest" the close relatives and affines and local men were opposed to the visitors. Payments 3, 4, and 5 (as well as the payments to the funeral teams) are largely conducted among members of the former group; payments 6 and 7 mainly go to people among the visitors. Altogether, this means a considerable drain on the resources of both the spouse's and the

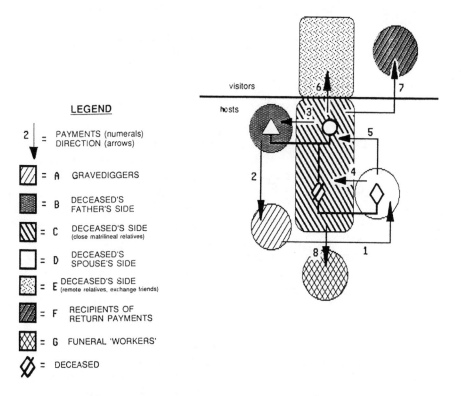

LEGEND

$2 \downarrow$ = PAYMENTS (numerals)
DIRECTION (arrows)

= A GRAVEDIGGERS

= B DECEASED'S FATHER'S SIDE

= C DECEASED'S SIDE (close matrilineal relatives)

= D DECEASED'S SPOUSE'S SIDE

= E DECEASED'S SIDE (remote relatives, exchange friends)

= F RECIPIENTS OF RETURN PAYMENTS

= G FUNERAL 'WORKERS'

= DECEASED

FIGURE 4. The social categories involved in complete mortuary exchanges.

245

Liep

deceased's relatives. A good deal of the valuables (stone blades, necklaces) and lower-rank *ndap* left by the deceased are thereby dispersed. (The *kö* and higher-rank *ndap*, however, are inherited, mainly by the deceased's children.) As there has been no time to collect contributions at tours of soliciting (the practice before other large prestations) people say that "a place is swept" after a mortuary feast. Yet, this is not the end of it, for weeks after the mortuary feast visitors may still show up at the deceased's village to cry at the grave and to claim restoration.

The prestations from the spouse's side to the deceased's side (payments 4 and 5) are returned when the widow or the widower dies. A man who marries a widow pays *tiye* (a somewhat reduced bridewealth). In addition, he must refund the widow's relatives the mortuary prestations they paid to her first husband's relatives.

When all the valuables have been presented and redistributed, the guests are served a meal of cooked tubers, which they eat on the spot before leaving.

THE FRESH AND THE DEAD: THE MEANING OF THE MORTUARY EXCHANGES

Informants offered various and not quite consistent statements about the purposes of these exchanges. It seems that no well-integrated explanation exists. I suggest that this complex of exchanges is exactly an ambiguous "custom." It follows an arbitrary scheme, faithfully reproduced in the main outline, but allowing for variation. It was developed out of bygone historical events, each affecting its features. Like other nonverbal communication these movements of valuable objects lend themselves to a range of interpretations. Several layers of meaning may be relevant, which may be variously stressed according to the situation and to the dispositions and strategies of the participants. I will discuss such layers under the three headings of reconciliation, reconstitution, and conclusion.

Reconciliation

The most obvious interpretation is that the deceased's relatives have suffered a loss. Those that pay are "sorry for them," and the payments are to be considered a compensation to soothe their bereavement. Especially the affines stand accused of having neglected to care for and protect the deceased—if they have not actually done him, or her, in! Through their prestations they counteract suspicions of malice. In a case in which a woman perished by fire, her husband's side made unusually large payments, evi-

246

dently for this reason.[19] In the same way the payments from the close relatives to more remote relatives and friends of the deceased among the visitors
may be seen as a gesture of appeasement. These people have also been "diminished" by the death and they arrive angry and vengeful. But they leave
in peace with valuables in their baskets. The prestations to the deceased's
side from the spouse's side, and the one from the deceased's side to his
or her father's side, may also be regarded as an acknowledgment of care
taken by the recipients for the other part. The dead person "looked after"
his or her spouse and was in the same way "looked after" by his or her
father.

Reconstitution

Through the death of the deceased a multitude of relationships have been
severed or damaged. Mortuary prestations, especially those given by the
deceased's close relatives to remote relatives and friends, may be seen as a
way of renewing or reconstituting these relationships. Strands in the network of relationships that centered on the deceased are taken over by the
living. Exchange items thereby in a way become icons embodying the
deceased's identity. (One informant said that a dead man was $k\bar{o}$ [inside]
a necklace he had received at his mortuary feast; the same expression is used
in the sense "equivalent to.") But such icons at the same time signify exchange relationships between living people.

For a surviving spouse the mortuary prestations made in his or her name
to the deceased's close relatives (payments 4 and 5) also—besides the element of compensation—substantiate the bond of filiation to the common
children. As noted, children possess identity vis-à-vis both their father's and
their mother's side, an identity that, I suggest, is to some extent ambiguous
and negotiable. Through the mortuary prestations the widow/widower, assisted by his or her side, "pays for" the right to "care" from the children.
Again, the prestations substantiate a right of access for the surviving spouse
and the children to trees and land used by the deceased. When the widow
or widower dies the direction of the affinal mortuary prestations is reversed.
If the husband died first, his children, by participating in the return payment
to his side, can prolong their use right to his trees and land. Yet by clinching
the first mortuary payment the return payment also signifies a closure of
an exchange cycle. Sometimes, therefore, a son may renew his claim to land
rights by making an additional mortuary payment (*taaka tii*: payment 4),
thereby opening a new cycle ("making a new point").[20] (I also observed an
instance in which a man used this opportunity to back up his rights vis-à-vis
his wife's side at the mortuary feast for his widowed mother-in-law.) Sometimes adult children do make their own separate *taaka tii* already at the
death of their father while their mother is still living. One of my informants

compared this aspect of the mortuary prestations, in which the payment refers to rights *in personam* and over things, to "income tax."

Conclusion

Informants explained that the payment to the deceased's father's relatives from the deceased's relatives—the *yi-yem kpaatii* ("leg-paying mortuary line")—is made to "close the door on the father's people."[21] The payment means, they said, that the deceased "goes finish" from his father's place. It is to "remove his legs from the father's land." Today, I think, this is only to be understood figuratively. Men often say that they garden on a piece of land because their father's or mother's father used it before. Rather than a complete severance of the relationship between the deceased's father's relatives and his descendents (matrilineal and filiates), I see the "leg payment" as marking a formal conclusion to the mutual obligatory exchange commitments between his or her father's relatives and his or her own based upon the marriage of the deceased's parents and maintained by the bond of filiation to the deceased. (There may, of course, remain similar commitments based upon other affinal or filiative bonds between the two sides, for example, if the deceased have surviving siblings.) The cycle of reciprocal exchanges was established by the deceased's parent's marriage and continued into the next generation. I have explained that affines contribute reciprocally to the payments each side undertakes, and that filiates contribute to, and share in, payments in which their father's subclan is involved. Adult children contribute to the mortuary payment for their father at his death. Men may later, through a special version of pig payment, transfer stone axes and necklaces to patrilateral relatives, a transaction that is seen as "paying for their father" (and also for use rights to his land). Conversely, children (mainly sons) inherit valuables from their father. They do so either directly, before or after his death, or indirectly, through the later return gifts, mentioned previously (payment 7), of prestations given to others at his mortuary feast. I interpret the "leg payment" as a clinching gift that concludes this long and many-sided cycle. To some degree it counteracts any surplus flow of wealth from the father's subclan to its filiate and frees the deceased's subclan from further claims from the father's side.

This element of closure is a principle that it seems people feel should govern all mortuary exchanges. We have seen that the mortuary prestations from the spouse's to the deceased's side must be returned at the death of the surviving spouse. The elders try to reconstruct who provided and received each of the ten *ndap* of the *taaka tii* and the other valuables of the *tpi tomü*, and equivalent pieces are returned to the original contributors (or their heirs) from the original recipients (or their heirs). We have also noted that some of the payments the deceased's relatives make are returns of valuables formerly received by the deceased at earlier mortuary feasts. In fact, all mortuary payments (except those for funeral services) are supposed to be either *ku* (fresh), that is "new points," or *ndo* (dead), that is, they *mbgene* (square) old ones. In a way mortuary payments represent the substitution of an aspect of a person by objectified value. But this should only be temporary. No definitive alienation should be possible. In the last instance life must tally with life and valuable with valuable.

At a general level it thus seems that the Yela maintain that the manifold exchanges set off by the death of an individual—resulting in debts that may be outstanding for many years and linking each particular mortuary feast to many others—should conform to a structure of symmetrical exchange. This scrupulous insistence on symmetry maintains an equilibrium in kind in the long term and thereby a form of social equality. In the mortuary complex no group should be able to employ wealth so as to make others permanently indebted and inferior. This emphasis on mortuary reciprocity gains further significance when it is seen as the culmination of a cycle of affinal prestations—after the initial bridewealth payment—that is likewise characterized by delayed symmetrical exchanges. When prestation is thus regularly checked by counterprestation in kind, an overarching hierarchy based on complementary exchange is effectively held at bay.[22]

CONCLUSION

In the first part of this essay I outlined a social structure based on asymmetric exchange between wife-givers and wife-takers of products of the land against foreign "prestige goods." If such a structure is regularly reproduced, it will tend to establish unequal rank between the givers and receivers of wives. Descent and the connection of people to land will be associated with the female line, and political power will appear as the relation of "father" to "child." Chiefly providers of prestige goods will stand as "fathers" to local land-owning and wife-giving communities. The sons of chiefs will go to reside avunculocally and succeed their mother's brothers as local headmen. It all becomes part of a logical system of hierarchy connecting rights to land and its products, descent structure, marriage alliances, affinal exchange, rank differentiation, and political power.[23] An approximation to the model of such a system is found in Kiriwina. If my hunch is right, what we are witnessing elsewhere in the Massim are various examples of the obfuscation of this hierarchical logic. I have discussed some of the ways this may be done. The analysis of Rossel mortuary exchanges provides one example of the dematerialization of hierarchy. Here, affinal exchanges are turned into delayed equivalent prestations in kind and "the door is closed on the father's people," thus repudiating a perpetual bond of filiation of the wife-giving to the wife-taking group. By such measures the reproduction of unequal relations between local descent groups is prevented.[24]

I must stress, however, that I am speaking of the containment of a structure of inequality between *descent segments* of society, what could be called a "mechanical" hierarchical structure. This does not prevent the development of other forms of inequality.

First, it is clear that the delayed symmetrical structure of Rossel mortuary exchanges is only grossly defined in terms of descent categories. These *do* figure as a framework for conceptualizing and performing exchange, but the identity of individuals is not solely determined by descent group membership. In the capacity of filiates children may reclaim valuables that their deceased father gave away at earlier mortuary feasts. They may also inherit from their father *kö* and high-rank *ndap*, which do not circulate in the mortuary sphere. Thus, there is some blurring of the picture of exact balance between descent groups, which at first appears to govern the mortuary exchanges. Again, we must remember that it is possible for people to reopen otherwise closed cycles, by presenting "fresh" mortuary payments. This gives able individuals scope for employing valuables strategically and exploiting debt.

Second, there may at one level of exchange—between descent groups—exist an overall equality, while at another—between elder and younger—there is access to wealth on unequal terms. I have just repeated that mortuary gifts, formerly given by people who are not deceased, are returned to their heirs. In many cases younger people may wait for years, after the death of their relatives in the former generation, before they inherit these valuables. Thus, there is a delay of inheritance that tends to make valuables circulate in the hands of the elders. By the time the "younger" generation has gained access to this wealth, they are themselves "elders."

Outside the mortuary circuit necklaces and axe blades circulate mainly, it will be remembered, in payments for houses and canoes. It is only mature men who are able to amass the wealth to pay for these items of status property. Younger men do most of the labor in building them and acquire valuables in return. Although this is difficult to demonstrate from my material, it stands to reason that there must be a general tendency for these valuables to flow from the younger men toward the elder at the mortuary exchanges, to balance the opposite flow of valuables in payments for house and canoe work. By employing their hard-earned axe blades or necklaces in contributions to mortuary prestations, younger men may gain cumulative standing as responsible kinsmen and exchange friends: that is, become social elders themselves.

Exchange practices on Rossel work against a "mechanical" structure of ranked descent groups, but they do not prevent the reproduction of a different, more individualized and "statistical" structure of social differentiation. Here, a stratum of elders, and especially the most able financiers, acquires status and influence by manipulating exchanges. Such big man systems are the normal pattern in the Massim today, outside northern Kiriwina.

NOTES

Acknowledgments: I have been supported by various grants from the Danish Social Science Research Council and from the Australian National University. I thank the staff of the Institute of Ethnology and Anthropology, University of Copenhagen, for valuable comments during a presentation of an earlier draft of this essay. For corrections of language I am grateful to Michael Whyte.

1. I further discuss the phenomenon of hierarchy in the Massim and its devolution toward "great man" or "big man" forms in Liep n.d. The containment of hierarchy is also involved in my interpretation of the symbolism of a Rossel Island dance feast (Liep 1987).

2. Chowning mentions hereditary rank on Goodenough, in Molima, and in Wamira, on the mainland. It is remarkable that the term for the large food distributions—*sagali* in the northern Massim and the D'Entrecasteaux, *hagali, segaya*, or *zayaga* in the Louisiades—reappears as far away as in the Maori *hakari* (Mauss 1966:97, n.77).

3. The material on which this essay is based was collected during altogether twenty-three months of fieldwork on Rossel Island (eighteen months in 1971–73 and five months in 1980). My field base on Rossel was in Pum village at the north coast of the island, in the Wulanga Bay census ward. One circumstance has limited my observations of mortuary practices. During my entire stay in the field nobody died in Pum or the larger Wulanga Bay area! I have therefore never seen a death and I have only been present at two funerals, in another district. I have attended altogether eight mortuary feasts in the census areas of Morpa and Jinjo, but my inquiries were hampered by my limited knowledge of the genealogical connections of the participants. As in all my other investigations I worked through interpreters, not having attained fluency in the Rossel language.

4. Occasionally people honor a deceased person some years after the death by a *mbgamö* (small memorial feast) where cooked food is served. A man may, for example, make such a feast when the posts of his father's house are pulled up.

5. These claims to mutual kinship are founded on grounds such as that the two subclans are associated with the same, or contiguous, lands; that they share totemic species; or that a woman from one of the groups was adopted into the other when it was on the verge of dying out.

6. Another set of clan names are given to children by their mothers and are thus passed on inside the clan.

7. Compare Gawan *yaakara* ("to deny") for "public hearings or moots involving conflicts" (Munn 1986:309–10, n.8).

8. Armstrong writes *temewe* (1928:103) but *we* just means "area." See also Liep (1983).

Liep

9. Compare Molima *bwabwale* and Duau *bwabwali* (Chowning, Thune, this volume).

10. The status of both widows and widowers is marked by the wearing of *yede wũ* (mourning strings). The widow's mourning string is actually two rows of thin string tied over each shoulder and under the opposite armpit. The widower wears a single string around the neck. A man who marries a widow must make a payment of a single medium-rank *ndap* to her former husband's relatives "to cut her string." A widower who remarries similarly pays his former wife's relatives to remove his own string.

11. *kiyã-pü-dyuu* (untranslatable-pay-small heap).

12. It is curious that the deceased's spouse's side receives these solicitory *ndap* and not the father's people, who actually pay the gravediggers. It is just the custom. None of my informants could explain why!

13. *kpö-chiye-kpaatii* (gravedigging-mortuary line).

14. *yi-yem-kpaatii* (leg-giving [paying]-mortuary line).

15. *taaka tii*: probably derived from *too* (skin). Armstrong mentions flaying of the corpse in the funeral rites for a "chief" (1928:103). *tpi tomũ* (person-silent).

16. Unfortunately I was not able to record exactly who gave and received these solicitory *ndap*. I do not know whether they are presented only to the deceased's own close matrilineal relatives or also to the deceased's spouse's people. It may be that the deceased's people receive all of them and pass some over to the spouse's side. Neither do I know whether the funeral "workers" present such solicitory *ndap*, as do the gravediggers. Consequently the flows of solicitory *ndap* (except the ones from the gravediggers) are not shown on the diagram.

17. *tpodo-tii* (work-line).

18. This is a schematic outline. The distinction between close and remote relatives of deceased is in reality somewhat blurred. Thus, for example, a filiate of the deceased's subclan may receive an "ordinary set" from the deceased's spouse's people or directly from people of the deceased's subclan. How close or remote a relative is depends on genealogical closeness, residence, and especially, I suppose, actual former association of the person with the deceased.

19. Weiner mentions similar considerations in Kiriwina (1976:74); see also Thune (this volume).

20. I was told that in this case the return payment would go to the son's heirs at his own death.

21. Similarly the *lo'un* exchange in Muyuw mortuary ritual is said to "end the marriage between the deceased's parents" (Damon, this volume).

22. Note, however, that my informants tended to see things the other way round: they stressed the interest of people to *regain* their wealth. This would, with a little foresight, set a limit to greed. The deceased's kin may well restrict their demands at the mortuary feast, well knowing that sooner or later they will in their turn have to "work," that is, to collect the return payment.

23. The model of such a matrilineal "prestige good system" was first proposed by Ekholm (1977).

24. Another measure that would work against the reproduction of a stable

hierarchy would be a reversal of the wife-taker/wife-giver relation through patrilateral marriage. Indeed, classificatory FZ or FZD marriage is recommended on Rossel and classificatory MBD marriage regarded as not quite right. (The marriage of first cross-cousins is proscribed.) Statistically, however, there is only a slight tendency toward patrilateral marriage. An analysis of the marriage system on Rossel is beyond the scope of this essay.

Roy Wagner

Conclusion

The Exchange Context of the Kula

•   The symposium presented here represents one of the stated purposes of the Second International Kula Conference: the consideration of internal exchange as it relates to external exchange among societies in the greater Massim area. The explicit point of comparison addressed here is that of mortuary feasting and exchange, practices that take on a special emphasis in the Massim area, as in some other regions of Melanesia.[1] Mortuary feasts and exchanges are a widespread, if not universal, cultural form in Melanesia and are found, often in a considerably elaborated format, in the interior[2] as well as on the coast. They generally emphasize, and enact, a kind of summative or definitive resolution of the deceased and his or her social relationships. In some areas (often those of predominantly Austronesian language affinities), such as the Massim or Central New Ireland, the feasting and the resolution it enacts assume an enhanced significance as the generic or archetypal collective social event: the definitive feast. The death of a person—often a "big," or influential person—provides the foil for social and individual values and their production and reproduction. For this reason mortuary feasting provides an excellent monitor, or checkpoint, for the interrelation of internal and external exchange in these areas.

We are fortunate, indeed, then, that each of the foregoing studies represents intensive, long-term fieldwork of a very high ethnographic standard, and that all represent, in the aggregate, a broad cross section of the Massim area. Although there is considerable variation in the ways in which the authors have chosen to present their material, particularly in the ideological dimension, it should be kept in mind that ostensibly "similar" cultural forms often have very different local meanings. Frequently, too, there is much variation in the degree to which the validity of verbal representation is admitted at all within the local culture: this editor's Usen Barok informants, from Central New Ireland, insisted that the meanings of a public feast are contained in the images and objects presented and could not be adequately verbalized. The meaning of a feast or rite can also be "absorbed" in its accomplishment: the lifting of a taboo or the providing of plenty.

Nevertheless, the broad sampling of societies presented here provides an opportunity to draw detailed comparisons among their mourning rites and the social and cultural resolutions enacted in them, and to examine the range of variation for evidence regarding the large-scale relation of internal to external exchange. For a beginning, I shall consider the comparative morphology of mortuary feasting in its overall organization and staging.

COMPARATIVE MORPHOLOGY

A remarkably uniform general schema of mortuary feasting characterizes all of the Austronesian-speaking peoples covered in this symposium and seems to extend considerably beyond the Massim region. (Central New Ireland, for instance, shows a strong overall congruence with it.[3]) The Yela of Rossel Island, who are not Austronesian speakers, do not conform in their practice to the schema, though they show other kinds of affinities with mortuary feasting elsewhere in the Massim.

The series of mortuary feasts is differentiated into usually, and at least, three stages, or phases, of feasting (in the D'Entrecasteaux examples, there are four), each phase including one or more named events. The sequence as a whole organizes the stages by which a community at large or particular classes of people involved in the mourning, are released from taboos or restrictions assumed at the time of death. An initial stage of feasting begins at death, or immediately after burial, and may last from a few days to a week or more; a second stage, from a month to a year after the first, follows; and the final stage comes some time after this, upward of a year to a much longer time after the death.

The first stage generally includes an event that effects the lifting of a collective, communitywide mourning restriction on collective activity, movement, or, most commonly, work involved in food production.[4] This is true of the Normanby *Basa*, Kaduwagan *Govan Vanu*, Vakutan *Mwagula Valu*, Tubetube *Mayaumate*, Muyuw *Ungayay*, and Vanatinai *Jivia*. This stage may also include the assumption of restrictions by principal mourners, or rites of appeasement, divination, or inquest (as on Rossel) regarding the

TABLE I
Comparative Morphology

Bwaidoka	Normanby	Molima	Kaduwaga
Wake	First phase:	Wake	First *Sagali* *Sekowau*
Burial	Burial feast	Burial	*Puya* *Sagali Vegua*
Matailuwana	*Basa* Lifts village mourning	*Vegabu,* *Gabugabu* Mourning assumed	*Govan Vanu* Fishing to release village from mourning
Venimaikola			
Enkovekovekuboma	*Dalauwa*	*Ve'enovila* Widow released from seclusion	Second *Sagali* Secluded mourners released from restrictions
Towatowa Food taboos imposed	Second phase: *Bwabwali* Removal of mourning from spouse's father's lines	*Ve'alaupa* Widow/ widower released from mourning	*Vatu Sepwana* *Nitutula Sepwana* *Sagali Nisanadobu*
Gufa			
Gufayafi			
Alakuku Lifts *Vewawana* taboos	Third phase: *Sagali*	*Sagali*	Third *Sagali* *Lagila* *Katupwakau* *Laka* *Dani*
Bwabwala Lifts *Valevaleta* taboos	Fourth phase: *susu* feasts itself		
Inua Disposal of relic			

Vakuta	Tubetube	Muyuw	Vanatinai
Yawari	*Wali*	*Ungayay* Lifts taboo on gardening	*Jivia* Lifts taboos on self-feeding, leaving village
Mwagula Valu Lifts *Borabora* taboo	*Mayaumate* Lifts general (fires, gardening) taboo	*Anagin Tavalam* Lifts taboos on eating coconuts, moving *kula* valuables	*Velaloga* Allows widow/widower to bathe, leave hamlet
Sakula Kola Permits mourner to bathe	*Ligaliga Boaboa* Cleaning of widow/widower	*Lo'un* Release of widow/widower from mourning	*Ghanrekereke* Lifts taboo on cooking in deceased's house
Kaptunila Papa Release of mourner	*Ligaliga Olo Olo* Frees widow/widower from mourning restrictions		*Verada*
Kawasa			*Zagaya* Lifts final restrictions on widow/widower
Ulusila Wadola Lifts taboo on mourner's eating yams	Soi		
Vakakaiya Release of restrictions on mourner			Rossel
			Funeral
Sagali			*Yaaka* (Inquest)
			Kpakpa (Mortuary feast)

257

death. The second stage usually includes a rite of washing the widow/widower or other principal mourners, removing them from confinement, or lifting some, or all, other restrictions upon them. This is found in the Bwaidoka *Bwabwale*, Normanby *Bwabwali*, Molima *Ve'enovila*, Kaduwagan second *Sagali*, Vakutan *Kaptunila Papa*, Tubetube *Ligaliga Boaboa*, and Vanatinai *Velaloga*. In Molima, on Muyuw, and Vanatinai, the widow/widower is not released until after this, at the final stage. The third (in Molima the fourth) stage is a much larger event, involving long and intricate preparations, and is usually held in commemoration of a number of deceased persons.

The terms *Bwabwale-Bwabwali-Boaboa*, and those including *papa* in a compound form, appear to form a cognate series designating a feast at which the spouse of the deceased undergoes cleansing or at which some or all mourning restrictions are lifted from him or her. It is possible that the Rossel Island term *Kpakpa* (mortuary feast) is also related to this series. The more widely shared cognate, designating the most general and public of feasts (usually the third stage), and also the generic for "mortuary feast," is represented by the series *Sagali-Sagal-Zagaya-Soi*. It is found, in one form or another, in all societies reported on here except Bwaidoka and Yela (Rossel). In Kaduwaga and Dobu, *Sagali* is the generic term for "mortuary feast," and on Muyuw it is *Sagal*. Clearly the *sagali* term involves a larger conception (except possibly for Bwaidoka) than *Bwabwale*; it is a term for a number of feasts or a feast for a number of dead. Whether these cognacies and similarities are based on common cultural or linguistic roots or are the results of "borrowing" among peoples in trade contact, we may never know. It seems likely that both conditions might reinforce one another.

The overall similarities are apparent enough: a series of feasts immediately following the death culminating in the lifting of a community taboo, a second stage some time later releasing the principal mourner or mourners and long-held food taboos, and a final, large-scale distribution of raw food for the generic dead. The concerted symbolic and social activity that serves to "construct" this typical sequence is, however, rather different in content and conception, if not in feature, from one society to another, and underlying similarities in format can easily conceal, as well as reveal, details of variability. This consideration introduces a second area of comparison: that of the organization and significance of internal exchange.

THE SOCIAL SIGNIFICANCE OF MOURNING

In all of the instances considered in this symposium, dual social categorizations play a predominant part in mortuary feasting. Several sets of these may come into play in the course of feasting, and more than one may be active in a given feast. However ad hoc the mourning categorizations, they inevitably present significant kin and social structural oppositions in a ritual transformation, so that the respective ritual and secular involvements of a given relationship stand in a motivating relationship to one another. The "social organization of mourning," the way in which mourning tasks are construed in terms of social categories and their effect on those categories, shows considerable variation across the range of the Massim. It constitutes the staging, and the dynamic, of internal exchange.

In Bwaidoka, the matter of which kin categories shall be fitted into the mourning role of *Tomotavuna*, "buriers," is a matter of choice; they can be a dead man's agnates, or "mother's people," though the latter, as "wife-givers," are preferred, as it is felt they *should* receive the buriers' payment. (Bwaidoka is the only patrilineal instance discussed here.) This degree of optation is fairly unique. In Kaduwaga, in the Trobriands, where an elaborate set of four mourning categories is recognized, the conventional format of four matrilineal clans is condensed into two moieties: Malasi-Lukuba and Lukwasisiga-Lukulabuta. Hence the ritual adaptation of social categories involves a more explicitly structural assumption of duality here than elsewhere. Mourning-specific social categorizations are found largely in the D'Entrecasteaux and the Trobriands—the western limb of the region under consideration. Elsewhere ordinary kin categorizations are used, or the "buriers" are simply an associated *susu*, like the *yanasa* of Tubetube, or the *bukuna* of Normanby.

Likewise the western limb of the Kula—the Trobriands and the northern D'Entrecasteaux—focuses a good deal of mourning activity around relics or objects taken from the body of the deceased. In Bwaidoka, the relics are retained throughout the mourning period, to be burned at the *Inua*, the last feast, for "owners" of the death alone. The *mwagula* of the Trobriands is a mourning necklace incorporating relics of the deceased (the Molima *mwagula* is free of these); it is worn throughout the mourning period, and its wearer or wearers are compensated at the final *sagali*.

Food, and especially elaborate puddings such as *moni*, plays a central role in all Massim mortuary feasting and in the exchanges that articulate it. But, except for the Kula valuables given as compensation in the Trobriands (*Sagali Vegua* in Kaduwaga, *Kulututu* or *Ninaboila* in Vakuta), and in the settling of marriage debts in Molima, the exchanges in the Trobriands and the D'Entrecasteaux are exclusively focused on food and other elements of domestic production. A full appreciation of the degree of cultural concern and elaboration in these areas, respectively, can be gained by a reading of Michael Young's *Fighting with Food*,[5] and of the discussion of skirts and skirt distribution in Annette Weiner's *Women of Value, Men of Renown*.[6] Montague's and Campbell's accounts in this study give a sense both of the centrality and of the regional variation of this culminating feat of women's productivity.

Mortuary exchanges in Bwaidoka take the form of payments by the *toinavuvuna* ("owners of the death"), the patrilineage, or subclan, of the deceased, to the kinsmen, friends, partners, and creditors of the latter, but principally to the *tomotavuna* (buriers). Ideally, the buriers should be "mother's people" of the deceased, so that the large payment they receive serves as a final compensation to them as the "wife-givers" of the deceased's mother. But they need not be mother's people, and the exchanges are thus ideally and conditionally kin exchanges.

The sequence of exchanges has a redistributive quality: the large *Matailuwana* and *Luwana* payments are followed by the *Venimaikola*, in which food is given to the owners' exchange partners to reciprocate their contributions; and the later, large *Gufa* (which also includes wealth objects) is followed by a similar reciprocation in the *Gufaiyafi*. In the *Bwabwale* feast, which lifts the *Valevaleta* taboos, raw food is given to the buriers, who pass it on to their own exchange partners and only consume food after these have reciprocated. Although the net result is an outlay of food and food products by the owners, much of their exchange "universe" is activated in the process.

The bilateral Molima of Fergusson Island likewise stage their mortuary exchanges in terms of a task-specific duality: the *valevaleta* (mourners or sitters) and the *geyawuna* (workers or eaters). The former category includes parents, children, siblings, and the surviving spouse of the deceased; the latter, as in the ideal case in Bwaidoka, the "mother's people." Molima mortuary feasts are given for the *geyawuna*, in return for their services, and they receive the property of the deceased (including wealth objects) as well. The final feast, the *Sagali*, is quite different, however. Organized by an aspiring *kaiwabu*, it is generated by the competitive energies of *'asa vaivai* (affinally related villages). The interaction, including "opening gifts," rivalry, and initiation of marriages, eventually leads to gifts of valued foods by the sponsor in order to secure the reciprocation of a yam harvest, which constitutes the core of the *Sagali*. Thus the Molima move, in the course of their feasting and through the exchange of food, from the resolution of a previous marriage to affinity and initiation of new ones.

Thune's analysis of Normanby mortuary rites reveals a process by which the deceased is serially divested of historically developed relations in *susu* other than his or her own and relegated to an anonymous, ahistoric matrilineality. Feasting opposes the *susu* of the deceased in turn to *bukuna* (distant *susu* mates and members of formerly associated *susu*, who act as buriers), to the *susu* of the deceased's spouse and/or father, to a generalized, areal audience, and finally, as in the Bwaidoka *Inua*, to itself. The exchanges consist of food, especially pork and large yams, and, as in Bwaidoka, seem largely to be redistributive, with the number of participating "parties" a matter of conventional definition. Thus in the first phase, the deceased's *susu*, together with its affines, make a prestation to the *bukuna*, together with *their* affines; in the second phase, affinally related *susu* contribute food to that of the deceased, which presents the assemblage to the *susu* of the spouse and/or father, which then distribute among *their* affinally related *susu*. The third phase is three-party because the *susu*, after assembling the contributions from affinal groups, presents the totality to a generalized audience (the third party).

The compensation of "buriers" and of close, lateral kin (here "father's people"), which are ideally collapsed together in Bwaidoka and Molima, is done separately on Normanby by stages. The redistributive nature of the exchanges makes use of present affinal relationships to resolve those involving the deceased; because the *bukuna* are in fact more distant *susu* members and members of formerly affiliated *susu*, present affinal relationships also serve to define the *susu* against these vestiges of history.

Of the four mourning roles recognized on Kaduwaga, in the Trobriands, the mourners comprise the "nurturers" of the deceased—*kakau* (spouse) and *makapu* (parents and those parents' same-sex siblings)—and are the chief recipients of exchanges. The deceased's siblings and male matrilineal kin are *tosagali* (payment makers). The other significant party is that of the affines of the deceased. In the first *Sagali* the *tosagali* provide raw and cooked food for those who give skirts and fiber bundles to the chief mourners and relic wearers and are themselves given wealth, coconut trees, or land by the affines as compensation for allowing someone in their care to die. Finally, the affines fish and distribute their catch to the village to lift the general mourning, and the *tosagali* compensate them with pudding. The second *sagali* involves the making of *sepwana* skirts and their presentation to mourners and those who have done funeral services; the *tosagali* compensate them with areca nut and pudding. The third *Sagali* includes three feasts at which the *tosagali* reward grave tenders and relic wearers with puddings and other delectables.

The *tosagali* receive wealth compensation from affines of the deceased and prepare and give food compensation to mourners and grave tenders and to those who provide them with skirts and skirt material. Payment is centripetal here rather than centrifugal, as on Normanby, and the focus is on the productive acts of food preparation and skirt making. Montague's eloquent analysis of *kanua* food and the mortuary significance of eating does much to interpret and explicate this emphasis.

The general pattern of exchanges in Vakuta, the southern extremity of the Trobriands, is similar: except for a payment (*Kulututu* or *Ninaboila*) by the principal mourner's kinsmen to allay sorcery accusations, the exchanges involve items of domestic production. The exchanging parties are the *torikariga* (owners of the death), the deceased's clanspeople, and the kinspeople of the principal mourner—wearer of the *mwagula* artifact—

ideally the spouse or father of the deceased. The first phase of the Vakutan sequence includes gifts of uncooked food and fish from the clan of the principal mourner to that of the *torikariga*, in order to release mourning taboos, as well as the payment of wealth to allay suspicion. Later the clan of the *torikariga* gives mature coconuts (or yams) and skirts to all who participated in ritual mourning and to the principal mourner for distribution to his clan, at the end of seclusion. The second phase begins with solicitory gifts (a *sepwala* skirt and taro pudding) by the principal mourner's clan, and a reciprocating taro pudding given in return by that of the *torikariga*. Two to three months later the solicited gift of a yam pudding by the deceased's clansmen releases the mourner from a restriction on eating yams, and afterward the distribution of skirts by these clanspeople to the principal mourner and his clan accompanies the lifting of all restrictions from the mourner. The final *sagali*, one to ten years later, involves the distribution of yams, skirts, and cooked and raw food by the deceased's clanspeople to those of the principal mourner, and also the distribution of cooked food to women of the village.

Like the Kaduwagan exchanges, those of Vakuta center on the solicitation and enactment of feasts correlated with the lifting of restrictions, culminating in the general distribution of skirts and yams by the deceased's clan. The final Trobriand *Sagali*, with their competitively motivated yam harvests and extended webs of skirt-making obligation and participation, celebrate the conclusion of mourning through massive coordinations of sociality and domestic production.

As we move eastward from these western termini of the Kula, we encounter, at Tubetube and at Muyuw, a very different way of talking about, and of conceptualizing, mortuary feasting. As Macintyre puts it, the operant concepts of mortuary exchange are also those of *kune* (the Kula) and marriage; they are spatial and treat relationships as roads. Death, in the expressive idioms of Tubetube as well as Muyuw, is a blocking of these roads, the felling of trees across them. The mortuary sequence is thus a process of opening these roads, or paths. As relationship is centrally involved here, in its resolution or renegotiation, so owned Kula valuables, *kitomwa* on Tubetube, *kitoum* on Muyuw, move through the exchanges: they become roads, or paths, like marriage, and like the Kula.

Exchanging parties on Tubetube include the *susu* (matrilineage) of the deceased; their *yanasa* (paired matrilineage), who act as "buriers"; and the *susu* of the widowed spouse. As the body is being mourned, affines (the line of the widowed spouse) decorate it with shell valuables, given as *lowalowa*, to be retained by the bereaved *susu*. At the *Mayaumate* feast, members of the deceased's *susu* prepare pork and vegetable food brought by grieving relatives and present it to the *yanasa*, in return for their mourning and burial services. The two later feasts concerned with the lifting of restrictions from the widowed person (*Ligaliga Boaboa* and *Ligaliga Olo Olo*) are accompanied by gifts of yams and a pig by the lineage of the widowed person to that of the deceased. The final *Soi*, given for the dead "of a generation," is redistributive: "honored guests" bring pigs and yams, and these are redistributed to them, together with contributions from the *susu* of the deceased. The overall pattern is for affinally related *susu*, especially that of the widowed spouse, to present to the *susu* of the deceased, which then makes a feast of it or redistributes it.

As in marriage or the Kula, however, prestations involve "roads," human relationships, and these entail debts and binding obligations. This is especially true of the *lowalowa* gift of shell wealth given before burial; it is usual to treat this as *yaga* (a gift that creates a debt), and when given by the widow of a deceased man, it secures rights of usufruct for her children in some of their father's land. The *yaga* must then be reciprocated by a similar (shell wealth or pigs) *maisa* payment made later (perhaps as a funerary *lowalowa* or an affinal prestation). Thus *lowalowa* takes its place in what may be a complex, Kula-like exchange relation between *susu*, in terms of which its status may be redefined. In the case of an in-marrying male, the *susu* can use his death to pass *kitomwa* on to its children via the *lowalowa* and its reciprocation and secure for them usufruct rights in the process.

Affinal relationships on Muyuw are likewise defined in terms of a Kula-like circulation of valuables, established through *takon* (gifts of *kitoum* [personally owned valuables] that make affines into *sinvalam*). The Muyuw mortuary sequence draws upon existing *sinvalam* relationships in order ultimately to resolve those of the deceased's parents with a final *takon*. The principal parties here are the *dal* (subclan of the deceased), those (affines) in *sinvalam* relationships with them, and other relatives who are not *sinvalam*: at the final, *Lo'un* feast, the *tokowadan* (deceased's mother's side) and *tokobinin* (father's side) are significantly involved. For the first feast, *Ungayay*, pigs and *kitoum* are brought as *siwayoub* (funerary gifts) by close affines, and raw pork is distributed to all who came to cry. At the second feast, *Anagin Tavalam*, a host takes upon himself the debts of the deceased and receives large prestations of pig and vegetable food from his *sinvalam*; these are distributed to non-*sinvalam* who cried at the Ungayay. (The support of guests requires a considerable outlay by the host in addition to this.) The final feast, *Lo'un*, concludes with a *takon* exchange in which "female things" are given by the mother's to the father's side, and "male things," including *kitoums*, are given in return.

Muyuw mortuary exchanges are structured around the *sinvalam* relationships created by the internal circulation of Kula valuables against food, and they culminate in an exchange that resolves the *sinvalam* relations of the deceased's parents. Thus the whole context, as well as the purpose, of mortuary exchange is created by the exchange of valuables and the "roads"

263

of this exchange. The closure of *sinvalam* relations in the *Lo'un* appears, at least initially, as the opposite of the Tubetube *lowalowa*, for the latter is generally interpreted as an opening gift. But the *lowalowa* may also be given as the *maisa* (reciprocation) of some earlier *lowalowa* and therefore also serve to achieve closure, or resolution, of interlineal relations. This, in turn, suggests a more general resemblance between the two regimes: in both cases the "road," the interplay of obligation and expectation with respect to Kula valuables, spans generations and links critical events in one life course with those of another. Mortuary feasts on Tubetube and Muyuw punctuate a longitudinal, interlineal "Kula" that runs perpendicular to the interisland one; a *kitoum* or *kitomwa* is a valuable that is "attached" for this kind of circulation.

To the southeast of Muyuw and Tubetube, on Vanatinai and among the Yela people of Rossel Island, and beyond the circuit of Kula exchange, the transgenerational linkage persists in the honoring (and remuneration) of the father's (matri) line. This involves the "thanking," as the Vanatinai say, of the father's people "for marrying the dead person's mother." On Vanatinai it is a patrilateral cross-cousin of the deceased, who has acted as "father" throughout the deceased's life, who ideally "eats the feast" of the dead and receives the largest compensation. Wealth objects (stone axes, axe blades, and shell wealth of various sorts) are the central focus (but by no means the only one) of these transactions. An emphasis on the mediated transmission of imperishable wealth objects via kin exchanges, and of chains of obligation and expectation among lineages regarding such valuables, thus extends beyond the limits of the Kula itself. The difference, of course, is that the valuables used on Vanatinai and Rossel are not "attached" Kula valuables.

A comprehensive analysis of the indigenous significances of such exchanges, and of feeding the "father," has been made by Debbora Battaglia for the people of Sabarl, near Vanatinai.[7] Although the Sabarl exchanges differ in some details from those of Vanatinai, Battaglia's study rounds out the symbolism of a southeastern Massim system with an elegance and force unattainable in a comparative essay such as this.

As on Sabarl, the parties to mortuary exchange on Vanatinai include the matrilineal kin of the deceased, those of the spouse, and a category of the deceased's patrilateral cross-cousins, represented by a specially selected "father" (male or female) known as the *tau*.[8] The flow of valuables is from the affines ultimately to the *tau*. Unless displaced (against the counsels of custom) by a prepossessing matrilineal claimant, the *tau* "eats the *zagaya*" and receives the payment of valuables at the culmination of the mortuary sequence.

Death places the surviving spouse and his or her kin in the position of having to validate their innocence of ill intentions by making *muli* (large) prestations to the matrilineal kin and *tau* of the deceased. Immediately after the death, the affines become the principal "mourners," unable to feed themselves and completely under the care of the deceased's kin. Released from the self-feeding taboo in the *Jivia* (first mourning), the surviving spouse remains in the custody of the deceased's kin, to be released from restrictions on bathing, shaving, and leaving the hamlet at the later *Velaloga* feast. The *Ghanrakerake* feast, which follows, allows the deceased's dwelling to be used for the storage and cooking of food. At each of these feasts, large prestations of valuables must be made by the affines to lift the restrictions upon the mourners. The culminating *zagaya* is, like its Sabarl counterpart, an orchestration of "immanent reciprocity," and it is likewise the occasion at which a large payment of valuables is made to the *tau*. But at the Vanatinai *Mwagumwagu*, at which this occurs, the valuables are placed on the mourners, who are said to be physically "given," together with the valuables, to the *tau*.

This is most significant, in that the valuables as well as the mourners themselves are tendered unto the kin of the deceased in expiation of the culpability of the spouse and his or her relatives. Both, together, are offered to the *tau* as a return on the care and generosity this relative has shown over the lifetime of the deceased. Nowhere is the general Massim tendency to draw upon existing affinal relationships for the resolution of previous ones more explicitly or dramatically demonstrated. Through the reversal, noted by Lepowsky, of their normal relationship (affines do not eat together), the mourners are coopted into a hostage feeding relationship in which they are compelled to the kind of generosity that the *tau* has rendered freely when the deceased was alive. The objects and receipts of this artificially constructed "hostage" feeding relationship are then given over to the *tau* in compensation for his or her efforts.

Mortuary practices among the Yela of Rossel Island do not correspond to the pattern of the Austronesian-speaking Massim peoples, in which seclusion and constraints imposed on mourners are lifted in a protracted series of feasts. The seclusion of the Yela widow proceeds unaffected by the mortuary feast. The funeral and the single *Kpakpa* (mortuary feast), held a week later, are pervaded by suspicion, tension, and confrontation, as relatives fault each other for the death and are in turn faulted by arriving visitors. At both events, the tension resolves into a *Yaaka* (inquestlike argument) concerning the circumstances and causes of the death. This is followed, at the feast, by the mortuary exchanges.

Parties to the exchange include the deceased's clanspeople—matri-relatives, those of the father's side, and the deceased's spouse and his or her relatives. Although the patrilateral cross-cousins do not play the role of a ritual "father" here, as on Sabarl and Vanatinai, they are included as a special category, that of gravediggers. In terms of social categorization,

265

then, Yela mortuary exchanges resemble those of their Austronesian-speaking neighbors.[9]

The similarity is sustained also in the manner and content of the exchanges. The prestations are laid out together, in a formal pattern according to a fixed mnemonic, and, except for informal supplementation, are given simultaneously, as in the "immanent reciprocity" of the climactic mortuary feasts on Sabarl and Vanatinai. Four basic payments are made, each by one party to another in sequence. The smallest is made by the gravediggers (patrilateral cross-cousins) to the spouse of the deceased, the largest by the spouse's side to the matriclanspeople of the deceased, the next largest by the clanspeople to the deceased's father's side, and a somewhat smaller payment by the latter to their offspring, the gravediggers. These may be supplemented by other and additional payments, including prestations made by the deceased's clan to remote relatives and friends of the deceased. When the amounts given by various sides are balanced out, the significant increments include what Liep terms a major payment, from the spouse's side to the deceased's matriline, and a minor payment, from the matriline to the father's line. The direction of these increments is likewise characteristic of the southeastern terminus of the area under consideration.

Liep's interpretation of the significance of these prestations likewise recalls the patterns on Sabarl and Vanatinai. The "major payment" by the widowed spouse and his or her side substantiates rights in the children and also usufruct rights in trees and land of the deceased. The "minor payment" to the father's side, made to "remove the legs" of the deceased from the father's land, appears as the transgenerational conclusion of the cycle begun with the marriage of the deceased's parents.

Rossel Island, the location of the only non-Austronesian-speaking society considered here, furnishes, like the nonmatrilineal Bwaidoka and Molima in the D'Entrecasteaux, the variation in one particular necessary for a "controlled comparison." For the Yela of Rossel are matrilineal, and the Bwaidoka and Molima are Austronesian. It is highly significant, then, that in spite of considerable differences in the morphology of feasting on Rossel, regional regularities in the social and ideological articulation of feasting override considerations of descent type or linguistic affiliation. The Bwaidoka and Molima resemble the other societies on the western limb of the area in this regard, and the Yela resemble the others at the southeastern terminus. I shall return to this most important ethnographic fact in the following section.

Before doing so, however, it is necessary to consider some general points about the social significance of mourning in the Massim area. First and foremost, mourning involves the moral and emotional consequences of death, and its social and ideological organization accommodates the activities and compensation of those who handle and bury the corpse, cry over it, or undergo privation in consideration of personal or community grief. Highly charged emotional states are engendered, assumed, or perhaps in some cases only pretended to, and their anticipation, enactment, or containment constitutes much of the drama and motivating force of mortuary feasting. Many of the details described here can only be comprehended in terms of this drama and motivation. Social articulation and ideological transformation work their particular magic *through* these motives and stages, rather than alongside them.

The second point is that, by making mortuary feasting into the generic, collective social form (especially in the case of the various *sagali*-type culminating feasts), these societies expand and elaborate upon the significance of death. It is not so simple as to say that death is "for the living," although that truism holds, of course. It is rather that the social person of the deceased (the aspect of a person that participates in the personae of others) is not diminished, but expanded to the limits of his or her social circle. All "participate" back into the social persona that heretofore participated in them, so that their mourning becomes the purely formal and social enactment, or construction, of the deceased. To the degree that mortuary feasting becomes the central point of collective social ritual, its entailed expansion of the individual into a generalized social significance becomes the point of origin of society. The dead are truly ancestors, each "renewing" society in his or her turn, because society is all made of them. In this regard the social significance of death is that it is the focal point, and its rites the epitomizing forms, of the social assimilation of the individual person.

The third and final point is that this social enactment of the *plurality* of the person[10] via the dramatization and resolution *in detail* of his or her relationships and obligations realizes the mutual encompassment of individual and society. It is in its general aspect the precise opposite of the Durkheimian notion of the division of labor, with its entailed hierarchy. For, instead of the differentiation of persons on a quasi-permanent basis according to the (ranked) roles and tasks of an organic society, mortuary feasting involves the collective enactment of the relationships and obligations of a person by society. The paradox, from the standpoint of the received Western ideology of society as the "artificial" product of collective action, is that the reverse appears to be true here: the *individual* as the product of collective action. But this "obverse" perspective would seem to represent as much a distortion as the assumption of purely social ends. In fact, either a completely "societal" or a wholly "individualist" mortuary practice could be seen to allow leeway for hierarchy to develop. What prevents it from being realized is a cohesively ("watertight") reciprocal mutuality of individual (or person) and society. The two are symbolically, so to speak, a single figure, whose integrity manifests the strains of reconciliation, reconstitution, and closure discussed by Liep in his concluding analysis of Rossel mortuary exchanges.

The principle of social hierarchy is not only, as Liep has suggested, implicit in much of Massim social usage (either historically or conceptually), it is integral to it. The problem is not with the realization of hierarchy as a social effect—as the prestige accruing from exchange, as incremental personal status—but with the relative unlikelihood of this effect's surviving the fact of personal death so as to form the basis of class inheritance. The mortuary exchanges considered here give good evidence of why this should be. Death is the point where the person as a focus and nexus of social relationships is resolved in terms of those relationships; the effect of social hierarchy "goes into" the resolution as two goes into an even number, leaving no remainder. Thus hierarchy is brought to a perfect resolution by the very forces that engender it. Clastres's thesis of "societies against the state" might best be understood in a heuristic sense here, for if there were a truly "antihierarchical" principle or tendency at work, it would be even more difficult than otherwise to account for the *Guyau* of northern Kiriwina, or the pretensions of Kalauna, as described by Young,[11] on Goodenough Island.

THE EXCHANGE CONTEXT OF THE *KULA*

Taking into consideration the circumstance that many or most major prestations will be raised (and often, later, redistributed as well) through current affinal and other exchange relationships, it is nevertheless important to establish exactly where a prestation, or series of prestations, is understood socially to originate, and who is understood to receive it. Given that all, or most, people concerned in mortuary feasting will be involved in the exchanges, how is their involvement formalized? What regional patterns or regularities, if any, can be recognized in the material discussed here?

Reviewing the accounts summarized in the previous section, it is apparent that three general kinds of categories recur again and again: those of the deceased's own kin (clan, subclan, lineage), the side or unit of the complementary parent of the deceased (usually the father, but the mother in Bwaidoka and Molima), and the surviving spouse and his or her close kin. In the D'Entrecasteaux and on Tubetube, the categorization is compounded in one way or another by the designation of "buriers," ideally the side of the complementary parent in Bwaidoka and Molima (thus furnishing the rationale for their compensation), and more distantly related clanspeople on Normanby (*bukuna*) and Tubetube (*yanasa*). The "gravediggers" of Rossel add a fourth category, that of patrilateral cross-cousins, to the three major parties.

Over and above such details, the distributional pattern of overall exchange organization among the societies represented in this study is clear and unequivocal. It divides the Massim area into two distinct regional types of mortuary exchange and exchange organization. The distribution is geographical over and above any consideration of linguistic affiliation or mode of descent and extends beyond the circuit of the *kula*, which straddles it. The distinction involves the type of goods upon which the exchanges focus, the direction of perceived obligation, and the organization of the exchanging parties. As these factors seem to be intrinsically linked in each case, a brief characterization of each might serve to establish the distinction more precisely.

For the societies situated in the western portion of the area under consideration here, the D'Entrecasteaux and Trobriand islands (Bwaidoka, Molima, Normanby, Kaduwaga, and Vakuta), the mortuary exchanges focus primarily on foods, foodstuffs, and other forms of perishable wealth. The organization of the exchanges is binary, the party contributing the major payment being the clan or lineage of the deceased. In the Trobriand examples the recipient party is the lineage of the spouse, the deceased's affines (who tender a somewhat lesser amount in return). In the D'Entrecasteaux examples, the recipient party is the line of the complementary parent (for instance, the mother's people) in Bwaidoka and Molima, and either the father's line or that of the spouse on Normanby.

Mortuary exchanges in the societies in the eastern section of the study area (Tubetube, Muyuw, Vanatinai, and Rossel) focus more emphatically on imperishable wealth objects, such as Kula valuables, axes, and axe blades (though foods, foodstuffs, and nurturance play an indispensable part in the exchanges). The organization of the exchanges is ternary (if only potentially so on Tubetube), the clan or lineage of the deceased being the *recipient* (rather than the donor, as to the west) of the major payment, some or all of which must then be given to the line of the complementary parent (father). Thus the major payment originates with the line of the spouse of the deceased, whereas the unit of the deceased acts as a pivot or mediator, relaying the wealth, in turn, to the father's line. (The tendency to treat the Tubetube *lowalowa* as a *yaga*, requiring later *maisa* reciprocation, renders the *susu* of the deceased pivotal there, too.)

If the contrast of "mourning with food" (to paraphrase Young's title) with "mourning with objects" exaggerates the rites, respectively, of the western and eastern regions (for all Massim peoples mourn with food), then perhaps the comparison can be drawn more aptly in terms of person-object relations. For the type of mourning relic (or compendium of relics) known in the Trobriands as *mwagula*, and focal to mortuary rites in much of the western region, makes an object out of parts of a person, whereas the mortuary prestations on Sabarl and Vanatinai create a human simulacrum out of axes, making a "person" out of objects. The difference is that the

269

personified object, the *mwagula*, shares the fate of the person—it is laid to rest after the mourning is over, but the axes that objectify the person are kept and reassembled at (other people's) future objectifications. Thus the western object of mourning transactions moves in the direction of the deceased, toward the grave; whereas the eastern objects move *against* the flow of life, from the spouse's unit through and via the mother's to the father's, and thence onward, retracing another life.

Hence the tendency of mourning objectification in the eastern area is congruent with the movement of imperishable wealth objects, minimally ternary in that each participant mediates the flow from a giver to a (necessarily different) recipient. The western personification corresponds to the essentially binary and limited exchange of perishable wealth. The end of mourning there often leads to the splendid isolation of the Normanby fourth phase, when the *susu* feasts itself, or the Bwaidokan *Inua*, in pointed contrast to the final pandemonium of giving that Battaglia has termed "immanent reciprocity" on Sabarl.

Although many of the peoples under consideration here (Bwaidoka, Molima, Vanatinai, and Rossel) do not participate directly in the Kula, it is in the context of the Kula that the contrast in internal exchange described here acquires its relevance. For the "eastern" form of mortuary exchange, a mediated counterflow of imperishable wealth objects (affines → maternal line → paternal line) against the flow of reproduction (father-mother-spouse), amounts to an internal "scale model" of the Kula, whereas the "western" form, with its essentially redistributive tendencies, is quite different.

For peoples participating in the Kula, a regime of internal exchange that models the Kula always retains the potential of preempting the larger exchange cycle by "attaching" valuables for mortuary purposes. On Muyuw this is the sense of the *kitoum*, a valuable reclaimed by its owner for the more elemental obligations of internal exchange. Malinowski speaks of the practice of interdicting the outflow of Kula valuables (and amassing as many as possible) for a final mortuary feast as extending around the ring as far as Kitava (to the east of Boyowa) and Tubetube, yet unknown in Kiriwina or Dobu.[12]

Mortuary cycles in the eastern limb of the Kula circuit (Kitava-Tubetube) have the effect of "pulsing" the Kula, damming the circulation of armshells and necklaces, and then suddenly releasing them in waves that travel around the ring.[13] As these societies model the Kula in their internal exchanges, then, so do they model the *flow* of the Kula upon their internal (mortal) cyclicity, causing dearths (and, at least on Muyuw, alienations) of valuables for their deaths, plenitudes for the resolutions of those deaths. Overall, the effect is like that of the escapement mechanism on a clock, which slows the uncoiling of a tightly wound spring so that, in a manner of speaking, our (social, conventional) time can catch up with it. Because of the reciprocal and reflexive modeling, the Kula is a kind of vital or mortal "clock" that ticks out the crises of its eastern participants.

Is it not, then, merely these people's system of delayed mortuary exchanges? The suggestion makes sense particularly in view of the Muyuw notion of the *kitoum*: that Kula valuables in circulation may always be recalled by their original owners for use in internal exchanges. But, although it provides an ostensible motive and point of origin for the Kula, such a suggestion does not explain why it exists in the form that it does, or who might have arranged such a "revolving credit association."

It would appear, rather, that the element of "pulsing" and delayed mortuary exchange plays a significant or crucial role in providing the irregularities or asymmetries in a system whose "rules" (particularly as a template for the Maussian canons of reciprocity) are phrased in terms of regularity and symmetry. A wave of arms shells released in one direction by a mortuary resolution, and a counterwave of necklaces released simultaneously in the other, generates imbalances and asymmetries (promises in exchange for valuables) over most of their respective courses and a potential for symmetry (valuables for valuables) only where the two waves meet again. Although the concentrations tend to attenuate in time, the ticking of the mortal clock regenerates wave and counterwave with their entailed asymmetries again and again.

An alternative way of understanding the creation of asymmetries involves the generation of imaginary wealth objects. The release of large numbers of arm shells and necklaces simultaneously in opposite directions assures the maximal degree of nonhomogeneity in their distribution around the ring (large clumps of each meet each other at only two places, rather than smaller aggregates of each meeting at all points on the circuit). Consequently, most exchanges involving these valuables consist of an arm shell or necklace given in return for a promise of one of the other kind: an anticipated or imaginary valuable. (Generally the promise is sealed by the giving of a lesser valuable, Malinowski's *korotomna*.[14]) Given the strategies of successful negotiation in the Kula, considerably more of such imaginary valuables are generated in the process than "real" counterparts forthcoming to substantiate them. Enforced separation of relatively large concentrations of the two kinds of valuables provides an enhanced opportunity for the generation and negotiation of imaginary wealth objects.

Whether one is disposed to view the Kula as an intensive competition to realize and validate promises of this sort or as the husbanding of the relationships through which they proliferate, a mortuary "pulsing" of the Kula can be seen as raising the tension (and the ante) in both instances.

Wagner

Like joking and other institutionalized "violations" of relationship, these engineered stoppages provide a foil for the activation of the relationships themselves, putting the actors, so to speak, on their mettle.

Understanding the role of mortuary "stoppages" in this way helps to clarify the (at least) equally significant role of participating societies on the western limb of the Kula. For theirs is the positive, dialectical countersurge, identifying with the movement of the Kula and with its expectations, often to the extent of criticism or attempts to "force" the blockade. The impetus is no less important than its foil (though of course the "impetus" on a given occasion may include all those Kula participants not involved with a particular death).

Considered in its own terms, the Kula is a self-defining and self-validating value system. In a recent study, *The Fame of Gawa*, Nancy Munn speaks of value levels as "the relative extension of the spacetime,"[15] adding that "*extension* means here the capacity to develop spatiotemporal relations that go beyond the self."[16] Models of this sort, which reflect the system's own condensation of time, distance, movement, and social relationship within a very comprehensive notion of "value," are likely to find more resonance with indigenous concepts than questions and answers based on linearity and causality. Hierarchy is realized and permitted, or "enabled," though contingently, within the recursive sweep of the Kula over "spacetime," and stoppage, as we have seen, gives rise to a greater potentiality of flow in its strangely curved value continuum.

But the exchange context of the Kula has an outside as well as an inside. The contrasting regions of binary and ternary mortuary exchange evidenced here extend beyond the Kula itself, and valuables that now move with the Kula (such as the *bagi* necklaces manufactured on Rossel Island), as well as others that seem to have done so in the past (such as axe blades from Muyuw), often circulate in this wider area as well. It is only in the perspective of the wider region, in fact, that the contrast can be fully established. For the eastern antithesis to the western *mwagula* (the object made of personal relics) is the Sabarl and Vanatinai "person" made of axes, located outside the Kula ambit.

The reader may have surmised that neither Muyuw nor Tubetube fit particularly well into this "eastern" modality. To be sure, both societies emphasize circulation of wealth in their mortuary exchanges, and in both cases the major increment moves from the side of the affines to that of the deceased's relatives. But the ternary organization of the parties is contingent (the Tubetube *maisa* [return payment] can only be seen as going to the parent's side if one changes generational perspective; the Muyuw payment to the father's side does not involve *kitoum*), and it could be argued, especially for Muyuw, that the significant content of the exchanges is actually food.

This suggests, in turn, an influence of the Kula itself within the scheme of mortuary values. For the interdiction of Kula trafficking, the amassing of valuables for the final feast, and especially the attachment of valuables as *kitoum* or *kitomwa* all amount to a coopting of prestige or valuation from the Kula for mortuary purposes on Tubetube and Muyuw. Are the objectifying "constructions" of the deceased out of axe blades on Sabarl and Vanatinai, and the similar outlays of wealth on Rossel, equivalent statements of value by peoples who have no Kula valuation to coopt?

Questions of this sort inevitably raise the issue of whether the Kula is an artifact of the regional contrast in internal exchange, or whether that contrast is in some sense an effect of the Kula. If the Kula is not necessarily a floating credit system for mortuary exchange on its eastern limb, is it not perhaps possible that that object-centered exchange tradition is itself a reflection or sublimation of the Kula? Prudence suggests that, cultural valuation being the sensitive register of influence and counterinfluence it is, the effects go both ways. We may, in other words, be dealing with elements of feedback or schismogenesis that move in several dimensions at once, producing, among other things, an eastern "epicenter" of person/object relations that is necessarily outside the Kula itself.[16] It is not unlikely that the differential weighting of kin obligations and relative distance from the mainland mass play parts in these relations also.

NOTES

1. Neither feasting nor exchange at death is confined solely to Austronesian-speaking peoples, and certain large-scale similarities suggest that these are old and widely dispersed cultural forms in Melanesia.

2. Significant examples from the interior would be Heider (1970:146–68), Williams (1940:121–32), and Brown (1961:77–96).

3. See Clay, (1986) and Wagner (1986). Princeton University Press.

4. The Daribi people of Mt. Karimui, Simbu Province, observe a similar taboo on any sort of work following a death and preceding burial.

5. See Young (1971).

6. See Weiner (1976).

7. See Battaglia (1985).

8. Among the Usen Barok of New Ireland, this same term, *tau*, is used for the father's sister, who is spoken of as the "female father" and stands in an especially warm and nurturant relationship, a feeding-relationship, to one.

9. The atmosphere of accusation surrounding mortuary observances, as well as the traditional cannibalism, slaying of the suspected sorcerer, and costly compensation to his relatives all recall Lepowsky's account of Vanatinai.

10. I am very much indebted to Marilyn Strathern for the insight germinal to this notion: that the person ("dividual" in Marriott's sense) is plural, and the "collective" unitary (Personal communication 1987).

11. See Young (1983c).

12. See Malinowski (1922:489–93).

13. This effect is achieved, to a lesser extent, by *marriage* exchanges in Dobu (Persson 1983:35–36).

14. See Malinowski (1922:355).

15. See Munn (1986).

16. Concerned, that is, with the construction of personal values out of objects *apart from* their Kula valuations, as against the Trobriand-D'Entrecasteaux creation of object values out of personal relics, which can comfortably exist *within* a Kula framework.

Bibliography

Affleck, D. 1983. "Manuscript XVIII–Informant on Customs and Practices of the People of Woodlark Island, by Carol Salerio." *Journal of Pacific History* 18(1):57–72.

Armstrong, W. E. 1928. *Rossel Island.* Cambridge: Cambridge University Press.

Balibar, E. 1975. "On Reproduction." In *Reading Capital* by Louis Althusser and Ettienne Balibar. Translated by Ben Brewster. London: New Left Books, 254–308.

Battaglia, D. 1983. "Projecting Personhood in Melanesia: The Dialectics of Artefact Symbolism on Sabari Island." *Man* 18(2):289–304.

———. 1985. "We Feed Our Father: Paternal Nature among the Sabarl of Papua New Guinea." *American Ethnologist* 12(2):427–42.

Berde, S. 1974. *Melanesians as Methodists.* Ph.D. dissertation, Department of Anthropology, University of Pennsylvania.

Black, R. H. 1957. "Dr. Bellamy of Papua." *Medical Journal of Australia* 2(6):232–38; 279–84.

Bloch, M., and J. Parry, eds. 1982. *Death and the Regeneration of Life.* Cambridge: Cambridge University Press.

Bromilow, W. E. 1929. *Twenty Years among Primitive Papuans.* London: Epworth Press.

Brown, P. 1961. "Chimbu Death Payments." *Journal of the Royal Anthropological Institute* 91:77–96.

———. 1970. "Chimbu Transactions." *Man* 5(1):99–117.

Campbell, S. F. 1983a. "Attaining Rank: A Classification of Kula Shell Valuables." In *The Kula*, edited by J. W. Leach and E. R. Leach. Cambridge: Cambridge University Press.

———. 1983b. "Kula on Vakuta: The Mechanics of *Keda*." In *The Kula*, edited by J. W. Leach and E. R. Leach. Cambridge: Cambridge University Press.

———. 1984. *The Art of Kula.* Ph.D. thesis. Canberra: Australian National University.

———. "A Vakutan Mortuary Cycle," this text.

Capell, A. 1969. *A Survey of New Guinea Languages.* Sydney: Sydney University Press.

Chowning, A. 1960. "Canoe Making among the Molima of Fergusson Island." *Expedition* 3:1.

———. 1962. "Cognatic Kin Groups among the Molima of Fergusson Island." *Ethnology* 1:1.

———. 1978. "The Massim as a Culture Area." Paper delivered to the First Kula Conference. Cambridge: Cambridge University.

275

————. 1983. "Wealth and Exchange among the Molima of Fergusson Island." In *The Kula*, edited by J. W. Leach and E. R. Leach. Cambridge: Cambridge University Press, 411–27.

Clastres, P. 1977. *Society against the State*. Oxford: Blackwell.

Clay, B. J. 1986. *Mandak Realities*. New Brunswick, N.J.: Rutgers University Press.

Damon, F. H. 1979. "Woodlark Island Megalithic Structures and Trenches: Towards an Interpretation." *Archaeology and Physical Anthropology in Oceania* 14(3):195–226.

————. 1980. "The Kula and Generalized Exchange: Considering Some Unconsidered Aspects of the Elementary Structure of Kinship." *Man* 15:267–94.

————. 1982. "Calendars and Calendrical Rites on the Northern Side of the Kula Ring." *Oceania* 52(3):221–39.

————. 1983a. "Muyuw Kinship and the Metamorphosis of Gender Labourer." *Man* 18(2):305–26.

————. 1983b. "The Transformation of Muyuw into Woodlark Island: Two Minutes in December, 1974." *Journal of Pacific History* 18(1):35–56.

————. 1983c. "What Moves the Kula: Opening and Closing Gifts on Woodlark Island." In *The Kula*, edited by J. W. Leach and E. R. Leach. Cambridge: Cambridge University Press, 309–42.

Eggan, F. 1954. "Social Anthropology and the Method of Controlled Comparison." *American Anthropologist* 56:743–63.

Ekholm, K. 1977. "External Exchange and the Transformation of Central African Social Systems. In *The Evolution of Social Systems*, edited by J. Friedman and M. Rowlands. Pittsburgh: University of Pittsburgh Press.

Eyde, D. B. 1976. "Dualism in Trobriand Culture." In *Directions in Pacific Traditional Literature*, edited by A. Kaeppler and H. H. Nimmo. Honolulu: Bishop Museum Special Publication 62.

Fortune, R. [1932] 1963. *Sorcerers of Dobu*. New York: E. P. Dutton & Co.

Fox, James J., ed. 1980. *The Flow of Life: Essays on Eastern Indonesia*. Cambridge: Harvard University Press.

Friedman, J. 1981. "Notes on Structure and History in Oceania." *Folk* 23:275–95.

Goodenough, W. H. 1955. "The Pageant of Death in Nakanai." *Bulletin*, University Museum, University of Pennsylvania 19:18–43. Reprinted in L. L. Langness and J. C. Wechsler, 1976, *Melanesia*. Scranton, PA: Chandler.

Heider, K. 1970. *The Dugum Dani*, New York: Wenner-Gren, 146–68.

Hertz, R. 1960. *Death and the Right Hand*. Translated by R. Needham and C. Needham with an Introduction by E. E. Evans-Pritchard. New York: Free Press.

Huntington, R., and P. Metcalf, eds. 1979. *Celebrations of Death: The Anthropology of Mortuary Ritual*. Cambridge: Cambridge University Press.

Hutchins, E., and D. Hutchins. n.d. *Kilivilan-English Dictionary*.

Huxley, J., ed. 1935. *T. H. Huxley's Diary of the Voyage of H. M. S. Rattlesnake*. London: Chatto and Windus.

Iamo, W. 1981. "Death of a Kinsman in a Keakalo Village." Paper delivered to the Second Kula Conference. University of Virginia.

Irwin, G. 1983. "Chieftainship, Kula and Trade in Massim Prehistory." In *The Kula*, edited by J. W. Leach and E. R. Leach. Cambridge: Cambridge University Press, 29–72.

Jenness, D., and A. Ballantyne. 1920. *The Northern D'Entrecasteaux*. Oxford: Clarendon Press.

———. 1928. "Language, Mythology and Songs of Bwaidoga, Goodenough Island, S.E. Papua." *Journal of the Polynesian Society* 37.

Jones, D. 1981. "Body-building in Melanesia." Paper delivered to the Second Kula Conference. University of Virginia.

Kirkpatrick, J. 1979. *The Marquesan Notion of the Person*. Unpublished Ph.D. dissertation, University of Chicago.

Kuper, A. 1982. *Wives for Cattle: Bridewealth and Marriage in Southern Africa*. London: Routledge & Kegan Paul.

Leach, E. R. 1957. "The Epistemological Background to Malinowski's Empiricism." In *Man and Culture*, edited by R. Fifth. London: Routledge & Kegan Paul, 119–38.

———. 1966. "Virgin Birth." *Proceedings of the Royal Anthropological Institute*. London: 39–49.

———. 1982. *Social Anthropology*. New York: Oxford University Press.

Leach, J. W. 1978. "Review of A. Weiner, *Women of Value, Men of Reknown*." *Man* 13:1.

———. 1983. "Introduction." In *The Kula*, edited by J. W. Leach and E. R. Leach. Cambridge: Cambridge University Press, 1–26.

Leach, J. W., and E. R. Leach, eds. 1983. *The Kula: New Perspectives on Massim Exchanges*. Cambridge: Cambridge University Press.

Lepowsky, M. 1981. "Fruit of the Motherland: Gender and Exchange on Vanatinai (Sudest Island)." Ph.D. dissertation. Department of Anthropology, University of California, Berkeley.

———. 1982. "A Comparison of Alcohol and Betel Nut Use on Vanatinai (Sudest Island)." In *Through a Glass Darkly: Beer and Development in Papua New Guinea*, edited by M. Marshall. Monograph No. 18. Port Moresby: Institute of Applied Social and Economic Research.

———. 1983. "Sudest Island and the Louisiade Archipelago in Massim Exchange." In *The Kula*, edited by J. W. Leach and E. R. Leach. Cambridge: Cambridge University Press, 467–502.

———. 1985. "Food Taboos, Malaria, and Dietary Change: Infant Feeding and Cultural Adaptation on a Papua New Guinea Island." *Ecology of Food and Nutrition* 16(2):105–26.

———. 1987. "Food Taboos and Child Survival: A Case Study from the Coral Sea." In *Child Survival: Anthropological Perspectives on the Treatment and Maltreatment of Children*, edited by N. Scheper-Hughes. Dordrecht, The Netherlands: D. Reidel.

———. 1989a. "Gender in an Egalitarian Society: Lessons from a Coral Sea Island." In *Beyond the Second Sex: New Perspectives on the Anthropology of Women*, edited by P. Sanday. Philadelphia: University of Pennsylvania Press.

———. 1989b. "Big Men, Big Women and Cultural Autonomy." In *Big Man*,

Great Man, Culture Hero, edited by P. Brown and J. Watson. Oceania Monograph Series. Sydney: Oceania Publications.

―――. 1989c. "Soldiers and Spirits: The Impact of World War II on a Coral Sea Island." In *The Pacific Theater: Island Representations of World War II*, edited by G. White and L. Lindstrom. Pacific Monograph Series. Honolulu: University of Hawaii Press.

―――. n.d. "Sorcery and Penicillin: Treating Illness on a Coral Sea Island."

Liep. J. 1981. "The Workshop of the Kula: Production and Trade of Shell Necklaces in the Louisiade Archipelago, Papua New Guinea." *Folk* 23:297–309.

―――. 1983. "'This Civilizing Influence': The Colonial Transformation of Rossel Island Society." *Journal of Pacific History* 18(2):113–31.

―――. 1987. "A Performance in Petticoats: Reversal and Reciprocity in a Rossel Island Dance Feast." *Folk* 29:219–37.

―――. n.d. "Great Man, Big Man, Chief: A Triangulation of the Massim." In *Big Men and Great Men: The Development of a Comparison in Melanesia*, edited by M. Godelier and M. Strathern. Cambridge: Cambridge University Press.

Lithgow, D. 1976. "Austronesian Languages: Milne Bay and Adjacent Islands (Milne Bay Province)." In *Austronesian Languages: New Guinea Area Languages and Language Study*, vol. 2, edited by S. A. Wurm. Pacific Linguistics, Series C-No. 39. Canberra: Australian National University, 441–523.

Macgillivray, J. 1852. *Narrative of the Voyage of* H.M.S. Rattlesnake, *Commanded by the Late Captain Owen Stanley, R.N., F.R.S. etc. During the Years 1846–1850: Including Discoveries and Surveys in New Guinea, the Louisiade Archipelago, etc.*, 2 vol. London: T. and W. Boone.

Macintyre, M. 1983. *The Kula: A Bibliography*. Cambridge: Cambridge University Press.

Macintyre, M., and Young, M. 1982. "The Persistence of Traditional Trade and Ceremonial Exchange in the Massim." In *Melanesia: Beyond Diversity*, edited by R. J. May and H. Nelson. Canberra: Australian National University Press.

Malinowski, B. 1922. *Argonauts of the Western Pacific*. London: Routledge & Kegan Paul.

―――. 1926. *Crime and Custom in Savage Society*. London: Routledge & Kegan Paul.

―――. 1929. *The Sexual Life of Savages*. New York: Harcourt Brace & World Inc.

Mauss, M. 1967. *The Gift*. Translated by Ian Cunnison. New York: W. W. Norton.

Maybury-Lewis, D., ed. 1979. *Dialectical Societies: The Gê and Bororo of Central Brazil*. Cambridge: Harvard University Press.

Metcalf, P., and R. Huntington, 1979. *Celebrations of Death: The Anthropology of Mortuary Ritual*. New York: Cambridge University Press.

Montague, S. n.d. *The Trobriand Society*. Ph.D. dissertation, University of Chicago.

Mosko, M. S. 1985. *Quadripartite Structures*. New York: Cambridge University Press.

Munn, N. D. 1986. *The Fame of Gawa: A Symbolic Study of Value Transformation in a Massim (Papua New Guinea) Society*. New York: Cambridge University Press.

Persson, J. 1983. Cyclical Change and Circular Exchange: A Re-examination of the Kula Ring." *Oceania* 1:32–47.

Powell, H. A. 1969. "Genealogy, Residence and Kinship in Kiriwina." *Man* 4:177–202.

Rathje, W. L. 1978. "Melanesian and Australian Exchange Systems: A View from Mesoamerica." *Mankind* 11:165–74.

Róheim, G. 1937. "Death and Mourning Ceremonies of Normanby Island." *Man* 37:49–50, 184.

———. 1946. "Ceremonial Prostitution in Duau (Normanby Island)." *Journal of Clinical Psychopathology and Psychotherapy* 7:753–64.

———. 1950. *Psychoanalysis and Anthropology*. New York: International University Press.

Rosman, A., and P. Rubel. 1978. *Your Own Pigs You May Not Eat: A Comparative Study of New Guinea Societies*. Chicago: University of Chicago Press.

Sahlins, M. D. 1976. *Culture and Practical Reason*. Chicago: University of Chicago Press.

———. 1981. "The Stranger-King: Dumezil among the Fijians." *Journal of Pacific History* 16:107–32.

Schlesier, E. 1970. *Me'udana (Sudost-Neuguinea). Teil 1: Die soziale Struktur*. Braunschweig: Albert Limbag Verlag.

Scoditti, G., with J. Leach. 1983. "Kula on Kitava." In *The Kula*, edited by J. W. Leach and E. R. Leach. Cambridge: Cambridge University Press, 249–73.

Seligman, C. 1910. *Melanesians of British New Guinea*. Cambridge: Cambridge University Press.

———. Unpublished diaries. Haddon Library, Cambridge, England.

Thune, Carl. 1980. *The Rhetoric of Remembrance: Collective Life and Personal Tragedy in Loboda Village*. Ph.D. dissertation, Princeton University.

———. 1983. "Kula Traders and Lineage Members: The Structure of Village and Kula Exchange on Normanby Island." In *The Kula*, edited by J. W. Leach and E. R. Leach. Cambridge: Cambridge University Press, 345–68.

Van Gennep, A. [1908] 1960. *The Rites of Passage*. Translated by M. Vizedom and G. Caffee. Chicago: University of Chicago Press.

Van Wouden, F. A. E. [1935] 1968. *Types of Social Structure in Eastern Indonesia*. Translated by Rodney Needham. Koninklijk Instituut voor Tall-, en Volkenkunde Translation Series, vol. 11. The Hague: Martinus Nijhoff.

Wagner, R. 1986. *Asiwinarong*. Princeton: Princeton University Press.

Weiner, A. 1976. *Women of Value, Men of Renown*. Austin: University of Texas Press.

———. 1978. "The Reproductive Model in Trobriand Society." In *Trade and Exchange in Oceania and Australia. Mankind* Special Issue. 11(3):175–86. Sydney: Sydney University Press.

———. 1980. "Reproduction: A Replacement for Reciprocity." *American Ethnologist* 7(1):71–85.

———. 1983. "A World of Made Is Not a World of Born: Doing Kula in Kiriwina." In *The Kula*, edited by J. W. Leach and E. R. Leach. Cambridge: Cambridge University Press, 147–70.

Williams, F. 1940. *Natives of Lake Kutubu, Papua*. Sydney: Oceania Monographs.

Young, M. 1971. *Fighting with Food: Leadership, Values and Social Control in a Massim Society*. Cambridge: Cambridge University Press.

———. 1983a. "Ceremonial Visiting in Goodenough Island." In *The Kula*, edited by J. W. Leach and E. R. Leach. Cambridge: Cambridge University Press, 383–410.

———. 1983b. "'The Best Workmen in Papua': Goodenough Islanders and the Labour Trade, 1900–1960." *Journal of Pacific History* 18(2):74–95.

———. 1983c. *Magicians of Manumanua: Living Myth in Kalauna*. Berkeley: University of California Press.